MOTHER COW, MOTHER INDIA

MOTHER COW, MOTHER INDIA

A Multispecies Politics of Dairy in India

YAMINI NARAYANAN

STANFORD UNIVERSITY PRESS

STANFORD, CALIFORNIA

STANFORD UNIVERSITY PRESS
Stanford, California

Printed in the United States of America on acid-free, archival-quality paper

ISBN: 9781503634367 (cloth)
ISBN: 9781503634374 (paper)
ISBN: 9781503634381 (ebook)

Library of Congress Control Number: 2022019296

Library of Congress Cataloging-in-Publication data available upon request.

Cover design: Jason Anscomb

Cover images: iStock

Typeset by Newgen in Adobe Caslon Pro 10.75/15

CONTENTS

TABLES AND FIGURES

MOTHER COW, MOTHER INDIA

INTRODUCTION

THE DYING, NEWBORN Holstein bull-calf lay on his side, small head extended upward on the hot sands of the Jaipur live "cattle" market. Saliva and froth dribbled out of his mouth as he panted slowly and feebly. He was emaciated, skeletal, barely holding on to his life by a thread. His black and white soft skin, exposed to the harsh Rajasthani sun, was surprisingly clean, though covered thickly with flies who buzzed in droves around his mouth and mucous-laden eyes, which were cloudy and dull, staring unseeing into the distance.

Thick rows of buffaloes, cows, and their infants were tied close together in pairs near the trucks or in groups, their faces tightly harnessed together down to a low stake on the ground. These animals could scarcely raise their heads or shift even a couple of steps to the side, remaining that way for hours until sold and loaded onto cramped trucks. It looked chaotic, hot, dusty. However, as I was to learn, an organized method of buying and selling these animals was in place. There was already a ring of vehicles around the entire periphery of the market, mainly large Ashok Leyland trucks and smaller Tata Tempos, standing empty, or in the process of offloading animals. More trucks continued to drive in, every inch of space packed with animals. At the gate, there was a small shack where market managers and a veterinarian sat at a table, stamping "fit-for-transport" certificates, without which it was illegal to transport live animals. Throngs of middlemen stood nearby, bargaining on behalf of dairy farmers, butchers, and transporters, negotiating the price for these certificates to be illegally stamped. Past these clusters of chained mothers and calves, the animal market broke into open space.

Next to the dying calf, a female black and white cow lay in the middle of the exposed space, stretched out with her legs extended and neck arched, eyes rolling right to the back of her head, exposing only the whites. Her swollen udders hung heavily onto the scorching sands, which were steaming hot even through my sandals. Foam frothed from her mouth, and her entire body shook with her labored breathing.

Manil, a Jaipuri animal activist, leaned over quietly to me. "Mother and son, no doubt," he whispered. "She must have given birth only one day or even only a few hours ago. They were transported in that condition, neither could withstand it."

I bent down and softly stroked the tiny calf's forehead. He barely registered my touch, already halfway across into another world. "He is going to die," I choked to Manil, barely able to get the words out. *Do not cry!* I thought furiously to myself. It was the first instruction every animal activist across India gave me. *Do not cry, do not shout, do not show any emotion in these places. Do not out yourself.* A series of muffled grunts made me look up and I saw a small, struggling calf at the edge of a cluster of cows, a few meters from me. A skinny, spindly female calf, her ribcage sharply visible, and barely bigger than the dogs on the streets outside the cattle *mandi* (market), pulled with force on the one foot of rope tethered around her neck to the fender of a Tata Tempo. She strained between her mother's front legs toward the heavy udder at the back, just out of reach. The desperation in that tense, hungry little body was palpable.

The "cattle" market continued to swirl and heave at a careful distance from the dying cow and her baby as they lay exposed under the blazing desert sun with no shelter, no water, no mercy. No veterinary care was administered to the mother and infant; the vet's role here—as in any space of animal production—was to keep the economics of animal commodification, in this case, the buying and selling of these bovine bodies, moving as efficiently as possible.

Farmers, butchers, and middlemen hovered around as we asked to whom the cow and calf belonged; no one answered, or they pretended they did not know. The mother and her newborn would lie there until death came, hours or even a day or so later. If they did not die by the end of the market day, they would be loaded onto the trucks and slaughtered at one of the thousands of illegal abattoirs in Jaipur and the surrounding regions. Otherwise, tanners and butchers would come to take away the bodies of the mother and son, too sick, weak, and broken to cope with the abject and brutal realities of being commodified for the dairy industry, and rejected as "discards."

"WE TREAT COWS LIKE GODS IN INDIA!"

I was astounded, in 2010, when an Indian colleague mentioned in passing at a conference at Stanford University on religion and nature that he did not consume dairy "because of the way cows are treated in India." We were in a group outside a lecture hall; I was close enough to catch the end of his sentence, and if I had so chosen, to turn around and ask, "*What?*" He was a brilliant mathematician; his work mapped onto naturecultures in ways I could not, at the time, fully understand. He certainly did not research animals; I knew no one at the time who did, and I could not have remotely foreseen that (other) animals could be, and in fact, already were, increasingly prominent subjects of political discourse and scholarship. It was the first time that I had heard such a notion explicitly stated. Did I intuit that if I dared to ask, behind that question lay a realization of violence that I would have scarcely known how to comprehend at the time? My question unasked, I pushed back into the theater with the rest of the group. It would be a few years before the truth of his words would confront me viscerally.

However, his words, stated so simply as fact, and my disbelief remained with me. *What do you mean, the way cows are treated in India? Aren't they worshipped and treated as gods?* As images of violence, abjection, and mistreatment witnessed routinely through the years flitted hazily through my head, this internal conversation continued to reverberate in a circular way . . . *and anyway, what does that have to do with not eating butter in America? Surely American cows are treated well?* Unbeknownst to me, the seeds of what would become this book had been quietly planted.

On the whole, I did not spend too much thinking about the lived experiences of other animals, even as they were so palpably part of multispecies environments and lives in India. Was it the very ubiquitousness of their presence that rendered them unseeable? I certainly could not recall any instance when other animals were introduced into our social, political, or religious imagination as moral, or even sacred beings, whose wellbeing was our ethical responsibility. There were still moments, however, when animals themselves cut into my psyche, making me aware of their suffering. In the last few years, particularly since 2014, against increasingly shrill political and populist discourses on cow protection in India, hidden memories of the abuse of cows started to surface frequently in my mind. Significantly, as I would come to realize later, my childhood memories of urban India failed to include buffaloes, already and always erased from public recognition and concern.

As a child in Chennai, I vividly recall a young native cow hit hard by a car or a truck, downed and bleeding profusely in the middle of Mount Road, the city's largest and busiest thoroughfare. She arched her neck back, blood drenching her body—the bright red a stunning contrast with her white skin—as it flowed down her distinctive hump. She had been hit perhaps only minutes before. Vehicles and pedestrians sped past without slowing. Perhaps several hours or even days later, when the cow was dead, the Chennai Municipal Corporation would come to haul her corpse away. Another time, on a scorching summer day in Delhi, I remember a pregnant cow desperately licking drops of water from the bonnet of a freshly washed parked car.

I recall, when I was engaged in field research on an entirely different area of study, passing an urban gaushala in Jaipur, recoiling, and walking away in disgust from the stench of ammonia that emanated from the dung-covered, urine-puddled cement structure. Gaushalas are widely understood as shelters for old, sick, and retired cows and bulls, based on the Hindu ethic of reverencing cows as sacred. They are different, however, from other farmed animal sanctuaries in that they are also involved in dairy farming. As I passed that gaushala on that day, not without shame, I found that at least part of my contempt was directed at the single thin white cow, a mixed crossbreed, who was chained there, streaked with her own feces and mud.

In recent years, the idea that cows are sacred to Hindus and therefore deserving of special protection is so deeply volatile and contested in intra-humanist identity politics that even the irony of such a debate is lost. Cows can be witnessed daily, foraging in the decomposing stench of the neighborhood trash, ingesting plastic, glass, nails, and even toxic hospital waste.[1] Despite their hypervisibility in Indian landscapes, it is rarely understood that these individuals are intricately enmeshed with India's milk industry—and even rarer still, worldwide, to consider the extractive violence of dairying itself, and its direct connection to slaughter. Humans tend to regard milk—the breastmilk intended for the newborns of other species—as much our birthright as water. The mythologies we choose to cultivate in different places and believe thus become even more powerful than the palpable realities that we may directly witness. So it is that our gaze can glaze over at the arthritic, hungry, abandoned "dairy" cow limping painfully on the hard bitumen of India's thickly polluted cities, until she blurs into an abstraction to resurface in India's national imagination as "our" revered (lactating) mother. Conspicuously, buffaloes are mostly missing from political outrage against cow slaughter even though buffalo milk is over-represented in Indian dairying, the largest in the world. Buffaloes do not even feature as an abstraction; conveniently, they can be legally taken to the abattoir when discarded by the dairy industry.

In the main, the notion that cows in *India* could be mistreated at all usually provokes stunned disbelief from Indians and non-Indians alike. And, indeed, that was precisely my response when confronted with my Indian colleague's assertion to the contrary. In the Hindu-majority country, *cows are mothers, cows are gods.* Cows are so holy that their slaughter attracts criminal penalties in most Indian states, a remarkable legislative protection for a farmed animal enmeshed in any production.

In some Indian states, the sale, consumption, and even possession of beef—a product that can be (more) obviously linked to the slaughter of the cow—can attract higher penalties than the trade in some narcotics. The lynching, rape, and killing of vulnerable humans in the name of cow protection cements the perception that cows in India have rights and security unparalleled for species otherwise designated "farm," "food," or "dairy" animals, and indeed, for some humans. The idea of protecting, and even reverencing the "sacred" cow makes it possible to be convinced of a scenario in which cows in India enjoy freedoms and even lifestyles unimaginable elsewhere. In India, above any country on the planet, cows are treated *well*. Or so the narrative goes.

Indeed, in recent years, the rhetoric of cow protection has provided almost theatrical landscapes for political violence against Muslims and Dalits, accused of slaughtering cows by Hindutva nationalists. *Hindutva* is a highly pervasive and influential form of Hindu nationalism that political economist Prabhat Patnaik describes as "almost fascist in the classical sense."[2] Those perceived to be involved in cow slaughter, or the consumption of beef, are now frequently subjects of this extremist violence.

In one case in January 2016, a Muslim couple, Mohammed Hussain and his wife Naseema Bano, were attacked by seven *gaurakshaks* (or self-styled "cow protectors," also commonly referred to as cow vigilantes) from the Gauraksha Samiti, a local right-wing and Hindu nationalist cow protection organization, at the Khirkiya station in central Madhya Pradesh. The men boarded the train and insisted on searching through the bags of passengers for beef. Hussain was beaten up when he abused the vigilantes for pushing his wife around roughly. Eventually a constable came to their rescue. Laboratory tests later revealed that the meat was buffalo flesh.[3]

Subsequently, in the same year, four Dalit youths were severely beaten in Una in Gujarat state by vigilantes when they were "caught" skinning a dead cow. Dalits, formerly of the "untouchable" caste, continue to be one of the most severely marginalized and vulnerable human communities in contemporary India. A significant feature of Dalit labor is to remove cow carcasses from public spaces. A video of the assault was taken by the gaurakshaks and uploaded on Facebook, "to showcase their 'bravery' and to serve as a warning to others who do not treat their holy cow with due reverence.'[4] Ironically, the video was circulated widely by the Dalits themselves on social media at a time when mainstream media coverage was negligible, leading to mass fury against the cow protectors, and widespread outrage from the Dalit community throughout India. Protestors marched through the city of Ahmedabad, shouting slogans and armed with sticks to intimidate.[5] They dumped whole cow corpses outside the collector's office at Surendra Nagar, while shouting, "*Tumhari mata hai, tum sambhalo*" (your mother, you take care of her).[6]

Such "disciplining" by cow vigilantes is hardly limited to extreme beatings. In 2015, the problem of cow vigilantism exploded into a major issue of extreme human rights violations when Mohammed Akhlaq was killed in Dadri district in Uttar Pradesh state by a lynch mob on suspicion of slaughtering a calf for beef. In 2016, a group of cow vigilantes thrashed and killed Mohammed Mazlum Ansari, a thirty-five-year-old man, and Imteyaz Khan who was only twelve years old, accusing them of selling bulls for slaughter.[7] Their bodies were then hung from a tree by the fanatics as a warning. In the same year, Hafiz Junaid, a sixteen-year-old Muslim boy, was murdered on a train in Haryana state when a mob started to taunt him and his friend, claiming that their bags contained beef. When they resisted, a large crowd attacked them. In 2017, Pehlu Khan, a Muslim dairy farmer in Alwar, Rajasthan, was killed by a lynch mob on suspicion of smuggling cows for butchery. In 2019, the Rajasthan High Court posthumously acquitted him of the charges, ruling that Khan was transporting the animals for dairying, not slaughter.[8]

Nor is this violence in the name of cow protection restricted to men of marginalized communities. In 2016, a Muslim woman and her fourteen-year-old cousin were accused of eating beef, and they alleged that they were gang-raped by a group of Hindu cow protectors for their "crime."[9] Two other Muslim women were severely beaten on the Mandsaur railway station platform in Madhya Pradesh when thirty kilos of beef were discovered in their bags. The women claimed that the assailants were from the Hindu nationalist Bajrang Dal party. Subsequently, "a state BJP [the Hindu nationalist Bharatiya Janata Party] leader had admitted that the Bajrang Dal members were indeed present on the platform, since they 'helped' the police with such incidents," though he denied their involvement with the beatings, and blamed the public.[10] The Home Minister Bhupinder Singh condemned the attacks, but dismissed them as "minimal."[11] He said, "The beating was minimal. The women, with whom these incidents occurred, have also accepted it. The mistake was of the women's [*sic*]." Mobile phone videos, however, clearly show the women being slapped, punched, cornered, and kicked.[12]

In early 2019, Human Rights Watch released an extensive report on the steep rise in hate crimes and gross human rights infringement since Narendra Modi came to power in 2014.[13] The report states, "there was a nearly 500 percent increase in the use of hateful and divisive language by elected leaders—90 percent of it by BJP leaders—between 2014 and 2018, as compared to the five years before the BJP was in power."[14] Such violence-inciting speeches are delivered overwhelmingly in the name of cow protection. In 2017, Raman Singh, the Chief Minister of Chhattisgarh state, declared, "We will hang those who kill cows."[15] Vikram Saini, a Member of the Legislative Assembly (MLA) from the BJP from Uttar Pradesh state threatened, "I had promised that I will break the hands and legs of those who do not consider cows their mother and kill them."[16] Another BJP MLA from Rajasthan promised, "I will say it straight out, if you smuggle and slaughter cows, then you will be killed. The cow is our mother."[17]

Underscoring all of this violence in the name of protecting cows is *one* specific racist, casteist, and sectarian obsession: that "Hindustan is for Hindus."[18] The bovine body represents Mother Cow *as* Mother India—implicitly a racially pure, "upper-caste" Hindu Mother India.[19] The sentient, living (dairy) cow is a living embodiment of *Hindustan*, the "land of Hindus." Allowing the cow to be slaughtered amounts, in effect, to sending the Hindu cow-mother-nation herself to the abattoir.

The realities of human rights violations, sectarianism, and casteism in the name of cow protection, and the rewriting of Hindu history by its extremists to advance the narrative of a cow-revering, cow-protecting Hindu civilization has been analyzed extensively. The most popular and controversial of these works, historian D. N. Jha's *Myth of the Holy Cow*, uses archaeological evidence to demonstrate that the Vedic Brahmins consumed beef, offered cow sacrifices to the gods, and beef was a ritual commodity. The politicization of cows as sacred, and beef as profane, is a modern narrative born of a specific "upper-caste" Hindu Renaissance during the British rule of India.

In *Buffalo Nationalism*, Dalit activist and scholar Kancha Iliah also traces how the sacralization of the cow became political, particularly over the colonial era. Simultaneously, the buffalo became invisibilized in "Hindu literature, Hindu tradition, Hindu culture,"[20] even though buffalo milk historically and contemporaneously constitutes the greater part of Indian dairying, and buffaloes are regarded as sacred by many agrarian castes like the Yadavs.[21] Many key Hindu scriptures reference the buffalo in reverential terms too; in the *Vishnu Puranas*, Surabhi, the cow-goddess "was the mother of cows and buffaloes."[22] Some states also conditionally protect buffaloes from slaughter. Nonetheless, caste politics—both Brahminical and Dalit—rely on the differentiation of the cow and the buffalo, including their color, to realize the politics of *humanist* differentiation and exclusion. Viewing the cow and buffalo through the "unquestioned binary of sacred and profane, spiritual and economic animals" is an ongoing legacy of "hegemonic Brahman and Brahman-inflected scholarly writings [that] have divided the bovine world in precisely this way."[23] In a similar way, Iliah too contrasts the exaltation of lighter-skinned Brahmins and cows, with the simultaneous devaluation of darker-skinned Dalits and buffaloes, and asks, "Is it not that it is a black animal indigenous to this land and thus repugnant to the foreign invaders, and has been rewarded for its patient service by being regarded as the symbol of all evil?"[24] Iliah notes that the "racist mind has been extended even to the animal world."[25] However, in this foundational opus on racism and animals in India, Iliah does not consider what the extension of such racism to the animals might also mean for the animals themselves.

Studies on the hyper-politicization of beef in India also miss reflecting on the strategically de-politicized and de-racialized nature of its *milk* production and consumption, warranting the need for a "milk politics." Indian dairying comprises a racially and religiously segmented production supply chain, which weaves through an intricately interwoven informal and formal political economy. It is precisely this segmented supply chain that makes the impossible possible in India, that is the enablement of the *idea* of a supposed "no-slaughter" milk economy, through circulation modes that selectively visibilize, and then *racialize* the slaughter-end of dairy production. In his book *Every Twelve Seconds* on the politics of concealment in industrial slaughter, Timothy Pachirat explains that, at their core, ideas of human civilization are fundamentally concerned with the *concealment* of violence, not its eradication. Pachirat argues that:

> power operates through the creation of distance and concealment and that
> our understandings of "progress" and "civilization" are inseparable from,
> and perhaps even synonymous with, *the concealment (but not elimination)*
> [emphasis added] of what is increasingly rendered physically and morally
> repugnant. Its alternative counters that power operates by collapsing dis-
> tance, by making visible what is concealed.[26]

In India, the ideas of civilizational progress of both the secular state and Hindu political narratives are linked to dairy production. Dairy occupies a vital status in the religious imagination of Hinduism, as well as other Indic religions like Jainism, where cow milk is treated as a sacred commodity. As such, a focus on unveiling the hidden weight of dairying for the animals, and the gendered and reproductive violence involved in the production of what Carol Adams calls "feminized protein,"[27] is highly overdue. In India, the politicization of "cow politics" as a two-dimensional issue, in its simplest form as Hindutva versus secular politics, has allowed *milk* to be depoliticized as a product that contributes to violence to animals, a gendered, racist, and anthropocentric neutralization of harms intrinsic in dairying. Politicizing milk—in contrast to beef—forces us to consider the *living* lactating animal's vulnerability as a "dairy resource," as well as those of racialized humans entrapped in specific segments of Indian milk production.

In India, racism operates *as* sectarianism or communalism, and indeed, casteism. Zaheer Barber argues that religion is inadequate to explain the communal tensions between Hindus and Muslims; rather, in

India, religious identities are mobilized to construct "racialized identities of 'imagined communities.'"[28] The Hindu state specifically relies upon the continuous creation of internal "enemies," produced both through the "'racialization' of Muslims and 'ethnicization' of Dalits."[29] In the former case, the ostensible "differences" between Muslims and Hindus are amplified; in the latter, "the radical difference of Dalits" from Hindu society is repressed "to incorporate them within a Hindu multi-caste and patriarchal family."[30] In recent decades, there are growing concerns that these types of racial or casteist oppressions may be more accurately described as fascism.[31] Such racial, casteist, or, indeed, fascist violence intricately entangles and weaponizes not only vulnerable humans, but also farmed animals who are already enmeshed in the violence of animal agriculture.

As a "farm" animal who is bred in the millions annually in India and worldwide, the extraordinary distinction bestowed on the cow, in contrast to other mundane "food" animals like chickens, buffalo, goat, sheep, pigs, ducks, fish, among others, warrants deeper scrutiny. In the main, political scholarship and analyses on cow protectionism in India have tended to regard cows exclusively as instruments of communal, casteist, and fascist violence—and ignore not only the buffaloes but also other animals enmeshed in dairying such as sheep, goats, and camels. The realities of these *living, sentient animals*, entrapped both as "production" resources, and as weapons of religious ultranationalism and fascism, have almost never been a focus of what has been hitherto a manifestly humanist political discourse. It would seem as though animals, other than human beings, have no stake in their own lives, and "cow politics" can be debated only in terms of bovine bodies as landscapes for intra-humanist oppressions.

Decades of rich feminist, sociological, and political scholarship point out that in being used as *tools* of fundamentalist, racial, patriarchal, or fascist violence, women, for instance, are also *subjects* of such violence.[32] The bovine, of course, is not merely political capital. In India, "livestock," including but not limited to "dairy" animals, contribute to about a quarter of the total earnings from "agriculture and allied activities."[33] Dairying is one of the largest rural employers in the country. What of these nonhuman animal subjects who are mobilized as symbolic, cultural, and productive capital in oppressive human identity politics and development discourses? What then of the sacred cow and the despicable buffalo themselves?

It may seem grossly incongruous—even offensive—to focus on cows and buffaloes when horrific violence against racialized and casteized humans is being perpetrated in the name of protecting cows. However, bringing the bovines into focus as subjects in the discourse on their "protection" can—and, this book argues, *must*—change the entire political discourse on humanist identity politics of power, powerlessness, and privilege. Undertaking the "dangerous work"[34] of subjectifying animal bodies, and considering the "animal" in political studies, and in turn, the "political" in animal studies,[35] can richly deepen our understanding of how power operates in complex configurations of anthropocentrism, sectarianism, casteism, and patriarchy that constitute oppressive institutions—whether fascist movements or animal agriculture—in eerily similar, and mutually reinforcing, ways. It offers a basis for rethinking Indian politics as a *multispecies* terrain, needing to intersect with critical animal studies to be understood in its entirety. When viewed with animals' interests in mind, the notion of "protecting" the cows or other animals begs a greater clarification of what, exactly, their "vulnerabilities"[36] are at human hands, against which they require protection.

Without diminishing the violence committed against racialized and casteized humans in what has been rendered an ethnonationalist, even fascist project of cow protection, *Mother Cow, Mother India*, then, calibrates our attention on the *cows* and *buffaloes*. It frames the animals as key political *subjects* in cow protectionism discourses, rather than treating them, hitherto, as merely objects of political analysis. It emphasizes human–animal hierarchies and relations—in this case, a spectrum of human–bovine relations—as also political. Specifically, this book's central claim is that the framing of the cow as "mother" is one of human domination, wherein the cow is simultaneously commodified for dairy production, and weaponized to create a Hindu state.

Mother Cow, Mother India shows that *species* is crucial for the fullest understanding of how fascism, religious extremism, and nationalism operate. When the species in question is a farmed animal, fascism and nationalism become interlocked with the institution of animal agriculture, in this case, dairying. The book demonstrates that the hyper-politicization of beef in cow protection discourses and practices obscures that the heavily state-subsidized *dairy sector*, India's primary bovine industry, itself requires the slaughter of cows, buffaloes, sheep and other animals used for milk production. To acknowledge the role of milk in cow slaughter, however, places the Indian state in a fraught position. Cow milk, in addition to being widely consumed as a mundane dietary product, is revered by Hindus as sacred. As a vector for the indistinguishably interconnected religiopolitical and commercial value of bovine bodies, the cow's *motherhood* becomes a vital resource for both the secular Indian and aspiring Hindutva state. The fullest extent of anti-casteist and anti-fascist politics in India, must then also compose an *anti-anthropocentric* anti-Hindutva resistance.

Mother Cow, Mother India, then, undertakes a larger task of also bringing into focus *humans'* greater and collective accountability, not only as it pertains to violence based on race, caste, or ethnicity—but also as it is enacted based on species membership. This book explores questions that have almost never been raised in previous political scholarship on cow protectionism in India: What does it mean for an animal to be used in dairy production? What does it mean for a cow to simultaneously have a *sacred* status as "mother" and a *mundane* status as a "dairy" cow? How does the cow's exalted status affect the buffalo—and, indeed, the cow? What and who does cow protectionism "protect"—and what and who does it render vulnerable? The book introduces anthropocentrism to the landscape of political thought on cow protection, and asks: how will attention to anthropocentrism illuminate new ways in which casteism, communalism, and fascism operate in India and elsewhere? In turn, how do oppressive humanist practices that negate the nonhuman animal, directly sustain and reinforce these structures and conditions of violence against marginalized humans, and animals?

Anthropocentrism is "a form of human centredness that places humans not only at the center of everything but also makes 'us' the most important measure of all things."[37] However, the "us" by no means even includes all humans. Rather, it represents a membership of racially elite, gendered humans, such as white, male, or Brahmin, among others, and excluding other racialized, casteized, and gendered humans, and certainly nonhuman animals, as also worthy of moral and political consideration. As philosopher and ethicist Matthew Calarco reminds us, it is precisely *via* anthropocentrism that the "benefits" of human exceptionalism itself are unevenly distributed—across race, gender, ability, and, indeed, species:

> anthropocentrism refers to a set of ideas, structures, and practices aimed at establishing and reproducing the privileged status of those who are deemed to be fully and quintessentially human. . . . What is included and excluded under the rubric of the human shifts over time, and group belonging expands and contracts. . . . [38]

A critique of anthropocentrism allows us to more fully understand how the disruption of human rights that is embedded in cow protectionism, may not in fact, be different from the damage of fundamental interests of other animal beings. Article 3 of the Universal Declaration of Human Rights declares that "Everyone has the right to life, liberty and security of person."[39] In *Pathologies of Power*, medical anthropologist Paul Farmer writes that "the most basic right—the right to survive—is trampled in an age of great affluence."[40] The notion of human rights allows us to reflect on the experience of *suffering*, and the power (and powerlessness) that causes such suffering, beyond "a small slice of civil and political issues."[41] It unveils the historical hierarchies *between* humans that endure into the present that make it, as Farmer argues, one of the most critical issues of contemporary times.

Advancing the scope of the fundamental prerogatives of human beings through an acknowledgment of "sentient rights," political theorist Alasdair Cochrane argues that "human rights are not qualitatively distinct from the basic entitlements of other sentient creatures."[42] Anthropocentrism undermines, in fact, the "the fundamental mission of the human rights imagination [of] checking the excesses of power on vulnerable life."[43] Rather than resulting in the dissolution of any human rights, a shared resistance between subaltern humans and animals might strengthen interspecific alliances that are necessary to undo the violence of anthropocentrism itself.[44]

Indeed, if non-recognition of the "unthinkable (unspeakable)" identities—race, gender, nationality, religion, class, and ability[45]—is foundational to their oppression, then *species* perhaps epitomizes the unthinkable in identity politics. Humanist discourse and language is complicit in normalizing human exceptionalism, and sanitizing the commodification and production processes involving farmed animals. Female human mammals have "nipples" and "breasts," as distinguished from females of other species in forced reproductive labor who have "teats" and "udders." Other sentient animal subjects are neatly displaced as objects and human property by referencing these individuals as "it." The flesh of cows and buffaloes becomes packaged as "beef," their infants are sold as "veal," and their lactate is "dairy" or seemingly innocuously, "milk," distinguished again from *breastmilk*, explicitly a newborn's nourishment, which remains associated mostly with humans who lactate.

Subjectifying individuals and species condemned as "food" may be one of the most subversive political acts of our times. This book thus undertakes a feminist's responsibility to tell stories[46] of those whose lives and deaths are obscured in animal agriculture—in this case, dairying—and to render "ungrievable" lives "grievable."[47] It recalibrates the focus on the individual animals who are incarcerated in farm spaces; it calls for noting, for example, and then politicizing the bellows of a chained mother whose nipples are attached to a hissing, sucking milking machine but whose newborn infant is nowhere to be seen. It is this mother and her absent calf who are at the heart of India's entangled political economy and religious traditions.

DAIRYING: THE WHITEWASHING OF GENDERED, SEXUAL, AND REPRODUCTIVE VIOLENCE TO ANIMALS

The blind spot in India's cow protectionism discourse, politics, legislation, and practices has always been the inconvenient fact of the living cows and buffaloes used for dairying—those sentient, *alive*, and vulnerable animals who are forcibly bred in the millions to serve India's milk sector. India has the highest "livestock" population in the world at 536.76 million (excluding chickens and fish), of which bovines—including cows and buffaloes—comprise approximately 303.76 million,[48] making it the largest global owner of these species.

Invoking the Orwellian concept, Kathryn Gillespie argues in her book *The Cow with Ear Tag #1389*, that milk is the product around which humans employ the most "doublethinking," our ability to "gloss over inconvenient or unsavory truths,"[49] which is vital to sustain oppressions and injustices, whether upon humans or nonhumans. Doublethinking is an intuitive way of acknowledging the reality, which we must quickly deny, to render our own choices bearable.[50] We know, of course, that "milk" is the lactate of another species, a vital source of a newborn's nourishment for months, or even a couple of years, until the natural weaning of that infant can occur. Nonetheless, it is rarely properly understood or acknowledged that cows, buffaloes, goats, sheep, camels, and other animals used for "dairy"—just like humans who can lactate—do not produce milk "naturally"; they have to be continuously and deliberately impregnated in order to keep them lactating. Following a pregnancy of nine months, these mothers are usually impregnated within two months, so they are often pregnant *and* lactating at the same time for most of their short lives.

We are, no doubt, at least dimly aware that the mother-infant bond would have to be disrupted in some manner in order for humans to consume the mother's milk instead. There can be no dairy production in any form without removing the infant immediately from the mother forever, or at least severely restricting their access to the mother. In a classic reversal of the female infanticide prevalent in patriarchal human societies in India (as females are seen as an economic liability[51]), male infanticide is prolific globally to serve dairying, bulls being an economic drain on the milk sector. Newborn males are usually starved to death, or butchered to serve the veal industry, and the female infants are recycled back into dairying. Notably, while beef is hyper-politicized to serve Hindutva politics, there is silence on veal, a product that can be immediately traced back to the dairy sector. Globally, "veal calves" are the discarded males from the milk industry.[52]

We don't, however, dwell too much on what happens to the mother or her calf as a result of this commodification of her milk, nor the normalization of such capitalization of a "food" exclusively meant for a newborn's consumption. In the main, the idea that milk extraction from an animal for human consumption involves *violence* against the mother or her infant is frequently met with surprise, or even offense by lay-persons, nationalists, and scholars alike; it is regarded as a grossly "hyperbolic"[53] exaggeration. The moral affront that could come from considering the *abjection* of the separated mother and newborn that makes dairying possible is therefore elided. The suggestion that any "dairy" animals, anywhere, endure unnatural lives, and suffer intensely when forcibly and repeatedly impregnated, and then when denied the right to suckle their own infants, becomes so bewildering that it is almost impossible to take seriously.

Unlike the commodification of animals as "meat," which obviously requires their death, the capitalization of products derived from *living* animals for human profit and consumption is seen as benign and non-violent because it allegedly involves an activity that the *living* animal does *naturally*—albeit, of course, for their biological young. Human consumption of animal milk, as well as avian ova/eggs, may even be seen as an embodiment of a mutually beneficial relationship between humans and these animals, whereby animals are believed to enter into a relationship of exchange with humans. In the case of animals in dairying, this "exchange" is their reproductive labor—their lactate and their infants—for the "care" that humans give them.

A rich tradition of feminist work has outraged, rightfully, against the multiple violences of patriarchy as "a system of interrelated social structures which allow men to exploit women."[54] This "system" has been almost singularly responsible for sustaining and legitimizing the violent commodification of women's reproductive and gendered labor, and capabilities, as resources to cement patriarchal power structures, including but not limited to both capitalism and religious fundamentalism. However, this framework of patriarchy does not protect other animals from the gendered violence that humans perpetrate upon them. There is breathtaking racist, casteist, sexist, and *humanist* privilege in curating what constitutes violence, *who* is violable, and *how* and *to what extent* such violations may be recognized as occurring at all.

Our *species*-engendered violence to other animals and their infants, I suggest, needs its own term. Over the course of my research, I found myself increasingly preoccupied with the idea of "anthropatriarchy"[55] to explain the total human ownership of living animal bodies as resources; their reproductive systems, germplasm and ovum, labor, familial relationships, and even their genetic material. This absolute control of sentient bodies is the foundation of animal agriculture, and is enabled by humanist frameworks that privilege not only human exceptionalism, but, as I was to learn, also racial exceptionalism.

Is such violence something that only humans experience? Is the term *violence* reserved only for describing ways that humans are harmed and abjected? I don't believe that such an idea can be sustained. Other animals are also subjects of profound violence, experienced both emotionally and physically, when their familial or herd bonds are disrupted. Like animals of our species, other animals, too, experience the violence of enslavement, abduction, physical invasion, and emotions like fear, terror, and the madness of being caged and incarcerated, all of which individual animals in dairying and other "food" production routinely endure.

However, advertising and public relation campaigns that the dairy industry worldwide has been running for decades present images of the cows whose maternal bonds they violate and disrupt as cheerful, beaming, and just *happy* to be lactating floods of their milk for human consumption. A popular French cheese brand goes so far as to call itself "Laughing Cow," depicting a cartoon of an inanely grinning Holstein mother, who is only too thrilled to caricature herself by wearing the round cheese packages, containing product made from her lactate, as ear-tags. That these heavily lactating mothers have just given birth, are still in physical agony from labor and mastitis, have had their newborns forcibly removed, and are most likely bellowing in terror for their infants, are fully obscured by a tinnitus-like chant from the dairy industry, telling us in ever greater pitch that these mothers are *happy, happy, happy, happy, happy, happy, happy, happy.*

At an elemental level, *all* races of humans who consume the lactate of other mammals exploit them as their "mother." However, this chant of happy cows acquires a particular shrillness in India through its depiction of cows as reverenced and loved "mothers" of humans, a misleading and cloying framing. "Indian" cows are not only *happy* but their sense of fulfillment is almost spiritual, evocative of the supreme contentment of a breastfeeding mother nourishing and caring for her infant in physical and emotional safety. The sense of maternal satisfaction of cows bred for the dairy industry in India is presumably unparalleled, revered as they are by their human "progeny" on par with the respect accorded to the most treasured relationship in intra-human relations—as "mother"—or indeed, even above a mother, as a "goddess."

Dairying is, in fact, founded upon violating what we humans generally regard as the most inviolable of relations for our own species—that between a lactating mother and her suckling infant. To obscure this violence in India, not only is the cow's motherhood celebrated as unconditional love for her *human* progeny, but the maternal instincts of other mammals used for dairying are not seen as worthy of any consideration. Thus, an entire spectrum of "violence against certain lives and bodies can become so normalized that it is not viewed as violence,"[56] let alone as the kind of violence that constitutes one of the most enduring anxieties of the feminist movement. In its failure to acknowledge the gendered, sexual, and reproductive violence that humans inflict on animals of other species, exemplified in dairy production, *mainstream feminism*, too, can be uncomfortably, even dangerously, *similar* to *mainstream patriarchy*.

These uncomfortable moral complexities do not feature in political discourses of cow protectionism, even as they are played out on the bodies of the lactating cow and buffalo, and their missing calves. Where the "consumption" of the cow as "mother"/"goddess," and cow as milk-machine is indistinguishably blurred, it can be even more difficult to "see" the violence done in plain sight to *bovines* as mothers of *other bovines* in the milk industry. To understand what the embodied experiences of the animals are, in political and production practices, and why they are important, this book focuses not only on the animals themselves but also the activists who advocate for animals.

"*DO NOT OUT YOURSELF*": THE SILENCING OF ANIMAL ACTIVISTS IN COW PROTECTIONISM

Do not out yourself—implicitly as someone who cared about other animals—I was warned by animal activists, while visiting live animal markets and other sites of animal production. However, the broader human society, driven by the consumption of animal bodies and products, also does not want the animal activist to *out themselves*. The activist who advocates for "food" animals especially, occupies a "killjoy"[57] position at the human dining table, and is an exceptionally inconvenient presence for states and governments who instrumentalize animals as vectors of development and various kinds of nation-building. The presence of anyone who draws attention to and challenges the violence perpetrated by humans against other animal bodies for food is so exceedingly uncomfortable that our social and legal systems can go to great lengths to silence and even criminalize animal activists, intensifying the trauma that comes from even bearing witness in this work.[58]

Being an animal advocate can bring on an overwhelming and almost unendurable sense of trauma[59], "loneliness" or "madness."[60] Animal activists experience intense, ongoing suffering which includes "sadness, grief, depression, anxiety, dread, horror, fear, rage, and shame; intrusive imagery in nightmares, flash backs, and images; numbing and avoidance phenomena; cognitive shifts in viewing the world and oneself, such as suspiciousness, cynicism, and poor self-esteem."[61] In *Aftershock*, LGBTQ and animal activist pattrice jones argues that even the therapy for sufferers of post-traumatic stress events is inadequate for animal activists, as their everyday reality itself is profuse with continuous "nightmarish" triggers, surrounded by the normalization of animal consumption, and routinization of intense animal suffering.[62]

The social ostracization of animal activists can be deeply sexist. In *Animaladies*, Lori Gruen and Fiona Probyn-Rapsey unpack and triangulate the three aspects of the term that have often come to characterize animal activism—animal, maladies, ladies. They write: "*Animaladies* highlight how pathologizing human–animal relationships blocks empathy toward animals because the characterization of animal advocacy as mad, 'crazy,' and feminized distracts attention from broader social disorder regarding human exploitation of animal life."[63] Labelling animal activists as "mad" in particular, has long been a way of "disciplining the movement."[64] The "'madness' of our relationships with animals intersects", they write, "with the 'madness' of taking animals seriously" at all in scholarly work.[65]

This censure of animal activists is not merely socially or emotionally ostracizing. Since the widespread proliferation of factory farms and animal slaughterhouses in the United States in the 1990s, it has become common to criminalize animal activism, branding those who bring light to the realities of *farmed* animals in particular, as *ecoterrorists* or *animal rights extremists*.[66] In many US states, what are termed *ag-gag* laws deem it unlawful for activists to film, photograph, or otherwise document acts of animal cruelty in sites of animal production and slaughter. In Australia, many ag-gag laws have already been passed, or are currently pending consideration in various state parliaments.[67] Thus the messenger, the animal activist who bears witness and then reports uncomfortable realities that may lead to questioning the whole idea of "food" animals at all, is punished for being what every other industry would deem a "whistleblower."

In India, animal activism has been made synonymous with right-wing extremism. In their analyses of the ethics underpinning human–animal relations, it is not uncommon for scholars to unselfconsciously collapse *all* Indian animal activism with right-wing extremism, and accuse animal advocates of sanctioning ostensibly only "narrow" forms of relatedness, this narrowness being one of no *intentional and premeditated* harm and violence to other animal bodies. Where one might be more vigilant about collapsing human rights activists with religious extremists, Indian political and anthropological work often seamlessly equates "Hindu nationalists—and their animal-rights activist allies,"[68] or "Hindu nationalists and animal rights activists around the world."[69] Animal activists in India, then, who have no right-wing sympathies, and who may in fact be human rights advocates themselves, are ungenerously dismissed as extremist—a move that justifies not taking seriously the important work they are doing for animal liberation, and the implications of this work for human social justice movements. This book rejects the tendency to collapse animal activism in India into one monolithic group, offering instead a nuanced account of these very different factions: separating out, on the one hand, "violent and xenophobic Hindu nationalists"[70] who might instrumentalize cow protection for violent racist and casteist ends (often referred to as gaurakshaks or cow vigilantes); and on the other side, animal activists who have dedicated their lives to the alleviation of the suffering of animals, often at the cost of their own mental, emotional, and physical wellbeing (and whom I refer to as *animal activists* throughout the book), while acknowledging that even within these two very broad categories, there may be variations in motivations, tactics, and perspectives.

Why do animal activists undertake work that almost dehumanizes them, and exposes them to widespread ridicule and risk for showing empathy with other animals? Through her work with animal activists in India, cultural anthropologist Naisargi Dave highlights the compulsion to respond—it is almost impossible not to—once that which is hidden by institutional structures is unveiled. In her extensive interviews with animal activists at all levels—from powerful politicians and philanthropists, to workers and volunteers directly involved in risky undercover work or animal care, Dave highlights a common "coming out" story in the recounting of animal activists—the act of *witnessing* animal suffering, an act of looking that is more than observational. There is a moment of "locking of eyes" between the human and the individual animal that is both intensely intimate and political, as "the human's knowledge is not of all animals in general, but of this animal, at this moment."[71] Such recognition demands, herewith, action and responsibility from the person. To counter the carefully hidden violence of routine animal agriculture, Pachirat too emphasizes the urgency of a "politics of sight" to make "*visible what is hidden*, and the need to breach, literally or figuratively, these very zones of confinement and invisibility, in order to bring about social and political transformation."[72]

The logic underpinning such a politics of sight—and one that motivates undercover animal activist exposés—is that once the suffering that animals routinely experience in farms and slaughterhouses is revealed, it will incite—indeed, almost inevitably force—radical change in people.

To a significant extent, this strategy is successful, evidenced by the palpable growth globally in consumer awareness about animal welfare, the proliferation of vegan products in supermarkets, and also, indeed, in the tightening of state-supported ag-gag laws that impose extreme penalties on activists for bringing the violence inherent in animal farming to light. Nonetheless, what of places, including India, where intensive and continuous confinement of animals—in small cages, on short ropes, in overcrowded housing—can be publicly and routinely witnessed? What of spaces where open slaughter, certainly of small animals like chickens is normative? Where live chickens can be weighed alongside potatoes in roadside stalls, where one can carefully examine and select each wide-eyed, panting chick as one would apples, and seeing through unseeing eyes becomes an everyday reality?

Political scientist Jan Dutkiewicz offers a meticulous analysis of the US-based Fair Oaks Farm, which *invites* the public for a tour of their factory farm where pigs are raised for meat and cows for dairy, as a counter to the undercover investigations of animal activists. In actively revealing that which is supposed to be hidden, the *live* openness can also instigate a counter and oppositional politics of sight in its normalization of such violence, such that it is not conceptualized as violent practice. In fact, video witnessing of violence can provoke greater shock than the live witnessing of the same event. As Dutkiewicz writes, "The politics of sight is not only about seeing and not seeing, but about understanding and *interpreting*, about a rhetoric that narrates what is seen [emphasis added]."[73] Dutkiewicz notes the careful curation of the farm tour, and the sanitized presentation of seemingly bland facts about pig bodies that anesthetizes any hesitation or horror in consuming the piglets and their young mothers, who were being observed. In this way, live "revelation [operates] as normalization,"[74] explaining the desensitization that may be necessary to sustain farm work.

This politics of open sight and revelation is epitomized in the normalization of violence that constitutes dairying, and through sentimental narratives of "free-range," organic, farm-fresh, "family owned," or indeed, the "mother" or "sacred cow." Popular representations of the milk sector worldwide present wholesome, nurturing, green images of an industry that has been aptly described as "dark and dairy"[75] for both the violence experienced by the animals, and the walls of secrecy and complicity—conceptual, political, physical—within which it is shrouded. These carefully crafted depictions of "dairy" animals in advertising, politics and popular media in India and elsewhere is increasingly countered by the political activism of animal rescue groups, who video-document the intensely unsanitized, raw realities of mothers, fathers, and their infants entrapped in dairying. The capacity to circulate on social media the video evidence of the sufferings of farmed animals has brought on an unprecedented capacity to bear witness to their realities.

In 2016, the Federation of Indian Animal Protection Organizations (FIAPO) started campaigns called #DontGetMilked and #WhiteLie, mobilizing people to "Ditch dairy and go vegan," based on extensive documentation of the routine cruelties to buffaloes and cows in dairy farms (see figure 0.1). First Information Reports (FIRs) filed by activists

FIGURE 0.1 *A FIAPO anti-dairy campaign at the Asia for Animals Conference in Kathmandu, 2017.*

Source: Photo taken by author.

in India on cruelties in dairying, live animal markets, transportation, and slaughterhouses; court cases documenting the sale of cows and calves by temples and gaushalas to abattoirs; video and photographic documentation of the conditions of buffaloes and cows by animal activists in these spaces; and the stories of various animals rescued from dairy farms into animal shelters, illuminate an entirely different aspect of what has come to be known as "cow politics" or "beef politics" in India. It was here, in the highly political spaces of animal sanctuaries and shelters, and in conversation with animal activists, that I commenced this research.

ENCOUNTERING ANIMALS: THE GENESIS OF THIS RESEARCH

In 2013, I visited an animal shelter for the first time. During interviews with residents of the old walled city of Jaipur on how religion impacts urbanism and determines sense of place, belonging, and access,[76] I learnt, unexpectedly, about electrocuted monkeys. Leaping macaques and langurs in the old heritage spaces of Jaipur would frequently be electrocuted on the naked electric wires that crisscrossed thickly over the tops of buildings. Oftentimes the victims would be mother-and-infant pairs. The "lucky" monkeys would die immediately; the unlucky ones would survive third-degree electric burns, and die a slow death from infections, septicemia, starvation, and attacks from other monkeys, dogs, vultures, and humans. These accounts were related to me in purely anthropocentric terms; understandably, the power cuts as a result of the electrocutions were an inconvenience to the more privileged human inhabitants of the space. However, I could not get the picture of the surviving burnt monkeys out of my head. What happened to them?

At last, I was directed to Help in Suffering, one of the country's oldest animal rescue shelters founded by the British animal activist Crystal Rogers in 1980. As I stepped down from the auto-rickshaw in front of the gate, several barking dogs ran up to me, some hobbling on three legs and leaping around exuberantly, a typical welcome, I was to learn, in animal shelters in India. A retired army colonel volunteered his time to manage the shelter. When I explained the purpose of my visit—my curiosity, really—he gently said, "It is not just the monkeys."

What followed was nothing short of life-changing—a grisly tour of the injuries and traumas inflicted by humans on other animals, and the lives and deaths of nonhuman animals in spaces dominated by humans. Puppies and kittens crushed and paralyzed by moving vehicles; thin, diseased, and limping dogs, including abandoned pedigree "pet" breeds; monkeys, dogs, and cows burnt by acid or boiling water or oil attacks for venturing too close to human habitations when looking for food; "riding" camels with broken nostrils after the ropes threaded through them were pulled violently to make them move faster; emaciated and severely injured donkeys with fractures from carrying loads for India's large brick and construction sector; large numbers of male calves discarded by dairy farmers (always cow calves, as the buffalo calves are sold more easily and openly to the veal market); pigeons with shredded, bloodied wings from the glass-coated twine of soaring kites flown during festivals; and "free-roaming" cows catatonic with chronic colic pain caused by forty to sixty kilos of plastic waste in their four-chambered stomachs.

Nonhuman animal lives are intricately enmeshed in the cultural, political, urban, and technologized worlds of humans, both in India and throughout the world. Yet, in the main, the existence of these living animals is obscured and erased from human imaginations. Their lives are deemed morally irrelevant, even as the realities and conditions of their lives are directly a result of human activities. I peered into the cage of a dog with a severe case of mange—she weakly raised her head as my shadow fell over her thin body, holding my gaze directly for several seconds before dropping her head in exhaustion back onto her thin jute bed.

It was clear to me that day that a vitally important story was waiting to be told of a massive, diverse political group, so severely marginalized as to be almost invisible, awaiting due recognition. As "already subjects of, and subject to, political practices" that determine the conditions of their lives and deaths, animals *are* indeed political subjects.[77] I could, however, scarcely begin to imagine how or what form this scholarly centering of animals as political actors might take.

A year later, I made contact with Pradeep Kumar Nath, founder of the Visakha Society for the Protection and Care of Animals (VSPCA) in Visakhapatnam in Andhra Pradesh state. He patiently answered my emails regarding his Facebook posts on various issues of animal cruelty. I sensed that this might be a critical place to begin my research. I arrived in his small office, which was overcrowded with files, an ancient computer, and two semi-paralyzed street dogs. Pradeep himself, a slender man with curling hair, sat hunched over his table. When I entered at the designated time, he looked up slowly.

"Oh, you are here," he said. And then, with no trace of malice or irritation, he told me, "I really don't want to speak to you."

"Oh!" I said, confused. "Uh, should I come later if this is a bad time?" I stammered, my mind already racing to potential "wasted" days of precious fieldwork time.

Pradeep sighed, a heaving weary exhalation. "Every day is a bad time in this field. You are here, now you might as well stay."

Now even more acutely conscious of wasting this man's time but my need for knowledge eclipsing my hesitation, I told him I knew nothing, nothing at all about the lives of animals in our country. "Tell me everything," I begged. Pradeep sat back and for the next four hours, he spoke of some thirty years of suffering, his own trauma as witness and activist, melding with the suffering of animals he tried to save. I sat immobilized, my head and heart pounding. He told me of the seven cobras he had rescued with their fangs pulled out, and mouths sewn tight by cobra charmers. Wild-caught for tourism, these cobras usually die of starvation and stress after a few weeks of display and entertainment. When the stitches were removed, they yawned wide in relief, the worst stink he had ever encountered emanating from their small mouths. Too sick for rehabilitation, the snakes were euthanized.

He spoke of the young goat in a Kali temple who was killed as a sacrifice, literally by a thousand cuts with a blunt knife. The crowd turned upon Pradeep with sticks and knives when he tried to save the animal.

I learnt of the cat meat trade in India's southern states, where cats would be hunted, stolen or abducted, thrown into sacks and bashed repeatedly against walls to kill them, or be roasted alive. "They believe that the more the animal has suffered, the sweeter its meat," he said. He recalled enduring the violence of pig slaughter while taking an exam as a university student. "Pigs are difficult to kill, and she screamed, screamed like a human. Do you know a pig's scream is like a human screaming?" In drawing attention to the human-like screams of the pig, Pradeep was not intending to anthropomorphize the pig as much as to plead for *empathy* for the pig, to indeed emphasize also, the pig-like screams of the human.

Pradeep described breaking into a backyard slaughterhouse where a live cow was being skinned alive and carved, even as her small calf shook violently in terror, watching the assault on his mother, on unsteady feet. "It was like walking into a surgery theater," he said. "They had cut into her, she was alive, her skin had been peeled off, and she was putting everything into staying alive for her calf. *Her eyes were fixed on her calf only.*" This sentence would continuously reverberate like thunder in my head over the next several years, as humans would blithely talk to me of the cow as *their* mother. The dying cow who was being stripped of her very flesh was putting every effort into trying to save *her baby, her biological infant*, the only progeny who mattered to her.

He told me of the bulls used for traction in agriculture. The diversion of young bulls to pull the plow for agriculture is seen as a "humane" alternative to slaughtering them as "bobby calves" or dairy waste, and is as romanticized in Indian national discourses as the lactating cow. Pradeep described how the bulls were castrated while conscious, and then beaten and broken into total submission to drag a plow weighing several tonnes through waterlogged paddy fields for hours every day. Often, their harnesses would not be removed at the end of the day, forcing them to keep standing all night before another day of hard labor. In a state of chronic starvation, the bulls often collapse in the fields, when they are carted off for slaughter. "You look into the bull's eyes, he is begging for mercy," said Pradeep.

Later in the day, Pradeep took me to visit VSPCA's animal shelter at the Kindness Farm, an unexpectedly arcadian sanctuary across eight acres in the outskirts of the port city of Visakhapatnam. Generously large by the standards of most Indian animal shelters, it was home to over 800 individual animal refugees of different species. "I have a surprise for you," Pradeep said. We turned a corner to look straight into an enclosure full of almost a hundred emus, native birds of Australia, staring at us with a slightly demented gaze, pressing against the fencing in curiosity, or for food. Originally exported by Australia for what was to become a failed experiment in emu meat and eggs, these birds were hatched in India, many with disabled legs, and rescued en route to their slaughter. I felt sickened by this sight of international trafficking of animals. I felt distressed by the complicity of global human institutions that, through a "visa," gave me full right to return to Australia but not the naturally vastly free-roaming native emus, permanently exiled, and incarcerated as refugees in a densely overpopulated Indian city.

I returned to my hotel room, sat on the floor, and wept for several hours. Upon these animal bodies, entire systems of human life were founded. I could scarcely believe the multiple privileges of being born upper-class, "upper-caste," and above all, being born a *human animal*, where not even being born female had ever deprived me of access to a wholly privileged life. Why me, and why not that cow? Why me, and why not that pig or emu? I returned the next morning to the VSPCA office, with no more clarity about what to do. "Shall I write about the goats?" I asked Pradeep. "Or the cobras? Oh god, how about a comprehensive study on all animals?"

We went back to the Kindness Farm that afternoon. As we walked, and Pradeep narrated the rescue stories of different animals as we met them, he gave me what was to be the first critical piece of advice in advancing this study. "Focus on the cows," he said.

> The cow has become so political that the animal has been lost. The animal is lost even though it is in full focus. The cow is an example of how totally we can lose the animal even while making the biggest issue out of it. The cow issue has colored matters for all other animals also. Even we as animal activists do not know how to respond to this. There is maximum confusion with the cows. Do the cows.

And so, four years after my Indian colleague explained that he did not eat dairy because of how cows are treated, I set out on a path of research and activism that would lead to this book.

With "beef lynchings" beginning to surface in the news with alarming frequency, combined with news reports of India's rapidly growing beef exports, a focus on cows seemed timely. In 2016, the U.S. Department of Agriculture's seminal *From Where the Buffalo Roam* report would confirm that India had become the world's leading beef exporter in 2014.[78] I started to focus on the ways in which cows were referenced in political, media, and anecdotal discourses—the spotlight almost always being on their trafficking for slaughter, which, I was to realize much later, defined the final stages of a *dairy* production continuum. It would be even later when I realized that my research, too, had almost risked missing the presence of buffaloes in India's cow politics, despite their singular part in beef exports specifically.

It was around this time that the second critical piece of methodological advice came from Dawn William, managing director of the Blue Cross of India, Chennai, when I visited the shelter a few months later. An ex-military man turned animal activist, Dawn exuded a no-nonsense demeanor. As I began asking Dawn about what he knew about cow trafficking in Tamil Nadu, he stepped in, turned the interview completely around, and began firing questions at *me* about what I had learned so far—and *how* I had learned it. "I heard . . .," I told him. "I spoke to . . .,'" I explained. "I read . . .," I stated.

Dawn held up his hand, and gave me advice that only an animal activist, fully immersed and engaged politically in the daily realities of the animals, could offer. "When you come back after finishing this study, I don't care what you conclude," he said. "But I don't care for *opinions*. I don't want your *opinion*. People don't hesitate to have opinions about animals without seeing what they actually go through. You decide what you want, but *see* everything first. See whatever you can. And only then you decide."

WITNESSING ANIMALS: SPACES, POSITIONALITY, AND
METHODS OF RESEARCH

Dawn's advice to heighten the focus on animals as subjects has had the deepest imprint upon this research, shaping every aspect of the three years of empirical, archival, and ethnographic work that focuses the *cows* and *buffaloes* in India's cow protection politics. Ethnography is a popular research method, particularly in anthropological work, to study humans and their cultures by observing them. The researcher, in so far as possible, aims to position herself as a member of this society, in an attempt to understand their cultures and politics from their standpoint. Since 2010, the sub-field of multispecies ethnography[79] has become increasingly popular, which aims to observe other animals to inform research. This methodological trend, however, is far from unproblematic in the field of animal studies and splinters almost neatly into two further subfields based on the politics of each.

It was crucial for this book to veer away from mainstream forms of multispecies ethnography, a methodological intervention that has become yet another way of instrumentalizing other animals to understand the *human condition*. As such, it has an "extremely narrow agenda"[80] that, in effect, reinforces human domination, human–animal binaries, and does little, if anything, to address the deeply uneven and naturalized[81] hierarchies that exist between human and other animals. At its core, it often reflects the reluctance on the part of individual researchers to consider their own personal objectification of animals by eating them or their products, and "unwillingness to actively work to undo their internalized speciesism."[82] In maintaining and legitimizing human supremacy, and correspondingly, animal abjection, such multispecies ethnography often deeply harms other animals by reinforcing their status as abject to human animals. Unsurprisingly, such work does not attempt to engage directly with animal activists.

The use of cows in Indian historical, political, and anthropological discourses to understand intra-human politics and hierarchies is precisely an enactment of such unselfconscious ethnographical anthropocentrism. Cows are instrumentalized as a way of articulating India's intra-humanist politics to the extent that discourses on "cow protection" have been rendered almost incoherent when read against what might constitute genuine vulnerabilities for the animals themselves.

By contrast, this book is a conscious and deliberate attempt to engage in "posthuman ethnography"[83] or "politicized multispecies ethnography"[84] that explicitly chooses to challenge the overt or covert anthropocentrism in social sciences research. In being consciously focused on exploring genuinely ethical and respectful human-to-animal relations and improving the lives of animals, these methods are political in their dedication to advocacy for other animals. This work is necessarily mindful about working "emotionally"[85] with animals as a way of understanding, in so far as possible and witnessable, the full extent of their rich emotional lives. In working this way, I have not "refused the risk of an intersecting gaze [with another animal] . . . and in response undone and redone [myself]."[86] It is arguably more coherent scholarship and politics to make legible the realities of the animals involved in cow protectionism. To persist in an endeavor to dismantle the chains that hold human minorities abject *without* sacrificing the interests and lives of animals is certainly more challenging, but ultimately more meaningful to the fullest ethical possibilities and responsibilities of feminism, social justice, and emergent multispecies democratic politics in India and elsewhere.

I conducted my research for this book between 2014 and 2017, during exceptionally troubling political times. It was in 2014 that the National Democratic Alliance, led by the BJP came to power, and Narendra Modi became the prime minister of India. The study was conducted in a sociopolitical climate where ultranationalist Hindu narratives and practices of cow vigilantism were on the rise, violently marginalizing minorities who were depicted as killing cows.

My own foray into the world of animals—and cows specifically—became open to political interpretation. I am a member of the "upper-caste" Brahmin community that has been historically and politically associated with cow protectionism. My intellectual curiosity made sense to some Hindu ultranationalists; as a Brahmin, I'd naturally, they assumed, be concerned about the preservation of the cow, and by extension, the restoration of the Hindu civilization. Others viewed my work with skepticism for the same reason. Some Dalit colleagues initially responded with fury. "How dare you think about animals before thinking about us?" a senior political student leader at Hyderabad's Dalit-majoritarian Osmania University asked me in understandable anger.

The directness of the question froze me. I genuinely wanted to understand the complexities of diverse Dalit worldviews on how animals constituted their politics and sociologies. And yet I froze because my caste rendered my inquiry—undertaken during a time of rising violence in Hindutva cow vigilantism, no less—instantly suspect, a cliché, and even potentially, yet again, an assertion of Brahminical dominance, a caste often associated with knowledge and learning. It was a powerfully humbling reminder of how the shrill political and self-righteous narratives of cow protectionism had rendered the idea of a genuine anti-caste animal politics implausible. "I have not come to reinforce any hierarchy," I pleaded. I truly wanted to arrive at a rounded understanding of cow protectionism beyond the one-dimensional account of Hindu and Hindutva groups. It was in this spirit of bringing the most marginalized into focus as political actors, even as they were among the most exploited as political and economic resources, that I also trained my focus on the animals. I had explicitly set myself the difficult task of *not* defaulting to the people versus animals impasse, "solutions" that I believed to be improvisations at best.

However, in that moment, my stammered explanations were of no consequence. It was the dominance of a particular intelligibility—perceived Brahminical vested interests—that was being rightfully challenged. On what basis could I, who comes from a caste whose humanity was realized, presumed and unchallenged, suggest that we also need to move to categories beyond "the human," when the humanity of those against whom cows were weaponized, was constantly under attack? This central objection raised a profusion of other questions for me. Would my plea for animal liberation make me culpable in rendering more vulnerable those who were already dehumanized in the name of animal protection? Did animal liberation inevitably clash with Dalit liberation? And what did animal liberation, and specifically that of the cows, mean for "upper-caste" politics and culture? Did it strengthen Brahminism—or could it possibly bring hitherto unchallenged Brahminical practices around animal exploitation into question? Could such a scrutiny offer anything meaningful to Dalit politics? How best might I—and must I—use the unearned privileges of my birth in negotiating the landscape of unfathomable violence in which both humans and animals were enmeshed, and where Hindu nationalists often featured prominently in perpetrating that violence?

I had no answers to these questions that raced through my head that day. The only respectful or adequate response I could offer, I understood, was to engage in "a politics of listening."[87] I needed to speak less and remain uncomfortable. And as I listened, I learned about the myriad ways in which pain and humiliation upended the lives of these students and scholars, as they told me of their grief over the then recent suicide of University of Hyderabad Dalit PhD student Rohith Vemula whose scholarship was suspended on a charge of being supposedly involved in "anti-nationalist" politics; their rage at the news of a Dalit woman being stripped and forced to drink urine by a "higher" caste couple in Madhya Pradesh[88]; daily reports of police torture of Dalits; and then, in their personal lives, pointedly being served on disposable paper plates in a friend's house; the social prohibition against entering many temples; and insolent treatment at every institution, from the university to the hospital to the police station. Against this context, the targeted beef bans being instituted in state after state at the time brought on another slew of humiliation, rage, and fear, reinforcing the multiple oppressions of casteism that Dalits experience from virtually every caste deemed "higher."

Caste, broadly, is a system of social organization that is "invested in purity, pollution, endogamy, hierarchy, and inflexibility locked in the rigidity of birth."[89] Caste organizes society throughout Asia, Africa, and North and South America, though the way it negotiates and maintains a hierarchical social system in a manner that explicitly produces "outcastes" has rarely been studied outside of India.[90] Though a fifth of the world's human population may claim a caste identity,[91] casteism has not been taken as seriously as racism. At the United Nations World Conference Against Racism, Racial Discrimination, Xenophobia, and Related Intolerance (WCAR) in Durban in 2001, some 300 Dalit representatives from India and Nepal described casteism as a "descent-based discrimination", and made a landmark appeal for the international recognition of casteism as oppressive identity politics.[92] This demand remained unmet due to vociferous resistance from the Indian government at the time.[93]

Caste's primary distinction from race lies in the notion of "purity"; as Suraj Yengde explains, "Belief in the *purity of soul and blood* affirms the raison d'être of the caste system [emphasis added]."[94] The most pernicious impact of such sociobiological purity in India is the production of the outcaste through "untouchability," or "the practice of excluding, from social or religious life, people who are believed to be *permanently impure*."[95] Such ideas of purity and pollution are solidified *via* labor,[96] differentiating those who might own cows and dairy farms for instance, from those who engage in slaughter or tanning labor, even as these "pure" and "impure" activities *together* compose the dairy production continuum.

Animals, I would learn over the years, are not incidental to caste politics. Animals, in fact, are used as core political metaphors to sustain the typologies of *many* polarizing caste-based nationalisms in India, and to maintain adversarial caste positionalities and hierarchies.[97] While the abjections of racism might rely on comparisons with the animal—the figurehead of the black and the animal being a classic example[98]—casteism operates somewhat differently. In the logic of casteism, humans of *all* castes are explicitly interlinked with animals; the noteworthy distinction lies not in the human-to-animal comparison itself, but *which* group of humans are related with *which* species of animals. In her opus *Hindus: An Alternative History*, Wendy Doniger notes that certain animal species and certain human castes are politically connected in the Atharva Vedas based on purported shared social qualities. For example, "lucidity or goodness or intelligibility (*sattva*), energy or activity or passion (*rajas*), and darkness or inertia or entropy (*tamas*)," respectively dominate in cows and Brahmins; horses and Kshatriyas (warrior-castes); and dogs and low castes.[99] Notably, in the Hindu imagination then, other animals are *also* born into caste, and inherently carry the admirable or stigmatizing qualities of their particular caste.

In exploiting their political and affective labor to sustain differentiation in identity and nationalist politics, animals are used across the caste spectrum.[100] The politics of differentiation certainly has a purpose; as Dwaipayan Banerjee reminds us, it allows "those that are seen as radically different as having the capacity for coherence"[101]—including, arguably, radically different *nonhuman animals*. Equally, he explains, in fixating on difference, politics gets "fetishized",[102] and in caste and communal politics, the *animal* too becomes fetishized.

Caste, of course, cannot be read exclusively through the animal, as indeed, the animal is also not defined solely by caste, though each is essential to the fullest understanding of the typologies of caste and species. Introducing the animal body into political debate *only* through caste, religion, or race, also forecloses the possibility of *species* having their own legitimate presence, in their own right, in radical democratic politics, however uneasy, messy, and complicated. Animals are subordinated not only by casteism or communalism, but centrally by the implicit nonhuman othering of humanism[103] itself. Instead, it is only through presence of "the animal" as his own sovereign body in political debates and praxis that the complex task of important and meaningful interspecific alliances[104] between animal activist groups and some of the most marginalized human groups may be creatively imagined.

That day in Osmania, as student after student recounted the events that led to the annual beef festivities as Dalit resistance in the university campus, I thought of the intricate and abject ways in which "untouchability" continues to pervade and shape socio-political life in contemporary India *via* the animal body. It was clear that beef had been weaponized as a core vector of "untouchability" in India—and beef consumption had thus been rendered an explicit act of Dalit resistance. Hindutva oppression thus becomes enacted in different ways against the subaltern human body, and the subaltern animal body, even as both are tightly enmeshed in the perpetration of violence against each other. Against this bifurcated oppositional framing of the cow and the Dalit, it becomes all the more important to be attuned to creative and meaningful ways in which interspecific solidarity may be imagined and enacted. Banerjee writes, "any politics of thick solidarity should acknowledge anthropologies (in the plural)," specifically those born out of colonialism and other oppressions.[105] Inspired by postcolonial law and feminist scholar Maneesha Deckha's call to "*centralize* the dynamics of race and culture" in feminist animal studies, I left Osmania with a solidified commitment to foreground caste and religion in my study, critical to avoiding the legitimate charges of ethnonationalism and elitism.[106]

The animal, however, and the farmed animal in particular, is also subordinate to *human* oppressions; as critical animal geographers Collard and Gillespie write, "entrenched hierarchies between humans and other animals are a defining feature of our relationships."[107] Could a radical humanist politics of thick solidarity, then, find its fullest expression by being in relation through allegiance and solidarity with radical animal politics and extending fellowship to nonhuman others, in what are multispecies social and political worlds? Through the years, I would speak to diverse caste and religious groups throughout the Indian dairy production continuum with different economic interests in the *cow commodity* that would each be narrated and justified in differential caste terms. And I would come to understand that in India, a *politicized* multispecies ethnography was also an *anti-caste* methodology, in its plea to *all* caste groups to take seriously the de-commodification of animals in order to undo the violence of anthropocentrism , a necessary precursor, as I would come to believe, to dismantling caste itself.

The exploitation of cows and buffaloes for milk production is not confined to any one Indian state; thus, it became necessary to engage in a pan-India exploration, the first of its kind that sought to understand how actual buffaloes, cows, bulls, and their calves were embroiled in India's bovine industrial complex as (re)productive, religious, and political capital. I visited the states of Delhi, Uttar Pradesh, Haryana, Rajasthan, Gujarat, Maharashtra, West Bengal, Tamil Nadu, Kerala, Karnataka, Telengana, and Andhra Pradesh. Although this research by no means covered the full extent of the bovine industrial complex in India, Uttar Pradesh, Rajasthan, Maharashtra, and Gujarat are among the leading dairy-producing states.[108] Uttar Pradesh, Rajasthan, Haryana, Gujarat, and Maharashtra were also particularly volatile landscapes of Hindu ultranationalism where stringent cow slaughter and beef bans were enacted during this time.

As Communist Party-ruled states where the killing of cows was permitted, Kerala and West Bengal have some of India's few licensed cow slaughterhouses. Kerala is one of the highest consumers of meat, including beef in India, and is the leading state for cow slaughter.[109] West Bengal serves as a conduit for cross-border trafficking of cows and other animals into Bangladesh. In 2019, news reports emerged that the Indian Border Security Force had found cows with crude explosives attached to their necks in West Bengal near the India-Bangladesh border so that rescuers, whether cow vigilantes, animal activists, or military personnel, might be blown up along with the animals.[110] However, "misdirection" through the media is often an endemic political game throughout local, state, and global geopolitics.[111] State institutions, including the police, assert that cow smuggling finances terrorism,[112] a charge then used to justify increased militarization of contested international borders based on the ostensible "illegal" smuggling of cows.[113] However, the experiences of border security and transporters in negotiating the "smuggling" and "seizure" of cows blurs the bovine body as sacred or commodity, disrupting the legal/illegal binary that frames the "cattle trade" in the India-Bangladesh borderlands.[114]

To develop deeper understandings of how cows are enmeshed in politics, I focused this research on what I classified as spaces of "production" and "protection" in these states. These sites are located in the continuum of informal, semi-formal, and formal political economies. Dairying may be semi-informal but legal; the transportation of animals between sites along the dairy production continuum falls in the shadow zone of legality, illegality, and even criminality as the purpose of movement is not always clear; and under India's cow protection laws, the slaughter segment of dairy production generally falls in the black/illegal economy. "Protection" spaces such as gaushalas also fall in twilight zones of authorized/unauthorized, and even legal/illegal. As dairy production spaces, gaushalas are not immune to the realities of market logics that require the disposal of unproductive animals.

I visited "production" sites such as dairy farms, licensed and unlicensed slaughterhouses, frozen bovine semen farms, state animal husbandry departments, veterinary and public health departments, agricultural and dairy research institutes, and "cattle" *mandis* in different states. I spoke to dairy farmers, dairy owners, dairy economists, veterinary and bovine genetic scientists, transporters, middlemen, and butchers. In all sites where living animals were present, I spent hours *with* them, to observe animal behaviors, bovine-to-bovine engagements, and bovine interactions with the human workers. Collard and Gillespie write, "Attention to these contact zones and to the fraught power relations existing in them is a key feature in a critical geographical multispecies ethnographic approach."[115] The observation method "allows the time to learn animal gestures, expressions, and sounds that we can use in many ways to further our understanding," to ensure that "humans and animals can achieve 'operative understandings' that not only make routine interactions possible but also provide insights into the animal mind."[116] Like Pachirat's ethnographic account of human labor in a US slaughterhouse, "[m]y account relies . . . on context, with an emphasis on little things and multiple voices, and with a tolerance for ambiguity."[117]

To understand bovine realities in empirical and conceptual spaces of *protection*, I visited animal sanctuaries, gaushalas and gosadans (municipal gaushalas), Hindu temples, police departments, and highway commissions. I went to gaushalas, managed by temples devoted to the cow-loving god Krishna, or managed by Hindu political parties, state municipal corporations, private owners, and Hindu trusts. I interviewed managers, workers, priests, and devotees about their ideas and practices of cow protection, and about their understandings of the concept and role of gaushalas. I spoke to gaurakshaks and activists from animal welfare organizations like FIAPO, Animal Welfare Board of India (AWBI), and the Humane Society International India offices, and critically, the local animal shelters and gaushalas of different cities.

My explicit positionality in all spaces varied based on my intuitive sense of the place and relational dynamics. The purpose of the interviews—to understand the production and protection conditions of animal existence—was explained candidly throughout, to both productionists and protectionists. This was a routine inquiry at the time as media interest in cow transporting, and the halting of trucks by animal activists and cow vigilantes, was high.[118] I intuitively relied on political ethnographer David Tittensor's advocacy for trust and reciprocity while doing ethnography in difficult or hostile climates.[119] In my respondents' counter questions to me, they too drove the conversation, and made decisions about entering our dialogues of reciprocity and trust.

Some of the respondents gave permission to be identified. Others, including many government officials and those working in the disposal end of dairy production (including those operating in authorized slaughterhouses), did not. However, regardless of whether this permission was provided, only the names of those respondents who are already recognized in the media for their work have been identified in this book. These names are used in full; in all other instances, names have been anonymized through the use of *a changed first name only*, as the intent is not to personalize or individualize any aspect of the cow protection or production complex. Rather, the focus is on the systems and processes of the entangled informal and formal economies that are normative in all animal farming in India, and indeed, globally.

FOCUS on the cows. Pradeep's words still reverberate in my mind, even years later. *Focus on the cows.* What does it look like to *focus on the cows and buffaloes, the animals,* even as they are prominently embedded in fraught landscapes of human political conflict? It is impossible to disentangle the bovines themselves from the political, religious, and economic context in which they are situated. To understand their lives and experiences, it is necessary to trace how the lives of cows and buffaloes are shaped by legal, political, and economic histories of modern, independent India.

CHAPTER 1

DAIRY POLITICS AND INDIA'S MILK NATIONALISMS

THE SEAMLESS CONTINUUM OF INDIA'S MILK-AND-BEEF ECONOMY

India's status as one of the world's largest milk producers, beef exporters, and leather producers—industries that are substantially sustained by the mass slaughter of bovines—implausibly coexists with its legislative prohibitions on cow killing. Some twenty-eight Indian states and union territories have legislation that fully or conditionally prohibits the slaughter of cows, bulls, and calves, and criminalizes beef production and consumption.[1] States like Chhattisgarh, Maharashtra, Gujarat, Karnataka and Madhya Pradesh also regulate the slaughter of water buffaloes, indigenous to South Asia. Many states criminalize the consumption of beef sourced from cows. In 2015, Maharashtra state banned the sale and consumption of beef, an offense that could attract up to five years in jail.[2] Later in the same year, Haryana state enacted the Haryana Gauvansh Sanrakshan and Gausamvardhan Act of 2015, which doubled the penalties for cow slaughter to Rs 100,000 (approximately US$ 1,390) and up to ten years' imprisonment. In Gujarat, cow slaughter is punishable with life imprisonment under the Gujarat Animal Preservation Act of 1954, as amended by the Gujarat Animal Preservation (Amendment) Act of 2017. An imprisonment penalty of seven to ten years has been included for transporting beef (i.e., the flesh of cows, bulls, bullocks, and calves).[3]

In a stunning paradox, however, in 2014 the cow-protecting, beef-criminalizing, Hindu-majoritarian nation emphatically placed itself on the global beef production map as the world's leading exporter. India's production peaked at 4,250,000,000 metric tonnes of beef and veal in 2017.[4] Of this amount, less than 50 percent, or 1,849,000 metric tonnes of beef and veal were exported,[5] and the majority was consumed domestically in India. Much of India's beef is extracted from water buffaloes;[6] however, there is evidence that cow beef constitutes a significant part of exports.[7] Indeed, based on increasing suspicion of contraband cow beef exports, the Indian government directed the Agricultural and Processed Food Products Export Development Authority (APEDA) in October 2015 to test animal flesh at export ports to ensure it was not cow meat.[8]

India's meteoric rise in beef production had been ongoing for several decades prior to its peak in 2014, even preceding the liberalization of its economy in 1991. In 1997, India became the world's largest milk-producing country, a title it has since held consistently.[9] Several years later in 2001, the National Commission on Cattle was established as an agency of the Department of Animal Husbandry, Dairying and Fisheries (DAHD), Government of India, in recognition of the use of cows in India's "agricultural and rural economy," and to respond to "persistent demands . . . to prevent their slaughter."[10] The Commission's report calculated the birth rate of the total estimated population of cows in India over a five-year period between 1987 and 1992, based on a calving rate of fifteen to eighteen months.[11]

They estimated that there is a shortfall of seven crores (70 million) cows, which cannot be attributed to natural death alone, even allowing for an exaggerated infant mortality rate as high as 50 percent. Akin to Amartya Sen's conception of "missing women" in South Asia to explain the region's skewed sex ratio due to female infanticide and feticide,[12] it is possible to conclude that there are "missing cows" in India due to illegal slaughter.

How is this possible in a country that ostensibly imposes stringent criminal penalties on the slaughter of cows, bulls, and calves, and the possession, consumption, and sale of beef? The answer: through cow slaughter on an industrial scale that operates via complex and widespread networks of underground trafficking in the black and gray economies. And in India, the core of this intricate, unauthorized—even criminal— transport economy for cow slaughter is, in fact, *not* the hyper-politicized beef industry.

India's cow protection laws and political discourses entirely sidestep one critical fact.

The *dairy* industry is a slaughter industry, no less than the beef industry,[13] and India has the largest dairy herd in the world.[14] India has consistently had the largest "beginning stocks" of bovines in recent years, giving it a competitive edge in all leading bovine industries, whether milk, leather, or beef (see table 1.1). India is second only to the European Union in dairying, and has maintained constant growth in milk production, even throughout the global pandemic in 2020–21 (see table 1.2). In 2020, the top importers of dairy from India were: United Arab Emirates, Bangladesh, United States, Bhutan, Singapore, Saudi Arabia, Malaysia, Qatar, Australia, and Oman.[15]

TABLE 1.1: *Beginning stocks of "all cattle" (million)*

Country	2019	2020	2021	2022
India	302.70	303.20	305.50	306.70
Brazil	238.15	244.14	252.70	264.10
China	89.15	91.38	95.62	99.50

Source: USDA Foreign Agricultural Service. n.d., b. Custom Query: "Animal numbers, cattle beginning stock." Retrieved 28 January, 2022, from https://apps.fas.usda.gov/psdonline/app/index.html#/app/advQuery.

TABLE 1.2: *Milk production by the leading dairy nations, 2019–2021 (million tonnes)*

Country	2019	2020	2021
India	191	194.8	199
European Union	147.1	149.67	150.05
United States	99	101.2	102.6
China	32.9	35.5	35.7

Source: USDA Foreign Agricultural Service. n.d., c. Custom Query: "Dairy milk fluid, production." Retrieved 28 January, 2022, from https://apps.fas.usda.gov/psdonline/app/index.html#/app/advQuery.

TABLE 1.3: *Numbers of "milch" or "dairy" cows, buffaloes and goats in India, 2019 (million)*

"Dairy" animals in India	2019
Milch cattle (cows) (in milk and dry)	74.18
Milch buffaloes (in milk and dry)	51.17
Milch goats (in milk and dry)	69.65

Source: Department of Animal Husbandry and Dairying, 2019, *20th Livestock Census: 2019 All India Report*. Animal Husbandry and Dairying Statistics Division. Ministry of Fisheries, Animal Husbandry and Dairying, Government of India, New Delhi. Retrieved 5 July, 2022, from https://dahd.nic.in/sites/default/filess/20th%20Livestock%20census-2019%20All%20India%20Report_0.pdf.

India has conducted a livestock census every five years since 1919, although the most recent census was released after a gap of seven years, in 2019. The 20th Livestock Census[16] notes that the numbers of "milch" or "dairy" cows and goats has increased since the previous census conducted in 2012, though the number of buffaloes has remained stable (see table 1.3). Notably, the number of exotic crossbreed cows has increased by 32.2 percent since the 2012 census—a trend that will have a pronounced impact on the nature of cow protection politics. Intriguingly, the 2019 census notes an unexplained 42 percent drop in the population of male buffaloes.

It is impossible to be the world's largest dairy farm without being among the world's biggest bovine slaughterhouses. It is impossible to sustain dairying, an industry which *requires* continuously impregnating and breeding ever larger numbers of animals, without slaughtering the "useless" males and "spent" females. It would be uneconomical to divert resources such as feed, shelter, housing, and (human) labor toward animals who are deemed "spent." Once too weak and malnourished for further childbirth, or if born male, these animals will be moved from the dairy farm to the slaughterhouse in one seamless and cooperative continuum. The profits from selling "unprofitable" cows and buffaloes from dairying are used to buy more of these animals for the milk sector. As Bazzoli et al. note, "The sale of cull cows contributes to the overall profit of dairy herds."[17] Leather, beef, veal, gelatin, and even the sugar industry, which uses bone char from bovine bones to refine white sugar, are *by-products* of Indian dairying, and in fact are what make milk cheaply available. In India, it is the *dairy* industry that is vital for the flourishing of *all* of India's other booming bovine industries—and these, in turn, sustain dairying.

INDIA'S "DAIRY" COWS, THE WORLD'S LARGEST BEEF SECTOR—AND THE SILENT VEAL INDUSTRY

India's significant dairy achievements are highly exciting prospects for Indian domestic and global beef production. The sheer scale and speed of India's status as a global beef producer is remarkable *for a country that rears no cows specifically for beef.* In two short years between 2013 and 2015, Landes et al. note that "India increased its share of world beef exports from just 5 percent to about 21 percent."[18] What is remarkable about India's leading beef exports is that its own bovine breeding policies do not cater to such production at all. Notably, other leading beef producers such as Australia, Brazil, and the United States have booming breeding industries oriented around cows specifically raised for beef production. It is a trait of modern, scientific animal agriculture to breed animals to extract very specific consumable features and qualities from animal bodies. Globally, as Gupta et al. note, "Historically, there was little distinction between dairy and beef cattle, with the same stock often being used for both meat and milk production, but now cattle are bred specifically for meat or milk."[19] India's competitive edge in beef exports comes *despite* the fact that it has to compete against other "beef" countries that breed cows for their flesh, *and* it has to contend with disadvantageous pricing for Indian beef.

When specifically farmed for beef production, cows are bred for traits like lean muscle and other physical features such as "carcass weight, which has good heritability, and eye muscle area, rib and rump fat."[20] It is important that cows bred for beef have qualities of "tenderness, marbling, and muscle deposition that correspond to differences in growth rate, weight at the time of slaughter, and fatness at slaughter."[21] Certain breeds of animals bred for meat, including cows, have to endure double-muscling,[22] a cultivated genetic trait that results in the development of a double layer of muscular tissue in these young animals, leading to acute infant or childhood arthritis and the inability to even move normally. These deliberately produced disabilities[23] for "meat" are exemplified by Cornish Cross chicks or Pekin ducklings who attain infant obesity at lightning speed so that these chicks and ducklings can be killed for their flesh at only eight weeks to be sold as "chicken" or "duck" meat.

Indian beef, though, is sourced from the worn-out bodies of overworked, emaciated buffaloes and cows bred for dairying, whose "meat" is of poorer quality compared with the flesh extracted from cows bred specifically for beef. Indian beef is comparable, for instance, to the "chicken meat" from the scrawny bodies of egg-laying hens. Much of India's exported beef is carabeef (buffalo beef), which is regarded as inferior to cow beef and hence priced lower than beef from competitors like Australia and Brazil (see table 1.4). Meat and Livestock Australia, a public authority that researches and promotes the meat industry in Australia and internationally, explicitly notes the dairying foundations of India's beef sector as sourced from buffaloes, though it chooses to remain silent on the role of cows in both the dairy and subsequently the beef sector:

> As water buffalos account for around 45% of the dairy herd in India, *the growth in Indian buffalo meat production is largely driven by the expanding dairy industry. It has benefited indirectly from the improvements in dairy farm management*, veterinary care, genetics and nutrition, along with private investment and government support *in the dairy sector*. [Emphasis added][24]

How, then, does India manage to rate as a competitive beef country (that is, make as much or more money from its exports as its competitors) when its unit value for beef is almost half that of its competitors? For markets and production lines that are global in scale—or in other words, for "globalized value chain(s) relying on economies-of-scale production"[25]—any form of seeming "disadvantage," including low-quality products, can in fact be extremely profitable. The flesh of cows emaciated from the dairy industry is globally used as ground beef, and it is precisely this cheap meat that supports the global fast-food industry. In Gillespie's work on the lives of "dairy" cows in the United States, a

TABLE 1.4: *Global beef pricing per unit (US$/kg)*

Country	2019	2020
India (boneless frozen buffalo)	2.92	2.85
Brazil	3.90	4.45
USA	5.61	7.06
Australia	5.54	5.86

Source: Meat and Livestock Australia. 2020. Global Snapshot: Beef. 2019 data. Retrieved 30 July, 2022 from: https://www.mla.com.au/globalassets/mla-corporate/prices--markets/documents/os-markets/red-meat-market-snapshots/2020/global-beef-snapshot-jan2020.pdf. Meat and Livestock Australia. 2021. Global Snapshot: Beef. 2020 data. Retrieved 11 February, 2022, from: https://www.mla.com.au/globalassets/mla-corporate/prices--markets/documents/os-markets/red-meat-market-snapshots/2021/global-beef-industry-and-trade-report.pdf.

milk farmer told her, "If you are eating a burger from a fast-food joint, you're most definitely eating a dairy cow."[26] Indeed, America's appetite for burgers is so vast that although it is the world's largest consumer and third largest exporter of beef, it is also the world's largest *importer* of beef—for its hamburger economy. The US *Beef Magazine* explains, "The import side seems harder to understand but it mostly relates to the hamburger market. . . . We don't produce enough cull cow meat."[27] Beef-breed cows raised for high-quality beef in the United States would not be "wasted" on something as unprofitable as ground beef. Thus, "cull cows," or discarded "dairy" cows are killed and then exported by top "dairy" countries like Australia to the United States to meet this demand. Meat and Livestock Australia confirms, "Manufacturing beef for burgers and other processed beef products make up a large proportion of Australian beef sold into the foodservice sector in the US."[28]

So too in India, what would logically seem a challenge for beef production in fact becomes its competitive edge. The disadvantageous pricing of Indian beef becomes an advantage in the Southeast and West Asian markets that seek large quantities of cheap beef.[29] Within India, too, the growth in the domestic meat market is linked to the rapidly growing demand from fast-food enterprises.[30] Ironically, while fast-food outlets within India are not allowed to serve beef burgers, it is likely that dead cows and buffaloes from India's dairy sector are serving the hamburger market internationally, given this is one of the commonest uses of "cull cow" (or "dairy" cow) beef.

To make profits comparable to its competitors—or in other words, to rate as a leading "beef" country—India slaughters a stratospherically high number of diseased, broken, "spent" buffaloes and cows discarded by the dairy sector. In fact, as early as 1999 when India opened its doors to foreign investment, including in animal production and slaughtering, leading animal rights advocate and then union minister Maneka Gandhi had warned, "Indian meat is priced far lower than that from any other country—at only 40 percent of the world market prices—so we have to kill two to three times the number of animals to earn the same from meat export as any other nation."[31] As per United States Department of Agriculture (USDA) Foreign Agricultural Service estimates for 2018 and 2019, India was the third largest bovine slaughtering country after China and Brazil (though there is no breakdown of what kind of bovine breeds are slaughtered in India) (see table 1.5).

However, a resounding silence across Indian politics, dairying, and beef production is the *veal* industry, founded upon the flesh of baby "dairy" calves. More than beef, it is *veal* that links undeniably with the dairy industry; veal comprises discarded male calves born in the milk sector. The idea of veal production, however, is a source of unease across the dairy and meat industries of the world. In the US, Gillespie notes, "there is a direct, yet uncomfortable, link between the production of

TABLE 1.5: *The top bovine slaughtering countries, 2019– 22 (USDA Foreign Agricultural Service)*

Country	2019	2020	2021	Forecasted 2022
China	47.50 million	46.65 million	47.40 million	48.30 million
Brazil	40.65 million	39.41 million	36.50 million	37.70 million
India	**38.60 million**	**35.80 million**	**38.60 million**	**40.00 million**
Argentina	13.95 million	14.00 million	13.00 million	13.100 million
Australia	9.04 million	7.56 million	6.35 million	7.05 million

Source: USDA Foreign Agricultural Service. n.d., a. Custom Query: "Animal numbers, cattle, total slaughter." Retrieved 12 February, 2022, from https://apps.fas.usda.gov/psdonline/app/index .html#/app/advQuery.

dairy and veal. Dairy farms do not publicize this link, given decades-long public concern over the ethics of veal."[32] Neither India's APEDA, nor the UN Comtrade show veal on their product databases on India. A category for "calf slaughter" on the USDA database, like "cow slaughter," comes up as zero for India, though USDA includes a category "Production (calf crop)" which showed 69 million infant heads (both buffaloes and cows) for India. However, official information for India is conspicuously silent about their fate. In comparison, in 2019 the leading dairy producer EU slaughtered 6.38 million calves out of a total of 28.58 million calf heads,[33] making EU the leading (albeit documented) veal producer.

The economic realities of the imbrication of the dairy-to-veal/beef production continuum are elided in the Indian Constitution. On the contrary, Article 48 of the Constitution implicitly makes provisions for enhanced scientific dairy production, making the cow's body an explicit "warscape" in India's competing milk-based nationalisms. The buffalo's body remains, in the main, an unnoted casualty.

ARTICLE 48 AND INDIA'S MILK NATIONALISMS

Article 48 of the Constitution of India is dedicated to directing and making recommendations for cow protection legislation in Indian states. As the realities of the dairy economy in India are so obfuscated—the dairy sector is predicated on the cyclical slaughter of "surplus" cows, bulls, buffaloes, and calves—it is not immediately apparent that the provisions of Article 48 are inherently contradictory in *simultaneously recommending the breeding of bovines, and the prohibition of their slaughter.* As it would be incongruous to impose a uniform national law based on Hindu sentiments in a multireligious secular democracy, Article 48 is placed as part of the Directive Principles of State Policy[34] in Part IV of the Constitution, which cannot be directly enforced through the courts. It is left to each state to enact the Directive Principles as legislation.[35]

Article 48 contains the directives regarding agriculture and animal husbandry, where it recommends that the states "endeavour" to

organise agriculture and animal husbandry on modern and scientific lines and shall, in particular take steps for preserving and *improving the breeds*

and prohibiting the slaughter of cows and calves and other milch and draught
cattle [emphasis added].[36]

The drafting of the Constitution in 1946 was led by Dr. B.R. Ambedkar, the renowned Dalit jurist, economist, and political theorist who was
appointed by the Congress party as the Chairman of the Constituent
Assembly. Ambedkar was a passionate social reformer, working against
the oppressive discriminations of untouchability, the notion that a group
of the *homo sapiens* species could be so "pure" that they could be contaminated, indeed, *desecrated* by the mere touch, presence, or even shadow of
an inherently befouled human group. In his work *The Untouchables: Who
Were They and Why They Became Untouchables?*, Ambedkar introduced
the concept of the "broken men," referring to the "defeated tribe" of the
Dalit community who became "broken into bits" due to the oppression
of untouchability.[37]

Beef consumption became the chief feature that distinguished "untouchable" from "touchable" Hindus in terms of caste, no matter how
"low" caste they might be otherwise.[38] In his extensive analysis, Ambedkar argues that the "touchable castes," including the Brahmins, had historically consumed beef.[39] The "upper-caste" revulsion against beef consumption was, in fact, conceptualized as a strategic political ideology
as part of a Hindu Renaissance in the nineteenth century in the British
colonial period. As such, Ambedkar himself was wholly against a ban on
cow slaughter as it reinforced a starkly oppressive caste hierarchy.

The remaining membership of the Constituent Assembly, at first
glance, also does not seem the obvious cohort to usher in a ban on cow
slaughter. Hindu nationalists, mainly from the far-right All-India Hindu
Mahasabha, in fact comprised only a minority of the Constituent Assembly; the Congress party constituted 80 percent of its membership.[40]
The Constitution came into force on 26 January 1950, and Article 48 was
voted in with the overwhelming support of the Congress party.[41] Why
did such dichotomous political ideologies *both* have nationalist investments in the cow in India? The symbolism of the cow, indeed, was essential to all forms of Indian nationalism—Hindutva, Congress, and
modern development nationalism.

Cows, Hindutva-Aryan Fascism, and the Making of Indic Hindu Anti-Semitism

In the aftermath of the destruction of the 500-year-old Babri Masjid (mosque) by Hindu fanatics in Ayodhya in 1992, anxieties across secular political discourses became heightened that what is manifesting in India may no longer be explained as communal riots, or even Hindutva extremism but a calculated project of Aryanic fascism,[42] with explicit "ideological links and parallels to Italian and German fascism, including anti-Semitism."[43] In his edited collection *Fascism: Essays on Europe and India*, Jairus Banaji argues that what has fueled fascism in India historically is "the abject humiliation of being what seemed like a permanently colonized, dominated people that the Hindu Mahasabha sought to transcend by its targeting of 'the' Muslims and real Muslims."[44] In other words, fascism in India masquerades as communalism, and in recent times, Banaji notes, "The culture of communalism is also at least as widespread in India as anti-semitism ever was in Germany, especially after the war."[45]

In his highly influential work *Hindutva: Who is a Hindu?*, Vinayak Damodar Savarkar, regarded as the ideological father of the Rashtriya Swayamsevak Sangh (RSS), a party affiliated to Hindutva values, describes a Hindu as one "who inherits the blood of that race whose first discernible source could be traced back to the Vedic Saptasindhus . . . who has inherited and claims as his own the culture of that race as expressed chiefly in their common classical language Sanskrit. . . ."[46] Savarkar distills the "essentials of Hindutva—a common nation (Rashtra) a common race (Jati) and a common civilisation (Sanskriti). All these essentials could best be summed up by stating in brief that he is a Hindu to whom Sindhusthan is not only a Pitribhu [Fatherland] but also a Punyabhu [Holy land]."[47] As claimants to "Hinduism [being] the religion of a superior race, namely the Aryan race"[48], this belief allows Hindu nationalists to assert that the geophysical entity of the Indian state is a Hindu state.

The Hindutva concept of the "pure" Hindu race and nation, started to solidify around the idea of shared Aryan ancestry during the Hindu Renaissance, making anti-Semitism as relevant to Hindutva fascism as

it was to Nazi fascism.[49] Anthropologist of Indian Jewish culture Yulia Egorova writes, "beginning from the 1930s Indian Muslims begin to be directly compared to European Jews in the rhetoric of the nascent Hindu right."[50] Hindu fascism seeks to reconceptualize—or more accurately in their vision, *restore* India as "Bharat," or a Hindurashtra, a pure Hindu nation-civilization. In this ideology of racial Aryan purity, non-Aryan, implicitly Semitic, and explicitly Muslim contaminations of the Hindu state are not to be tolerated.[51]

Cows, intriguingly, have been intensely exploited in both Nazi Germany and the aspiring Hindutva India in the hardline vision of Aryanic fascism. In Nazi Germany, auroch cows, also known as "Heck cattle" (or even "Nazi cows"), were back-bred in the 1930s by Nazi-sympathizing German zoologists Lutz and Heinz Heck to represent "Aryan qualities" of courage, aggression and domination.[52] The Aurochs were bred to replicate fierce and "wild cattle" in terms of "anatomy, genomics, behavior, and ecology."[53]

So too in India, the "Mother Cow" is invoked as an exceptional nation-building resource, albeit for an upper-caste Aryan Hindu, and feminized "Mother India." Akin to ways in which European Aryan *humans*, and Hindu Aryan *humans* were projected as different in (noble) temperament as respectively "active and combative" and "passive and meditative" to construct the Aryan civilization,[54] even as they purportedly shared a genetic ancestry, so too the European Aryan *cows* and Hindu Aryan *cows*, respectively, replicate these characteristics. In contrast to the Germanic Aryan cow with their associations of aggression, the Hindu Aryan cow is associated with elevated spiritualism as mother and goddess.

However, tracing the place of cows in India further back in history, it can be seen that they were, in fact, no more reverenced or protected in premodern Hindu society than any other animals, and in fact, were explicitly killable by Hindus in precolonial India. As D. N. Jha notes in his *The Myth of the Holy Cow*:

> the holiness of the cow is elusive. For there has never been a cow-goddess, nor any temple in her honour. Nonetheless the veneration of this animal

has come to be viewed as a characteristic trait of modern day non-existent monolithic "Hinduism" bandied about by the Hindutva forces.[55]

Since colonial times, "Hindu history" was rescripted by Hindu nationalists, and cow protectionism became a calculated political development driven by right-wing activists who "tried to use the movement for their own purposes."[56] As part of the explication of Hindu racial purification and preservation under Dayanand Saraswati in the nineteenth century, cow protectionism started to be formalized as a Hindu revivalist movement.[57] Cow protectionism as a Hindu nationalist project had to define itself *against* something, and this was, unsurprisingly, the Muslims, Christians, as well as Dalits. Simultaneously in this era, Dalit resistance movements started to mobilize against the Brahminical humiliation of the Dalit community as backward, uneducated, and untouchable, bringing forth what Anupama Rao calls "the intellectual formation [of] caste radicalism."[58]

Against this context, cows, and beef consumption, become weaponized as instruments of Brahminical oppression *and* Dalit resistance. Jha notes, "one law book describes a cow killer as a leper (*kusthi govardhakari*) and another treats beef (*gomamsa*) as 'the worst form of cursed or abominable food.'"[59] Jha further writes, "The Vyasasmrti. . . categorically states that a cow killer is untouchable (*antyaja*) and even by talking to him, one incurs sin; it thus made beef eating one of the bases of untouchability from the early medieval period onwards." Consuming beef was as repulsive as eating any "food offered by a *candela* [untouchable]," requiring the performance of penances by the "upper" castes to ritually cleanse themselves.[60]

In his *Sacred Cows, Sacred Places*, one of the most highly regarded studies on the sanctity of cows and gaushalas, Deryck O. Lodrick notes that the "Muslim invasion," and later, the British colonial rule, were impetuses to establish the cow as a signifier of racially pure upper-caste Aryan Hindu identity.[61] However, as Morrison writes, tales of "the past that never was, a problematic and unenlightened era, or a golden age prior to the decay brought about by modernity [or] colonization"[62] are political. They are intertwined with advancing the power of groups invested with such narrations at the cost of obscuring diversity and contradictions to such chronicling. "Not only does the first part of that construction falsely reduce and homogenize diverse and dynamic histories, but the second part builds on the problematic logic of succession."[63] Morrison writes:

> Happy indigenes living in harmony with nature were rudely interrupted by colonial intervention which brought about deforestation, degradation, and a breakdown of traditional forms of management and self-governance. . . . The "Hindu Eden" of the timeless precolonial was followed by a loss of innocence and massive destruction of environment laid entirely at the feet of the foreign intruder. That such a vision biologizes social distinction and naturalizes power relations might go without saying; that it is simply false as a historical vision, must, however, be emphasized.[64]

The patient and self-sacrificing Mother Cow invoked several layers of national purity for different political stakeholders—moral, spiritual, religious—and caste. In his article "Cows, Congress and the Constitution," political theorist Ian Copland argues that the insertion of the anti-slaughter clause of Article 48 does, however, indicate the growing influence, and one of the early victories of the Hindu Right in independent India.[65] For Hindutva patriots, the freedom of the Indian nation went deeper than merely unshackling from the British; it required the restoration of the pure Hindu state that purportedly existed prior to the arrival of Islam on the subcontinent. If the cow evoked "Hindu purity" for the Hindu Right, the Congress likewise also instrumentalized the cow as evocative of self-reliance and moral purity, the two virtues that were claimed by the freedom movement, albeit for very different agenda.

Cows and Congress Nationalism
As galvanizing patriotic capital, the cow appealed as much to the secular Congress nationalists as to their Hindutva counterparts, despite their contrasting political standpoints. The Indian National Congress, formed in 1885 in British India, was the first modern political party in

the country, which subsequently not only led India to freedom, but also significantly influenced freedom and decolonization movements in a number of former colonies, including South Africa, and even the civil rights movement in the United States led by Martin Luther King.[66] Mahatma Gandhi was one of the most important Congress leaders, and his conception of *sarvodaya*, the social upliftment of all, especially the most severely socially and politically marginalized citizens, became one of its core political ideologies.[67] The present constitution of the Indian National Congress, in contrast to Hindutva nationalism, explicitly advances "secularism, socialism and democracy."[68]

On the one hand, the Congress party, "the most prominent and successful movement of anti-colonial nationalism in the twentieth century," aimed to represent Indians regardless of "social, occupational, class, religious or caste differences"; on the other, it shared a complicated relationship with Hindu religion and traditions.[69] In his analysis of Hindu nationalism in colonial India, William Gould writes that this was because the concepts of "Hindu" and "Hinduism" "had fluid descriptive and representational meanings in this period."[70] Therefore, writes Gould, "the activities of Congress spokespersons, through deliberate and public uses of religious symbolism, were accommodated into understandings of 'Hindu' traditions,"[71] inviting engagement with a spectrum of communities.

Symbols like Gandhi's spinning wheel, the home-grown khadi fabric, and the allegory of the Salt March evoked the purity of India's precolonial culture, and centered a commitment to serve the material needs of the poorest, and most oppressed of Indians. Brown and Fee describe how Gandhi's spinning wheel, for instance, galvanized the moral force of Indian independence:

The image of the emaciated, almost naked, and obviously non-violent Gandhi hard at work at his spinning wheel had an electric effect on millions in India and across the world . . . and starting in 1931, his traditional spinning wheel became the primary symbol on the flag of the Provisional Government of Free India.[72]

While they remain important cottage industries, the spinning wheel and homespun khadi cloth retained symbolic and emotional, rather than material significance beyond 1947. However, the "lively materiality" of the cow for milk, and the bull for traction had a more enduring impact on nation-building, through both "Gandhian philosophical musings used to establish a newly independent India, or contemporary Hindu nationalist political posturing."[73] Contemporaneously, too, "milk [was] promoted to enhance growth and development in India, to solidify India's position as a 'developing nation' and even its place among the world's growing 'superpowers.'"[74]

The directives in Article 51A(b) of the Constitution impose a fundamental duty[75] upon Indian citizens to "cherish and follow the noble ideals" that inspired the "national struggle for freedom." The struggle included the protests against cow slaughter and the 1857 revolt by the Indian soldiers of the British colonial army, triggered by the use of beef and pork-coated cartridges. This call appealed equally to the Congress and Hindutva nationalists who each mobilized these events to articulate the Indian state. Like the Hindu nationalists, the Congress likened cow protection to the protection of the Indian nation, the cow's milk becoming symbolic capital for the Congress as well:

> the concept of "mother cow" could be twinned with the often used depictions of "Mother India" and the life-giving, pure quality of cow's milk could be associated in the minds of audiences with the purity and strength of the nation, not to mention the strength of the Congress.[76]

Article 48 thus reflects an uneasy attempt to mediate secular democratic and Hindutva nationalisms by simultaneously recommending breeding bovines for dairying, and prohibiting their slaughter. In *India's Agony Over Religion*, Gerald Larson analyzes religiopolitical crises like the 1992 demolition of the Babri Masjid to demonstrate the real struggles of a secular Indian state whose only option was to act wittingly or unwittingly in the interests of a religious group, rather than remain neutral.[77] Political analyst Shivam Vij regards cow protectionism as one of the most polarizing tools of political segregation between Hindus and Muslims, even above the destruction of the Babri Mosque.[78] Seen this way,

Article 48 epitomizes India's "agony" in attempting to achieve a middle ground in polarizing sectarian issues.

However, Article 48 is also deeply controversial when we consider what the secular nation was promising: a "no-slaughter" dairy industry. Though the cow was an object of "contention" between Hindus and Muslims, it was clear that a slaughter ban could not meet the economic objectives of dairying or agriculture.[79] Indeed, there was no doubt, even during the euphoric years of India's consolidation as a secular democratic republic through its revolutionary dairy expansion through the 1960s and 70s, that maintaining a ban on cow slaughter while encouraging the breeding of more animals for traction and dairy production was a scientific impossibility.[80]

These contrasting Hindutva and secular nationalisms, then, which invoked the idea of "purity" in different ways, were soon cemented into deeper intractable political tensions around cow slaughter when the newly independent Indian state started to commercially invest in dairy farming as part of its development agenda. If the cow protection movement itself developed as a "modern" discourse in colonial India where the cow was a political resource, it was to encounter frictions with another type of modernity—the dairy industry—in postcolonial independent India. If the anti-slaughter clause of Article 48 was important for Hindu nationalism, then its breeding clause became equally crucial for developmental nationalism when dairy engineer Verghese Kurien's innovations with a milk farmers' cooperative in the 1950s transformed the nation into the world's largest milk producer. In independent India, the body of the cow and the buffalo was to experience one of the most intensely extractive forms of commodification yet. However, it would be the cow who would become a living material landscape of volatile and conflicting nationalisms.

Cows and India's Development Nationalism
In the early years of Indian independence, when the nation was still importing powdered milk from the West, the small dusty outback town of Anand in Gujarat state unexpectedly rose to prominence as a site for the enactment of the development nationalism of the newly independent country. The story of what was to become Anand's monumental place in

modern India's history of development and progress is intertwined with that of a man named Verghese Kurien. Born to a Syrian Anglican family in 1921, Kurien earned a degree in mechanical engineering though he lost interest early on. He applied to the Indian government for funding to study abroad, and was awarded, much to his utter dismay, a scholarship in dairy engineering, of all things, at Michigan State University. This random act of fate was to turn the tide of development in newly independent India when he was sent to Anand for his first posting upon his return from the United States.

In 1949, Kurien became a pivotal figure in Indian dairy protectionist politics when he was appointed as Dairy Manager and Chief Technologist by Tribhuvandas Patel, a dairy farmer and a founding leader of the Kaira District Cooperative Milk Producers' Union Ltd.[81] Patel organized a boycott of milk production in 1946 to protest the authoritarianism and dominance of British cartels,[82] and Indian dairying continues to be enmeshed in explicit tones of patriotism and nationalism. Kurien is credited with the metamorphosis of the Kaira Cooperative into Amul, the largest dairy farmers' cooperative in the world.[83]

The 1950s and 60s were a crucial era for the material dimensions of Indian nationalism—food scarcity, hunger, nutrition and sustenance—in the postcolonial project of nation-building in an era of agonizing Cold War dependencies.[84] Food security was a core part of India's great "romance with developmental planning"[85] in the 1950s. In the additionally fraught years of war with Pakistan in the 1960s, the then prime minister Lal Bahadur Shastri's rallying cry *"Jai Jawan, Jai Kisan"* (glory to the soldier, glory to the farmer) knotted together food and national security itself.[86] The Green Revolution, driven by the agricultural scientist M. S. Swaminathan, began the transformation of Indian agriculture into a more industrialized form in the 1960s through the use of genetically-modified high-yield seeds, intensive use of chemical fertilizers and pesticides, and irrigation. Indian women, notes historian Benjamin Siegel, were "saddled with the burden of remoulding the diets of their husbands and children [for] the bodily transformations that would help realize the goal of national self-reliance."[87] Subsequently, they were also "saddled with the blame" when these food security projects failed.[88] In the following decades, environmental feminist Vandana Shiva would deliver scathing critiques of the Green Revolution, charging the technologies with impoverishing the soil of essential nutrients, destruction of ecosystems, causing severe malnutrition, farmer suicides, and exploitation of women's labor.[89]

It was against this landscape of fraught national, food, and gender politics that Indian dairying—or what would come to be known as the White Revolution—started to be formalized and commercialized from the 1950s, heralding the remaking of bovine bodies, labor, and their genetic material itself. In 1965, Prime Minister Shastri sanctioned the creation of a National Dairy Development Board (NDDB) to oversee the establishment of cooperatives like the Kaira Union throughout India.[90] Kurien was appointed as its chairman. In 1970, the NDDB launched its watershed program Operation Flood, to eliminate India's reliance on the import of powdered milk from the West. This was perceived as the removal of a major shackle of India to Western colonialism. Freedom via a protective milk-producing "mother" was a crucial sentiment in the early decades of the nation's birth as a free, self-governing country. Operation Flood highlighted Indian dairy products such as curds and ghee, which were pivotal in the nascent identity construction of the young nation.

Operation Flood heralded a specific Indian form of industrialized dairying—simultaneously grassroots *and* one of the world's largest in scale and size, through scientific breeding technologies. India began to witness the onset of "the industrial processing of traditional products through the cooperatives" and the emergence of a more organized milk sector.[91] Cooperatives form a central feature of India's dairy economy, generating enormous value for the country and providing employment and income for a large sector of the population. As such, developments in dairy production such as those innovated by Kurien and Patel have had significant impacts on the industry's value, and employment opportunities for rural communities. Kurien claims in his memoir that, "The dairy cooperative movement, inspired by Amul, is India's largest employment scheme and has more than doubled farm-family incomes."[92]

Kurien celebrates the dairy cooperative federation, which advanced India's stratospheric rate of milk production, as a "movement" that exemplified far greater change:

> What then was the Kaira Cooperative? It was certainly not only about milk. It was very soon becoming an instrument of social and economic change in our rural system. It was evolving into a programme that involved our farmers in their own development.[93]

However, as dairy cooperatives grew and started to modernize, following in the steps of other leading dairy producers, the necessity of slaughtering "unproductive" cows quickly became a volatile issue. As a dairy engineer and a pragmatist, Kurien pointed out that cow slaughter was imperative to keep dairying productive; *"My brief was to prevent any ban on cow slaughter. It was important for us in the dairy business to keep weeding out the unhealthy cows* so that available resources could be utilized for healthy and productive cows [emphasis added]."[94] However, this demand went against the very grain of the Indian independence movement, which, as we have seen, gained its moral force and momentum through the use of the resonant symbol of the cow to embody the cause of different nationalisms.

The utilization of the cow as sacred-political-economic resource, and the simultaneous erasure of the cow as a *being* by both the secular democratic Indian state, and the aspiring Hindutva state, is exemplified in the competing nationalist visions of Kurien and M. S. Gowalkar, then head of the RSS. Both men were self-stated patriots, committed to lifting India out of the depths of poverty and debt in which the nation found itself after independence, albeit with contrasting visions for the new nation. Kurien was a secular nationalist and Gowalkar was a Hindu nationalist. Both were staunch proponents of empowering India through the principle of *swadeshi* (the concept of self-reliance, specifically on indigenous products, and the local labor of one's own country). Thus, both Kurien and Gowalkar regarded their similar and yet differential instrumentalization of the cow as a labor of patriotism.

In 1967, both men were invited by then prime minister Indira Gandhi to be part of a committee to examine a national ban on cow slaughter,

after thousands of rampaging *sadhus* (holy Hindu men) attacked the Indian Parliament a year earlier in 1966, demanding such a ban. The committee consisted of men who *all* had economic or political investments
in objectifying the cow. Along with Kurien, who as chairman of the
NDDB, explicitly had an investment in cow *slaughter*, the cow protection committee comprised Ashok Mitra, chair of the Agricultural Prices
Commission; the Shankaracharya of Puri, one of the titular religious
heads of Hinduism; H. A. B. Parpia, director of the Central Food Technological Research Institute, Mysore; and M. S. Gowalkar, head of RSS
Gujarat. Unsurprisingly—and akin to influential all-male policy forums
debating issues of significance to women—no member was an animal
activist with an inherent recognition of all animals as valuable in and
of themselves, regardless of their utility to humans. Interestingly, no reports were ever submitted by the committee, although the men met for
twelve years; most information is, in fact, contained in Kurien's memoir.

Kurien documents his unlikely friendship with and mutual respect
for Gowalkar, who campaigned against cow slaughter. Kurien recalls
Gowalkar's rationale to keep the cow alive, based on her *living* utility
as an inherently valuable political capital to unify "Bharat" or a Hindu
India:

> I started a petition to ban cow slaughter actually to embarrass the govern-
> ment. . . . Look at what our country has become. What is good is foreign;
> what is bad is Indian. . . . If this nation does not take pride in what it is and
> merely imitates other nations, how can it amount to anything? Then I saw
> that the cow has potential to unify the country—she symbolises the culture
> of Bharat [Hindu reference for "India"]. So I tell you what, Kurien, you
> agree with me to ban cow slaughter on this committee and I promise you,
> five years from that date, I will have unified the country. What I am trying
> to tell you is that I'm not a fool, I'm not a fanatic. *I'm just cold-blooded about
> this. I want to use the cow to bring out our Indianness.* So please cooperate with
> me on this [emphasis added].[95]

Kurien claimed that even as he admired Gowalkar and his patriotism, "Of course, neither did I concur with him on this nor did I support
his argument for banning cow slaughter on the committee."[96] Kurien

proceeded with his visions for dairy expansion, which enacted the Constitutional mandate for scientific breed development by sourcing technical know-how from dairy leaders such as New Zealand and the United States.[97] His strategy included the development of artificial insemination and frozen semen technologies for strategic breeding for increased milk production.

The cows born from these developments in animal genetics would be predominantly Jersey and Holstein Friesians (breeds not native to India) as well as water buffaloes, who would together come to be increasingly represented in Indian dairying. As of 2013, it was estimated that "Exotic and Crossbred animals contribute nearly 21% of [India's] total cattle population."[98] They included these imported breeds, as well as those crossbred with native Indian breeds. In the case of buffaloes, the Murrah is the most exploited breed in Indian dairying for her substantial lactative capacity and the higher fat content of her milk.

As the economic and logistical problem posed by large numbers of unwanted bovines became more pressing, these "foreign" cows would become particularly vulnerable to illegal trafficking and slaughter, when even Hindu farmers, in their desperation to dispose of "dry" animals, would resort to conceptually distinguishing the sacrality of the "Indian" cow from the mundanity of the "foreign" cow.[99] Buffaloes, on the other hand, necessitated none of these overworked conceptual distinctions. As Hardy writes, "While cows are sacred, buffaloes are often considered merely economic—sometimes even demonic—by scholars and lay people alike,"[100] and can be trucked to slaughter without inconvenient moral twinges or fear of vigilantes.

The economic value of the cow's milk *and* her symbolic religiopolitical value is in a dangerous tension. Dairy production *depends* on slaughtering the cow once she is no longer productive; politically fetishizing the cow demands *no* slaughter. That is, logistic issues differentiate the utilization of the cow as an economic resource for a *secular India*, as distinct from the instrumentalization of the cow as a political resource to make a *Hindu India*. The former necessitates her slaughter to sustain an economically viable dairy industry. The latter demands the maintenance of her life, however abject. What, then, of the cow herself within this fraught context?

WHERE ARE THE ACTUAL ANIMALS IN THE (UN)MAKING OF THE INDIAN NATION?

What do we know about the historical and ongoing condition of the *animals* who were subsidizing milk production, and the making of the secular/Hindu nation, through the enforced labor of their bodies and the disruption of their family bonds? How do the animals fare when multiply objectified as commercial, political, and religious resources? As Nicole Shukin notes in *Animal Capital*, it becomes difficult to even conceptualize the violence of their commodification when animals—like India's "sacred" cows—have symbolic and cultural cachet, in addition to "production" value:

> animal signs and metaphors are also key symbolic resources of capital's re-production. Given the soaring speculation in animal signs as a semiotic currency of market culture at the same time that animals are reproductively managed as protein and gene breeders under chilling conditions of control, an interrogation of animal capital in this double sense—as simultaneously sign and substance of market life—emerges as a pressing task.[101]

There is thick confusion or ataxia around *seeing the animal*, and particularly, seeing the violence done to an animal held up to Godliness and reverence, and positioned as a lauded nation-building resource. This is evident even in Mahatma Gandhi's attempts to mediate a middle path wherein the cow could be used as an economic resource, and simultaneously to reject a use that he recognized was violent. As a devout Hindu, he too regarded the cow as sacred, and invoked the image of the gentle, loving, mothering cow to further the cause of independence and his campaign for *ahimsa*, the ethic and practice of nonviolence toward all living creation, including other animals. For Mahatma Gandhi, the cow, "a poem of pity,"[102] was a natural symbol of nonviolence, and he held that *ahimsa* could not be achieved without cow protection.

However, he was also acutely aware of the different forms of violence done to the cow, *especially* for milk. Cow protection, he argued, would be achieved through *tapascharya* or active, deep meditation and self-reflection on the part of the Hindu—and not through harassing

Muslims. Gandhi rejected the communalism that became associated with cow protection through the propagandist works of Hindu nationalists, and pointed out, as early as 1917 in a speech in Bettiah, the violence done *by Hindus*, to bovines used for traction and dairy:

> Hindu society has been inflicting terrible cruelty on the cow and her progeny. The present condition of our cows is a direct proof of this. My heart bleeds when I see thousands of bullocks with no blood and flesh on them, their bones plainly visible beneath their skin, ill-nourished and made to carry excessive burdens, while the driver twists their tails and goads them on. I shudder when I see all this and ask myself how we can say anything to our Muslim friends so long as we do not refrain from such terrible violence. *We are so intensely selfish that we feel no shame in milking the cow to the last drop. If you go to dairies in Calcutta, you will find that the calves there are forced to go without the mother's milk and that all the milk is extracted with the help of a process known as blowing.* The proprietors and managers of these dairies are none other than Hindus and most of those who consume the milk are also Hindus. *So long as such dairies flourish and we consume the milk supplied by them, what right have we to argue with our Muslim brethren?* [emphasis added][103]

Gandhi's thinking, however, reflects the classic confusion that typically marks any discourse on animal welfarism, where the reduction of nonhuman animals to property—and the violence inherent in such an objectifying status—is so entrenched in anthropocentric worldviews that, despite earnest efforts, it remains largely unaddressed. Vegetarianism was an integral part of Gandhi's striving toward *ahimsa*. Far from constituting a passive mode of being, *ahimsa* is understood as an active and engaged practice in Asian religious thinking, and at least until recently, the "most notable application [of ahimsa] comes in the form of vegetarianism."[104] Gandhi did reflect on the abuse of buffaloes, and it is clear that he had some notion that an *ahimsic* lifestyle must include the rejection of the consumption of animal milk. In his autobiography, Gandhi regretted having consumed cow and buffalo milk when he was ignorant about the abuse meted out to bovines. He took to drinking goats' milk, but subsequently acknowledged that he had indeed broken the spirit of his vow to never consume the milk of other animals:

For although I had only the milk of the cow and the she-buffalo in mind when I took the vow, by natural implication it covered the milk of all animals. Nor could it be right for me to use milk at all, as long as I held that milk is not the natural diet of man.[105]

Confusingly, Gandhi nonetheless advocated breeding for dairy production as an integral part of India's national development and its freedom movement. That dairy could be *inherently* profuse with gendered, reproductive, and sexual violence to the mothers, infants, and males trapped in production apparently never occurred to him. Rather, Gandhi considered breeding reforms as social reforms in human interests, and as a salient duty of Hindus:

> I would, if I could and had the necessary time at my disposal, engage the various cow protection bodies in reforming the pinjrapoles [animal shelters], in imparting to the people scientific knowledge of cattle-breeding, in teaching cruel Hindus to have compassion for their cattle and in making available pure milk to the poorest child and to the sick.[106]

Interestingly, Gandhi advocated the cessation of buffalo breeding and in effect, her liberation, recognizing that domestication—in this case, for dairy production—was fundamentally and inevitably violent to the domesticated animal. Gandhi pleaded that breeding might thus be limited to only the cow, whom Hindus at least had a recognized obligation to protect. Gandhi thus asked for:

> the stopping of buffalo-breeding in her own interest. In other words it meant freedom of the buffalo from its bondage. We have domesticated the cow for our own uses and therefore it has become part of our religion to protect her. It was my object to show that in trying to breed the buffalo, as we do the cow, we might lose both. [107]

In contrast to Gandhi's painstaking efforts to formulate ethical practice in farming animals, however fraught, Kurien's memoir is a stunningly unselfconscious obscuration of the living animals upon whose bodies the nation's milk empire was built. The title of Kurien's memoir *I Too Had a Dream* (2005), nostalgically draws on the visionary civil rights activist Dr. Martin Luther King Jr.'s famous "I Have a Dream" speech, in which he called for an end to the continued oppression and marginalization of Black Americans, and for freedom and equal rights in a land rife with racial violence. The speech is regarded as a definitive moment in the American civil rights movement. Kurien's clear reference to the civil rights movement is intended to draw attention to the oppressed state of India's poor in the early years of independence. In framing dairying as the liberator of humans, however, its role in the commodification of bovines—ushering in an unprecedented era of intensive animal exploitation in India—goes entirely unremarked.

Kurien recounts his indignation at being selected by the Indian government for a scholarship to study dairy engineering when he "didn't even know what a cow looked like."[108] The animal was not of interest to him, beyond her capacity as a milk machine. Indeed, as far as the living animal was concerned, his "patriotic" approaches to building an India self-sufficient in milk were ruthless. For instance, to encourage dairy producers to farm enough milk from their animals, he lobbied for the central government to heavily cut import subsidies.[109] The suffering of animals in bonded servitude is swept away as the dairy cooperative movement is narrated as a second independence movement whereby poor farmers were able to source fairer prices for the milk; as Kurien writes,

> This I learnt very early on through my years of working closely with . . . the farmers of Kaira district: *true development is not development of a cow or a buffalo* but development of men and women. However, you cannot develop men and women until and unless you place *the instruments* of development in their hands, involve them in the process of such development and create structures that they themselves can command [emphasis added].[110]

However, the claim that it is possible to advance the wellbeing of vulnerable humans through the oppression of even more vulnerable animal others is problematic. Kurien himself acknowledged that milk was a luxury product that could not claim exceptional nutritional benefits over plant protein and fats. He also accepted that animal milk was produced for elite humans by the labor of poor humans.[111] The role of enforced animal labor, of course, did not merit recognition.

Milk contains two important nutritional components—fat and protein. Milk fat is three times the price of vegetable fat, and even as Chairman of India's dairy board I was unable to put forward the thesis that milk fat was superior to vegetable fat. It is not. However, the protein efficiency ratio of milk is slightly better than vegetable protein. These arguments, however, hold no meaning for a starving man and it is unrealistic to say that this expensive food must be eaten by the poorest of our poor.[112]

A mix of perceived or real insults from the West, a particularly sensitive issue in the early years of independence, drove Indian dairying. When Western nations raised the objection that a poor country like India should not be investing in milk, Kurien took that on as a personal challenge, but also a challenge on behalf of the Indian state. The concerns of Western detractors were driven by the fact that milk could not address chronic malnutrition entrenched in the country; however, nations like Switzerland and New Zealand were also unhappy about the potential loss of income from a decline in Indian imports of dairy, and lobbied hard against Indian dairy development. Against the advice of Western critics who "airily recommended" that India disinvest in buffalo dairying (as it was assumed that buffalo milk powder could not be manufactured), Kurien and dairy engineer Harichand Meghaa Dalaya managed to successfully dehydrate buffalo milk into powder.[113] In the 1950s and 60s, the dairy cooperative in Anand developed "condensed milk after a Nestlé official (to his later dismay) unwisely said it was too delicate to be made by 'natives,' and later, baby food from buffalo milk against the advice of Glaxo."[114]

Kurien's anger at the blatant racism contrasts with the unselfconscious speciesism, disregard, and contempt for the animals used to build the Indian state. To describe his approach in challenging Western racism, he invokes speciesist metaphors denigrating and crushing bovines, "Rather, the more monstrous the crisis, *the more tempted I am to rush at it, grasp it by the horns and manoeuvre it until it gives me what I want!* [emphasis added]"[115] At another time, he describes his offense at KGB security constantly shadowing his team during a visit to the Soviet Union, "By that evening I was completely fed up *of being herded around like cattle* and I decided that nobody was going to take us for granted just because we were Indians [emphasis added]"—or in other words, regarded *like cows*.[116]

In his memoir, Kurien does not once discuss the conditions of the animals entrenched in dairying. He explains that it was clear from the outset that the free-ranging dairying practices that prevailed in New Zealand were not an option in India. He doesn't, however, elaborate as to what was standard practice for bovine welfare in India. Presumably highly limited grazing gave way to increasingly confined operations, to the zero-grazing and concentrated feed systems that are now pervasive in the Indian dairy sector:

> we could not give each cow or buffalo one acre of green grass, where all that cow had to do was graze on it, morning, noon, and night and produce 40 litres of milk a day. That type of dairying was obviously not for us.[117]

In truth, Kurien could not have afforded to get involved with the sobering realities of the animals who were instrumentalized in his grand visions of nation-building. Consider India's ongoing and projected dairy expansion plans, for instance. Continuing to follow the Constitutional mandate to breed "scientifically", India is currently in the middle of its hitherto most ambitious dairy development program to date—Mission Milk, also known as the National Dairy Plan (or White Revolution II), an ambitious tripartite collaboration launched in 2012 between the NDDB, Government of India, and the World Bank, with an investment of ₹ 2242 crore (US$ 306,316,994).[118] In 2016–17, Mission Milk led to production of 146.31 million tonnes of milk,[119] which went up to 187.7 million tonnes in 2018–19.[120]

THE *INDIVIDUALS* IN THE AGGREGATE OF SCIENTIFIC BREEDING FOR DAIRY

A "large" dairy farm in Australia or the United States might contain tens of thousands of cows, and a "small" milk farm might hold 500 or fewer cows.[121] The Mudanjiag Mega Dairy in China, a US$ 161 million collaboration between Chinese and Russian investors, is celebrated as the world's biggest industrial milk farm with over 100,000 cows.[122] In India, a "large" dairy operation, whether formal or informal, might use a mix of 200 to 500 buffaloes and cows. A typical "small-scale" dairy farmer might in fact own only one or two cows or buffaloes, reared within the spatial and social confines of the family in their small backyard. According to a Food and Agriculture Organization report, "Small and marginal farmers own 33 percent of land and about 60 percent of female cattle and buffaloes," and "Some 75 percent of rural households own, on average, two to four animals."[123] However, the sheer number of dairy farms, with animals held mostly in continuous and lifelong zero-grazing conditions, contribute on an informal but *also* industrial scale to the dairy economy in India.

It is easy to forget amid the numbing and blurring effects of statistics, numbers, economics, and science that these plans involve the forced impregnation and births of millions of sentient *individual* cows, buffaloes, bulls, and infant calves. As Kenneth Shapiro notes, "We lose the sense of an individual animal's life when he or she is placed in, really lost in, an unfathomably large aggregate."[124] How would the trajectory of Indian and, indeed, global political debate begin to change when the very foundation of any animal production—breeding—begins to be read politically?

It became clear that I needed to understand the implications *for the animals* of the Constitutional mandate to "breed scientifically." Unexpectedly then, and with hindsight, unsurprisingly, I found myself directly encountering bulls, in a frozen bovine semen farm, where the bulls are "milked" for their semen. Bulls and the quality of their semen are the crux of the dairy industry's advancement. However, the lived realities of bulls used for dairying is rarely known or discussed in the public imagination. Anticipating and worrying only about the female animals I would encounter in my research, I felt unprepared to witness the palpable suffering and distress caused to teenage bulls for dairy production. At the start of encountering the lived lives of individual animals throughout the dairy production spectrum, it began to dawn on me that the different activities that comprise dairying—especially scientific breeding—are profuse with *"gendered commodification"* and *"sexualized violence"* (emphasis in original text) for the animals.[125] It is to these animals and the spaces and experiences of their breeding that I now turn.

CHAPTER 2

BREEDING BOVINE CASTE

SCIENTIFIC BREEDING FOR DAIRYING

A striking aspect of a bovine semen farm, as opposed to a milk farm, is how devoid of living animals this production site initially seems to be. A semen processing station is a technologically sophisticated space with advanced and expensive machines that filter and process ejaculates of raw semen from young bulls. Highly educated, white-collar professional men and women in white coats and face masks, with advanced degrees in animal genetic science and reproductive technologies undertake the scientifically precise task of semen collection and processing. This semen will be transferred into hundreds of thin straws that will be frozen and stored in liquid nitrogen until they are eventually used to artificially inseminate (AI) the females. These laboratories contain no animal bodies, and have no smell, feces, urine, or animal sounds. Nor do poor, low-waged human laborers work at the start of the dairy production line. These spaces are pristine, clean, and cool, the only sounds being the muted hum of advanced machinery and air conditioners.

I was at a semen extraction station in Tamil Nadu state to learn about the science that drives the breeding logics of the dairy industry. There, I was to glimpse the young bulls only briefly, tightly tethered and enclosed in hot sheds at the back of the laboratories. I was startled by the sheer magnificence, beauty, and good physical health of these young animals, so accustomed had I become to seeing emaciated, often limping and dung-streaked cows and buffaloes in dairy farms. Later, at closer quarters, I would see bulls demonstrating stereotypic behaviors including repetitive head-swaying, head-banging and other "apparently functionless behavior patterns" that arose from a confined animal's "lack of control over its environment, frustration, threat, fear, and lack of stimulation," "forced proximity to humans," and no natural social contact with their own.[1]

What I was witnessing was part of the "scientific breeding" mandated by Article 48 of the Constitution of India for improved dairy production, where bulls whose genetics are deemed ideal to sire high-lactating cows are farmed for their semen. Once the bull is ejaculated by a human, this semen is then placed into the vagina of recipient cows and buffaloes. It is the selective and strategic breeding of cows and she-buffaloes with bulls *through* human intervention that is, in fact, responsible for the phenomenon of particular breeds of cows and buffaloes who lactate so profusely beyond the purposes of suckling their biological young, that they can sustain the possibility of a *dairy industry* at all.

In popular imaginations, however, not only does a cow continuously lactate, but "nature" intends that a cow "gives" excess milk beyond her infant's requirements for human consumption. Interestingly, I had not heard this justification for the consumption of goat, buffalo, or sheep milk—nature's intentions mattered little for these species. In the case of cows, this "surplus" milk may, without ethical dilemmas as regards her biological infant, be unproblematically diverted for the consumption of human beings.

Furthermore, in India, Hindu religion offers a commonplace landscape of symbols and stories evoking hyper-lactating mythological cows, which might unselfconsciously cement perceptions of such naturally overflowing milk production by the *modern* cows bred for dairying. Such images are frequently used by state-sponsored commercial dairy enterprises. Kāmadhenu, for instance, is known as "the mother of all cows"[2]; her overflowing udders make her the "source of all prosperity,"[3] the "cow of plenty,"[4] and the "satisfier of all desires."[5] Kāmadhenu is the "wish-fulfilling cow,"[6] the "wish-granting cow,"[7] the "wish" being humans' desire for her milk and associated dairy products. Evoking the natural abundance of the mythological lactating cow, the Goa state government's dairying project is called the "Kamadhenu Scheme," which requires that dairy farmers "[u]ndertake to strictly stall feed the animals and not allow open grazing."[8] In 2013, the Uttar Pradesh state government also introduced a "Kamdhenu Yojna" scheme to breed young bulls with "superior" semen quality.

The reality is that cows and buffaloes, like human and other mammals, naturally lactate only in amounts generally required for the nutritional needs of their growing infant. The amount of milk produced as a result of a *natural* mother–newborn lactative bond is entirely unsatisfactory to make for an economically viable dairy sector. Females who might lactate sufficiently to nourish and grow their infants—but not in copious amounts to satisfy human demand—are deemed genetically "inferior," contributing to dairy losses. Through scientific inter-breeding of selected males and females, therefore, the natural tendency of mammals to lactate in sufficient quantities for their newborn's nourishment after giving birth is manipulated in domesticated species like buffaloes, goats, and cows to make them *hyper-lactate*. Caton provides a simple definition of "breeding" and explains how science helps to maximize those desired physical traits of animals efficiently.

> *Breeding*, or the human activity of influencing the reproduction of domesticated animals for *the exaggeration or continuation of desired qualities*, is perhaps as old as domestication itself, but science identifies specific technologies to make "breeding on scientific principles" or scientific breeding.[9]

Breeding along "*modern and scientific lines*" as mandated by Article 48 simply advances the fundamental objective of breeding, that is, breeding for specific consumable physical traits of the animal body in exponentially exaggerated form (such as hyper-obesity) and/or quantities (hyper-milk/egg production) through advanced biomedical and reproductive technology. As author of *Pure and Modern Milk*, Kendra Smith-Howard writes, "'cows' bodies [became] standardized and modified by human action, and yet their natural attributes [to lactate] remained critical to dairy production."[10] Scientific breeding is especially vital for the dairy industry. Bovine genetics scientist Ricardo Stockler explains that bovine reproduction for increased milk output is, in fact, the most researched area of animal breeding:

> *Reproductive efficiency is one of the most important factors for successful cow–calf and dairy enterprises.* Certainly, in the absence of reproduction, there is no cow–calf or dairy enterprise. During the 1950s, frozen bovine semen was developed and artificial insemination with progeny-tested bulls became recognized as effective in making more rapid genetic progress for milk yield and beef production. [emphasis added][11]

India, of all developing countries, provides one of the most extensive AI programs to support the crossbreeding of native Indian bovine breeds "with the semen of exotic breeds like Holstein–Friesian, Brown Swiss and Jersey."[12] The purpose of such crossbreeding is to introduce genetics that will allow more efficient and voluminous milk production into native breeds. Gupta, Gupta and Chaudhari write, "In India, zebu nondescript cows are crossed with exotic breeds, like Holstein–Friesian, Brown Swiss, and Jersey bulls or their semen, to enhance the milk production potential of the progeny."[13] The sperm quality of the bull is crucial to determining the quantity of milk production in the females. To this end, "elite" bulls are "milked" via various forms of human-aided ejaculation for semen. The report of the Sabarmati Ashram Gaushala (SAG), one of India's most advanced bovine reproductive and semen extraction stations, explains, "To sustain and improve the [milk] productivity of the population, the prime need is to produce high genetic merit bulls and disseminate the semen doses produced from these bulls to the farmers."[14]

A select number of bovine breeds are represented in Indian dairying. As per the Annual Report of SAG for 2012–13, the semen farm at SAG "maintains a diverse germplasm (20 breeds of cattle and buffaloes) to cater to the artificial insemination needs of the dairy farming community."[15] These include Indian genus like Gir, Kankrej, Red Sindhi, Sahiwal; the "exotic" foreign cows like the Holstein–Friesian (HF) and Jersey; and Murrah buffaloes, who are among the most hyper-lactating and favored breeds in Indian dairying. The most favored breed worldwide is the Holstein cow. Together with the buffalo, the Holstein has rapidly started to become one of the most popular cows to breed in India. Phillips notes,

"Selection for high milk yield has been the major emphasis of breeders in the past, which has tended to favour large dairy cows, such as the Holstein–Friesian breed."[16] Selective breeding has increased the fat content of the Holstein's milk from "below 3.5% to nearly 4.0%."[17] Along with buffaloes, this makes Holsteins an attractive source of ingredients for fatty, luxury products like cheese, ice cream, and sweets. Many of India's native bovine breeds are endangered due to dairying, including the Pangunur, Red Kandhari, Vechur, Bhangnari, Dhenani, Lohani, Rohjan, Bengal, Chittagong Red, Napalees Hill, Kachah, Siri, Tarai, Lulu, and Sinhala.[18]

The science of breeding bovines scientifically in India has long been regarded, however, as a service to the nation, an act of patriotism that is inflected by Hindu sentimentality, whether by those sympathetic to secularism or Hindutva politics. Mahatma Gandhi famously declared that gaushala maintenance, for instance, was "not merely a religious issue. It is an issue on which hinges the economic progress of India."[19] SAG, intended by Mahatma Gandhi as a "model" gaushala, is today focused on "improving the socio-economic conditions of the milk producers in the country . . . [by] improving the genetic potential of cattle and buffaloes in the country."[20] In its report, SAG declares its commitment to continually advance its scientific breeding methods based on demonstrable success in other leading dairy-producing nations:

> High levels of productivity in dairy cattle in dairy advanced nations has been achieved primarily through continuous use of genetically superior bulls produced through field programs like Progeny Testing (PT) and Pedigree Selection (PS) and by continually increasing the proportion of breedable animals under Artificial Insemination (AI) services.[21]

What does scientific breeding mean for the animals involved? How does it contrast with natural breeding in free herds? As bovines have been domesticated and commodified for so long, few studies can tell us about bovine sexuality and sociality in natural herds. Most dairy herds are female-only, or contain very few bulls. However, we do know that mating between a cow and a bull would normally involve an elaborate series of behaviors in which species-specific forms of selection and agency are present.[22] Bulls demonstrate specific behaviors toward mate selection: sniffing the cow's urine, sniffing and licking her genital area, putting his head on a cow's pelvis, and some real or sham mounting attempts multiple times to check that the cow is physiologically and behaviorally receptive.[23] A bull may also "guard" his chosen female and keep her away from the herd (and the other bulls).[24] When the cow is in *estrus* or sexually receptive, "females play the major role in soliciting sexual partners and often form a sexually active group that stays within visual contact of the bull or bull group."[25]

In dairy farming, these natural mate selection processes become messy, time-consuming, and above all, the pairing of two individuals, depending on their breed and individual physical qualities, may not result in "elite," hyper-lactating females. Therefore, humans intervene in the sexual encounter between bulls and cows to orchestrate selective breeding.

At the start of my research, I was keen to understand how the bulls fare in scientific breeding for dairying. The conditions of hyper-confinement that virile young bulls experience to support the dairy industry is almost entirely unknown by the milk consuming public. At the slaughter-end of milk production, bulls are made "absent" once born; however, at the breeding stage of dairying too, they remain conceptually absent.

"SEMEN EXTRACTION" AND THE "MILKING" OF BULLS FOR DAIRY

As compared to the two-hour tour of the semen processing laboratories, my visit to the actual ejaculation center was very quick. It was empty of the animals at the time; young males are usually ejaculated by human workers twice a day, in the morning and evening about four times a week. They would be used for about six years, depending on optimum semen quality. The accompanying scientist led me out of the labs to a narrow-corralled pathway which led to a structure that reminded me of a merry-go-round. The bulls would obediently go in a line around this roundabout to rise on their hind legs, one by one, to mount a dummy cow.

The scientist showed me what looked like a giant beige sock, but was, in fact, a sophisticated temperature-controlled "vagina" for the bull's penis, simulating the warmth and moistness of a cow or a she-buffalo vagina. Once the bull had ejaculated into the sock, his semen would be quickly transferred to sterile containers and passed through a window between the ejaculation station and the laboratories for processing. As for the bull, he would be led away, out of sight, to be chained to his feeding trough or small enclosure until his scheduled afternoon ejaculation. Except for the ten-minute walk around the roundabout to the dummy, young adolescent, highly hormonal bulls might spend close to twenty-three hours being continuously chained and restrained.

The impact of such incessant, enforced ejaculation on individual animals can be devastating. In the US, a Holstein stud bull Picston Shottle was continuously abused for years for his ejaculate; he had fathered "more than 100,000 female calves in 20,000 herds in 22 countries." It was reported that "The animal died, possibly of exhaustion, in 2015."[26]

The first "stud" bulls I saw at close range were in a semen extraction farm in Maharashtra state. The bulls in a semen farm are magnificent creatures. I gaped when I saw some of the largest, strongest, healthiest—and also crazed and frustrated—animals I had yet come across. Enormous young Holstein, Jersey, Gir and Red Sindhi bulls, and Murrah buffaloes were tethered tightly in rows in stalls. Some of these animals had small concrete enclosures with strong gates, which they frequently charged in their desperation to break free.

In the prime of their youth, most of these males were eighteen to thirty-six months of age. We walked past the stalls first at a safe distance, as a strange presence—that is, mine—might add to the bulls' agitation. However, many of these young animals seemed already stressed. Bulls are territorial creatures and cannot tolerate the tension of being herded together. Face harnesses secure some of the particularly "intractable" bulls to the ground on either side with short taut ropes, such that the bull cannot even turn his face to the right or left and see his neighbor—though he can sense, and know, that a male, perhaps a rival, is immediately to his side. The only movements possible under these conditions are rising, sitting, and leaning forward into the feeding troughs. Burned into my memory is a wide-eyed "stud" buffalo, straining fruitlessly but forcefully at his short nose leash, almost out of his mind from boredom and agitation, and unable to move an inch except for the repeated, raving bobs of his head.

We made our way to the enclosures, each containing one caged bull adjoining the others. As we passed one enclosure, a large Holstein suddenly charged at the gate with full force, making all of us jump violently. He then reared on his hind legs, his forelegs against the wall, and snorted in agitation. Across from the Holstein, a Pandherpuri buffalo, with his magnificent sword-like horns, stood absolutely rigid in his small stall, his bloodshot eyes radiating anger. At that moment, I felt that I could see hatred in that young buffalo's eyes, a perfectly understandable and rational response in the circumstances he was in, I thought.

This way of describing what I understood the bull to be experiencing may be met with the charge of anthropomorphism. However, despite "the prevailing notion . . . that animals are more like zombies or robotic machines capable of responding only with simple, reflexive behaviours," animal science writer Virginia Morrell argues that animals are, in fact, deeply "self-aware and very likely conscious of their actions and *intents*."[27] Reading a bull's response as angry or full of hatred need not be read as attributing human characteristics to animals, but rather can be understood as trying to recognize *bovine* emotion on its own terms, albeit interpreted imperfectly through our human lens. "*Context matters*," emphasizes Barbara King, in developing an understanding and empathy for animal emotions,[28] and the context for farmed species is one that seeks to exploit them in harmful ways. Drawing upon the findings of ethology, King concludes:

> if we spend time with animals and watch them closely and persistently, our own eyes will tell us that grief and jealousy, joy and anger, are real because the animals themselves tell us so. Anthropomorphism from this perspective is not just misguided but fatally anthropocentric; it takes as a starting point that emotions are *human* emotions whereas in fact, our species has no rights of ownership over the kinds of emotions we are discussing here [emphasis in original].[29]

I wondered how these males were subdued to milk them for semen. At a veterinary college in Tamil Nadu, I asked the dairy department if I might be able to witness semen extraction. The college housed all manner of tied animals to train future generations of dairy scientists.

The bulls had already been ejaculated that morning, I was told, however I could stay and observe semen collection from the male goats. A scientist in a white coat and I walked to a rectangular concrete section where about ten goats were tightly tethered to the fencing around the space. These adolescent males can never be released, the scientist told me; bull or goat, they were likely to attack each other in these confined spaces.

A worker untied a goat and pulled him to the middle. He placed a dummy mount at the center, and started a high-pitched whistle to sexually arouse the teenage goat. The man watched the goat's penis alertly; as it became erect, his whistle became ever shriller. The goat half-closed his eyes and started to arch his back; as he approached climax, he leapt at the dummy with his forelegs, and the scientist caught his ejaculate into a sterile sock with perfect timing, not a drop spilled. Within seconds, the worker pulled the goat back to his spot and tied him. The goat continued to arch his back, eyes fully closed, for another couple of minutes. The animal almost immediately forgotten, the scientist had already started to make his way back to the lab with the precious semen, which had to be stored right away in temperature-controlled conditions for processing. Outside the goat enclosure were two chained young, healthy Jersey bulls. They were infants still, at about four months of age. They had recently been purchased so they could be trained for the sexual labor of ejaculation when they were still relatively small and docile.

In India, semen is mostly extracted through the traditional method of a bull mounting a dummy cow and ejaculating into an artificial temperature-controlled vagina. Forebodingly, electroejaculation,[30] a widely used method in the West where "mild" electric shocks of 12 to 24 volts are administered via the rectum to force ejaculation,[31] is becoming common in India. In humans, this is recognized as a painful method of semen extraction requiring general anesthesia when performed on human males,[32] though it is not administered to male animals in farming. A scientist at a leading dairy research institute told me that electroejaculation had begun to be applied to disabled young bulls who may not be able to mount a dummy to ejaculate. He explained: "when the bull is exceptionally good but is unable to donate naturally. Let's say an excellent bull has a femur bone fracture and is unable to deliver natural service. It's a loss for AI. So then electroejaculation is done."

The semen from some "stud" bulls can be extremely lucrative. The ejaculate of Yuvraj, a famous Murrah stud buffalo in Haryana state, is estimated to be worth US$ 3,000 per 10–12 ml.[33] If he cannot be sexually aroused by a human, then Yuvraj is electroejaculated.[34] Each straw containing his sperm costs about US$ 6, which is about ten times as expensive as straws of semen sourced from other bulls.[35] Yuvraj is regularly paraded at agricultural shows where he "wins" cash prizes of thousands of dollars for his owner; pictures show him chained on short ropes as an exhibit at shows while men ring around him with pride, basking in his reflected glory,[36] and perhaps, at the same time considering themselves even more virile for so "emasculating" a bull in chains.

Bulls in semen farms are thus used for about ten years until their semen quality starts to decline with age. Bulls used for semen extraction are often incapable of living in mixed-sex herds, having never been socialized into natural interactions with females (or males). A *pinjarapole* (animal shelter) in Gujarat showed me a single large Jersey bull from a semen station, standing slightly apart from the rest of the herd in an enclosed area. He was, thus far, their one and only successful integration, possibly because he might have been an especially docile bull. At the Blue Cross in Chennai, Dawn William showed me seven young Holstein bulls of "inferior" genetic merit who lived in a small bachelor herd in a confined space at the shelter. These caged bulls, released by the semen farm, were comparatively "fortunate"; most bulls are "sold," a euphemism for slaughter. A dairy research scientist in Haryana had told me "I don't agree with the gaushala concept, economically it is not practical and doesn't make sense. The unproductive cattle are still eating valuable green fodder which could be diverted toward productive cattle." Semen stations would prefer to sell their bulls to the abattoir as each animal can fetch a high price, rather than send them to gaushalas. An animal husbandry scientist in Chennai explained: "A high-yielding Jersey *maadu* [cow] can cost 4 to 5 lakhs. Even the cheaper *maadus* can cost [from] 40,000 rupees to 1 lakh. *Beyond this, there is no worth or protection. It is not worth more than this*" (emphasis added).

Once the semen is extracted from the bull, and processed, it is packed in straws and stored in liquid nitrogen until it is time to inseminate the female. This human-driven AI is necessary in animal farming, as stressed, "restrained females do not present the ideal mating stimulus" for bulls, and the cows may present "antagonistic" behaviors, thus compromising the conception.[37] Scientific dairy studies themselves reveal that even in mixed free-ranging herds, conception is often unsuccessful because cows can and do *choose* to resist the advances of bulls.[38]

Scientific breeding for dairy, I would learn, has further insidious impacts on the lives of these animals, as Indian dairying requires a workaround with regards to the irregularity imposed by the provisions of Article 48 that encourages the breeding of cows and discourages their slaughter. Therefore, those who engage in dairying in India, including in gaushalas, find it necessary to curate bovine *breeds* in terms that are reminiscent of Hindu caste, where different bovine breeds become socially hierarchized as more or less valuable—and grievable—than others. Caste (re)produces humans who might be "less than" fully human, and this social inequality sustains Indian capitalism.[39] So, too, the social differentiation of bovine breeds based on their perceived *sacrality* makes it possible to reconceptualize some breeds of bovine as *less than* (sacred) *cows*, or even, *not cows*. Scientific breeding of bovines in India, then, does not merely (re)produce dairy. Breeding for dairy in India could be said to breed the *bovine caste* that Indian dairy capitalism requires.

NEGOTIATING SACRALITY IN BOVINE BREEDS: THE
SCIENTIFIC BREEDING OF CASTE IN INDIAN DAIRYING

In India, caste differentiation and the opportunities it affords for discrimination, favor, and exploitation, provides the primary labor and resource to sustain the market and the capitalist development economy.[40] These ways of differentiating and ranking human bodies and labor become mapped onto *bovine* bodies and labor, illuminating how multispecies caste sustains market capitalism, and specifically dairy capitalism in India. In their analysis of how diverse nonhuman natures (both ecologies and bodies) are exploited for capitalist production, animal geographers Rosemary-Claire Collard and Jessica Dempsey point out that the nonhuman *form*—or the commoditized body—is not only affirmatively valuable. Rather, they write, "to accumulate capital, capitalism needs the diverse materials and creative forces of natures *ordered in a variety of positions within society*, not just as commodities" (emphasis added).[41] In other words, animal bodies do not just have a direct productive value for capitalism; they are also useful when "superfluous" or as "waste."[42] The afterlives of bovines as "a range of new commodities comprising bone, fat, flesh, and skin," for instance, play a vital role in sustaining dairy capitalism,[43] though in India, the refashioning of cows as "waste" for profit is not a straightforward economic logic.

In Indian dairying, where cows are legislatively protected from slaughter on account of being regarded as holy, it becomes necessary to find means to negotiate this sacrality as a selective rather a universal characteristic of *all* cows. This is by no means a modern socio-political practice; what constitutes the sacrality of some bovines and the mundanity of others has historically always been related to power struggles between human groups. The buffalo was once also regarded as sacred, by the Indigenous people of the Indus Valley civilization.[44] The buffalo even had a place in key Hindu scriptural works. The *Srimad-Bhagavatam* is one of the most important scriptures celebrating the life of Lord Krishna, popularly known in the Hindu imagination as the lover of cows. Passages from the holy text suggest that the buffalo was equally beloved to Lord Krishna, a sentiment that is obscured in contemporary religious narratives that associate only the cow with Krishna. An evocative passage describes Krishna amid the cows *and* buffaloes:

> The cows had bells with different shapes and sounds around their necks and feet. Headed by their group leaders, they went back to Vraja. The cows walked on Krishna's right side and the buffaloes on His left side. The residents of heaven mistook the cows to be the white Ganga and the buffaloes to be the black Yamuna.[45]

When the nomadic "early food producers"[46] began to settle, heralding cultivated agriculture, they needed protection from "evil spirits, disease, and pestilence," and the pastoralists who continued their traditional way of life using settled lands that they viewed as common grazing. Conflicts between the settlers and the Indigenous pastoralists became *animalized* when the cow and buffalo, respectively, became their symbols, signaling the start of "gory and violent buffalo sacrifices"[47] by the settlers, who would eventually become the "upper" castes. The late Vedic scriptures began explicitly to twin the protection of the cow-owning Brahmins and the cow. These dual protections—protecting the Brahmin *human*, and the cow *as* Brahmin—were eventually advocated as the core duties of Hinduism itself.

In the *Vishnu Purana*, cows are expected to be venerated along with the gods, Brahmins, saints, elders, and holy teachers.[48] The *Mahabharata* (*Anushasana Parva* 24–7) states: "Obstructing provision of water to thirsty cows should be considered equal to the sin of killing Brahmins." The *S'rîmad Devî Bhâgawatam* states: "To abandon the Bhaktas, the devotees, is to incur the great sin due to the *murder of a Brâhmin, the killing of a woman*, the drinking of liquors and *the killing of a cow*."[49] In the *Garuda Purana*, Garuda asks, "what is the path of misery in the world of Yama [god of death] like?"[50] Garuda learns that the following misery is the consequence of killing a cow: one is reborn "humpbacked and imbecile,"[51]; and one who strikes a cow or a Brahmin with their foot is "(re) born lame and deformed."[52] It is difficult to conclusively date the *Garuda Puranas*, though they are believed to be at least as early as the first millennium of the Common Era.[53] Thereafter, the concept of the sacred cow was firmly established in Brahminical doctrine.

Thus, the fatalism of casteism becomes constructed in the *animal body* as inevitable and "natural", as a result of her birth. Challenging the idea, however, that there is anything "natural" about caste, Dipankar Gupta notes, rather, that it is "political power that decides which castes will be superior. . . . Political power turns difference into hierarchy."[54] In India, political power has historically referred to economic power, that is, ownership of land[55] and bovines.[56]

In modern, independent India, however, the ownership of cows would soon become an economic drain rather than a benefit, if they could not be slaughtered once they had no productive value for dairy. Thus, the *breed* of the cow, rather than the species per se, would become a salient sociobiological point of differentiation where some breeds of cows were more valuable than others. The sustained focus on science as rationale in India's breeding policies for bovines, by subtly bringing together *"improving the breeds and prohibiting the slaughter of cows and calves and other milch and draught cattle* [emphasis added]" in Article 48, allowed Hindu nationalists to use the veneer of science to claim the national interest of the whole of India, to justify their interest in prohibiting cow slaughter.[57] The intersection of science and Hindu religion is, in fact, "integral to the Hindu nationalists' cow protectionist discourse that supports vigilante violence today."[58] As Adcock explains:

> breed improvement made it possible for cow protectionists to secure the imprimatur of the state for their efforts, apparently vindicating cow protection's central claim: that their concern with cattle is not a matter of private Hindu sentiment, but is in the material interest of the country as a whole.[59]

The charter of cow protection as mandated in Article 48 would come to mean a reconceptualization of the cow in practice, by differentiating between breeds—or *castes*—of cow. The taxonomic classification of cow breeds based on their ostensible physical, psychological, or affective characteristics is not necessarily scientific. Breed is largely determined by humans' subjective view of animals' physical and behavioral characteristics, meaning that "categorization based on breeds is an imprecise taxonomical system [which has more] to do with human perception and social construction than with science."[60] These idiosyncratic groupings of the perceived physical characteristics of bovines, possibly biased and prejudiced, become extrapolated to different cow breeds and buffaloes as a form of sociobiological classification, by referencing their *purity* and *impurity*—classic markers of caste.

If caste contains the potential to *dehumanize*, it also carries the possibility of *de-animalizing*, a fundamental act of species elision that is violent to other animals. Through the association of humans and animals, caste is sustained by simultaneously dehumanizing, sub-humanizing, and animalizing *humans*, and *humanizing*, sub-humanizing, and *de*-animalizing *other animals*. In being linked with specific human groups to render them admirable (for example, the cow with the learned Brahmin, or the horse with a noble Kshatriya), or subhuman (for example, the pig with the unclean Dalit), animals—including the holy cow—have to be correspondingly de-animalized—*debovinized* in this instance—through a denial of their species-being. *Debovinization* can be understood as a stripping, or a de-recognition of inherent bovine vulnerabilities, which denies cows and buffaloes their species truth. Significantly, the violence of debovinization manifests both through sacralizing some breeds of cow as mothers or goddesses, and denigrating other breeds of cows, as well as the buffalo.

The "Brahmin" Cow, the Jersey Cow, and Casteized Speciesism
It was at a Hindu temple that I first heard the idea that not all cows were sacred; some breeds of cow, in fact, were to be regarded with the same contempt meted to the buffalo by "upper-caste" Hindus or Hindu nationalists. A gaushala official in Visakhapatnam hastened to clarify that not every cow was special—it was only the native Indian purebreds who truly qualified as the sacred mother goddess. He expressed a sentiment that was to be oft-repeated in these conversations at other temples, gaushalas, and even among Hindu cow-vigilantes: "*Desi* [Indian] cow is not a cow, she is not an animal, she is a goddess, she is a mother. Only Jersey cow is an animal." A gaurakshak I met in Hyderabad got frustrated when I unwittingly kept referring to the "animals" he rescued from slaughter trucks. He had proudly taken me to several gaushalas that held the cows that he had rescued; curiously, all the chained individuals were native breeds. He finally erupted, "*Desi gai janwar nahin hai! Desi gai tho Ma hai!*" (The Indian cow is not an animal! The Indian cow is a mother!). Indian historian Mukul Kesavan notes that the political sentiment attached to cows in India is reserved for Indian breeds only:

> [It] is a specifically Hindu sentimentality about Indian cows. For Hindus, the *desi* [Indian] cow is a beautiful thing. Its large eyes, its calm, its matte skin tinted in a muted palette that runs from off-white to grey through beige and brown, its painterly silhouette with its signature hump, make it the most evolved of animals.[61]

This was, I was soon to realize, a recurrent theme even in temples and gaushalas, bastions of the Hindu duty to protect cows, ostensibly unconditionally. The "Indian" cow would be spared—or denied?—her latent *bovinity.* By elevating her to the highest and most respected human status—mother—or even above humanity, as goddess, the cow no longer belongs to the biological category of a cow. As a "goddess," the purebred cow is conceptually transformed into a sacred being. At a gaushala I visited in Mathura, where cows evoke the legendary loving relationship between Krishna and his bovine "mothers," the manager regarded the native Indian cow as being on an almost transcendent level of consciousness: "Pure breeds are more peaceful, intelligent . . . even the presence of a cow is very pure, auspicious. They live on a higher plane of consciousness, and in their presence, we are elevated too."

How does an individual cow experience, or indeed endure, this exalted status? Perhaps the most viscerally confronting sense of entitlement to exploit the "mother" cow in the name of sustaining the enforced cow mother–human child relationship was brought home to me in a gaushala in Kolkata (formerly Calcutta).

I carefully walked the wet, slippery stone steps smeared with feces, urine, and water to the back end of the gaushala, where milking cows were tied to short ropes and closely packed against each other, leaning over empty feeding troughs on both sides. All the cows were native breeds. Not one calf was seen near the lactating mothers. Muffled sounds emanated from the last line of cows on top of the steps. As I drew closer, I saw that an emaciated sickly cow had keeled over and was suffering a massive epileptic fit, eyes rolling, mouth foaming heavily, and milk spurting from her udders at the same time, mixing with the urine and dung. The other chained mothers around her watched impassively. "A cow has fallen!" I shouted in panic. A few workers came running. "That's okay," one laughed. "She fits like this for half an hour every day when you start milking her. Then she stops and then we can finish milking her."

The gaushala manager explained later that the rescued cow had been in the shelter for more than four years, had always shown "weakness" during milking time, and they were not worried. "But why do you still get her pregnant, then, if she cannot handle it?" I asked. "Oh, she can handle it," the man said. "*She is a mother; mothers can sacrifice anything for their children!*" (see figure 2.1).

FIGURE 2.1: *A sick and lactating "Mother Cow" suffering seizures from being made repeatedly pregnant at a Calcutta gaushala.*
Source: Photo taken by author.

The severely sick cow is refashioned as an agential, self-sacrificing mother of humans, eliding her species-specific suffering as a recently delivered, weakened cow suffering postpartum complications that probably required emergency hospitalization. Sacralizing an animal as divinity/mother/goddess is a process of objectification,[62] and objectification, regardless of purpose or process, is generally profuse with violence.[63] It was precisely the objectification of this sick cow as "goddess" that made her continued exploitation possible, affording her no protection from—and, in fact, increasing her vulnerability to—the double exploitation of being a "sacred" cow *and* a "dairy" cow.

Simultaneously, the interlinked religiopolitical economy of Indian dairying has to be circumspect about conceptualizing the sacrality of the cow and its attendant "protections." While the laws make no distinction between the breeds of cow, the cold economic logic of disposal and profit becomes necessary to find workarounds to render at least some cows ungrievable, if not explicitly killable, for milk. Not all cows, it turns out, are Brahmin "mothers" of the Hindu universe.

A manager of a regional gaushala in Rajasthan told me, "We don't accept the Jersey as a cow." *"Bechari hai, haan, lekin uska jaath sahi nahin hai"* (she is innocent, yes, but her caste is not right). A few months later, I visited a gaushala in Kolkata whose manager echoed these sentiments, emphasizing a classic concern of casteism—impurity. He said, "Cross-bred—even the *shabdh* [word] is wrong. It shows cross-contamination, mixing." Both these gaushalas milked their cows for dairy and addition-ally bought milk from commercial outlets—which likely contained milk from cows *and* buffaloes—to make sweets. Nonetheless, distinguish-ing the Jersey from the native cows was important—there was simply not enough physical space or economic resources to accommodate the sacred status of *all* cows. Some cows, therefore, had to be conceptually de-sacralized. As no scriptures differentiated between breeds of cow, the recourse, therefore, was to reconceptualize the Jersey as *not a cow*.

I spoke to a Mumbai-based Hindu political party worker whose team regularly raids loaded trucks to inspect them for trafficked cows. His work starkly illustrated how the rescue labor of Hindu groups is different to that of animal activists, and is specifically in the service of the Hindu state. However, here too, Hindu political rescuers would be forced to make distinctions based on the breed of cows, given that the numbers of "dairy" animals needing rescue always vastly outnumbered the capacity to rehabilitate them. If the captured truck additionally contained buf-faloes, or non-bovines like the camel, they might, if possible, be sent to an animal shelter, or more often than not, returned to the butchers. Their gaushala in Maharashtra state shelters only native cows. "Where do you keep the Jerseys?" I asked. "We send them to another gaushala, keep them separate. We don't allow them to mix with the *desis*," he said.

Many gaushalas keep the native and non-native breeds separate, housing the Jerseys where possible out of compassion but when con-fronted by an acute lack of space or resources, which was almost always the case, it would be the native cows who would be prioritized. The cow vigilante explained—correctly—that there is no specific religious obli-gation to recognize the Jersey breed as divine; he regarded the foreign

Jersey and Holstein crossbred cows as a modern "concept." Thus, he concludes, there is no spiritual directive to rescue them:

> We don't think of Jersey cow as a cow. In the Puranas or any of our scriptures, there is no reference to the Jersey as divinity. It is our [native Indian] cow that is sacred, supreme, and godliness incarnate. The Jersey is artificial, like you have created a new concept.

In being regarded as a human-conceived "concept," the Jersey is not only *not* perceived as godlike but ironically, is even considered demonic. A temple manager in Mathura, the birthplace of the cow-loving Lord Krishna, put it bluntly. "Jersey cow is like a *churail* [monster]. There is nothing divine about her."

Most striking, perhaps, was the assertion I heard from a political party worker, that the very fact that she produces a high yield of milk—ironically, through forced human genetic manipulation of her body—indicates a voluptuousness, an excess of greed, and a lack of restraint. The Jersey cow's milk, while economically attractive, is spiritually base. The man told me, "She gives a lot of milk but she is like a demon, a *rakshas*! Her milk is poison."

The *de-animalized* and *sacred* status of the Indian/Hindu cow emerges as a contrast to the *animalized* and *demonic* status of the crossbred/Jersey bovines—in both cases, the cow is *debovinized*. Not dissimilar to the sacred cow who is not a cow but a goddess, the Jersey is *also* stripped of her innate "cow-like" qualities. Thus, the Jersey mother is not just a "socially inferior" cow, but, indeed, not even a cow at all. Instead, the party worker reserves for her the most stinging insult; this cow is "only" as good as a buffalo. In ascribing the qualities of the buffalo's milk to the milk of the Jerseys, the manager emphasizes "purity" to rationalize the stratification of these breeds:

> You see, Jersey cow's cow [calf] is not a cow. These features [of purity and godliness] will not be there in a Jersey cow. Jersey cow is as good as a buffalo. Their milk will not have same qualities, they cannot bear this atmosphere [Indian heat]. . . . Jersey is from America. It will give larger

quantities of milk but it will not have the same qualities as Indian cow milk, its milk is [only] as good as a buffalo's.

While gaushalas separate native and non-native cows, dairy farms notably do not. While human entanglements with different breeds of cow define their existence so centrally, it was in a dairy farm that I got to witness how these cows were entangled with *each other*. I leaned against a tree in a dairy farm in Himmatnagar in Gujarat and watched a group of cows in a small fenced area; while crowded into the space, at least they were not tied. A single dark-honey toned Gir cow stood among the black-and-white dappled Holstein mothers. The Gir was exclusively for the private use of the dairy owners; the milk from the Holsteins would be diverted to the local dairy cooperative at the end of each day. Despite having more than forty lactating mothers, the farm had only three newborn calves, all Holstein girls, tied away from their mothers in separate pens. Many of the cows looked prematurely aged with concave hips, acute limps, and low-hanging udders, all signs of over-milking.

I noticed after a while that the Gir had a clear and definite friend in the group. She trotted faithfully behind a particular Holstein cow who moved briskly from the feeding trough to nose through some greens on the ground, then over to me, hoping for some food. This Holstein moved with confidence and surety, and the Gir cow seemed to feel safest near her. After some time, these two cows moved under the single tree in the yard for the shade, each carefully grooming the other, nuzzling and licking each other's faces for minutes on end. I leaned against the fencing, and drank in the sight greedily. I had heard so many political, religious, cultural, and dairy economics narratives, separating and hierarchizing the Gir and Holstein—high caste/low caste, Indian/foreign, pure/impure, more-than-a-cow/barely-a-cow—and yet these two beautiful pair-bonded animals themselves only saw comfort, love, and family in *each other*. The ways in which the Gir and Holstein, *as cows*, were knotted up together in their lives and bodies were not acknowledged by human institutions as morally relevant; in fact, their bonds were routinely and violently disrupted by enforced human "entanglements" in the production process that were racial, gendered, and casteist.

The Debovinization of Buffalo Caste

If the Jersey cow evokes social aversion for Hindu purists, the highly productive and commercially valuable buffalo is even more innately contemptible. In what could not be a more baldly antithetical contrast to the celebrated framing of the cow as a "goddess," the first description of buffaloes in a Hindu temple was a literal evocation of "shit." A temple manager in Visakhapatnam was explaining the differential caste status of cows. When I asked him about the buffalo, he flinched slightly and sat right back on his chair, arms folded. Intriguingly, he informed me that buffaloes are repulsive because they eat their own excretion, a disgusting product that was associated with humans from the former "untouchable" caste:

> I don't want to use the word but the buffalo is inferior, it is a low-caste animal, it—what shall I say?—it eats its own shit. You are a lady and that's why I didn't really want to speak my mind in front of you. But this is the reality. It eats its own shit.

The extraordinary evocation of the shit-consuming buffalo is far from innocent or true. Like beef, feces, particularly human feces, is a weapon of oppressive casteism. The poorest of the Dalit community are often forced into the filthiest of physical labor such as tanning, butchering, and fecal management; their handling of human shit is often with "their bare hands."[64] The image of the buffalo, so degraded and abhorrent as to apparently consume their own shit, was an unselfconscious reinforcement of the interlocked abject caste status of both buffaloes and the Dalits conceptually linked with buffaloes. Through her ethnographic work on the relationship between buffaloes and the "lower" caste Yadav community in Varanasi, Kathryn Hardy argues, "The refusal to see the buffalo as a meaningful animal is related to the refusal to see Yadavs as meaningful Hindus."[65] Excavating different narratives of relationality between *other* breeds of bovines and *other* castes of humans becomes a vital counter to the cow-Brahmin nexus that has come to be overwhelmingly present in Indian caste politics.

Unsurprisingly, then, the buffalo fails to achieve apotheosis like the cow.[66] In fact, the protections extended to the cow (and Brahmins) immediately led to an escalation of exploitation of the buffalo. As "upper-caste" humans turned to agriculture, they needed to protect their fields from pestilence, disease, and theft, and to depend on the monsoon and the land.[67] Fertility became a central concept of worship, signaling the start of the glorification of the Mother Goddess, or the bloodthirsty Kali or Durga. As an appeasement to this carnivorous goddess, and as a demonstration of power over the "low" castes, buffalo sacrifice to the goddess became common.[68] In an extraordinary contrast to the image of the cow as a pure, white-colored goddess, scriptures like the *Viṣṇu Purāṇa*, and the *Garuda Purana* describe a terrifying image of Yama the god of death riding atop a black, grotesque-looking monstrous buffalo heralding demise and violent destruction (see figure 2.2):

> Very sinful people behold the terrifying form of Yama—huge of body, rod in hand, seated on a buffalo,
> Roaring like a cloud at the time of pralaya, like a mountain of lampblack, terrible with weapons gleaming like lightning, possessing thirty-two arms,
> Extending three yojanas, with eyes like wells, with mouth gaping with formidable fangs, with red eyes and a long nose.[69]

Akin to the "untouchable" human, even the sight of whom or of their shadow was regarded as inauspicious, unlucky, and socially impure, the buffalo is also similarly stigmatized. In his 1904 book, *Beast and Man in India*, English art teacher John Lockwood Kipling observed that Hindus regard it as unlucky to keep buffalo and an ill omen to see one at first light.[70] Kipling reflected that the buffalo's ungainly shape, black color, and dingy tones make her the antithesis to the sacred cow,[71] that is, to "high" caste Hindus. The Mumbai political party worker who had taken me to gaushalas to see the cows he had rescued took pride in maintaining his sense of spiritual and social purity by taking care not even to know about buffalo rescues, for *even the knowledge of the buffalo was a contaminant.*

XL. Yama.

FIGURE 2.2: *The four-armed, dark-skinned Yama, god of death, rides atop a black buffalo. Dallapiccola 2010 cat. 9.72, painted in Tamil Nadu, c. 1850.*

Source: Reproduced with kind permission of The Trustees of the British Museum, museum number 1993,0806,0.72, 32.4 cm high, 29 cm wide

Don't ask me about buffaloes, I have no knowledge about them and I don't want to contaminate myself by knowing either. You ask me whatever you want about cows, and *desi* [indigenous] cows especially and I will be able to tell you. . . . But don't ask me about them, I don't know anything and I don't want to bother.

The base milk of the buffalo is as political as the holy milk of the cow. In a systematic stripping away of the divinities bestowed by Indigenous people upon the buffalo, products sourced from buffalo milk were regarded as a "desecration" if used as offerings to idols and in other sacred rituals. Post-Vedic literature such as the Puranas, particularly the canonical Viṣṇu Purāṇa, which was created around 450 CE, has references to the milk of buffaloes and other mammals (in Chapter 16, Book Three),, distinguishing these animals from the cows: "The milk of animals with undivided hoofs, of a camel, a ewe, a deer, or a buffalo, is unfit for ancestral oblations."[72] Buffalo milk, even as it is commercially valuable, is spiritually repulsive. This is not dissimilar to the rejection of foods cooked or even touched by the former "untouchable" caste; Anant notes, "The cooked food or the food prepared by a Harijan would be considered more polluted than the noncooked food or the food prepared by [higher] Caste Hindus, but served by or physically handled or accidentally touched by a Harijan."[73]

Nonetheless, the socially devalued milk of the buffalo, with its higher butterfat content, is a more expensive and profitable commodity than cows' milk. At the Barsana gaushala near Mathura, I met a devotee who was a dairy farmer and ran the local milk cooperative from his house, where farmers would bring milk twice daily. It would be weighed and systematically noted, and then sold to milk processing companies to pasteurize the milk, and make into "value-added" products like butter and ghee. At the end of each month, the farmers were paid out of the cooperative funds.

The cooperative owner offered to take me to his farm nearby, where he kept three buffaloes and three cows. All the animals were lactating mothers. The cows were allowed free range in an extremely small enclosed area; their tiny calves were in an adjoining pen. Each of the buffalo mothers and calves, however, were chained on short ropes in a line along the wall of the collection office. The intensive confinement of buffaloes compared to the slightly freer conditions of the cows was a striking feature of nearly every dairy farm I visited throughout the country. On this farm, the buffaloes were chained in such a way that they could only look to the front, and couldn't see their infants right behind them. As I walked past them, the mother at the front looked at me with bloodshot eyes, grunting and heaving at her rope. Her calf was right behind her, not even three feet away, but she could not reach her, or even turn around to see her.

The man saw me pause and look at this mother. All the mothers, cows, and buffaloes, were separated from their calves but at that particular moment, this buffalo mother was most visibly agitated as she grunted and pulled at her rope, trying to reach her calf. "She is a *badmaash* [trouble-maker]! She always behaves like this, bad-tempered," he said, clearly irritated as he waved his hand impatiently at me to follow him.

To highlight the fundamental differences between the milk of cows and buffaloes, the man explained that the buffalo's lactate apparently does not have nourishing features even for her own young. There was, then, no wrong committed in consuming a product that was not good for anyone, including her newborn. He referred to how a buffalo infant might be inclined to sleep after suckling, akin, indeed, to suckling infants of other mammals, including humans. He attributed to the mellow sleepiness of a suckled buffalo infant, however, the characteristics of slothfulness, and even alcoholism.

> Buffalo is thick-skinned. After drinking cow's milk, the calf is energized as the cow's milk is very light. But the buffalo calf will sleep like it is drunk or hungover after drinking his mother's milk. After drinking buffalo milk, the calf is slow like an alcoholic.

There needs to be no remorse in separating the buffalo infant from her mother, whose base nature will experience no grief. A gaushala manager in Thane in Maharashtra state, who also worked as a gaurakskak told me, "Buffalo has no love for her calves, she is not refined like the cow. She has no motherly feeling, she is nothing, she is just a *ghati* [coarse] animal." In brief phases, the casteist stigmatization of the buffalo has meant some temporary relief for these animals. The Gandhian mass mobilization to break down caste barriers had a brief role in the eschewing of buffalo meat because of these stigmas.[74] While the National Dairy Development Board (NDDB) is "seeking to maximize cow and buffalo milk production, there is simultaneously," writes Wiley, "an active anti-buffalo-milk consumption campaign in India that asserts that cow milk is superior to buffalo milk, especially in terms of its effects on mental abilities."[75]

INTERLOCKING CASTE, BREED AND SCIENCE:
ENCODING ANIMAL SUFFERING IN SCIENTIFIC
BREEDING FOR DAIRY
How do these animals, whose bodies have been physically manipulated, bred, and actively designed for dairying, endure their everyday realities? What are the consequences for the individual animals, I asked a dairy scientist in Tamil Nadu state? He was happy to explain at length. Due to abnormally high production of milk, mastitis or infections in inflamed udders are widespread, especially in Holstein, Friesian and Jersey cows.[76] Jersey cows are more vulnerable than other cows to human diseases like tuberculosis, and at greater risk of contracting Black Quarter or blood bone disease,[77] and Theileriosis.[78] Hereford and Friesian cows are susceptible to a range of eye and skin cancers.[79] It has been long noted that Jerseys, born without the fatty hump, are unable to withstand the fierce Indian summers, and Jersey bulls struggle when forced into labor in agriculture as traction machines.[80]

I sat in the office of this dairy scientist, stunned that he did not seem to be troubled by the sufferings of cows as a result of the breeding programs that were being supported in India (and elsewhere) in the name of dairy production. "How is the existence of these breeds kind or compassionate?", I asked. "How can we justify bringing forth breeds in whose genetics extreme physical suffering is already coded?"

The scientist, a Hindu man, replied: "*The question of kindness is a wrong one.*" Dairying, he was careful to emphasize, is a business, that is, not a charity. Kindness had no place in efficient manufacture and production, in this case farming, where lively bodies *were* the commodity. Any display of empathy or humanity to the "lively commodity"[81] where the systems of operation cause pain and suffering would significantly slow the rate and volume of production, if it didn't disrupt or halt it altogether. In the case of farmed animals, capital is extracted most efficiently from the lively body when their "bodies and functions . . . have been completely appropriated by capital, and, subsequently, put to use in a single way only, subordinating the total animal being *to this single productive activity* [emphasis added]."[82] Kindness compromised the efficiency of serving a singular production purpose because kindness *has no productive function*. For an animal used in dairy farming, the question of kindness was indeed a wrong one.

"This is the business model," he continued. "There is wear and tear, profit and loss in every business. We are also ethical, that is not the point."

The development of reproductive technologies for dairy extraction continues on an ever-onward march. The NDDB expected a demand of some 140 million frozen semen doses in 2021.[83] Indian exports of frozen semen are also expected to escalate as Indian indigenous breeds are highly desired in South America and elsewhere in South Asia.[84] To ensure the "conservation of the rich diversity of indigenous breeds" in India, while profiting from exports, the Department of Animal Husbandry and Dairying intends to establish protocols that differentiate germplasm for breeding and domestic use, and for export.[85]

In addition to bovine AI, already well established in India, plans are underway to cross-breed bovines—leading to greater numbers of mixed-caste cows who would never qualify for "protection" from Hindu purists and gaushalas—via embryo transfer technology (ETT) and in vitro fertilization (IVF). In 2020, the NDDB reported significant success with the production of calf embryos through these methods in its four frozen semen stations in SAG (Gujarat), Raebareli (Uttar Pradesh), Alamadhi (Tamil Nadu), and Rahuri (Maharashtra).[86] The laboratories in SAG are now so advanced that they can produce 12,000 mixed-caste embryos per annum.[87]

ETT is regarded as potentially the greatest breakthrough in animal breeding after artificial insemination.[88] In contrast to AI's primary focus on the virile bull and his sperm, ETT is focused on the fertile female and her ova, and the breeding of *hyper-ovulating* cows. Typical of mammals including humans, cows generally produce *one* ovum in each menstrual cycle.

Thus, where *one* cow might conceive *one* embryo through *one* insemination (natural or human-driven), a super-ovulating cow, ovulating six or ten or more ovum in each menstrual cycle, might conceive *six embryos or more* through a single insemination. These embryos would then be suctioned out of her uterus, and each transferred into a "non-descript" cow, or one who does "not belong to any definite breed"[89] (i.e., details regarding her features, temperament, bodily conditions, physical descriptions have not been formally listed or recognized), who would carry the fetus as her own. The "elite" hyper-ovulating cow would then be re-impregnated to conceive six more embryos, and so on. If the elite females are unable to produce such high numbers of embryos, the oocyte or unfertilized eggs would be removed from these cows, and fertilized under laboratory conditions through IVF, and the embryos would then be transferred into recipient cows.[90] In pursuit of such invasive and expensive dairy production methods, "The government of India has already sanctioned projects for the establishment of 30 IVF labs with 15 labs already operating."[91]

This unprecedented blow, this time to the mother–*fetus* bond, comes with immense physical and emotional violence to both biological and "non-descript" surrogate mothers. Large Holstein cows have one of the highest chances of super-ovulation,[92] and are used most extensively in ETT. However, when their large fetuses are placed into the wombs of other smaller breeds, the result is agonizing labor and delivery for recipient mothers. A study notes, "In the UK, for example, the use of beef-type heifers as recipients for embryos from large dairy breeds (e.g., Holstein–Friesian) and double-muscled beef breeds has occasionally resulted in a proportion requiring surgery to deliver the fetus."[93] If these "non-descript" surrogate mothers died, their deaths would carry no genetic losses to the dairy industry. If they survived delivering their calf, they would suffer the multiple traumas of being a "dairy" cow—the aftermath of a painful and complicated delivery, hyper-lactation, and above all, the separation from their calves.

As with humans and other mammals, roughly half the newborn cows and buffaloes will be male, as is necessary for successful species propagation. As public awareness in India (and elsewhere) grows about dairying's mass slaughter of male infants, a core dairy science focus now is the development of "sexed" semen. Animal scientists are trying to ensure that only female animals will be born, so that there will ostensibly be no dairy waste (male calves) to manage. In this sexing process, the Y chromosomes would be flushed out of a bull's ejaculate before it is inserted into a cow's vagina, leaving only X chromosomes, in order to exclusively breed female calves. Animal welfarists, who advocate that animals can be used as resources "humanely," present the idea of sexed semen as a win–win for humans *and* the animals exploited for their milk production—apparently, "we" (that is, cows and humans) could *all* have it *all*, as some form of mutually beneficial multispecies relatedness.

Such humane-washing obscures the fact that the increased number of females who will be born in this way will continue to suffer reproductive, sexual, and gendered violence, and emotional traumas, *always* a cold reality of dairying. Such narratives remain silent about the fact that sickly female calves will continue to be killed, and female cows sent to the slaughterhouse at a young age due to multiple injuries and ill-health as a result of their steeply increased lactation. Genetically manipulated species of animals have severe health issues compared with native breed animals.

While the breeding machinery of Indian dairying reproduces millions of cows and buffaloes, abstracted and faceless, throughout the years of dairy research, I would continuously witness the realities of *individual* cows, buffaloes and their calves who constituted the sum of India's industrial dairying complex. And I would be haunted by the reflections of Melissa Boyde, an Australian animal studies scholar, who has cared for a number of cows rehabilitated from dairy farming. Rescued from slaughter when they were deemed "spent" at about three years of age, these elderly cows—the fact of natural aging itself an extraordinary phenom-enon for a farmed species—are now between twenty-two and twenty-six years old, among the oldest cows in the world; older indeed, than any I had ever seen in India.

Cows, writes Boyde, are preoccupied and anxious about only one thing—returning *somehow* to their calf. Boyde writes, "'dairy' cows . . . may do the work required by the breeders but all the while are preoc-cupied by the question, 'where is home'—where is my calf, where is my herd—'and how do I get there?'"[94]

CHAPTER 3

MILKING

To milk (synonyms): *exploit, bleed, drain, extort, extract, suck, wring, impoverish, pauperize, overcharge, steal, leech, threaten, elicit, empty, evince, exhaust, express, fleece, siphon, draw off, impose on, take advantage, coerce, ransom, swindle, deceive, embezzle, take to the cleaner's, victimize.*[1]

I climbed into the animal ambulance just as it was about to pull out of the Blue Cross of India in Chennai. Dawn William had seen me getting out of my car in the animal shelter's parking lot just as the rescue team had been about to leave, and he called out to me. "Is it an emergency?" I asked, not even clear yet as to which animal we were going to rescue. "No, routine case" he replied. Blue Cross sent out their ambulances at least four or five times a day for this specific call, often being forced to turn away further pleas for such help. "But you need to see this."

It was a cow from one of the informal urban dairies in Manapakkam with birthing difficulties, I gathered, as we sped through the Chennai traffic. She had been roaming the streets, struggling to deliver for the last three days, before someone finally called the Blue Cross for help.

"Apparently her fetus is partially out but she can't push it all out," said Dawn.

"Half out fetus for three days?" I could not fathom this. I felt sure the caller had exaggerated, or even misunderstood.

The driver was on the phone to the caller, listening to directions. When we reached the spot, he leaned out, and called to some men on the street, "The cow with the leg out, where is she?" They knew immediately what he meant, and directed us; the entire street had seen her struggling for several days.

I walked quickly behind Dawn, the vet, and the para-vets as we made our way through a building to the back, near a rubbish heap. A thin white cow nosed slowly and painfully at the ground. "Her? . . ." I scarcely started to ask, when I stopped in shock at the sight of her vaginal region (see figures 3.1 and 3.2).

A small hoof, wet with rot and decay, poked out of her vagina. The team got to work quickly, loosely roping the cow around her neck so they could make her sit. I noticed the faint marks of *manjal* (turmeric powder) and *kunkumam* (vermilion powder) on her forehead and rump, anointed

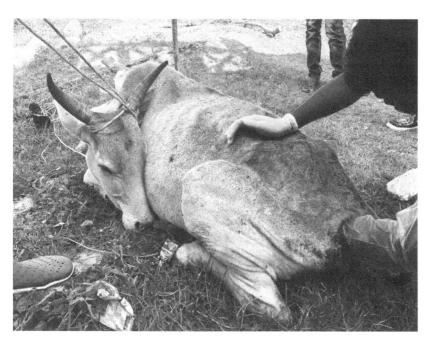

FIGURE 3.1: *The veterinary team preparing to pull the dead fetus from a cow. The faint marks of vermilion and turmeric powder on her forehead and rump are signs of her routine worship.*

Source: Photo taken by author.

FIGURE 3.2: *The rotten male fetus that was pulled out of the cow.*
Source: Photo taken by author.

some time ago as part of routine worship. The vet pulled on long surgical gloves all the way to his shoulder, and inserted his arm into the vagina to maneuvre the dead fetus so he could pull it out safely. The emaciated cow grunted mildly; she was too weak to resist. After a few minutes, the vet calmly and steadily pulled the fetus out halfway; seconds later, the decayed corpse—brown with rot, slimy with decayed fetal membrane— was fully out. The stench was visceral.

The cow feebly moaned, and laid her head on the ground. The vets started to administer fluids and pain relief as a small crowd gathered to watch, shaking their heads at the putrefying fetus, eyes still sealed, the little jaw seemingly broken.

The cow's condition, I learned, was called dystocia, "when it becomes difficult or impossible for the cow to deliver the calf without assistance. It can occur in the first or second stage of labor," when her cervix begins dilating and the contractions commence.[2] Among the main causes of dystocia are large fetal size, incorrect position of the calf at different birthing stages, twins, or uterine inertia, when "the uterus will not contract, or becomes 'exhausted.'"[3]

This fetus was severely underweight and emaciated, the vet told me; the fetus's size was not the issue. He estimated that this cow was about five years old, and this was likely her third or fourth pregnancy. "She is weak, weak, weak!" said the vet. "Up to 80 percent of her rumen is filled with plastic."

The vet explained that as is the case with thousands of pregnant and lactating "dairy" cows scavenging for food in rubbish throughout the country, the pregnant mother had consumed so much plastic that she had been unable to absorb even what edible scraps she did find. Severely weakened as a consequence, she had suffered extreme uterine inertia during labor. "She has insufficient nutrition—no nutrition, you could say. There is no microbial activity, no metabolism, no digestive capacity, no nutrition absorption. She is emaciated." said the vet.

I started to rapidly google the condition on my phone. As per dairy science studies in the United States, up to 50 percent of heifers, or cows delivering for the first time are at high risk of dystocia, also a leading cause of calf death.[4]

"Is that the same here?" I asked the vet.

"Fifty percent? I would say, 80 percent, 90 percent of the cows suffer this in Chennai!" he said. "The risks are anyway high, on top of that, what chance do these cows have?"

In the case of humans, maternal mortality refers to "when a pregnant or birthing person dies during pregnancy or up to 42 days after the end of pregnancy from health problems related to pregnancy," due to inadequate or no access to maternal care before, during and after pregnancy.[5] In a dairy farm, there is virtually no maternal veterinary care for what can be a medically complex phenomenon like pregnancy and birth, particularly for first time expectant mothers; therefore, the vet explained, bovine maternal mortality is in fact one of the leading causes of death on a dairy farm.

"Is she in pain?" I asked.

"Surely, surely." He replied. The vet explained that the cow was almost undoubtedly septicemic, a condition where her blood was infected.

In this condition, she would likely soon slip into shock and coma, and die on the rubbish pile in about a week or so. Blue Cross, already overflowing with animals like most shelters, could not take her, although they would come every day to administer pain relief, antibiotics, and palliative care.

The cow had curled her head against her body in exhaustion as a man held a drip over her. The vet and I walked over to her fetus, and I tried not to breathe in too deeply. The vet pointed to the broken jaw. "Someone, maybe the farmer, has clearly tried to pull it out, someone without expertise, the stress has caused it to suffer badly in the end," he said. Unable to extract the fetus, or perhaps realizing that the cow had no hope, she had been abandoned, her fetus likely in a state of acute distress, if not already dead by that time.

We looked over the little body in silence, the loud din of the city traffic sounding in the distance. The vet put on his gloves again, bent over, and raised one fetal hind leg slightly. I could just about glimpse a tiny scrotum.

"Boy," he said, briefly. "Anyway he had no chance."

MATERNAL VULNERABILITY OF A "DAIRY" COW: INVISIBILIZED FACETS OF COW PROTECTION POLITICS

It is the cow's maternity that ostensibly qualifies the Mother Cow for "protection" in India. It is also the cow's maternity that is of central interest in a dairy farm, through the acts of conception, birth, delivery, and most importantly, her lactation. As we returned to Blue Cross with a lingering sense of unease and grief for the distress and pain of that cow, I pondered the maternity of the cow which simultaneously left her so vulnerable to human violence *and* supposedly protected her from it. The immediate risk to that cow was not slaughter, and yet her suffering was palpable—recognized and communicated in clear terms by the vet himself. What did this mother and her son need protection from? Who was protecting them?

"Nobody," said Dawn William at once when I asked him. "She has no protection. In fact, as long as she has even one drop of milk left in her, she has no protection. They [milk farmers] will put her through whatever torture is required to get it."

It struck me as he spoke that animals raised for dairy exist in a state of perpetual vulnerability and that the concept and practice of "protection" for the animals themselves—crucially defined *against* its interpretation and co-optation by "cow protectionists"—must surely rely on an informed understanding of these vulnerabilities.

Up to that point, I had spent a lot of time asking humans to explain their perception of the cow as their mother.

Now, a different set of fully formed questions articulated themselves in my mind: how might the *cow* or the *buffalo* experience maternity? How might maternity be understood as a window into the vulnerabilities that characterize the lives of bovines used for dairy? And what might this dimension of bovine maternity mean for India's cow protection politics?

"Maternity [can be] understood as the embodied experiences of being pregnant, giving birth, *and feeding and caring for infants* [emphasis added],"[6] writes Matilde Cohen in her work on the bovine maternal body in dairy production. Maternity is an intensely emotional phenomenon for the mother, writes Cohen, where the mother's role is not only defined by her breastfeeding but also by a deep desire to care for, and protect her child. It is, in fact, these nurturing and protective experiences that would go on to comprise the most enduring facet of maternity.

Dairy production is founded upon two foundational acts—impregnating a cow or buffalo repeatedly, to make them go through the high risks of labor to produce colostrum and lactate; and separating the suckling newborn from its mother in order to divert the milk for human consumption. No dairy farm—including in India—can accommodate the truest expression of maternity, namely, the strong bonds between a mother and her newborn, because the mothers *feeding and caring for their infants* would disrupt dairy production altogether.

The process of impregnation, birth, and milking subjects cows and buffaloes to a range of vulnerabilities, not only the extreme form of suffering that the dying cow in Manapakkam was experiencing. The everyday realities of dairy production so normatively contribute to their physical and emotional suffering that is almost becomes difficult to isolate and address any specific harm as particularly distressing to bovine mothers. Indeed, the experience of *being* a cow or buffalo on a dairy farm might itself be understood as constitutive of the bovines' vulnerability to "so great a violence that it has no clear beginning and end."[7] It is precisely these vulnerabilities[8] that make an animal profitable to humans. Anat Pick writes, "In their peculiar relations to human beings . . . as *agricultural*, medical, *symbolic*, and *emotional* fodder—animals are uniquely vulnerable [emphasis added]."[9] It is precisely the buffalo or cow's vulnerability in being a *lactating mother*, for instance, that is both a "mundane [and] highly lucrative fact."[10]

These vulnerabilities contrast—even get eclipsed—by popular perceptions and ideations of who these animals are, and what they supposedly represent. Ecofeminist Greta Gaard writes, "For too long, the dominant culture has childishly projected its own gendered image onto nature as selfless and self-sacrificing mother . . . or onto other mammal species, requiring the female bovine to symbolize maternal nature: mindless, patient, slow-moving, lactating."[11]

In India, dairy production is rooted in Hindu culture, where rhapsodic descriptions in mythologies have, for centuries, validated a lactational relationship of the cow with the human. Lactating breasts are an evocative embodied symbol of motherhood. The fetishization of the cow's breasts/udders in the scriptures (*Rigveda* 1.164.9, *Atharvaveda* 9.9.9, 4.39.2, and *Śatapatha Brāhmaṇa* 4, 5.8.10), indicate the extent of the cow's veneration as a *lactating* mother: "That the great Cow may, with exhaustless udder, pouring a thousand streams, give milk to feed us."[12] The cow's udder is "pure"[13] and "heavenly"[14], it swells with "lordly nectar,"[15] and the cow's milk is "nutritious, brightly shining, all-sustaining." The cow is eulogized as beloved, respected, and reverenced, as mother of the universe, and all creation itself.[16] In this galactic conception of motherhood imposed on the living "dairy" cow as a species and as an individual, the tiny atom of her own biological infant, her small starving calf straining for her full udder, is perhaps the most irrelevant and forgotten facet of her motherhood.

Gaard asks, "If we set aside this stereotype [of the self-sacrificing cow] and look into her eyes, what can we see?"[17] In other words, what if we were to ask: What makes a "dairy" animal *vulnerable*? How might cow *protection* be reframed, against a Hindutva political project of nationalism, and even a broader Hindu veneration of a cow as goddess, if it responded directly to the idea of *securing* a being against a vulnerability?

The vulnerability to the precariousness of life itself, by virtue of being alive and mortal, is a feature of *all* life. However, some lives are rendered vulnerable in specific ways based on how they are used by the political economy, and in a dairy farm, mothers and infants are rendered vulnerable from their forced alienation from each other; this mother-child estrangement constitutes the heart of dairying. In this chapter, then, I attempt to provide a fuller account of the vulnerabilities of maternal relations among cows, buffaloes, and their calves on dairy farms. I share stories, like the cow wandering the streets with dystocia, that relate the experiences of individual animals I encountered in order to illuminate some of the mundane vulnerabilities to which animals are subjected in dairy production spaces. Some of these stories are highly generalizable as common experiences of animals raised for dairy, while others are unique to the individual or geographic context in which they unfold. Together, they craft of a picture of how vulnerability characterizes the lives and deaths of animals in dairy production in India as elsewhere.

Despite my knowledge of what milking essentially involves—humans (and not the newborn calves) would "milk" the cow or buffalo by hand or machine—I ultimately felt unprepared for the vulnerability and suffering of mothers and calves that I would witness routinely on dairy farms. Over the years, I would see hundreds of cows and buffaloes in dark dairy sheds, tightly confined in what seemed like endless rows, bones and ribs visible, caked in feces, and their calves missing or chained and left to die if male, or sequestered together if female. The sheer mundanity of how nothing seems to *happen* on a dairy farm between milking hours would later be disrupted by my witnessing the vulnerabilities and suffering of the agitated mothers and calves *during* milking. While the scenes would repeat in dairy farms throughout the country, the seemingly unremarkable act of milking in a Visakhapatnam dairy farm would particularly haunt me over the years.

"WE ENCOURAGE NO RELATIONSHIP BETWEEN THE MOTHER AND CHILD"

It was not until more than halfway through my research that I happened to visit a private dairy farm *during* milking hours in the peri-urban outskirts of Visakhapatnam city. I was accompanied by Malathi, an activist and staffer at the Visakha Society for Protection and Care of Animals (VSPCA). The dairy farm was, by Indian standards, a large, "family-owned" farm, and contained about 200 lactating cows. No buffaloes were present here. The owner told me that this was because the local temples were among his buyers, and they would not use lactate that was at risk of being contaminated by that of buffalo mothers. The cows were housed in enormous sheds, and typical of many dairies I had seen before, tied tightly in long parallel lines, facing each other over feeding troughs.

We drew up to the parking area right outside the sheds and in front of the manager's office. Almost immediately, resonant bellows and high-pitched cries hammered incessantly into our heads. Malathi spoke in rapid Telugu to the manager, introduced us, and explained again the purpose of our visit; she had already spoken to him on the phone.

One of the workers signaled to me to follow him; he would show me around the cement sheds containing the chained cows. I lifted my salwar gingerly off the ground and walked carefully through rivers of urine and dung. As we entered the shed, the bellows of the mothers for their calves echoed across the farm, insistent and agitated.

Frantic vocalizing, stamping and grunting is not typical behavior of bovine mothers who are allowed to remain with their infants. An animal behavior study on the effects of separation on both cows and calves concluded that prior to separation, mother and child are bonded, and therefore quiet and mellow; indeed, "calves and cows rarely vocalized before separation."[18] Even dairy science studies, conducted as long as some forty years ago, report that bovine mothers and infants form powerful emotional attachments within minutes of birth,[19] and the forcible separation that ensues results in visible behaviors[20] that may be interpreted as traumatic for mother and infant. Immediately after separation, the "mothers bellowed, paced, and thrust their heads through the fencing in attempts to get to their calves."[21]

The agitation was significantly due to the fact that mothers in dairy farms have no opportunity to suckle their infants through the day. In a non-dairy situation, calves, like other mammalian infants including humans, suckle from their mothers all day at regular intervals for both nourishment and comfort. In a dairy farm, the buffaloes and cows are milked twice a day by humans for efficient milk collection, leaving the calves hungry and fearful, *and* the mothers in an acute state of emotional and physical pain. A study notes that the mothers' distress often peaked about eighteen hours after separation, due to "[u]dder discomfort [a euphemism for pain], associated with a lack of suckling or milking during the previous 12h [which] may explain this second peak."[22]

Up ahead, I could hear the commotion of grunts, bellows, and thumping hooves, as workers started attaching machines to the nipples of the cows. We began to walk carefully through the last row of cows. In addition to the tight face-harnessing, some of the more agitated mothers had both their hind legs tied tight together to eliminate any kicking and injuries to human laborers who went about the work of milking.

As I slowly moved through the shed, I saw that each cow, "mother" of the Hindu universe, seemed wary, angry, and frightened. One of the cows at the end of the feeding trough fruitlessly resisted her tight face harness, eyes bulging as she strained toward me. She was tied firmly with red plastic ropes on both sides of her face so she could barely look left or right, and there was even a rope threaded through her nostrils to discourage any resistance. But she did not break eye contact with me; it was I who could not bear to look into her eyes for more than a few seconds.

Waves of helplessness washed over me; I reached out and tried to scratch the sides of her jaw. But this mother was not interested in my weak gestures and she tried to back away in distress, snorting and breathing heavily. Even against a charge of anthropomorphism, I could have no doubt that every fierce and fruitless pull against her harness and her wild-eyed gaze said to me, "Get me out of here. I want my baby." As a heavily lactating mother, she would have delivered her calf recently, and what I was witnessing was her embodied desperation for her newborn.

I wanted to articulate a begging plea for forgiveness but I could not even begin to frame one without immediately feeling shame. Anything I tried to convey felt like a deep insult. Not for the first time, in the face of such palpable grief and suffering, I felt rage at my own species. But this was not directed at the workers who were also abjected, impoverished, and forced into positions where they became responsible for this level of violence. Instead, my disgust came to rest on those who profit from, and consume, the products of this suffering without thinking twice.

I tore myself away from her gaze and forced myself to keep walking. Through the cacophony, one particularly piercing cry rose and reverberated above the rest. I turned to the worker. "Which cow is that?" I asked nervously. "Is she okay? Is she sick? Why is she screaming like this?"

"Everything is fine," the worker assured me. "You walk carefully, don't fall."

We wound our way through the endless lines of the dark sheds; however, the cries of that particular animal continued to resound. "Which cow is that?" I again asked the worker. "Please take me to her."

I followed the man, careful to avoid slipping or an accidental kick, into a section that amazed me—a large bare pen full of calves with a large blue plastic drum of dirty water in the middle. Then as the scream rose again, the man pointed at an extraordinarily beautiful, very small, and very loud white-and-brown 10-day old male Jersey calf!

The sounds in the shed were, in fact, loudest near the calf pen, the high-pitched cries of the newborns, and the bellows of the mothers melding together. Calves like this one continued to be used as cogs in the machinery of dairy production because crossbred and native cows and buffaloes often cannot easily let down milk into their udders unless their infant is present. Calves are allowed to suckle for just a few seconds or minutes, barely long enough to begin satiating their hunger. Once milk letdown has occurred efficiently, the calves are roughly pulled away by their large ears back into the pen, and the milk machine is attached to their mother's nipples.

As with human mammals, natural weaning might occur when the calf is about a year old. Weaning is the time when an infant starts to consume foods other than her mother's breastmilk. "When this happens," states the Australian Breastfeeding Association in the case of humans, "*is really a decision that each mother and her baby make*, based on their personal circumstances" (emphasis added).[23] In the dairy industry, however, "weaning" is a business decision. Infants even on beef farms are separated early at about four to six months of age; on dairy farms, separation is usually on the same day as they are born.[24] Australian dairy scientist Clive Phillips writes:

> Feral cattle normally maintain cohesive matriarchal groups, with prolonged bonds formed between cow and calves. Since the bond between the calf and cow extends beyond provision of milk, weaning should be considered as occurring when the cow and calf are separated, which in dairy calves is normally at *about one to 14 days of age* [emphasis added].[25]

Breeds who have not been bred to hyper-lactate may find it difficult to produce milk at all, due to their anxiety at losing their calves. This is particularly true of buffaloes who have not been as intensively bred for milk production as the cows. To address this production problem, dairy farmers regularly engage in the practice of the *kaalbaccha*, which involves using crudely severed taxidermized heads of calves. Calves are starved to death, but their heads alone are preserved to place at the rump of the anxious cow or buffalo mother, so when she looks back, it appears that her calf is at her breast. The mother can smell the corpse of her infant, and will be fooled into allowing milk letdown. These practices are normative even in the cow-protecting state of Gujarat.[26] Amit Chaudhery, president of the People for Animals Gurgaon, writes in his eyewitness account of leasing *kaalbacchas*, a business in itself at the milking stage of Indian dairy production:

> At birth all calves are separated from the mother and allowed just enough milk to survive if they are female and none if they be male. Enterprising cowherds sever the heads of calves and tie them just near the rump of the cow to create the illusion of her calf as she turns to watch while they milk

the udders. The *pashu melas* [cattle fairs] at Fatehabad, near Hissar in Haryana and Sonpur in Bihar among several other places present this common
and sadly acceptable sight. In fact men ply the severed heads, renting them
out by the hour. Between garbage, polythene and severed heads India gets
her milk and milk products.[27]

On this farm, we learnt that a "pickup" came once a week for the
male and the sickly or underweight female calves (typically born of malnourished mothers). "What happens to them?" asked Malathi. "Once we
sell, we don't know," the manager replied. "They are maybe given to poor
farmers for agriculture purposes." As elsewhere,[28] dairy farmers in India
want to disassociate the idea of evocative maternal warmth projected and
exploited by the dairy sector, from the male infanticide, and the market
for veal and calfskin associated with it.

We stood in the pen before the loud little Jersey calf, watching as
he waited anxiously to be allowed his twenty seconds of suckling. He
had been left until last because he was being punished for being "a
troublemaker."

"He wants his mother," I said urgently. "Please let him feed," I
begged. The men around us laughed.

A persistent question driving my work has always been: *who was my
research for?* I sought to prominently draw the bovine mother and her
calf, at the core of India's cow politics but fundamentally invisibilized as
sentient subjects, into the political landscape. There was little doubt that,
from the outset of my research, such an approach would inevitably focus
on active advocacy in making explicit the annihilation of the mother–infant bond as *violence* to both. This approach was also vital to disrupting
what hitherto was a communal, casteist, and speciesist concept of cow
protection itself. Activist scholarship is sometimes charged with being
simplistic, often at the expense of accounting for social complexity.[29]
However, this itself is a reductive accusation, for it was activist research
that helped me to overturn the oversimplified conclusions of erstwhile
narrow, overwhelmingly human-focused analyses of the hate politics of
cow protectionism. As professor of anthropology Charles Hale writes,

"activist research methods regularly yield special insight, insider knowledge, and experience-based understanding."[30]

I could not buy this little calf his freedom, or secure his or his mother's release. I had no way of adopting them and personally taking responsibility for their lifelong care. The VSPCA, as we shall see in the next chapter, was already packed beyond capacity with discarded male calves. However, the urgency I felt to ease the immediate suffering of this infant was overwhelming. I was desperate for him to have at least one full meal before his death. I turned back to the manager.

"Please," I begged him. "One meal. Let him be near his mother at least once."

The manager laughed somewhat uneasily. "Okay, fine," he said. He nodded to a worker. As soon as the gate opened, the skinny calf raced out straight toward a brown Jersey cow. "She is not his mother?" I checked. "No, but he is hungry, it doesn't matter," came the reply.

It sure doesn't, I thought. The calf grunted, heaved, and pulled at the cow's teats. The cow tried to lick him but with her face tied tight to the stake in front, she could not reach him at her back. He suckled and suckled. Five minutes passed.

A small crowd started to gather around the mother and calf—workers, managers, activist, researcher—to watch the baby bull, his eyes closed, pulling vigorously at a cow's teats, an utterly remarkable act in a dairy farm. Even as the bellows of the other animals continued to reverberate, a pin drop silence fell upon our group of humans as we watched.

It was twenty-seven minutes before the calf finally broke away, exhausted and fully satiated, probably for the first and last time in his short life. *Twenty-seven minutes.* Twenty-seven minutes of getting to be a baby. Twenty-seven minutes of his absolute fundamental birthright to be near the comfort and breasts of this mother. If they had been allowed, mother and infant would probably curl up together now for a deep, comforting sleep.

In silence, we all regarded the young boy, mellow now, being pulled back to the pen, truly orphaned in every sense, by the dairy sector. I could scarce trust myself to speak. "Twenty-seven minutes," I said. "Did you know that? It takes at least twenty-seven minutes for him to have a full belly."

They shook their heads. No, they did not know. I did not know. Whether this particular calf took more or less than the "usual" time it takes for a bovine infant to suckle was hardly the concern. It was exponentially more than the dairy sector asserts a suckling calf needs. As in a blur, I recalled interviews with highly educated, upper-class dairy and animal husbandry scientists. "Few minutes of mother's milk is enough," one dairy scientist in Visakhapatnam had told me just days earlier. Few minutes was indeed enough, albeit for efficient milk letdown into the udders, so that *milking machines* could suck up the rest. The scientist continued, "If you want to be humane [i.e., also think of the calf's welfare], you can give ten minutes but who has the time when there are so many animals?"

The forcible separation of mothers and calves from each other results in at least two immediate, irreplaceable losses of critical maternal care for infants. Johnsen et al. write: "Weaning comprises two elements: the loss of milk provided and loss of care from the dam."[31] Colostrum, the first milk that mammals lactate, is vital for the health of their newborns, as it is the single factor in bolstering the immunity of the infant.[32] Colostrum is especially important for ruminant bovine infants for whom "no exchange of immune factors occurs in utero."[33] All transfer of "immunologic components"[34] occurs after the birth, through the newborn suckling the colostrum. "Achieving early and adequate intake of high-quality colostrum is widely recognized as the single most important management factor in determining health and survival of the neonatal calf."[35] In the early months, calves need *more* milk, especially colostrum, to sustain the growth spurt.[36]

Second, "allogrooming," or the combination of licking and suckling, is critical to the emotional health and development of the bovine infant,[37] and to the security of both the mother and her calf. Typically, these comforting and nurturing behaviors "[were] performed more within family pairs than unrelated cows and calves, indicating that the bond is specific to the dam and her calf."[38] However, in studies on herd behaviors, it was observed that some 95 percent of the time, cows engaged in allogrooming activity with at least one other (non-biological) calf, indicating that a tribal or communal system of mothering was crucial to both the overall development of the calf and feelings of security within the herd.[39]

Even if calves are not allowed to nurse, there remains a profoundly emotional bond between a calf and their mother. A dairy experiment in British Columbia explored whether there was benefit in reuniting mothers and calves, even if the infants weren't allowed to suckle.[40] They found that, regardless of the length of time for which they were separated, mother–calf attachments remained extremely strong.[41] When separated mothers and infants were allowed to reunite for a certain amount of time, the "dams" (mothers) would accept the calves immediately without hesitation,[42] and their bond was reaffirmed. Indeed, "even when nursing becomes irregular, the mother–calf bond persists throughout the animals' lives in feral cattle herds, and does not wane as new offspring are born."[43]

However, the freedom to engage in these caring, intraspecies relations is virtually impossible in a dairy farm, as the permanent physical separation of the infant from her mother is, as we have seen, the very foundation of this industry.

One of the farm workers came to me. This man was of the Mala caste, categorized as part of the scheduled castes in Andhra Pradesh.[44] Sweating profusely in the Andhra humidity and dressed in nothing but a hitched-up purple loin cloth, he was one of the millions who made a bare subsistence as a dung sweeper, feeder, and milker on the dairy farm. Part of his job was to load unwanted and downed cows and calves into the pickup truck each week.

By this time, darkness had started to settle around the humid sheds, and mosquitoes buzzed at our faces. The man who had perhaps the least decision-making power in the casteist, hierarchical structures of Indian dairying had something urgent to say to me. "We will try to give them a few more minutes," he mumbled, softly. "I will try . . . give them extra time together."

As the night fell, lights were dimmed across the cement cow prisons. I looked across at the little brown-and-white Jersey calf. He was curled up on his own in the corner of the cement floor, completely quiet now. But in a couple of hours, he would start his loud cries again for his next feed.

I wondered when the little calf would be sent away to the slaughter-house where he would face a more terrifying fate alone, to become veal or calfskin. I could have asked to touch him, stroke him, but *any* human touch on that little body felt contaminating. My eyes thick with tears, I imprinted that bright, spirited, beautiful brown-and-white calf in my mind. I prayed for his death to be quick, whenever it came.

We wound our way back through the rows of mothers who were packed tightly against each other in intensive confinement—all except a row in the middle of the shed, which was cleared of almost all but one tethered cow in the middle, eyes bulging and pacing the length of her short rope frantically. Her udders hung swollen and heavy.

"She is about to give birth, first time," said the owner, who was kneeling and observing her udders closely, even as I looked at her wide eyes, fearful and in pain. "Less than forty-five minutes now, I would say."

A cow or buffalo can labor for anything between two and twenty-four hours or longer,[45] a universally painful—indeed, agonizing—mammalian experience. Typically, during this stage, "cows will often separate from the herd and may be restless." In spite of the heaving contractions of the final stages of her labor, this young cow could do nothing to relieve her pain, tightly restrained as she was by the rope. Nearby cows across the feeding troughs on the other side stood still, alert. "You can stay and watch if you like," added the man.

I paused. "How quickly will you remove the calf?" I asked.

"Immediately," the man nodded. "We will give her a few minutes to clean, and then immediately remove. One of the workers will give the calf its first feed from a bottle."

"Not even the first feed from the mother?" I asked.

"No," he replied. "We encourage no relationship between the mother and child."

I thanked the owner, and quickly walked out.

As we left the gate, I noticed something I had not seen earlier in the evening, but which is a common sight in most dairies and gaushalas in

India—a tall statue of the blue-skinned Lord Krishna playing a flute as he leaned against a beautiful white cow. Then, as now, her calf was nowhere to be seen; she was frozen in time in her role as mother, solely to the human.

BREASTFEEDING AND SUCKLING: UNIVERSAL
MAMMALIAN RIGHT OR *HOMO SAPIENS* PRIVILEGE?
Much social engineering and marketing in India went into framing and naturalizing the lactate of other animals as the birthright of humans as much as human breastmilk. A marketing breakthrough signaling the growing success of Amul, one of India's dairy cooperatives, was through its foray into producing human infant formula using cow and buffalo milk. This phase of Amul's growth is described by the father of India's White Revolution, Verghese Kurien, in his memoir in a chapter titled "On a Roll." Creating and sustaining a human infant formula market was a clever commercial strategy that had to be introduced with gendered sensitivities. Anticipating feminist resistance to baby food in India as an implicit offense to *homo sapiens* mothers that their own breastmilk was wanting, Kurien writes, "We had to make the correct impression on the minds of mothers with new babies *without trying to undermine breastfeeding* [emphasis added]."⁴⁶

Amul shrewdly launched advertising campaigns, and introduced a breastfeeding guide called the Amul Baby Book, emphasizing the inherent and irreplaceable superiority of the biological mother's breastmilk for the newborn—albeit, of course, the human mother and infant. That the entire industry was founded on the violent disruption of the powerful mother–infant bond of one species to unselfconsciously eulogize another did not even dimly register in the Amul Baby Book. As Kurien explains, the Amul Baby Book went to great lengths to recommend the (human) mother's breastmilk as beneficial to her infant:

the Amul Baby Book [had] a chapter *exclusively dealing with the superiority of mother's milk*. Some years later we also brought out an advertisement in the press *advocating breastfeeding*. We took great pains to say that baby food was necessary only in those cases where the mother was unable to breastfeed. And to those who accused us of nearly monopolising the baby-food market, I always pointed out that the monopoly was held by *the mothers of India*, as 93 per cent of our babies were breastfed [emphasis added].[47]

In contrast to the celebrated "monopoly" over breastfeeding held by the human mothers of India, the bovine, ovine (sheep), and caprine (goat) mothers of India (and globally) are forced to surrender their infants *and* milk immediately after giving birth. Bovine infants are elided even while emphasizing human maternal care for their infants and fetuses by *using bovine lactate*. In his book, Kurien describes the nutrition training programs that the NDDB set up to help village women increase the milk output of buffalo and cow mothers. Even in comparisons of human and bovine motherhood, the object of maternal love and care is steadfastly the human. Kurien writes, "Could these women not relate all this to their own growing foetuses? Were we only discussing animal nutrition?"[48] The *animal mother* was a production machine whose nutrition was valued in terms of resource input to produce more lactate as salable capital; the *human mother*'s nutrition, in stark contrast, was a conduit of maternal relatedness, even to her unborn fetus.

"But cows give too much milk, the calf cannot finish it all! We *have* to milk them for their own good!" I would often be told. Or I might hear, "It is cruel to not milk the cow. She suffers if she is not milked." Or even, "If we let the calf drink as much as he wants, he will get diarrhea! You can *kill* the calf that way! Do you want me to kill the calf like that?" These refrains are common among dairy farmers and dairy scientists, and, indeed, consumers and devotees. One could be forgiven for believing that the cow's milk, so celebrated as human food, medicine, and sacred commodity, is poisonous for her own biological baby.

The modern "dairy cow" does lactate copious amounts of milk, unnaturally in excess of the amount her newborn might need. However, this is less out of a desire to suckle her human progeny, and more due to the fact that her reproductive system is deliberately overworked so that *normal* female mammalian functions—lactating *naturally* in quantities required for their infant—is no longer possible. Cows and buffaloes have been domesticated and strategically bred for dairying for so long that it is difficult to know what their normal lactation would be; the closest "natural" indicator is the "beef" cow (in this case, bred for her flesh, rather than milk) who would "naturally produce around 4 litres of milk per day."[49]

In contrast, dairy scientists Oltenacu and Broom note: "The dairy cow is producing considerably more milk than its ancestor would have produced. The amount is ten times the beef cattle average of 1,000–2,000 kg."[50] A "dairy" cow may peak at 60 liters per day, and average at the least, at "28 litres per day over a period of 10 months."[51] The findings of Animals Australia reinforce these approximate figures: "The modern dairy cow can produce about 28 litres of milk per day—that's fourteen 2 litre cartons of milk and *about ten times more milk than her calf would need*."[52]

The volumes of milk that modern cows produce can be staggering. The 2012–2013 Annual Report for SAG in Ahmedabad, one of the most advanced parent-breeding bovine stations in India, notes that the Holstein Friesian crossbred mother no. 45359982 produced a whopping 8,430 kilograms of milk,[53] and the other Holstein mothers consistently produced between 7,400 to 8,400 kilograms of milk annually. Although Holsteins' large physical size makes them more prolific milk producers, Jersey mothers also produce copious amounts of milk, despite their smaller stature, with an annual production of over 6,000 kilograms. Contrast this with the most "natural" cow we know, at least as regards lactation—the "beef" cow, at 4 liters a day, might produce *about 1,440 kilograms of milk for her infant.*

However, even this profusion of milk from the domesticated "dairy" cow is insufficient for humans. Across dairies and even in gaushalas, infants are usually separated from their mothers to prohibit even minimal access to their udders. I would visit gaushalas where the manager would point at a mother and newborn pair, ostensibly "together." They'd be tied to a different pole each, unable even to lick or sniff each other. Every drop of the floods that the cows have been engineered to hyper-lactate is intended for humans.

Globally, the number of lactations for cows in dairying, or the number of times they are made pregnant, has been continuously dropping as their high milk production causes a number of health issues that send them to slaughter early.[54] The drain on the bovine's physical health as a result of such abnormally high milk output is considerable. Animals Australia note: "

> Producing large quantities of milk puts a significant metabolic strain on the animal. The great weight of the udders often causes painful stretching or tearing of ligaments and frequently causes foot problems, such as laminitis. These foot problems can be associated with significant pain.[55]

Correspondingly, the age of first calving is also decreasing; in other words, the bovines are being made pregnant younger and younger. Farmers typically impregnate cows when they are just over a year old, at approximately fifteen months, so that the cow is about two at the time of the first birth.[56] In essence, cows are being genetically selected for their ability for early lactation *and* high lactation performance but with little concern for traits like longevity and what these lactations do to their bodies. After three or four pregnancies, these cows are slaughtered as their physical form declines quickly due to voluminous milk production. As Australian dairy scientist Clive Phillips explains:

> The risk of contracting mastitis, lameness, fatty liver disease, hypocalcae-mia, acidosis, ketosis and many other diseases *increases with milk yield*. As a result the mean number of lactations is only three or four in most developed countries, compared with more than ten for feral cows.[57]

Mastitis is one of the most widely reported physiological problems of lactating mothers in dairy farms and represents a significant vulner-ability from which animals used for dairying have no protection. Once I started to recognize mastitis—thickly veined, pink inflamed udders—I started to see it almost all the time. Some cows and buffaloes have dark red udders, indicating severe infection. Mastitis is an extremely pain-ful inflammation of the breasts/udders when the milk ducts become blocked. This condition is made even more painful during breastfeeding or milking. This blockage can occur for a range of reasons,[58] including poor drainage of the breasts/udders which can be caused by weak attach-ment of the baby at the breast/udder, or limiting the baby's time at the breast/udder, a universal practice in the dairy sector.

Dairying is an industry *that actively causes mastitis.* Calves typically suckle every two to three hours,[59] and mothers are at high risk of mastitis when they are not suckled for extended periods of time. Both the infection and the treatment are extremely painful for milking mammals,[60] whether humans, cows, buffalo, or sheep, among others. In Amir and Lumley's account of lactational mastitis in the case of humans, they quote a mother recalling, "I have never felt worse."[61]

A vet from a leading dairy research institute told me that most bovines with mastitis are never treated and continue to be milked, either by hand or machine, causing extreme distress to the mothers. If the mastitis becomes chronic, it may be time for the farmer to either sell the buffalo mothers directly for slaughter and dispose of the cows illegally through markets and slaughterhouses in the black economy or simply abandon them, as the resultant low and infected milk yields would mean that another pregnancy was not worthwhile. The vet told me that Indian villages are full of abandoned cows with acute mastitis. Where he was based in Haryana, abandoned cows suffering mastitis were "everywhere":

> They just leave the unproductive cows, they are abandoned. We can fill two trucks full of abandoned wandering cows just from this one village. Or they transfer the cows from one village to another at night, as the cows often wander into the fields and destroy the crops.

Not only cows but also male calves who need the protection of their mother and their herd to survive are rendered vulnerable and left to fend for themselves on the streets in a chronic state of starvation, from where they are most likely to be picked up by butchers under the cover of darkness. I was walking through the curving narrow streets of a dairy colony in Old Lucknow when I saw a man pulling a calf to the corner closest to the road and tying him up. I ran across the road and found three cows and three calves, mothers and infants tied separately, in his small courtyard. "Why don't you let him be near his mother?" I asked.

"I am only waiting for a few days for him to get a bit stronger," he replied. "*Usse vaise bhi chod denge*" (I am going to let him go anyway). He was being prepared for a life of precarity, begging, and beatings on the streets.

I looked at the thin little bull, about to become completely disoriented and lost among the heaving traffic and indifferent human public, never to see his mother again. "He will be picked up by the *kasais* [butchers]," I told the man. "You know he will be."

"Yes," replied the man, who had "let go" several calves before. "But what else can I do? He is no use to us."

The man himself, as so many others, lived in a state of vulnerability and precarity, being enmeshed in a complex web of informal livelihoods. At the same time, there was the reality that the calf was certain to die of starvation on the road, if not at the slaughterhouse. At less than a month old, he was not even capable of fully digesting food other than his mother's milk. A study on dairy calf welfare notes: "Calves are born with a physically and metabolically underdeveloped rumen and initially rely on milk to meet nutrient demands for maintenance and growth."[62] An animal husbandry director in Andhra Pradesh explained that infant calves do not have a fully developed digestive system and they are incapable of consuming anything other than their mother's lactate (or milk replacement formulas). At the least, he said, the calf should consume predominantly breastmilk for at least three months, already a drastically shortened timeframe compared with what a calf requires:

> Minimum three months it (*sic*) needs milk to develop its four stomachs. After the third month only, the gastric juices will start secreting to facilitate the digestion of the fiber. Till then it cannot digest anything. So, it needs to be with the mother for three months minimum. In the third month, the calf will start chewing the grass, and the gastric juices will start secreting and it can digest that grass.

These vulnerabilities, including metabolic hunger caused by the calorie-dense labor of lactation and pregnancy, a range of infection and disease, and, above all, maternal separation that are routine in dairy farms, are compounded by the intensive confinement of the bovines in authorized, and unauthorized/informal dairies or *tabelas* in urban and rural areas. This system, called "zero-grazing," is recommended by the Food and Agriculture Organization, which describes it as "a system where the cattle are usually kept in the farm and farmers bring the feed and water to the animals."[63] Such methods, where the animals are confined for life in sheds with no access to grass or pasture, are now adopted in countries from Ireland to Kenya. In an era of escalating climate change and desertification, zero-gazing (rather than a switch to alternative food systems) is gaining traction.[64] Zero-grazing is already normative in India. As I would come to see, buffaloes in particular are almost always continuously raised in confinement; it is rare to see free-roaming buffaloes on the streets of Indian cities. Cows, while also intensively raised, might sometimes have a more dubious and dangerous form of "freedom"—they would be turned loose to forage and be responsible for their own feeding, which often translates into eating plastic in urban rubbish heaps, as was the case with the cow whose story opened this chapter.

THE INTENSIVE CONFINEMENT OF DAIRYING

Incredibly, and unsurprisingly in hindsight, informal dairies can sometimes be as difficult for an "outsider" to access as slaughtering areas. As compared to the mega-dairy farms of the West, Indian dairy farms are overwhelmingly small-scale (commonly called *tabelas* in northern India, or *doddi* in Karnataka, for instance), usually located in the informal sector, and pervasive throughout rural, peri-urban, and urban India. A study on Indian dairy development notes: "One emerging trend in the Indian dairying scenario is the growing number of commercial dairy farms in the urban and peri-urban areas of the metros and big cities."[65]

Twice, plans to visit *tabelas* in Delhi fell through. An activist tried to organize a visit accompanying a veterinary team; when this did not materialize, she emphasized that it could be unsafe to go in for interviews alone. Heightened vigilantism in cities like Delhi has increased the presence of middlemen in dairying sites, sourcing animals for illegal markets where animals would be sold for slaughter. Some dairy owners, she said, were becoming aggressive to outsiders appearing in their areas. Finally, along with animal welfare officers from the Bombay SPCA, I visited my first *tabela* in Mumbai.

All cities, whether megacities like Delhi, Kolkata, and Mumbai, or smaller ones like Jaipur, Lucknow, or Visakhapatnam, have hundreds of illegal, highly intensive *tabelas*. They usually operate with the full knowledge of municipal corporation officers who might come down to threaten the farmers and extract bribes. These "dairies" contain anywhere from a couple to hundreds of animals, living out their lives in crowded dark, confined sheds in pools of their own urine and dung.

Often the first sign that a neighborhood contains *tabelas* is the sight of emaciated newborns tied seemingly randomly to poles on the road (see Figure 3.3). Walking through a well-known urban *tabela* area in Visakhapatnam, Malathi and I found six cows and six she-buffaloes stuffed inside a small, dark room in a building, perhaps originally intended to house motorcycles or bikes, covered in urine and feces, and, as usual, harnessed tightly by their faces to low stakes on the ground (see Figure 3.4). The dairy farm was so fully enclosed in the one dark and humid

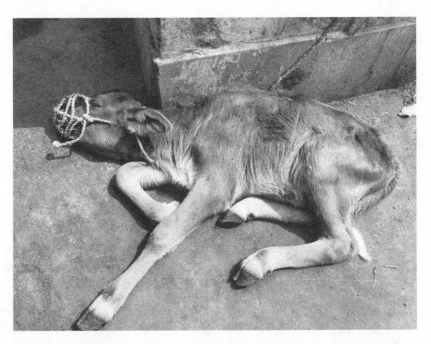

FIGURE 3.3: *Emaciated male calves left to die a slow death outside are often the first sign of an overcrowded indoor urban dairy farm in the vicinity.*
Source: Photo taken by author.

FIGURE 3.4: *Twelve lactating bovines tied and overcrowded in a steaming dark room in a Visakhapatnam dairy farm.*
Source: Photo taken by author.

room that we only became aware of it when we saw two skeletal calves tied to a lamppost outside, near a rubbish bin. One calf licked the dirty plastic drum repeatedly; the other was faint with hunger, eyes tightly shut and swaying ever so slightly as he stood in the almost motionless manner of very sick animals. Only an extremely slow labored breathing showed that he was even alive.

These *tabelas* sell cow and buffalo milk to meet customer demand for fresh milk, ghee, and paneer; cows' milk additionally serves the requirements of Hindu and Jain temples for *paal* or *doodh abhishekham*, where hundreds of liters of milk are poured over a stone statue or a *lingam*. Dairies—like butcher houses—thrive in specific caste or religion dominant neighborhoods, for instance, around the famous Kapaleeshwarar Temple in the largely Brahmin-caste area of Mylapore, or the Jain Temple in Sowcarpet where the high-dairy consuming Marwari caste community lives.

The first *tabela* that I visited in Mumbai held buffaloes. As far as the eye could see, row upon row of buffaloes were tethered with about two feet of rope and squatting next to each other. In total, 210 lactating or pregnant she-buffaloes lived—or rather, endured an existence—in the dark sheds in Kurla-Zari Mari. The ground was almost completely covered in a shallow pool of urine and dung. The under-bellies and even the backs of the buffaloes were thickly coated in dung, as they got sprayed with jets of urine and dung each time a neighboring animal stamped her foot, swished her tail, or made a sudden move. The restrained buffaloes could only sit or stand in the exact same spot. Indeed, even *tabelas* with one or two animals continuously chain them. Accompanied by the Bombay SPCA patrolling officers, we walked between the rows. The buffaloes leapt to their feet in fright, and tried ineffectually to make a run for it, their panic escalating because of their restraints, rows of heavy buffaloes bashing and knocking against their neighbors, sending up more jets of dung and urine. I was drenched in excrement after the short walk from one end to the other.

A squatting Murrah buffalo knocked her horns incessantly—bang, bang, bang, bang—against her cement feeding trough, which bore indentations from the steady banging over months, possibly years. Is it possible that these were signs of zoopsychosis, of madness, as ways of coping with the trauma she would have experienced? Zoopsychosis refers to the "involuntary repetitive movements," which are "symptoms of the trauma of being kidnapped, displaced, incarcerated, alienated, bored to death."[66] Zoopsychosis is experienced with great frequency by animals in spaces of extreme captivity, including farms, zoos, and laboratories. While there were hundreds of lactating mothers in the *tabela*, there were only seven calves in the dark shed, each painfully emaciated. One sleeping infant bull's neck was raised up the pole to which he was secured with a rope far too short for him to put his head down. A study of *tabelas* in Bareilly city in Uttar Pradesh revealed that calf mortality was 81.09 percent, as investment in "calf management" was considered "uneconomical."[67]

Many of the buffalo mothers in the *tabela* were about three or four years old. It was likely that at least one or two of their calves had already been sold and killed. It was likely that they might have another two or three pregnancies and thus two or three more years of zero-grazing confinement before their limping or even downed bodies, simply unable to rise again, were loaded into a truck for slaughter.

While I had been somewhat prepared at this point in my research for the crush of bovine bodies in the dairy farm, I was amazed to witness the intensive crush of *human* bodies, those of the dairy workers who lived confined lives on flimsy platforms, just beneath the ceiling of the sheds. Typical of many informal constructions, the roof was made of tightly woven dried palm leaves, tarpaulin, and dried buffalo manure. Below this makeshift canopy, a seeming labyrinth of rooms, or a "floor," had been constructed with wooden planks, where some forty workers lived, cooked, and slept with their meager belongings and cooking stoves. Alongside the buffaloes, these men too, were virtually imprisoned in dairy economies, vulnerable not only to the precarity of an informal economy that could not guarantee their employment, but also to working conditions that left them exposed to physical injury, or even a risk to life.

"What if a fire starts?" was my first question. I was truly shocked, finding it difficult to imagine how there hadn't been a cooking accident already, consuming both humans and bovines.

One man grinned. "We know how to manage, we manage," he said. He told me that they had migrated from Uttar Pradesh state in the north to seek work; the pay and working conditions had become so irregular and oppressive at home that these men, along with thousands from the state, had left to seek better opportunities in the south.

Like these men, most dairy workers are poor, landless, and of the "lowest" Dalit or Adivasi castes; it is more privileged castes like the Patels in Gujarat, for instance, who typically own the animals, space, and infrastructure of a dairy farm, and who predominantly comprise the decision-making membership of dairy cooperatives.[68] Studies of dairy management have emphasized the exploitation of poor "low-caste" dairy laborers from Uttar Pradesh, a state entrenched in casteist politics. "The farmers in the region are mostly illiterate and they are unconscious and unaware about processing, value addition of milk and milk products and current trends in dairy industry. So they do not get proper profit from their milk production."[69] Enmeshed in the precarity of the informal dairy economy, workers in farms, like those in slaughterhouses, are on low, subsistence wages and are not formally skilled.

While Kurien intended the dairy cooperatives as a way of democratizing social norms at the grassroots, there is evidence, even in the birthplace of Operation Flood, of the entrenched inequities of caste. The wealthier Patels and Patidars control most cooperatives in Gujarat and own most of the animals.[70] Middle-caste Hindus have gained most from milk cooperatives, which often disempower Christian, Muslim, or "low-caste" Hindu dairy farmers by excluding them from decision-making and representation. In half of the cooperatives that they surveyed, Dohmwirth and Hanisch found that there was complete caste homogeneity with no participation of Muslims or "lower castes." In addition, "presidents and secretaries belong to dominant or majority castes, indicating that men and women from scheduled castes often remain excluded from cooperative leadership."[71] "Lower-caste" dairy farmers frequently preferred to form their own cooperatives, as "upper-caste" managers often underpaid them for the milk they brought.[72] The dairy cooperatives did not pay farmers in a timely manner, re-entrenching caste inequalities where scheduled caste and scheduled tribe dairy farmers remain vulnerable to upper/middle-caste *dudhwalas* (milkmen) and dairy cooperative members.[73] "Lower-caste" farmers in Bihar, Punjab, and Uttar Pradesh, for instance, had limited or no opportunities to even become members of cooperatives.[74]

While *tabelas* are now no longer allowed within the metropolitan precincts of most cities, Dawn William told me that in fact, they exist throughout urban spaces in central nodes that allow for rapid transportation to various markets or slaughterhouses. Accompanied by a Blue Cross volunteer in Chennai, I peered into a darkened, humid room on the ground floor of a two-story block near the Mylapore temple to find seventeen young cows. We were alerted to the fact there were cows housed in that building by the presence of a single enormous Jersey bull tied tightly outside to be used for insemination. To subdue his agitation, he was tied by the face to the window of the building with a rope that was less than a foot long, pressing his face against the wall. I walked, stunned, from the back to the front; he looked at me warily with bloodshot eyes. He could do nothing except stand in that one position all day—he could not bend his head, or turn even slightly sideways. Presumably, a few hours of respite might come at night when he was allowed to lie down.

In another *tabela* close to Mylapore, lactating buffaloes and cows were chained around garbage mounds and cesspools under a suburban railway bridge. Every twenty or thirty minutes, the ground would shake and reverberate as a train screeched overhead, making me jump violently the first time I heard it. If the police or municipal health inspectors decided to visit, the *tabela* owner would be duly tipped off in time by someone on the "inside," and the animals would vanish, easily transported under cover to illegal slaughterhouses, operating in these cities.

While the buffaloes have no alternative to continuous confinement in cities, the sacred status of the cow can yield further opportunities for exploitation. As Hindu mothers, cows attract donations, and are used as begging props. After morning milking, *tabelas* with cows often "hire" out their mothers daily to the poor who take them to a neighboring temple, where they make money by selling greens and fodder to devotees to feed the cows. Violence against the animals abounds in these ostensibly pious transactions. In front of a wayside Ganesha temple in Kurla in Mumbai, we saw one cow among a group of cows with her face harnessed close to the ground by a half-foot rope. She could not raise her head, causing stress and pain to her back and shoulders. She was being punished with tight restraints for repeatedly straining at her rope, perhaps demanding to go back to her calf. Later, when we returned to the Bombay SPCA, we found a man had brought in his "begging" cow, her eyes crawling with live maggots. Despite the veterinarian's pleas that he leave her there as she was in agony, her owner insisted on taking her back after a few wriggling worms had been plucked from her eyes, as she was the source of his daily income. His eight-year-old daughter sobbed piteously for the suffering of the cow whom she loved. The desperation and vulnerability of all—the cow, the veterinarian and the little girl—was palpable as we parted ways.

There might be one exception to intensive incarceration. Both abandoned and lactating cows may be turned onto the streets to find their calories from the toxic waste that cities generate. Lactation is highly calorie-intensive labor,[75] where the females burn through several hundred calories a day, or even a few thousand in the case of large animals, by producing milk. It is difficult to overstate the raw, chronic, hormonally-induced levels of severe hunger that lactating females endure.

ABANDONMENT AND ABJECTION: A TOXIC DIET

I looked out of the car window in a traffic jam in Chennai to a sad but familiar sight. A white cow with fairly heavy udders stood on the footpath, tore a large piece of poster off the wall and ate it. She continued to tear off piece after piece, ingesting a lethal cocktail of ink, chemicals, glue, and paper. Another time, outside a *tabela* area in Jaipur, my activist friend Manil took me to a garbage dump where huge stinking mounds of plastic plates, spoons, and polythene from a recent wedding were piled high amid older decaying waste. As dusk started to fall, we saw several small male calves running to the dump to nose through the plastic to find any edible waste, forced to fend for themselves in the absence of their mother and the safety of their familial herd. When I visited the Kanha Upvan animal shelter in Lucknow, I found that they had framed the contents of what they found in an abandoned and starving cow's rumen as a sobering lesson on where waste, carelessly discarded, ends up. The display included large rusty nails, big pieces of glass, coins, and forty to eighty kilograms of plastic bags.

Plastic is an exceptionally serious environmental problem in India. The Ganga in India, and the Indus in Pakistan are among the ten rivers worldwide responsible for an estimated 90 percent of the plastics in the oceans.[76] Urban plastic waste is being generated on an unprecedented scale. In their *Waste of a Nation*, Assa Doron and Robin Jeffrey note that Chandighar city for instance, was producing "135,000 metric tons of waste a year" by 2017, half of which was plastic.[77] This waste was not disposed of; India has a waste disposal, as much as a waste production problem. Doron and Jeffrey write, "Animals still foraged, but they now risked blocking their intestines by eating plastic bags and other indigestible hazards."[78]

These free-roaming urban bovines and other animals risk physical abuse, and toxic environmental conditions to stave off hunger, being forced to "trespass" upon public and private human property. In *The Force of Falsity*, Amit Chaudhery (2014), president of People for Animals Gurgaon, describes the contempt with which the cows and buffaloes are treated as they attempt to share urban spaces with humans:

> every upstart colony in every shabby parvenu neighbourhood is intolerant of animals. Roaming cows are a very obvious victim of this condition. Robbed of grazing land and clean water, forced to subsist on filth, walk this country's pathetic roads only to be killed by callous drivers, beaten and shooed away by people, administered painful oxytocin injections to extract milk, compelled to deliver calves on streets, administered dhoomdev and phooka [blowing] to draw every drop . . . the litany is painfully long.

As concealed transportation to underground slaughterhouses is becoming difficult due to heightened vigilantism, the public presence of these animals on the roads has increased in both urban and regional India. On the highway from Udaipur city to Sirohi district in Rajasthan for instance, a route spanning the urban, peri-urban, and the rural, it is possible to see hundreds of bulls of all ages living in bachelor herds on highways, village roads, and in cities.

With productive "free-roaming" cows, farmers nonetheless find ways of somehow physically restraining them, so they are not tempted to wander too far in their desperation for food. Once, Malathi and I were going past a side street in central Visakhapatnam when she spotted what was to me an extraordinary sight, but one, she assured me, that was extremely common. We grabbed some bananas and walked to a garbage mound, where a brown Jersey cow, sniffing around the mounds of plastic and kitchen waste, was in real agitation. Her face was tied to her right foreleg (see figure 3.5). Thus, bent low with her face to her raised foreleg, she walked with an enforced limp. A small thin girl calf trotted near her. I held out the bananas, which the mother grabbed out of my hands and grunted agitatedly in rage—she tried to shake her head at us, and it was clear she wanted help. Malathi ran back to the car and procured a pair

FIGURE 3.5: *A "free-roaming" dairy cow with her foreleg tied to her face to limit her freedom. Her baby girl calf trots besides her.*
Source: Photo taken by author.

of scissors from the driver. They were blunt; even as the cow tried to headbutt Malathi in her agitation, Malathi managed to cut the cord and leap out of the way. The cow paced down the road, her calf close behind. Thereafter I was to see large numbers of cows and buffaloes, all with their faces tied to a foreleg so they could still manage to limp and forage in the garbage but would not be able to wander far.

Animal welfarists—those advocates who claim that it is possible to use animals humanely—will earnestly tell you that the best solution is for the dairy farmers to "just keep the animals," rather than selling them. "They are the ones making money from the cows, it's their responsibility and they should keep them," a middle-class activist who worked against cow slaughter told me. She herself bought and consumed milk from what she described as an "ethical" dairy owned by a wealthy Delhi social-ite—a dairy that reportedly keeps the male calves, although she could not answer how they could sustain the births of more males and post-menopausal cows, year after year. For most farmers, living on the edge of precarity, it is economically impossible to pay the ongoing expenses of caring for non-productive animals, and thus there is no choice but to discard or sell those animals who are no longer sources of income. The idea that poor, subsistence farmers should subsidize the cost of dairy farming and widespread dairy consumption by maintaining non-lactating animals reflects the unrealistic assumptions embedded in caste, class, and species privilege, and indeed, misconceptions about the basic facts of dairy production itself. It is the cows and buffaloes, however, who bear the brunt of the dairy farmers' frustration at the impossibility of making ends meet. At gaushalas and other animal shelters, it is possible to meet some of these "useless" animals who have experienced violence at farmers' hands—and to truly understand that dairy farmers cannot subsidize the milk sector.

I visited the Pathmeda gaushala in Rajasthan, a beautiful gaushala spread across 200 acres in the desert. In their "hospital" section filled with disabled, paralyzed, and severely injured animals, an indigenous female cow stood still, severely disfigured by an acid attack (see figure 3.6). The cow's skin was peeled raw and blistered, her ears had been burnt off by the acid, and her eyes—blind and the sockets now sealed with a plastic cap—bulged out. Starving and abandoned, she had wandered into a farmer's field at night for food, and had acid hurled at her as punishment. The gaushala staff said it could well have been a Hindu farmer who had attacked the cow, "Hindu, Muslim, it can be anybody, in fact, probably a Hindu farmer only as they are the ones who rear cows the most." Muslim dairy farmers increasingly avoid raising cows as they are vulnerable to vigilante attacks when it is time to dispose of the animals.

The human victims of acid attacks or vitriolage are mostly young women who are "out of place," though increasingly, children, older women, and men are targeted.[79] These attacks now extend to abandoned and destitute farmed species, who are forced to forage in risky sites in desperation. Concentrated hydrochloric or sulfuric acid can melt metal,

FIGURE 3.6: *An abandoned or starving dairy cow who became a victim of an acid attack for going into an agricultural farmer's field looking in desperation for food.*
Source: Photo taken by author.

and burns easily through fat, muscle, vital organs, and bone.[80] Most acid attack victims lose one or both of their eyes permanently.[81]

In addition to acid attacks, cows and other animals are subjected to other forms of violence to deter them from foraging in agricultural fields. At the time of my visit at Kanha Upvan rescue shelter in Lucknow, they had a heavily pregnant cow whose entire jaw had been blown to pieces by a crude bomb. This cow had broken into a field just outside the city. Farmers place explosives at strategic spots in their fields amid their crops to deter hungry farmed animals, typically abandoned cows or free-roaming pigs. The cow stood still, with tendons and muscle hanging from her jaw, blood dripping, two days after her rescue. "Why won't you euthanize her?" I implored the management. However, the euthanasia of animals is extremely rare in India;[82] it is often seen as an unethical, or even "lazy" Western approach to animal care. As a result, I'd constantly see animals of all species—cows, buffaloes, kittens, dogs—in states of extreme suffering, being forced to drag out their life in slow inches. Euthanasia of cows, in particular, can quickly become very political.[83]

Moreover, in the case of this cow, she was not "alone." "She has a calf inside her," I was told. "We have to give the fetus a chance to live." Even as they promoted awareness of the cows' vulnerability in consuming plastic, for instance, it was not necessarily connected explicitly to their vulnerability embedded in dairy farming itself, for which these bovines were bred. The shelter milked pregnant animals and sold the milk to customers eager to buy ostensibly ethical milk from a shelter rather than a dairy farm. The pregnant cow's maternal bond to her *fetus* was thus to be protected, and yet the routine and necessary disruption of the mother–infant bond—even in "humane" farming, however negotiated—did not bear the same respect. If anything, throughout India, I was to encounter even more extractive forms of milking "dairy" mothers.

OXYTOCIN: FOR EVERY LAST DROP OF MILK

At the early hour of 4 a.m., Sowcarpet area in Chennai city is nothing like the heaving, packed, polluted urban village hub that it would become later in the morning. The quietest, darkest, stillest hours of the day are perhaps the most stressful hours for hundreds of cows who live in this densely overcrowded milk enclave in Chennai. A volunteer-activist from the Blue Cross of India had picked me up, and we had traveled quickly across the multiple flyovers in the dark on his motorbike, reaching Sowcarpet in less than a quarter of the time that it might have taken us once the teeming, congested city came to life. We went straight to the small *chara* (greens) market just outside the Jain Temple, a few small vendors already beginning to lay out their wares. Devotees typically buy small bunches of greens to offer in handfuls to the chained cow "goddesses." Thus, it would not be unusual for us to go up to the cows to offer the greens, though admittedly, our piety at that hour was, perhaps, a bit unusual.

We started to wind our way through the empty, dark alleys, and in the dim street lights, soon began to see groups of one, two, three, and soon even ten cows and buffaloes, some heavily pregnant, and many with engorged udders, make their way to their milking spots. They knew where to go. These pregnant and lactating mothers were walking briskly and purposefully to start with, but soon the milkmen started to hit them hard on their bony backs with heavy sticks, making them break into a run.

One brown Jersey cow had such a ballooned-out udder that she had to splay her hind legs wide as she limped heavily along on the hard road. As I watched the fearful mother struggle to walk fast on the bitumen to avoid a torrent of whipping, I wondered if this might be her last cycle of lactation before being trucked to slaughter. Already moving with great difficulty and in agony, she was almost certain to be a "downer" cow soon, unable to stand from the repeated extractions of pregnancies and milking, or almost certainly, en route to the slaughterhouse. If she was trying to keep pace now to escape the blows on her back from her "owner," who was meant to care for her welfare, I could not begin to imagine the beatings this mother would have to endure from transporters and butchers as a downed cow, to make her final crawl to the kill floor.

Many cows and buffaloes were already chained to their spots and their emaciated calves occasionally stood tethered a few feet away, patiently waiting or straining for a suckle, or just curled up in a small ball on the hard ground. Some small calves stood near mothers who were already pregnant. Many other cows stood alone, their calves presumably sold to the veal market. I held out some greens to a pregnant cow whose back was concave from the heavy calcium leaching from her bones as a result of repeated pregnancies and lactations. No calf stood near her although she had engorged udders. She snatched the entire bunch out of my arms ferociously.

All around us milkmen in folded up *veshtis* and shirts bustled with large aluminum milking cans, a thick medical syringe stuck behind each ear. My companion nudged and pointed to the ground. As our eyes became accustomed to the dim street lights, I could see that strewn throughout the street, and across every street that we traversed thereafter, were empty, unlabeled white plastic bottles with red caps. They were once filled with oxytocin, the prescription-only drug that is widely and illegally injected by dairy farmers into lactating cows at least twice a day during morning and evening milking to increase milk production.

As we offered our remaining greens to the cows and patted the babies, we observed a farmer curl his entire fist around a large syringe. He raised his arm, and punched the injection hard into the side of the cow's neck folds. The tethered animal recoiled and jerked sideways in a futile attempt to get away. The man waited a few minutes, and then started to pull at her teats to drain her of milk. After she was depleted, he would dip the same needle into his bottle of oxytocin to inject the next cow.

What is oxytocin? As per the description in *Black's Veterinary Dictionary:*

> Oxytocin is a naturally occurring peptide hormone . . . excreted by all mammals for induction and maintenance of labor and promotion of milk ejection. It has an important pharmaceutical use in veterinary and human medicine. Treatment is via injection, intravenously, intramuscularly, or subcutaneously.[84]

Oxytocin is widely used in human and nonhuman animal maternity care to assist with uterine contractions in late-stage labor, as well as breastfeeding, where lactation does not occur naturally. In the dairy industry, *lactation is not allowed to occur naturally.* When the infant is removed from the stressed lactating mother, milk letdown into the udders might not occur easily. Oxytocin is also used to treat mastitis as "the stimulation of milk ejection . . . is correlated with increased pathogen removal from the udder."[85]

In India, the illegal use of oxytocin to force milk letdown in bovines has become ubiquitous[86] when the mother's capacity to suckle naturally is weakened or disrupted altogether. In another *tabela* close to Mylapore area in Chennai, some twenty-five cows were packed into a small shed with a tin roof atop a small hillock of garbage. Near the shed was a stinking pond that served as a receptacle for human and animal waste, and all types of garbage generated by the city, including soiled nappies, bloodied medical waste, plastic and rotten food. Skinny chickens and goats, also owned by the *tabela*, scratched around in the mounds of contaminated rubbish. Neela, the Blue Cross volunteer who had accompanied me, nudged me and pointed to the floor—it again took me a few seconds to register what he was pointing at, and then I saw them everywhere, the tell-tale small white plastic bottles with red screw tops—oxytocin.

Dawn William estimated that some 95 percent of the urban dairy farmers he has encountered through his field rescues use oxytocin, especially for milking buffaloes whose milk letdown is supposedly slow. William's anecdotal estimate corresponded with a study on commercial dairy farms in Bareilly, Uttar Pradesh, that reported oxytocin use being widespread among the "ninety commercial dairy owners in the Bareilly district of Uttar Pradesh" that they studied.[87] A study published by the Indian Council of Agricultural Research authored by an animal nutrition scholar, a biochemist, and a veterinary scientist, found in their study:

> In all the dairy complexes, the banned hormone oxytocin was used extensively, at higher doses (6–10 ml or even more), for let down of milk and same needle was used for all animals. Perhaps this could be one of possible reasons for high incidence of abortions (1–20%) at most of the dairy houses.[88]

In one of the most ruthless uses that I had heard, Dawn described oxytocin being forcibly administered even to nearly "dry" cows who were brought to the slaughter market at the infamous Pollachi *maatu chanthai* in Tamil Nadu, regarded as the cruelest of "cattle markets" by many animal activists in the state. Dawn saw a farmer with four tightly tied, emaciated cows in a Tata Tempo truck; he was shocked to see that the nipples of two of the cows, red with mastitis, were tightly sealed with duct-tape so that the last few leaking drops could be extracted before their sale for slaughter. The other two cows, however, had to be administered oxytocin to extract the last drops of milk. One was almost completely "dry." Dawn recalled:

> The farmer went to his thin cow and jammed the (oxytocin) injection into her neck. After some minutes he started milking her, but nothing came, only a few drops of milk. Then he yelled and abused the cow with filthy names, and you could see she was extremely terrified. He slammed another injection into her neck, and waited again. After a few minutes, still nothing, just some drops. She was milked dry, she had absolutely nothing. He started to slap and punch the cow's face in fury, screaming the filthiest abuses at her the whole time. Then he threw the can of milk with those

pathetic few drops in her face—she recoiled in terror but she was tied, where could she go? He screamed, "Don't think you can get away with this, bitch. You haven't got the better of me yet. I am selling you—you will make money for me yet!"

Routine intramuscular injections cause stress to the animals.[89] Dawn told me that the Blue Cross routinely receives abandoned cows with infected abscesses on their neck folds or hump. When the wound was cleaned up, there would be a broken needle embedded deep in the tissue. The illegal use of oxytocin in Indian dairying has become so prolific that the national government attempted to take steps to restrict its use.[90] In April 2018, the Central Board of Excise and Customs announced a ban on the import of oxytocin from 1st July 2018, to counter the illegal use in the dairy sector.[91] The Ministry of Health declared that only the public sector enterprise Karnataka Antibiotics and Pharmaceuticals Ltd would manufacture the drug for domestic use.[92] However, this ban had to be rescinded as it would have led to a shortage of oxytocin for treatment of mastitis and milk release complications in human mothers.[93] Oxytocin continues to be used widely in Indian dairy farms, in addition to the core extractions of forced birthing and labor, and mother–infant separation, which constitute dairying itself.

FOUR years after I commenced this research, I was in an "organized" dairy farm near Ahmedabad, only a couple of hours away from Anand, where Kurien started his dairy revolution. Italian and Danish dairy investors had started to provide generous subsidies to Indian dairy farmers to increase the volumes of milk per individual cow and buffalo mother. This meant a sharp uptick in the use of Holstein cows, who, through intensive genetic manipulation, could lactate a stupendous 30 liters of milk a day, even in widely observed conditions of under-feeding in India.[94] The owner, from the Patel caste—traditionally wealthy land-owners, proudly told me that he did not use oxytocin on his farm at all; he did not have to as the Holstein genetics allowed a voluminous milk letdown without oxytocin. Buffalo farmers, he allowed, had to use oxytocin twice a day.

As we walked through the rows of cows, right next to the entry on the far side of the rows where the sun poured through in full blaze, I almost missed an extremely tiny brown calf lying curled up on the ground; he looked like a small sack. I asked the owner if he was male; he confirmed that he was. Now three days old, the calf had been separated from his mother a few minutes after he was born; this Holstein newborn wasn't even required to stimulate milk letdown. When I asked what was going to happen to him, the man mumbled, "We will keep him, of course. He will live as long as he lives. Maybe we will give him to a gaushala."

I stopped the man, and looked him in the eye. "Let us not do this," I said. "We both know what will happen to him. There is not even one male animal on your farm. And the gaushalas are overcrowded— no gaushala will take a Holstein calf."

He looked away. "Yes, it is the reality, what can we do?" he mumbled. He said that male calves were taken to a market about twenty kilometers away. In the most curious of business sales—possible perhaps only in the Indian dairy industry—the farmer would *pay* the middlemen Rs 1000 for *them* to buy the calf; in other words, perform the service of removing "rubbish." "I don't know what they do with the calves, maybe they use them for *kheti* [agriculture]," he said.

We circled the other animals and a few minutes later, I returned on my own to the calf, wide-eyed as I approached. As I put my hand out to touch him, the baby immediately grasped it and started to suckle with his gummy mouth, my fingers yielding nothing, my heart pouring out grief. The calf rose unsteadily, and tied as he was to a short rope, stumbled a bit and stood, trembling, near a Holstein cow tied closest to him. She immediately began straining at her ropes, and licking his back repeatedly, sniffing him, nuzzling her head on him as much as she could. He was tied just out of reach of her udders. Heavily lactating herself, this mother's calf had already been sold or was dead.

A young female worker, about fifteen years old, and her father came and sat with me. They were of the nomadic Raika caste of Rajasthan, traditionally camel herders, who were losing their tribal way of life due to the onslaught of urbanization that eroded their forest rights. Classified as among the "other backward castes," (OBCs)[95] they were among the poorest of the social hierarchy of caste. "He is being starved," the man said to me. "He is a *ladka* [boy]. He will be dead in a month."

His daughter described what this month would look like for the neonatal male calf. "We give him 300 ml milk a day," she whispered. "Right now, he is drinking whatever we give him, in a week, he will become weaker, maybe only take 200 or 100 ml." In two weeks, she explained, he would barely be able to take in any milk at all. Not long after, the infant would be so weak that he would not even be able to raise his head, and would refuse feed altogether. He would be prodded every few days to check if he was alive—and he would be, barely breathing. "When he stops drinking anything, we know he will be dead in ten days," she said. Tanners from the village, also of an OBC caste, would come to take away his corpse.

The owner circled back. "I know this is wrong, it is difficult," he said. "I will give this calf some time with his mother." The man asked one of the workers to take him to his mother, tied at the far end of the other side of the farm. The man started to drag the three-day old by the rope, stumbling, unsteady. "Please lift him," I asked. As soon as he was placed near his tied mother, she started to sniff and lick him in great agitation.

What I did not foresee was the excitement of the chained Holstein mother next to her, who started to moo softly, reaching out to lick and sniff the calf herself. Cows are wonderful tribal mothers, and whether she believed his infant was hers or otherwise, this bereft mother, her own calf lost to her already, started to tremble violently at the sight of another infant of her own species.

The worker gave this cow such a stinging slap on the face that I actually jumped in fright myself. "*You* are not his mother!" he shouted.

The cow hastily retreated in fear, but then slowly tried to advance again toward the wide-eyed calf. The cow, as a *concept* in India, was "mother" of the Universe itself. However, in daring to show love to an infant she might have *naturally* helped to mother if allowed to be part of a free herd of cows, she received a blow. This cow had disrupted the order of the dairy industry, which could not bear to endure, even for a few seconds, the immense love, bonding, and care between a *cow mother* and her *cow calf.*

The primordial vulnerabilities of cows and buffaloes as *bovine mothers*, and the sufferings of their infants, lay bare the speciousness of the Hindu reverence of cows as "mothers" of humans. I did not believe that this was necessarily or always, willful duplicity; doublethinking, as discussed at the outset of the book is fundamental to sustaining dairying, anywhere. Framing the (dairy) cow as "mother" is simply another specific and imaginative—in this case Hindu—way of obscuring the real violence of dairy production, as is any disregard for the buffalo mother. Dairy farming, regardless of scale or geography, remains universal in its exploitation of the maternal body. In the case of humans, however, Katsi Cook argues for the iron-clad safeguarding of the mother's body, which she describes as the "first environment" of her infant—a vulnerability of mother and infant that is true regardless of species.

The intentional witnessing of the vulnerabilities of cows, buffaloes, and their infants in dairy farms brought into focus for me the various configurations of power[96]—both intra-human hierarchies of caste, class and religion, and even more specifically, the *human-animal*, including *human-cow* hierarchy that defines dairying in India. As Pachirat writes, where "physical, social, linguistic, and methodological distance and concealment [operate] as techniques of power, [attempts] to subvert or shorten this distance through a politics of sight are necessary and important."[97] Bringing to light their collective lived realities became critical in bringing to light a facet of cow politics that has gone almost entirely unremarked in Indian political discourse. If the vulnerabilities of being a "dairy" animal are taken seriously, then, it started to become clear to me, it would have to be a *milk politics* at the forefront of Indian identity politics that pivots around animal protection.

Across this conceptual landscape of the simultaneous objectification of the cow in India as milk machine and as mother-goddess, I tried to understand how cow protection was enacted. Singularly in India, cows will supposedly be retired and allowed to die at the end of their natural lives in gaushalas or cow shelters, a remarkable aspiration for any sustainable, profitable animal production sector. In other words, dairying in

India can supposedly occur on a continuum of birth and *life*, wherein the removal of death or killing from the milk production line is not a disruption of viable dairy production. If uniquely in India, cows can exit *production* spaces to move into *protection* spaces rather than slaughterhouses, then what do these sites of sanctuary look like?

CHAPTER 4

GAUSHALAS: MAKING INDIA "PURE" AGAIN

THE DEEP RED *pottu* smeared across the forehead of the small male Jersey calf had started to bleed in the rain, appearing as a premonition of a dark gash slicing his face. He stood still, patiently with three other males at the foot of the 1,000 steps that marked the ascent to the Simhachalam Temple in Vishakapatnam city in Andhra Pradesh. Simhachalam is the second most venerated Hindu temple in the state after the Tirumala Tirupathi Devasthanams, which is regarded in turn as one of the holiest Hindu sites in the world. Each calf was decorated with a garland of drenched flowers and holy *tulasi* or basil leaves, and glittery red ribbons. Following a cramped ride in the back seat of an auto-rickshaw (see figure 4.1) or even a long trek from a village in the peri-urban conurbation of Vishakapatnam, these newborn males from India's dairy sector would be transformed, briefly, into gods, in being donated by their owners to Simhachalam. Ribs protruded prominently from the sides of each calf. I reached out to rub one calf's back to find it sodden with rainwater. I did not know that calfskin could soak up so much moisture.

There was not a trough of water or a blade of hay nearby; three of the calves fell hungrily upon a large bunch of ripe bananas I offered. One small calf hung back in misery refusing even to smell the fruit. He caught scent of my extended hand and desperately suckled it for a couple of minutes before turning his small head away in disappointment; he did

FIGURE 4.1: *A Jersey calf being transported at the back of an auto-rickshaw to Simhachalam. It is common to find three or four calves stuffed into such autos during transport to the temple.*

Source: Photo taken by author.

not even yet have teeth. This calf was almost certain to die slowly from heartbreak and starvation. It was only nine in the morning, and these newborn infants would be joined by others throughout the day, often up to 200 calves on festival days. The Simhachalam Temple Gaushala would not adopt these abandoned calves as they were Jerseys. The temple gaushala was reserved exclusively for indigenous Indian cow breeds.

At the end of each week, a transfer truck from the VSPCA would take the orphaned Jersey calves away to a few acres of greenery at their Kindness Farm where they would join other rescued calves, the numbers increasing daily. Up to 40 percent of the youngest calves will die without their mother's colostrum and body warmth. These are the "lucky" males. Until a few years ago, they were being auctioned en masse by the temple on a weekly basis to intermediaries who would route them to slaughterhouses.

THE POLITICAL ECONOMY OF INDIA'S SACRED
DAIRYING: THE GAUSHALA-SHELTER-DAIRY COMPLEX
The fact that dairying in India is no more unique than anywhere else,
and is sustained by the same cold and mundane realities of slaughtering
"useless" animals as elsewhere, is often countered by the argument that
Indian dairying *is* distinctive because cows can be retired into gaushalas,
popularly understood as cow shelters. The dominant discourse circulating in Indian society is that there is no need for cow *slaughterhouses* because cow *shelters* can instead receive and sustain the millions of cows,
bulls, and calves annually rendered sick, prematurely aged, disabled,
emotionally broken, or orphaned by the dairy sector.

Confusingly, however, even as gaushalas ostensibly receive discarded
animals from dairying, they also operate *as* dairy farms. Even the Indian
state invests in gaushalas as part of its dairy development. In 1946, the
Ministry of Agriculture's Indian Council for Agronomic Research recognized their potential as breeding centers for high-yielding dairy cows.[1] In
1949, the Central Gaushalas Development Board was established to coor-
dinate financial support for breeding and dairying, which was further developed in India's second and third Five Year Plans between 1955 and 1966.[2]
In his book, C. Madan Mohan described gaushala development schemes
in Andhra Pradesh: "The *Goshalas* are serving as cattle-breeding-*cum*-milk
production centres and are supplementing Government efforts for supply
of good breeding bulls and increasing milk production in the state."[3]

At the same time, some 80 percent of the funds granted for animal
shelters by the Animal Welfare Board of India, a body under the Ministry of Environment, Forest, and Climate Change, are also allocated to
gaushalas.[4] This begs the question: what are animal sanctuaries?

Animal sanctuaries are generally understood as permanent or temporary refugee settlements where animals are liberated from intentional
human harms. They are also sites of captivity; the conditions of animals'
lives, including when and what they are fed; what sort of medical care
(if any) they receive; their housing conditions; and recognition of their
individuality, are fully regulated by humans.[5] Core principles of animal refuges include: non-exploitation of individuals; non-perpetuation
(i.e., animals are not bred); and awareness and advocacy, "challenging

conventional ideas of domesticated animals existing to serve human needs [including] Eschew(ing) use, sale, or other commercial activity involving animals."[6] In the case of farmed animals, the rehabilitation is precisely *from being farmed.* In farmed animal sanctuaries, putting the animals through forcible reproduction, the core of all farming activities, would recreate the very violence from which these animals needed rescue in the first place.

Gaushalas, then, are not animal shelters in the way that this term might be commonly understood. However, they are also not ordinary dairies as might be commonly imagined. An integral part of the Indian dairy economy, gaushalas produce "pure," "sacred" milk for use in ritual Hinduism. While commercial dairying peddles cows' milk as a nutritionally perfect food, a myth challenged by health science[7] and vegan studies,[8] gaushala dairying further commodifies cows' milk—albeit from native breeds—as *spiritually* perfect food. Hindus pour thousands of liters of milk, buttermilk and curds over idols on major festivals like Shivaratri or Janmashtami (the birth day of Lord Krishna), generating profits for dairy companies.[9] In a sycophantic twist, fans often drench statues and cut-outs of movie stars and politicians in hundreds of liters of milk, particularly in the southern states.[10]

Some citizens question the waste, arguing that the milk could be fed to malnourished children. An animal organization in Mumbai collects the milk from the temples to feed street dogs, despite the fact that dogs are lactose intolerant.[11] Very rarely does any institution—Hindu temples, devotees, or even animal welfare organizations and gaushalas—link the deprived *calves* to this profusion of waste. It seems important to maintain the cow–calf disassociation at all costs.

Gaushalas can perhaps be most accurately regarded as one of the oldest spaces of animal welfarism, a discourse that maintains that it is possible to exploit animals "humanely,"[12] "compassionately," or indeed, "reverentially." "Sacred" treatment of cows in gaushalas is made explicit through two acts—no slaughter, and the anthropocentrism of their worship. All other aspects of dairying—forced impregnation and breeding, removal of colostrum and lactate from the calves, and separation from their mothers—are routine.

However, what governs the logic of a gaushala as a *sanctuary* in India? From what and who are these animals receiving protection? Clearly it is not the dairy industry.

In *Sacred Cows, Sacred Places*, one of the oldest and most highly regarded studies on the sanctity of cows and gaushalas, Deryck O. Lodrick notes that gaushalas began to be regarded in the British colonial period as spaces in which cows were saved from *killing* by *Muslims* and *Dalits*,[13] a racial and casteist idea of "cow protection" that endures into the present. The presence of "rescued" cows in gaushalas is relatively recent, solidifying as such during the Hindu renaissance in the colonial period.[14] Indeed, even during my research, in places like rural Rajasthan, I found that up to 90 percent of the cows were born in the gaushala itself, complicating the site as housing rescued animals. Large bachelor herds of bulls and bull-calves, however, can be found abandoned throughout regional Rajasthan.

Forced to concede the realities of dairying, gaushalas, too, have been unable to separate themselves from the conjoined bedfellows of dairying—the beef, veal, and hide industries; male calves and unwanted females are often "sold or traded" by gaushalas.[15] When slaughter is prohibited, the number of ex-dairying animals needing rehabilitation far exceeds the limited capacity of gaushalas to house and feed them. The Satyam Shivam Sundaram Gau Seva Kendra, the largest gaushala in South India, can house only 5,000 cows.[16] In 2010, the International Society for Krishna Consciousness (ISKCON) Temple established a gaushala on the outskirts of the temple city of Tirupati in Andhra Pradesh state, which can shelter 2,000 cows.[17] Pathmeda, a beautiful gaushala spread across 200 acres in the desert in Rajasthan, shelters close to 20,000 bovines, all native breeds like Kankrej, Sahiwal, and Tharparkar. However, dairying discards hundreds of thousands of cows, calves, and bulls every year, all needing lifetime care. In all my travels, I found *one* gaushala that took in buffaloes, housing them grudgingly in dark sheds, out of sight. In a move that is economically efficient and seemingly pious, then, discarded male calves are often routed to the slaughterhouse via temples and gaushalas, co-opted into the cow slaughter economy as a smokescreen, exposing vulnerable groups whose labor sustains dairying to lynching and killing.

Gaushalas, as I discovered first in Simhachalam and then elsewhere in the country, are incredibly complex sites. In order to substantively comprehend a gaushala, it is important to look at them—and the animals that they house—through the multiple optics of commerce, theology, nationalism, casteism, and sectarianism.[18] At the center of all of this is dairy.

WEEPING TEMPLE CALVES: DAIRY CALVES WHO
BECOME VEAL

The 1,000-year-old Simhachalam Temple, built atop a hill twenty kilometers outside central Vishakapatnam city in Andhra Pradesh, is a rare architectural wonder of South India's medieval Chola dynasty. The temple is dedicated to the fourth incarnation of Lord Vishnu, the Varaha-Narasimhan, the man-lion, who descends to earth to protect his devotees from the evil ruler Hiranyakashipu. It receives thousands of pilgrims every day. In the sanctum sanctorum or the "womb" of the temple, the idol of the Lord is covered thickly with sandalwood paste, almost forming a small hillock, anointed thus as an act of piety. During the festival of Chandanaotsavam in the months of May and June, the sandalwood-anointing ceremony is celebrated on a spectacular scale, and the temple receives millions of devotees, not just from within Vishakapatnam or even Andhra Pradesh, but from throughout western and eastern India and beyond.

Alongside the pageantry, and beneath the perfume of sandalwood, a ritual is carried out in the name of auspiciousness and devotion throughout the year, peaking during the festival season in the sweltering month of May. Thousands of male calves are "donated" to the temple, some of them barely hours old, with their umbilical cords still hanging from their abdomens. The devotees who bring the calves to the temples are typically poor, small-scale dairy farmers who live in the peri-urban and rural areas of the states of Andhra Pradesh, Odisha, and West Bengal, as well as from the cities of Hyderabad, Vishakapatnam, and Vijaywada, among others. In a political climate where it is increasingly dangerous to directly sell cows to slaughterhouses—and in part due to guilt and sentiment—the farmers prefer to "donate" the neonatal bulls to gaushalas and temples instead. Suparna Baksi Ganguly, the vice president of the Bangalore-based animal sanctuary Compassion Unlimited Plus Action, said: "The villagers can't support the bull calves, so they donate them to the temples instead of selling them directly to butchers. *Donating* bull calves to a temple is a euphemism for sending them to slaughter [emphasis in original]."[19]

Previously, the calves were forced to climb the 1,000 steps to the hill-temple in the scorching summer heat. Invariably, many calves could not manage this trek, due to weakness from hunger and dehydration or fear. If the calf was small enough, he might be carried for some of the way, or dragged or pushed roughly up the steps, resulting in broken bones. Quite often, the calves would simply be discarded en route if taking them up to the temple proved too much trouble. One temple visitor noted, "The climb was easy but the road had more calves than men. Almost all of them were male. Some were lame. Many looked starved. I saw a few calves lying at the edges of the road with their legs broken."[20]

Unable to cope with the influx, the temple, for decades, used to sell the calves in a weekly auction. "All calves that were brought here were sold—all of them, *desi*, Jersey, it didn't matter—they would all end up in the slaughterhouse," said Pradeep Nath, VSPCA's founding director. As Pradeep explained, the orphaned calves become an unexpected and welcome "resource" to generate illegal wealth, once they become "temple property." After being sold, the sick calves would be dragged down the temple steps again for the final journey to the slaughterhouse. Pradeep described the intricate nexus between the temple authorities and the butchers in disposing off the bull-calves:

> Every week, anything between 50 to 200 calves are stolen from their mothers, [during] peak festival season, thousands of calves come at that time. Per day, May, June is the worst, when it is also 45 degrees [celcius]. They are crying and bleating for their mother, pushed up the stairs. And then they [the butchers] bring them down 1,000 steps again—what madness is

this. These temple calves end up in restaurants and cafés as veal, and are sold to butchers throughout the city. The temple is hand in glove with the cow mafia. We have rescued some 700 calves. Supposing a calf is donated on Monday, he will be taken to the slaughterhouse on Saturday, otherwise he is dying there [in the temple itself]. They get no milk, no water, they are just starving there. When you bring them to the temple, you know they are going to die. Either in the slaughterhouse or from starvation.

In 2010, VSPCA embarked on a long legislative battle with the temple authorities to ban their auctioning of the calves, and instead, do what gaushalas are widely expected to do—care lovingly for the dairying "waste." In 2013, the temple made news headlines when it was reported that hundreds of calves had perished in the gaushala. The *New Indian Express* reported: "the deaths have occurred due to scarcity of fodder and water, cramped spaces and the unbearable heat turning the cowshed, which houses more than 500 cows and calves, into an oven."[21] In their report, the VSPCA stated:

> The temple goshala is unimaginable in its horrific conditions. Up to 700 calves—many injured, diseased, and handicapped—are boxed into less than half an acre of land, competing for a [*sic*] limited hay and dirty water. Stress and competition for food regularly leads to stampedes [among the baby calves].[22]

The temple came under scathing criticism from political parties like the RSS and the BJP, and animal activist organizations like the VSPCA. In their defense, the temple argued that they did not invite dairy farmers to abandon their unwanted calves on temple grounds, and could not be expected to cope with the scale of the influx. When the gaushala was finally prohibited by the courts from auctioning them, the temple responded by neglecting the calves; though wealthier than farmed animal shelters, they, too, were ultimately constrained for space and resources. The VSCPA reports:

> And here they are left. On their own. For an indeterminate amount of time . . .. Temple authorities have no means or space to accommodate these animals—so the calves are just left there—tied to a steeple, awaiting their fate

in hunger, thirst, loneliness, and fear under India's blazing sun and stifling heat.[23]

By 2014, when cow protectionism became a rising Hindutva issue, Simhachalam had to tread the volatile landscape carefully. It subverted the issue of animal neglect and cruelty into one of *purity* or *impurity* of different breeds, invoking the same logic of social differentiation that, we have seen, is characteristic of caste. Differentiating between *purebreds* and mixed or other breeds not native to India, the temple made the decision to permanently close its doors to Jersey calves, one of the breeds of cow bred prolifically to sustain Indian milk production. The gaushala would only accept the native Indian bull-calves, washing its hands of the matter of the Jersey bulls.

The explanation of one of the temple officers at Simhachalam conflated economic pragmatism and religious and political Hindu sentiments, as he positioned the Jerseys and their milk as *spiritually* base in order to render these animals economically disposable. It was at the advice of the Hindu nationalist RSS party, he explained, that they ceased auctioning the calves, and faced with space constraints, also decided to stop accepting "non-Hindu" cows. The gaushala started a new campaign—notably, *not one* that illuminates the culpability of dairying. Instead, they emphasize: "do not bring Jersey calves" because Jerseys," he explained to me, are "not even cows." (See figure 4.2). The temple officer said:

> The RSS people had a relevant point—not to put the calves up for auction. By their demand only we stopped the auction. Earlier we used to put them all up for public auction. The decision was also made that we stop receiving Jersey cows. Jersey cows are not at all cows. Their milk is not at all pure. Then after that incident [of the media exposé and public outrage against Simhachalam's auction of the calves], we developed the infrastructure and started a campaign—"do not donate Jersey calves." We will not accept.

In response, the VSPCA started to take the Jersey calves away to the Kindness Farm. Malathi was responsible for overseeing the weekly

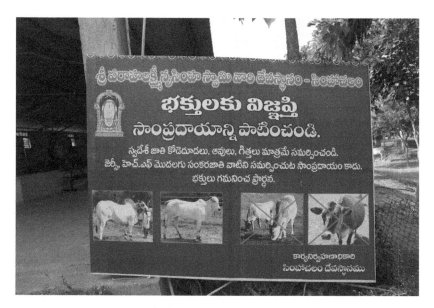

FIGURE 4.2: *Simhachalam Temple started a campaign prohibiting dairy farmers from bringing Jersey calves. The temple gaushala would accept only native calves.*
Source: Photo taken by author.

transfer of the calves, and she spent entire weekends at the temple to record the numbers of arriving calves, and talk to each farmer to explain what would happen to their "donated" calves. VSPCA's plea to the farmers was to keep the calves, a strategy Pradeep and I had endless discussions about. Dairy farmers, but especially poor farmers, could not afford to keep non-milking animals. Earlier, a dairy farmer in regional Andhra Pradesh had explained to me that it costs about Rs 6,000 (approx. US$ 90) per month to look after an animal, making it highly uneconomical to care for unproductive animals.[24] How would this approach sustain itself? As Pradeep admitted, it was the VSPCA that continued to take away the abandoned calves from the temple grounds every week.

Late in 2015, I accompanied Malathi to the Simhachalam Temple one Saturday. As soon as we stepped out of the car, a fat street dog raced up to Malathi, and flung himself on her. "Bandoo!" she screamed, laughing. Bandoo—literally *friend*—panted, licked, and jumped joyously around his beloved Malathi, who enthusiastically hugged and kissed him back.

The trio of us trooped to the temple entry at the foothills, me treading more carefully on the stone floor and steps, slippery with water, oil, calf diarrhea and dung, and streaks of wet mud. We tickled the rambunctious Bandoo while we waited for the calves to arrive.

Straight ahead of us was the ascent of the 1,000 stone steps to the temple on top of the mountain, most of which disappeared from view immediately as I looked up. I could scarce imagine small, newborn calves stumbling up each huge step, a trek that would induce burning muscular pain in minutes in a healthy adult human. As we sat at the bottom of the steps, I focused on Bandoo and his squeals, hoping that perhaps no calves would show up that day. Flies buzzed around small mounds of dung piles.

Before long, however, Malathi nudged me. "Yamini, look . . ."

A small black Jersey bull, with a thick coating of dust and a streak of red *kumkum* on his forehead, was being pulled by a man toward the steps, accompanied by his family of five. The young bull lowered his head and attempted to stand his ground; the man yanked at the rope around his neck more forcefully. "That way," interjected Malathi, pointing to the makeshift gaushala. The calf stumbled as he was pulled away from the steps and pushed through the gate, where he ran inside to get away. Eight calves were already standing dazed on the camp grounds, muddy with rain and dung. A roof of dried palm leaves covered some of the area; the rest of the camp would be exposed to the scorching Andhra sun as it rose later in the day.

"You know well what is going to happen to the calf," said Malathi. "So why do you bring them?"

It would be later that I would appreciate the weight of this simple exchange. The farmer was of the Mala caste of Andhra Pradesh, a designated scheduled caste, and an agricultural labor caste who (along with the Madiga caste) were almost bonded to landowners until as recently as the 1940s when they rose in revolt.[25] The man owned three cows, all Jerseys, and he regularly brought two or three calves to Simhachalam, as his forefathers had done, earning anything between US$ 300 to 500 a month by selling milk. Malathi was of the Pambala caste, also formerly oppressed and now reclassified as a scheduled caste, and her wage, similar to workers in under-funded animal shelters, was less than US$ 200 a month. The sole-earner, Malathi supported her entire family on her meager salary, leaving her in a highly precarious situation with no savings. These intricate forms of subaltern animal activism—regional, "low" caste, gendered, and frequently poor—are routinely ignored in the common dismissal of Indian animal activism as urban, elite, and upper class.

Malathi used to work in a women's NGO for slightly better pay; as an avid lover of animals, she also volunteered what time she could spare with the VSPCA. After two years of growing awareness of what animals endured largely unseen and unheard, Malathi could no longer deny that she wanted to work full time for the animals. This placed her as a stranger in at least two worlds: one, the familiar world of rural and semi-urban Andhra Pradesh where she now emerged as an animal activist; and two, in the English-speaking world of the state bureaucracy where she would go to fight or plead with multi-sectoral institutions—the police, or the state animal husbandry, municipal public health, and veterinary departments. Malathi never married; as a dedicated activist, first for women's causes and then for animals, there was never any question that she would. "I forget I am a woman, Yamini," she told me. "I have no fear. I only think of the animals and I have no fear."

The man mumbled, "I have brought him to God. Now it is up to God to look after him. Whatever happens is now God's will. I am okay with that." The man brought a calf or two to Simhachalam every year. His conscience—*manasaktchi*—made him bring the calves to the temples where he made no money, rather than selling them to a butcher. It was hard, he admitted: he would sometimes avoid the cow for a week if it seemed like "she knew," or if her grief—bellowing, sniffing in agitation, searching behavior—was too confronting. His brother, he said, donated a calf to Simhachalam once, and then never again. "What does your brother do now?" I asked. "He just lets them go on the road. Sometimes you can see them and feed them. Sometimes the calf even recognizes you and comes," the farmer said. It felt less like abandonment when the little bull was turned onto the street and the brother could still occasionally see the calf.

This Mala farmer preferred to send the calves to the temple. "There is a God, ultimately everything *is* in His hands," he insisted. The sense of fatalism—god's will, or *karma,* or destiny—was frequently evoked in my conversations with stakeholders in the dairy sector, whether farmers, devotees, animal husbandry professionals, or gaushalas. I would later be struck by Shaheed Tayob's observation that "situating animal and human life in a hierarchical relationship that is further subject to the hierarchy of an all-powerful god allows for an opportunity to recognise ethics within the practice of sacrifice."[26] The notion of a god who exercises meta-control of all life and death makes bearable the consequences of one's own decisions to engage in slaughter, or separate the calf from his mother. Yes, perhaps violence, abandonment, and death awaited the animals bred into dairying; however, it was, quite simply, their *fate,* and there was very little that anyone—certainly, any human—could do about it.

Human–animal relations, however, as indeed human–human relations, do not occur within sociological hierarchies alone. In the case of farmed animals, human relations with buffaloes, cows, goats, pigs, chickens, and fish, among others, occur in the conditions created by capitalization of animals, and state-subsidized breeding for their use and exploitation as living *and* dead products. The farmed animal is always a *commodity* in relation to the human, and their raising and slaughtering occurs in an increasingly neoliberal economy around dairy production. As Wadiwel reminds us, it is "difficult to disentangle the ethics of these encounters," particularly those embedded in capitalism, without "glossing over" the central relations of human domination in animal production.[27]

Ideas of multispecies entanglements around human–animal kinship, human sexuality (to justify human male violence to bulls in bull-racing or bull-taming "sports", for instance)[28] or human–animal–god relations (to justify animal sacrifice, or in this case, animal abandonment) as characteristic of human–animal *agricultural* relations convey "something important about the world [but] *they do not capture everything*" (emphasis added).[29] The notion of "ethics" as a measure of *relatedness* itself is non-innocent when it is understood and practiced as two distinct concepts in human to *commodity-animal*, and human to human relations more generally. The Mala farmer's decision (and that of so many others like him) was driven by the inescapable logic of the milk industry in a state that promoted dairying as a means of livelihood. Performing the same labor as his forebears and enmeshed in circles of poverty and exploitation, the farmer was trying to conduct an economic activity that did disturb his *manasaktchi*, as ethically as possible.

Later, I would come across a Muslim dairy farmer who had brought a bull-calf to the temple. "If there is a way to spare them, I am happy to take it," said the man. "I used to sell them—I did not know about this option." Ironically it was the rising vigilantism that brought the possibility of disposing of unwanted calves in this way to his attention. "I don't see that this is a Hindu tradition or Muslim," he said. "We take so much from the cows—it is not right to just use her like this if there is another way. This is better than selling. This is also difficult. But it is better." The man walked away after leaving his calf, not stopping for the *chai* that another farmer was buying for everyone.

By now, the calves had started to arrive almost continuously, and the ground was turning into a bog of urine and diarrhea. The bleating of the calves—for as infants, they bleat rather than moo—was incessant. A couple of them came sniffing toward our hands. The temple had been handed feeding bottles by the VSPCA; no one, however, was attending to these suckling infants. A few bales of dry hay were strewn around the area, which the calves were too young to eat. A large drum of filthy water stood in the middle of the makeshift camp. One black and white Jersey calf lay on his side, mouth foaming, eyes almost fully closed. A dark brown calf stood vigil over his dying friend (see figure 4.3); he did not move once from his side for several hours. Malathi shouted to a temple worker in Telugu; I handed him several wads of notes, and he soon returned with two feeding bottles for human infants, and a large sack of 500 ml milk packets—advertised as Jersey cow milk. We started to bottle-feed the calves, perhaps the only drops of the breastmilk of these Jersey mothers that might make it back to the infants of their own species. The calves suckled frantically, more gathering around us. I started to feel overwhelmed by grief and what felt like futility in addressing suffering of such mammoth proportions. I

FIGURE 4.3: *A young male calf holds vigil over his dying mate for several hours at Simhachalam.*

Source: Photo taken by author.

reminded myself that easing the suffering of any individual was worthwhile in and of itself. Suddenly, we heard a cacophonous din of drums as a small procession headed toward the temple.

Malathi jumped up. "Indian calf!" she said. "Go look!"

We ran out toward the temple steps again. Almost hidden in the middle of the loud procession was a very small, gray bull-calf, heavily decorated with metal ornaments from his forehead down to his hooves. A little hump protruded out of his back, the distinctive feature of native Indian bovines. He fearfully ducked his head this way and that, frantic to get away from the din of the resounding drums. He had to endure his "worship" first, however; the priest anointed his forehead with *kumkum*, and waved the *aarti* (the sacred fire) around him, as the drum-beats reached a crescendo. Heavy flower garlands were continuously added to the metal trappings as the priest chanted, weighing down the small calf's head. After several minutes of such torturous reverence, he was led away to the Simhachalam Temple's gaushala. If determined to be of adequately "high-caste" stock, he might eventually be made to perform as a stud-bull to impregnate females.

I watched the wide-eyed struggling "god-calf" and turned around in anguish to Malathi. Before I could say a word, we both spotted a black Jersey calf with a white patch on his belly and large, watering eyes, stumbling and falling on weak, spindly legs as he was dragged toward the camp. At one point, the little bull managed to sit on the ground, refusing to budge (see figure 4.4). He was roughly heaved up again, and dragged to the temple to be put through the ritual worship (see figure 4.5), a necessary psychological precursor to his imminent abandonment. As the temple drums clanged, he became visibly more agitated, lowering his head and trying to charge.

As he was dragged toward the makeshift gaushala, the farmer briefly loosened his grip on the rope around the calf's neck. In that instant, the calf bolted, racing out of the temple. I had seen numerous undercover

FIGURE 4.4: *A black and white Jersey bull infant who tried to stand his ground against entering the temple.*

Source: Photo taken by author.

FIGURE 4.5: *A calf being put through ritual worship prior to abandonment at the temple.*
Source: Photo taken by author.

videos of animals trying to escape slaughterhouses, but the irony of witnessing an animal—the progeny of the Mother Cow no less—fleeing a Hindu temple froze me. To my amazement, none of the temple workers followed him.

At a small table near the worship area, a man scratched off the seventieth calf to arrive that week, that he had just noted in his register. "Sixty-nine again," he laughed.

I stood shocked for a second, and then ran after the little bull, who was running confusedly through the chaotic parking lot, and straight into the oncoming traffic on the main road. Not taking my eyes off him for a second, I phoned Malathi. She sent the VSPCA workers in the transfer truck to us: they parked on the side and caught the frightened, resisting calf.

Over time, however, the options for the VSPCA—and the temple calves—have become limited and bleak as the Kindness Farm itself is packed beyond capacity. "If I take any more, I will be the one guilty of factory farming conditions," says Pradeep. "In fact, I think I am already guilty of it!" The sheer impossibility of ever having enough space to accommodate every animal bred is a daily reality for gaushalas and shelters.

The VSPCA now collects the Jersey calves weekly and donates them to tribal farmers in the hills around Visakhapatnam, on the understanding that the farmers will return them if they can no longer keep them. The hope is to rehabilitate the calves as "traction bulls" for agriculture, for which the humpless Jersey bulls are particularly unsuited. "There is no victory in these situations, we are forced into a hopeless situation, no matter what," Pradeep told me. The choices facing farmed animal shelters in under-resourced countries are without redemption: overcrowd the shelters, turn animals away or, once again, use them.

THE MOTHER COW–DAIRY COW HYBRID: CONFLATING
"CONSUMER" AND "DEVOTEE"

In the blue-tinged dawn of a cold winter morning, the car driver pulled into a parking lot to ask for directions from a *chai* shop, already open to serve the long-distance tourist buses. The driver got out, grabbing the bit of paper with the scribbled address of a major gaushala that I had given him. I glanced out of the window at the fog and then did a double take. I climbed out after him, and looked around, stupefied. Close to a hundred bulls and bull-calves of every age and condition—elderly, disabled, young adults, teenagers, and infants—had gathered into the empty parking lot, some huddled together in groups for warmth, some standing still, a few gathered hopefully in front of the *chai* shop. Two adolescent bulls had locked horns in front of an empty tourist bus.

Keeping a safe distance from this young pair, I went up to the *chaiwalla*. "They come here every night," he told me. All *avara gais* (stray cows), abandoned by small-scale dairy farmers, they would forage through the city's garbage during the day, retiring to the parking lot for the night. In a manner reminiscent of Hindu families abandoning widows in the sacred city of Benaras, he explained that people come from all over India to leave their unwanted cows and calves here. *"Achha khayal rakhenge*, they think they will be well looked after here." Every discarded animal, as far as I could tell, was of a native Indian breed.

I had arrived in Mathura, the birthplace of Krishna, one of Hinduism's most beloved gods. Krishna is also known as Gopala (protector of cows) and Govinda (lover of cows). He grew up with the cows and the calves, who loved Krishna as rapturously as he loved them. Brindavan or Vrindavan, the twin city of Mathura, is regarded as the earthly manifestation of Goloka, the celestial abode of cows. While Krishna is celebrated as a mascot in commercial Indian dairying due to his famed love for milk products, the way Krishna's story mirrors the embodied lives of the orphaned dairy bull-calves[30] in dairy farms is remarkably little noticed by the Hindu public.

Born in a jail that was also meant to be his slaughterhouse, the newborn Krishna was separated from his mother Devaki within minutes of his birth to save him from his murderous uncle Kamsa who had vowed to kill the newborn to take what was not his to take—the kingdom that was Krishna's inheritance. However, in the enforced separation of Devaki from Krishna, Kamsa also took away a more primordial birthright—the newborn Krishna's right to suckle his lactating mother. Subsequently, Krishna was lovingly raised on a dairy farm by his adoptive mothers, Yashodha and the cows. The toddler developed an unnaturally obsessive attachment to the breastmilk of Yashodha and the cows—folklore and mythologies affectionately recount how he would do anything to get it. The possibility that this frantic attachment to lactate might be a *traumatized* response to the newborn infant's deprivation of the breastmilk and comfort of his mother at birth is never raised in religious, political, or even feminist analyses.[31]

Popular religious stories almost entirely eclipse the bereft Devaki, whose grief at having never been able to suckle and raise her infants might be too uncomfortable to bear. However, the *Harivamsha*, the epilogue to the *Mahabharata*, offers a glimpse into Devaki's sorrow. It describes the visit of the sage Vaishampayana to the then adolescent Krishna, urging him to fight Kamsa for his kingdom, and to restore himself to his parents. Vaishampayana then prepares Krishna for the sight of Devaki. To describe the highest form of grief that a mother could experience at being separated from her infants, Vaishampayana invokes the analogy of a separated cow and her calf.

> O Govinda! *You will also see Devaki, who has not held sons at her breasts.* She is like a goddess, but is suffering, bereft of all her radiance. Because of grief on account of her sons, she has dried up. She wishes to see you. *Because of the separation, she is tormented by grief. She is like Surabhi, without her calf.* Her eyes are always overflowing with tears. She is always dressed in old garments. [Emphasis added][32]

The city of Mathura as I would come to see, was profuse with the commercialization of the image of the dairy-consuming toddler Krishna, often depicted as affectionately held by Yashodha or nuzzled by cows, on calendars in shops and markets, posters on walls and trees, and pavements overflowing with souvenirs. We got back into the car and drove on through the smog lingering on the sacred landscape of the city. Reaching our destination, we could hear the gaushala as we approached. Not the moos of cows, or the high-pitched cries of their calves, but devotional songs for Radha-Krishna floated through the cow shelter on loudspeakers.

A well-maintained gaushala by most standards, it was full of indigenous breed cows. Large, magnificent Kankrej cows from Rajasthan with massive curling horns effortlessly pushed the smaller Kapilas from Karnataka away from the feeding troughs. A white Kapila with her archetypal horns curling inwards snorted in protest but held her ground stubbornly while she waited for the bigger cows to finish. A beautiful honey-red-and-gold Gir cow from Gujarat stood nearby with eyes half-closed in the sunshine. There was not one Jersey or Holstein cow in this herd in Mathura, and I knew to expect no buffaloes there at all.

Many of the cows were lactating, their separated calves huddled in groups for warmth and comfort in an adjoining pen. The gaushala office had already given me permission to enter the calf pen to take photos if I wished. As I started to open the gate, a large white cow from the maternity pen snorted and stamped her hooves, bobbing her head up and down in anxiety; I did not have *her* permission. Her calf was among the infants. I hastily dropped the latch, and retreated. Though the cow had no way of physically stopping me, I had no desire to worry her.

A man drove up in a Toyota with a drum of *chappatis* (Indian wheat bread) as his weekly offering to the cow mother-goddesses, a standard offering though gluten and starch are not tolerated by the four-stomached ruminants. He held out a couple of pieces at a time to the nearest cows who whipped them out of his hands. We started chatting. Being with the cows, he explained, even for twenty minutes, "brought peace" to him. I asked him if he visited other animal sanctuaries. He was surprised. "No, of course not. I like all animals but they are not the same." To explain his "pilgrimage" to the cows specifically, the man detailed his love for cows' milk as a conduit that connected these cows as his mothers. He explained, "I drink a big glass of milk morning and evening. I like it. These cows are like my mothers. I come every weekend to feed them."

The framing of cows as "mothers" performs a subtle but critical political task of ascribing agency to the "dairy" cow, who ostensibly *wants* to be the (lactating) mother of humans. In her work on the spiritual significance of cows in Hinduism, Samantha Hurn argues that cows in gaushalas are self-determining entities who willingly "*provide* a surplus of milk for human consumers" (emphasis added).[33] Indeed, for the bovine, as imagined through human eyes, "The more one *gives* [to the human species], *the more one experiences a churning of the heart as the emotions intensify around the object of one's love*" (emphasis added).[34] As the man feels love for his (lactating) bovine mother, so too the suckling cow's churning maternal love is also projected on to her "child," that is, the human milk consumer.

Manufacturing the animal's "consent" through double-speaking in this manner is not unique to Indian dairying. It seems a universal, even innate human condition in which we are intuitively uncomfortable with what we do to other animals to commodify them as consumable resources. To muddy the forcible extraction from their bodies, fictitious and mythologized narratives of consent are produced, whereby the farmed animal willingly surrenders her body parts and products for human consumption. In his book *Farm to Fable*, Robert Grillo writes:

By portraying the relationship between farmer and the animals he exploits as consensual, we, as the consumers of his products, are misled into believing that other animals don't mind being used against their will, thereby reducing the issue to one of how we treat them. This has led not only to a wholesale denial of the value of their lives but also to a depraved standard of treatment we call "humane," which, if applied to our cats and dogs, would be considered torture and even sadism. And not only do we portray them as consensual, we embellish this fiction by portraying ourselves as their benevolent masters and protectors.[35]

The celebration in Hinduism of the lactating cow as *our mother* epitomizes this relationship of manufactured consent. As elsewhere, the "dairy" cow is not only drawn into a non-consensual *sexual* relationship with the human farmer, but in India, she is also forced into a non-consensual *maternal* relationship with the human, making human exaltation of cow motherhood, in fact, an act of domination over cows *and* indeed, other animals, as *their* motherhood is implicitly devalued. The Maan Mandir Gaushala in Barsana near Mathura states: "No living creature on this planet calls its mother, *"Maa"* except a calf (a baby cow) and a human being."[36]

Hindu scriptures solidify the idea that it is inherently in the nature of mothers—including cow mothers—to willingly sacrifice everything for their "children." A passage from the *Mahābhārata,* Book 13, Anusasana Parva, illustrates the concept of the *sacrificing, mothering* cow, whose motherhood is an instrument for resource extraction:

> They are the mothers of the universe. O, let kine [cows] approach me! There is no gift more sacred than the gift of kine. There is no gift that produces more blessed merit. There has been nothing equal to the cow, nor will there be anything that will equal her. With her skin, her hair, her horns, the hair of her tail, her milk, and her fat, with all these together, the cow upholds sacrifice. What thing is there that is more useful than the cow?[37]

"Upper-caste" Hindu male scholars reinforce such entitlements from female bodies. Entirely unselfconscious of the violent patriarchy in forcing a female into a non-consensual sexual and maternal relationship,

Panjak Jain describes the exploitation of every part of the cow's body as the cow's *duty*, as her "'bovine *dharma*' [or] a dharmic environmental ethics *for* cows . . . [inspired by] the inherent qualities and virtues of the cow, i.e., the dharma *of* the cows" (emphasis in original)."[38] Once framed as the cow's *responsibility* to "give," Hindus' material exploitation of the animal's body can become a loving act of receiving maternal care; as Jain writes:

> The cow *gives* [emphasis added] all of her belongings to humans: milk and other dairy products strengthen us, bullocks are utilized in farming, cow dung is utilized as a fertilizer, and urine is used as an Ayurvedic medicine. After her death, the cow's bones are utilized in the sugar industry, her skin is used in the leather industry, and her horns are used to make combs. . . . Indians do not just exploit cows for materialistic benefits but instead regard them as mothers.[39]

Such anthropatriarchal ideas make up the thick context of everyday realities in spaces that purport to *protect* cows. Unsurprisingly then, this theme recurred regularly in conversations with gaushala managers and priests, particularly in Krishna temples. The story of the human–child–god who was deprived of his mother's breastmilk and thereafter developed a great attachment to bovine lactate, is unequivocally interpreted as the righteous obligation *of* the cow to lactate for all humans. For an official of a Krishna temple gaushala in Visakhapatnam, the cow is merely performing "God's will":

> Every living entity is God's creation and is cooperating with God's plan. Every living entity has got its particular duty to do. Duty in the sense, it is to cooperate with the will of God. Like that cow has got its own set of particular duties. *One of her important duties is, the cow is giving us milk.*

As I watched the cows and their separated neonatal infants in the Mathura gaushala, I ruminated on the cow's "duty" to lactate for the Hindu, so much at odds with the Hindu's duty to care for and protect the cow and her calves.

"What happens when these cows stop milking?" I asked the manager in Mathura. "And what about their male calves?"

"We keep them, of course."

"Really? You have an area for *sandh* (bulls) and old cows? How many do you have?"

"Well, here we only have a few of them," he said. He later took me to see nine chained bulls, who were "working" animals, used to pull heavy carts of milk and sweets.

"What about the rest?"

"We have a large gaushala outside the city, near the jungle area," he told me. "There is room for thousands of cows there. No problem." I asked if it was possible for someone to take me to visit the forest gaushala. "*Dekhte hein*," he said. *We will see.* That visit never transpired.

As we continued to chat, we could see an argument developing between the watchman at the front gate and a man who had come with a dark brown Jersey calf. "He wants to leave the calf here," said the manager. "But how many can we keep taking? They want to make money from the cows, but don't want the responsibility of the calf, and think it is our problem, just because we are a gaushala. If I let one come, I will be instantly flooded with all the rest also."

"But won't he leave the calf on the road otherwise?" I asked.

"Yes. We cannot take every animal from the streets. Every day we get four to five cases of farmers coming with their old cows, male calves. No one brings a female calf. They try to say they found them on the road, they are sick and pretend they are rescue cases. But we take only the accident cases, not the sick or old," the man said. The gaushala was forced to operate on a triage system and take in only the animals in immediate need of attention—due to a road accident, for instance—rather than a sick animal, *for almost every animal on the road was sick*. The man continued, "Yes, this calf will go on the road but it is the calf's *karma* from there."

Karma was invoked again to justify the belief that the calf, his mother, and indeed, their whole species, were simply living out their predestined life as consumable and disposable resources for humans; that humans simply had no control over what is, ironically, the micro-controlling by humans of the breeding, and the births, lives, and deaths, of these domesticated farmed animals.

For indeed, cows, whether in gaushalas or commercial dairies, are resolutely human *property*.[40] Bovine sexuality, reproductive organs, ovum, germplasm, and genetic material, regardless of the site at which they are located, are capital or assets of their owners, according to the Livestock Keepers Movement that originated in India.[41] This global resource status applies to all bovines, including those in a gaushala, regardless of their human-imposed status as their "Mother." As *devotees* of the cow's motherhood, Hindus also become *consumers* of the cow's motherhood. Seen in this way, the sacred "Mother Cow" is indistinguishable from the mundane "dairy cow."

There is, however, one crucial difference between mundane and sacred cows that generates additional profits for the Indian dairy sector: the supposedly spiritual quality of the native cow's milk. A devotee from a Sri Krishna gaushala in Hyderabad told me, "Gaumata is our mother, her milk is our blessing." Later, at ISKCON in Mathura, a temple officer would tell me, "By consuming her milk, we get to benefit spiritually and physically as it is the purest food source in the world." I remembered an official from the Simhachalam Temple gaushala telling me, "Indian cow is very sacred, it gives A2 milk, its products are used for purification, its milk is a holistic food, cholesterol free, solution for several diseases, asthma, cancer."

Cow's milk typically contains two protein groups—82 percent casein, and 18 percent whey.[42] The casein has two variants—A1 and A2. Prior to domestication, all cows only produced A2 casein. There is some scientific evidence for the theory that the A2 beta casein is easier for humans to digest.[43] Akin to "organic" or "biodynamic" milk in the West which attracts a higher price, the "sacred" A2 milk of the Indian breed cows is regarded as a "spiritually" and scientifically superior product for human consumption.

The reality is more complex. Lactate from a spectrum of species, including the "Guernsey, Jersey, Asian herds, human milk, and others (sheep, goat, donkeys, yaks, camel, buffalo, sheep) contain mostly A2 beta casein."[44] However, about 8,000 years ago, "a natural single-gene mutation occurred in Holsteins, resulting in production of the A1 beta casein protein in this breed."[45] This genetic mutation was passed on to other breeds, and A1 is common in Western dairy herds. Now, with profligate crossbreeding in India, more than half of the Jersey breeds have the "A2 beta casein variant," and many of the native Indian breeds may, in fact, carry the A1 variant.

The spiritual value of the cow's milk is a crucial material in constructing the Hindu nation. In 2017, Justice Mahesh Chandra Sharma of the Rajasthan High Court created a stir when he declared in a 139-page judgment that the cow must replace the tiger as India's "national animal."[46] Unlike this other animal, the Indian cow is credited with mystical gifts, in a manner typical of fascism, racism, and indeed, anthropocentrism by invoking pseudo-science. Describing the qualities of the *panchagavya* or the five sacred products (milk, butter, ghee, urine, and dung) sourced from the native cow, the High Court judgment referenced German scholar Rudolf Steiner who stated that the cow "absorbs cosmic energy" by her horns. Later, the chief minister of Uttrakhand state, Trivendra Singh Rawat, declared that the cow is the only living being who inhales and exhales oxygen, and can therefore cure respiratory illnesses in humans.[47] With such extraordinary discourses around the cow, it is all too easy to see how the *actual animal* may be lost in the thick fog of propaganda and indoctrination among the highest judicial and legislative offices of the secular nation.

RAISING (AND DENYING) THE SLAUGHTER QUESTION

In temple after temple and gaushala after gaushala, I raised the fundamentals of dairy economics: that cows bred for milk would have to be moved down the continuum of dairy production and be slaughtered when and if the very purpose of breeding them—milk production—was not served. Rescuing unproductive cows from slaughter constitutes a disruption of the economic logic of dairying. Was it not the case that at best, only individual animals may be rescued from slaughter? Was it enough, then, to think of "protection" exclusively as "no slaughter"? Could we avoid recognizing our culpability in *breeding* animals for dairy in the first place?

At a major temple in the temple city of Kancheepuram in Tamil Nadu state, a mild-mannered, elderly Tamil Brahmin priest, who sat crossed-legged with me on the floor for our interview, actually leapt to his feet in rage when I raised these questions. *"Paithyakari,"* he hissed at me, an epithet reserved for "mad" females. *"Stupid* woman. Don't talk nonsense!"

So normative is the idea is that the cow's holy status is a good outcome *for the cow* that any suggestion to the contrary is almost viscerally offensive. Inherent in the idea of a gaushala as an alternative to slaughter for cows in dairying, however, is an implicit inverse acknowledgment that slaughter *is* the logical option for animals who cannot lactate. Then how, I persisted in asking, could the slaughter of cows alone be realistically avoided? I was continually provided with a mechanistic, formulaic answer, reducing "cow protection" to only one thing—no slaughter. An official of a Krishna temple in Visakhapatnam told me that milk, the primary reason for which cows are bred in India, is the "secondary point":

> Forget about the milk, milk is secondary; killing is bad . . .. You are highlighting the secondary point. Whatever the reason for killing, killing is bad; you stop the killing! . . . We will only continue to participate in educating that killing is bad.

A young boy walked past at this point with a small drum of ghee-laden *boondhi laddus,* a popular Indian sweet, and deposited a plate on our table. The priest had earlier explained to me that they used milk from the temple gaushala's cows to pour over the stone idols, and bought cows' milk from commercial dairies for their sweets. I politely declined the *laddus.*

"How is it possible," I asked the man, "that you don't think of these laddus as linked with cow slaughter when any number of gaushalas would never be able to take in and sustain each and every cow outside who is repeatedly being impregnated for more and more milk?" There was no option for these cows except eventual slaughter. "Fundamentally, then," I pressed on, "is it not possible that the *laddus* are responsible for cow slaughter, not beef? Cows are bred in India only for milk, not beef."

The man was outraged. "You are comparing beef with *laddus?* You are comparing *beef* with *laddus?* We see the cow as our *mother!* They [implicitly, the Muslims] see her as *meat!*" The priest refused to consider that *milk* and *meat* formed part of the same production continuum. When *only* slaughter is violent, and dairying is conceptually disconnected from the sole act that is defined as "violent," Hindu consumer–devotees, thus absolved, can pass the crucial slaughter-end of milk production as an unnecessary and malicious act of Muslims and Dalits. The man continued:

> Okay, maybe, maybe dairy is associated with cow killing. But you have to do something about them, who is actually doing the violence. We are associated with cow protection, not veganism! *Temple means cow protection. Otherwise, it is not a temple. Try to understand this basic point.* [emphasis added]

The "one doing the violence" is resolutely not the milk consumer. To the extent that Hindu temples might engage in any form of animal advocacy or even "cow protection," it would be limited to the single act of emphasizing "no slaughter." In fact, if their campaigns extended "cow protection" beyond this—namely, non-dairy or vegan campaigns—then, the man at the temple told me, the very perception of the temple as a Hindu sacred space would be threatened. When I asked how human consumption of bovine lactate might impact the calf, the answer made clear that it is commonly assumed that the cow produces far more milk than her biological infant needs. The modern, genetically manipulated cow who is bred to hyper-lactate at great physical cost to herself, is presumed part of the "system" of a prosperous Hindu universe overflowing with milk for her human progeny:

> But the calf is getting its milk, na. So we can have the rest. The problem is you don't have proper knowledge. No one is taking the milk from the calf. The calf is properly getting its quota. Say the calf drinks 3 liters, and the cow is giving 20 liters . . . okay, let's say it [*sic*] is drinking that much in the morning. How much milk do you think the calf drinks in the morning? The basic point is, the cow gives milk in excess of what the calf needs. That is the system!

The "system" of gaushalas is identical to the production systems of dairy farms. In most gaushalas, the calves, including newborns, are penned off from their mothers, or sometimes not seen at all. Gaushalas, like commercial dairies, brush off the need for the mother and infant to

FIGURE 4.6: *An overcrowded gaushala in Uttar Pradesh with thousands of cows as far as the eye can see.*
Source: Photo taken by author.

spend more than a few minutes together during milking time, which is necessary so that *humans* can milk the cow instead, once she lets down milk into her udders. I was often told that mothers would crush the calves, though these animals naturally live in large herds. Moreover, stampedes are more likely in the intensive, confined spaces of gaushalas and dairy farms, especially during feed time, than they are in nature.[48]

Gaushalas, particularly in cities, serve quite literally as sites of overcrowded, lifetime confinement for hundreds of ex-dairy cows (see figure 4.6). I visited a gaushala in Hyderabad which was originally a multistory car parking lot. On the ground floor, the parking spaces had been partially converted into a temple where a female white cow would be brought to be worshipped twice a day. Above, the parking-lot-turned-gaushala rose to three floors, and at each level, spaces were sectioned into pens where the cows were either continuously tied, or confined in groups. On a visit to this same gaushala a few years before me, cultural anthropologist Naisargi Dave witnessed a calf being eaten alive by maggots.[49] However, even here, stud bulls were used to impregnate cows, and as with other gaushalas, penned-off areas contained calves separated from their lactating mothers.

I reached the top floor, which had a wraparound balcony, with tree-topped views of Hyderabad city. A single large Holstein cow was tied with a short rope to a stake; the accompanying gaushala worker said that she had been chained continuously for the last 15 months since she was rescued. Dave describes the total and lifelong incarceration of the cows after "rescue" in these spaces of sanctuary:

> I had seen . . . cow shelters in which a cow will spend her entire life tied on a short rope to a stake in the ground in the darkness of a shed, periodically milked. Of all the things I have seen, the one thing I wish I could unsee was that. Saved from slaughter, yes, but for what? For life itself. For profit. To perform one's humanity.[50]

As the dairy industry erects structures to invisibilize, semi-visibilize, or normalize the realities of the lives (and deaths) of these animals, so too gaushalas have to find ways of hiding violence in plain sight. Immediately upon entering a gaushala once in Jaipur, I saw five or six beautiful, relatively plump calves in an open pen. Almost unvaryingly, the calves publicly displayed by gaushalas are indigenous breeds. Female vegetable sellers had set up mountains of greens and garlands, to sell as offerings for these "gods." Devotees would croon, bow in prayer, and feed them big lumps of *gur* [jaggery]. However, an activist from FIAPO and Help in Suffering AWO in Jaipur slapped his forehead in consternation when I described the seemingly cared-for animals. I had to learn to ask—casually—for the "other" calves when I visited gaushalas. They are often kept in dark sheds or overcrowded pens at the back, out of sight.

I got to see some of these "other" animals at a Calcutta gaushala. When I asked to see their calves, I was taken inside a dark building where the stench of feces hit me even from the outside. Tiny emaciated calves lay inside the hot room in pools of green, putrefying diarrhea, flies buzzing around their heads and bodies. Small bumps protruded from some of their backs, indicating their native caste. The calves jumped up in fear as soon as we entered and retreated, though a couple of thin calves, no bigger than large dogs, tentatively came forward to sniff my hand. "It's their feeding time anyway, let's let them out," said the worker who had accompanied me. He opened the door wide, and a stampede of calves of all sizes raced straight to the troughs outside which contained commercial formula, milled grains, and dirty water—presumably the reason for the pools of diarrhea inside the dank room. Then the worker pointed to something I will never forget.

An extremely tiny calf, her ribcage showing starkly, had broken away from the rest of the calves, and shot back into another dark, filthy room in that building full of cows. Amid the fifty large bovine bodies crammed in that space, the elfin calf had located her own mother. As I approached them slowly, the mother and calf watched me fixedly, with palpable trepidation, standing absolutely still. "Let her stay, give them some time together," I begged the worker. He agreed to give them 30 minutes until the feeding outside was over, before taking the sickly infant away from her lactating mother, back into the dark, diarrhea-filled room.

CONTAINING AND SAFEGUARDING THE (HINDU) COW-NATION

As I grappled with the notion that gaushalas could not be straightforwardly understood as cow shelters, I was surprised to learn that many Muslim families in different parts of the country run gaushalas. In late 2016, I arrived at a Muslim gaushala in the peri-urban agricultural outskirts of a city in Telengana state. In the standard design of most dairies and gaushalas, thin lactating cows were tied to low stakes along cement feeding troughs. Predictably, the newborns of these recently delivered mothers were nowhere to be seen. Skinny chickens and guinea fowl ran around outside the gaushala; a rooster perched on a sitting cow's rump. A searing white heat beat down more fiercely and mercilessly than almost anywhere else I had been. I immediately started a pounding migraine. The woman, noticing my considerable distress and nausea, brought out a large bottle of cold Thumbs Up, the Indian version of Coca Cola. At that moment, it was the most delicious thing I had ever tasted.

I looked around. A Hindu priest came in the morning and evening to offer *arati* to the chained cows, who were also milked at the same time. The cow worship draws a steady stream of Hindu devotees to the Muslim household.

"Why?" I asked the couple simply.

"The cow is our mother," explained the Muslim woman hesitantly. "She is our mother. That is why we worship her."

The efforts of the Muslim community in India to provide sanctuary to cows as peacekeeping is not new. The Mughal emperor Akbar and even the reviled Aurangazeb gave funds to gaushalas to earn trust from their Hindu citizenry. These precolonial peace offerings continued through British colonial times. Gaushala Mehrauli Dehat in South Delhi has been running for 128 years, now managed by an elderly Muslim couple who look after 1,300 ex-"dairy" cows[51]. Sarvath Ali, a Muslim man transferred two bighas of land in Muzaffarnagar in Uttar Pradesh state to Balaji Dham Temple as an act of *"gau seva"* (cow service) to build shelters[52]. The Shri Shyam Purushottama Gaushala, the largest in Alighar city, fails to receive the annual donations it needs from Hindus, and relies on additional funds from the Muslim community.[53] Mohammaed Atique who manages a gaushala in Jodhpur, finds it "absurd" that "Cows, whose milk is best after mother's milk, is used to spark communal tensions."[54] In 2017, a Muslim man, Jabar Jat, fasted for forty-eight hours in the Bhuj region in Gujarat to "spread the message of cow protection and communal harmony"[55]. Jat highlighted the risks for these animals (but not other species), eating trash and plastic at garbage dumps.

It is easy to appreciate how some Muslims might feel compelled to care for cows as appeasement, or indeed, like cow vigilantes, and even some animal activists who are steeped in the everyday politics of Hindutva, they might even be convinced that cows deserve more protection than other farmed animals. However, the Muslim labor of care for *only* the cow and as *mother*—rather than a rehabilitated farmed animal—also obscures the violence to the "dairy" cow, and ironically reinforces, in fact, the false and dangerous perception that beef consumers alone are responsible for cow slaughter. Against the economic logic of maintaining gaushala dairies, the blatant disposal of unproductive animals by Hindu gaushalas and municipal cow shelters may be riskier for Muslim gaushalas to undertake in an aspiring Hindutva state.

The inevitable sale of unwanted cows by temples and gaushalas has been ongoing for decades. In 2000, three years after India became the leading producer of milk, the landmark case, *Common Cause v Union of India*, heard by the Delhi High Court, uncovered that out of 89,149 bovines who had been sent to the Delhi municipal *gosadan* (shelter for ex-dairy cows abandoned on the streets), only 8,516 cows remained, with no information available about the fate of the remaining animals.[56] Florence Burgat noted in her study of gaushalas at this time: "In many goshalas, where the duty to protect cows is interpreted to such a narrow extent that it corrupts the spirit, these animals are not sheltered but are sent to the abattoir without arousing the slightest indignation on the part of cow worshippers."[57] In another key lawsuit in 2004, *Jaigopal Garodia Foundations v T. R. Srinivasan*, the Madras High Court found that gaushalas were selling cows to slaughterhouses[58]:

> the Temple authorities, in their anxiety to dispose of the large number of cows, tried to find out some person or the other who claimed that he is running the Goshala, who in turn actually received it for personal gains, either by selling them to third parties or by sending them to butchery. . . . Ultimately, the cows are being directly transported from Temple to slaughter houses by the persons to whom the Temple authorities handed over the cows.[59]

Cases of temples and gaushalas starving or selling cows for slaughter continue to emerge throughout the country. In early 2016 in Jaipur, some 8,000 cows died of starvation at the government-run Hingonia gaushala.[60] In September 2016, *India Today* showed footage of a gaushala operator in Uttar Pradesh selling a calf for beef.[61] In August 2017, reports emerged of cows starved to death at a gaushala run by a BJP leader in Chhattisgarh.[62] Another twenty-five cows had died from starvation, illness, or getting stuck in mud after heavy rains at a government-run gaushala in 2017 in Mathana village in Haryana state.[63]

To address illegal slaughtering, the BJP government in Uttar Pradesh, headed by the hardline Hindu nationalist Yogi Adityanath, created a Rs

600 crore (US$ 84.2 million) budget to subsidize gaushalas,[64] which is, in effect, a subsidy to the state's dairy industry. *It was not enough.* Indeed, since the slaughter bans, conditions in gaushalas have worsened due to overcrowding; the "stray cattle" problem has also grown.[65] Frustrated villagers locked up these abandoned cows in schools to prevent them from damaging crops,[66] a recurring issue everywhere in the country.

Forebodingly, gaushalas—akin to Hindu *shakas*—are used to give "a more systemic form" to Hindu nationalism.[67] As early as 2002, in the aftermath of the murders of four Dalit men charged with cow slaughter in Dulina, Haryana, the People's Union for Democratic Rights noted in their report that local gaushalas were using cow protection politics to instigate violent riots if they even "believed" that cows were being slaughtered by Muslims:

> For the Teekli Gaushala Committee members the location of the Gaushala and its role in protecting cows is lent a particular urgency by the fact that Mewat (where 4.6 per cent of the population is Muslim) is located immediately beyond the line of low hills behind the Gaushala. They constantly refer to the "border" with Mewat, a "border" almost represented as a battle line between the lands of "cow-protectors" and "cow-slaughterers." A segment of the dominant groups feel that Hindus could easily kill if they even "believed" that a cow had been slaughtered. There is also communal mobilisation based on concerted and deliberate representation of Muslims as "cow-slaughterers." This is evident in the recent high incidence of posters and hoardings depicting Muslims slaughtering cows with sharp-edged tools across the state.[68]

In view of such militarization, violent containment, boundary-marking, and propaganda, it was becoming clear that gaushalas do become sanctuaries—albeit for the cow–mother–*nation*, where the body of the (dairy) cow is, above all, a Hindu state. As I continued to probe into how "risk" and "danger" to cows, and therein their "protection," is conceptualized by Hindu nationalist groups, I was soon to encounter the most definitive political animal in the multispecies landscape of Indian nationalism—Mother India herself.

CHAPTER 5

"SAVE COW, SAVE INDIA"

BUNDLED UP IN a brown monkey-cap and a thick muffler against the January morning chill, Rana sat on the worn carpet of an office near the Janmasthan Temple in Mathura, the site of the prison where the god Krishna is believed to have been born. An old electric wire heater glowed a bright reddish-orange near him, hurting the eyes somewhat to look at it. He blew into his palms every now and again for warmth before writing on a thick ledger on the low floor-table in front of him. By day, he helped in the office; his family also owned a small grocery shop. By night, he led a team of eight or nine men who would "pilot" the streets of the twin cities of Brindavan and Mathura, and National Highway 19 (heading toward Delhi), looking for trucks carrying concealed cows. They would start their patrols around ten or eleven o'clock at night and continue into the early hours up to six o'clock in the morning.

"Could I join in the patrolling?" I naively asked. He did not answer. I tried again. "I promise not to get in the way. I just want to sit in the corner of the vehicle and observe."

"*Wohi tho* problem *hai*," he said. That is exactly the problem. It would, in fact, be a considerable inconvenience and burden to the gaurakshaks to have me in the way of what was likely to be the violent transformation of night-time roadways, side streets, and bovine bodies into communal warscapes. I presented an additional responsibility. "You can come on one condition only—if you agree to hold a gun. And use the gun if needed."

I must have visibly blanched at his words. I grasped at what might be the least offensive excuse to him. "I don't even have a license . . ." I trailed off feebly, realizing the foolishness of my words. Neither did he.

In states like Uttar Pradesh, Bihar and Madhya Pradesh where corruption is rife across government institutions, a thriving underground arms and ammunition economy bolsters lawlessness.[1] The illegal gun factories supply crude but deadly arms throughout India, and the guns are often gifts of political mentors.[2] Both vigilantes and butchers can be heavily armed, making any potential encounters tantamount to the risk of a warfare.

The man gave me a look. "Why won't you use a gun to save your mother? Are you saying you will *not* use a gun to save your mother?" I squirmed, uncomfortable with the turn in the conversation, and his "catching me out" as a *sickular*, an epithet often used by Hindu extremists to describe secularists as in the throes of sickness, or even contemptible.

I backed off on my request—I was clearly a disappointing soldier for the nation. Not engaging in a Hindutva-defined cow protectionist agenda was being defined as a lack of loyalty to the Indian nation—Mother India. Such rigid delineations are part of the deepening trend toward right-wing nationalisms globally. India's right-wing Hindutva movement is gaining rapid traction, polarizing religious and secular populations, and further entrenching and normalizing racist and casteist violence against Dalits and Muslims. As this violence and polarization escalates, and conversations proliferate on these dynamics and their consequences, it becomes all the more important to excavate the complex multispecies entanglements that contribute to these fraught politics.

To return to an earlier question in the book, then, how can we take seriously the ways in which the "dairy" cow has been instrumentalized for right-wing Hindu projects of violence, exclusion, and nation-making, *and* at the same time, take equally seriously the violence done to cows and buffaloes in routine dairying practices? It might appear that addressing violence against the cow detracts or takes away focus from important analyses of violence against humans. But without dismissing these profoundly important human politics, an excavation of the cow's role as a symbolic "mother" figure and in tandem with this status, as a real, embodied, suffering sentient being enriches and provides a much-needed deepening of understanding of these dynamics. Against this context, it becomes important to raise some vital questions. While the political role of beef in advancing Hindutva is well known, what of the political role of *dairy*, including in the state's official statements and documents? What are the motivations of vigilantes like Rana, whose work coincides with an ever-expanding dairy sector, and what are the implications and responsibilities of that for the Indian animal movement? And what does saving the Mother Cow as Rana described, mean for the future of the Indian state?

HINDUIZING DAIRY, ISLAMICIZING BEEF

"Save Cow, Save India!" is a widespread political sentiment that can be found in graffiti, posters on street-lights, and on social media platforms, a theme originating in the cow protection movement that dates back to the colonial era. For the past hundred and fifty years, political pamphlets, and even art and paintings, have depicted cartoon figures of a huge, black-skinned human meat-eater threateningly wielding a sword over a pure white cow goddess,[3] and towering over a smaller, fair-skinned, noble-looking "upper-caste" Hindu male, who bravely puts himself between the cow and the cow slaughterer. Images depicting "a cow in the act of being slaughtered by three Muslim butchers [titled] 'the present state' were circulated and exhibited at many meetings" by the colonial cow protection movement.[4]

These days, in a message circulated by the Hindu Janajagruti Samiti (which works "For the Establishment of the Hindu Rashtra" or Hindu Nation), a thought-bubble over a white cow says, "Oh humans, please have mercy on us and release us from the captivity of the cruel butcher."[5] A website titled "Struggle for Hindu Existence" depicts a saffron-clad arm holding back a knife-wielding green arm imprinted with the Islamic crescent from butchering a white cow draped in the Hindu swastika.[6] A twist on the popular patriotic song *"Vande Mataram"* (Glory to the Mother[land]) now reads as *"Vande Gau Mathram"* (Glory to the Mother

Cow).[7] Presses owned or supported by Hindu extremists publish incendiary books such as *A Hindu's Fight for Mother Cow* by Sanjeev Newar, which purveys itself as the "First book ever giving 94 ways to rip beeflover apart [*sic*]."[8]

In stark contrast to blatant threats to undo the "beef-lover," the "milk-lover" is allowed to naturalize and sentimentalize the violence inherent in breeding and slaughtering animals for their lactate. The milk-drinker is the fiercely loyal and protective "son" who will not tolerate his "Mother's" dishonor, much less her slaughter. The violent casteized and racialized depiction of slaughter workers as "other", combined with milk consumption as an accepted and *expected* form of reverence for the Mother Cow, obscures the violence inherent in dairying, and the fact that slaughter workers are an essential part of the milk production line.

Since the installation of the BJP-led National Democratic Alliance in 2014, anxieties in Indian intellectual thought have spiked about the growing muscularity of contemporary Hindutva extremism, which Edward Andersen and Arkotong Longkumer call "neo-Hindutva." They describe this phenomenon as "simultaneously brazen but concealed, nebulous and mainstreamed, militant yet normalized."[9] Contemporary or neo-Hindutva's widest expression today is in the form of violent cow protectionism; specifically, what can be understood as the overt Islamicization of beef— and a more implicit, covert Hinduization of dairy—is a core strategy.

The 2014 election campaign of the BJP prime ministerial candidate Narendra Modi took on a clear "Hindutva flavour."[10] In addition to using Hindu symbols and phrases to pepper his campaign speeches (including references to "Ram Mandir," "Ram Setu," "Ganga River," and "Cow and its Progeny"),[11] Modi charged the Congress with instigating a *"gulabi kranti"* or a "pink revolution,"[12] referring to India's growing beef exports from the flesh of slaughtered bovines. He accused the United Progressive Alliance government of providing subsidies to slaughterhouses and promoting meat export,[13] "both things being identified as 'Muslim.'"[14]

However, purveying the idea of the cow as mother is only fully successful when dairy is *also* politicized, albeit Hinduized; the Hinduization of milk and associated dairy products hardly ever receives a parallel critique. In the instrumentalization of bovines in contemporary

Aryan forms of right-wing ultranationalism and fascism—whether neo-Hindutva or neo-Nazi as in America's alt-right,[15] lactate meant for newborn cows has become weaponized to construct a racially "pure" nation for humans of Aryan descent. In August 2017 in the United States, hundreds of white nationalists, alt-righters, and neo-Nazis traveled to Charlottesville, Virginia, to participate in the "Unite the Right" rally. They congregated outside an anti-Trump installation and to protest the art, they glugged gallons of cows' milk as a symbolic demonstration of white superiority, targeting people of color, vegans who resist animal oppression for milk,[16] and of course, the animals used for dairying and their infants. This racist, speciesist and sexist alt-right act is based on an old belief that Aryan races, who have a greater tolerance for the lactose in cows' milk, are therefore superior.[17]

In India, the genius of Aryanic nationalism is manifest in both the obscurity and silence around the central role of dairy production in slaughter, and in the ostentatious and public celebration of milk as nourishing the nation and, specifically, the Hindu civilization. The consumption of cows' milk, writes historian Charu Gupta, was constructed in the colonial era, as necessary to build the healthy Hindu nation itself. Gupta writes: "The cow was now much more directly linked with building a strong nation, a nation of Hindu men who had grown weak and poor from lack of milk and ghee. For a body of healthy sons, cows became essential."[18] Milk, thoroughly *Hinduized* through the incessant and overt evocations of the mythological, ever-lactating Kamadhenu, and the fantastical and miraculous properties of milk itself, cements a specific relationship of the *Hindu citizen–child* and the *Hindu mother–cow–nation* as the only legitimate relationship of an Indian citizen with the Indian state.

The neat split of cow protection from dairy consumption, and in fact, the active *conjoining* of cow protection *with* dairy consumption has been a political strategy, particularly in states like Gujarat, home to India's dairy revolution, the National Dairy Development Board, and a vital seat of what would become the growth of Hindutva as a national project. In 2012, as Chief Minister of Gujarat, prior to becoming Prime Minister, Modi outlined his government's reasons for implementing cow protection; the core importance of Lord Krishna in the lives of Hindus, and "everything associated with him"—essentially, butter, cream and ghee.

> There is a huge presence of Lord Krishna in every aspect of our life. We not only revere Lord Krishna but also everything associated with him. Among other reasons, his association with cows made us to [*sic*] worship them as our mother. In Gujarat, we have left no stone unturned to protect "Gau Mata." We are the only state in India to enact a law for protecting the cow's progeny and ban cow slaughter. But, our work does not stop at preventing killing of mother cow but to also ensure their wellbeing. This inspired us to organize cataract operations for cows.[19]

The exaltation of bovine lactate continues to be central to the anthropatriarchal nation-making narrative of Hindu India. In 2017, the Hindu co-convenor Mahiraj Dhwaj Singh of the Muslim wing of the Hindu nationalist party Rashtriya Swayamsevak Sangh (RSS) announced that their annual iftar feast for breaking the daily Ramadan fast would celebrate dairy products to emphasize the message of "save the cow" to the Muslims.[20] In 2017, the RSS collaborated with the Pasmanda Muslim Samaj, a Muslim political party, to host a "milk" iftar, and break the Eid fast with a glass of cow's milk and sweets made of cow ghee (rather than dates, as per tradition).[21] The irony of unselfconsciously advocating cow destruction—by fostering consumption of the products that contribute to cow slaughter and are also sacred capital to Hindus—to the very community that they frequently accused of cow slaughter went unremarked.

In early 2021, the BJP-led government went to new lengths to entrench the *native* cow as emblematic of India, through a national exam on cow protection, which school and university students, politicians and bureaucrats—indeed, all citizens—were encouraged to take. The Rashtriya Kamadhenu Aayog (RKA), part of the Ministry of Fisheries, Animal Husbandry and Dairying, stated that "Union education ministers, chief ministers, state education ministers, chairmen of Gau Seva Aayogs of all states, district education officers of all states, principals of all schools, print and electronic media, NGOs and cow donors will be involved in this mammoth exercise."[22] The RKA helpfully provided a fifty-four-page study booklet, which included a substantial section differentiating the native cow from the Jersey, Holstein, and crossbred cows, wittingly or unwittingly curating these cows as at least ungrievable, if not killable. "Indian cows," it teaches us, "maintain hygienic [*sic*], hardy and clever enough not to sit at dirty places." The Jerseys and Holsteins, however, "are known to be very lazy and highly prone to diseases. It has also been seen that they attract infection by not being hygienic enough."[23] The Jersey also "Sits idle and [is] very inactive," and "No emotions [are] displayed by her."[24]

Unselfconsciously, the document goes on to assert the importance of five Hinduized cow products—*panchagavya* (milk, ghee, curds, dung, and urine of the native cow)—and notes, "None of the auspicious works of Hindus are complete without them."[25] It finishes on a rambling note, pointing to cow slaughter as the cause of earthquakes, and predictably, pinpoints *one* product sourced from cows—beef—as the cause of all physical and moral devastations afflicting the world today. In absolving milk consumers, including Hindus and Jains who commodify milk as sacred, of contributing to cow slaughter, the fetishization of beef as uniquely responsible for cow killing is a politically strategic way of framing Muslims and Dalits as the only killers of cows in the world's largest dairy nation.

In this way, it is the dairy industry—not the beef sector—that emerges as one of contemporary Hindutva's most vital foundations. In a neoliberalized Indian economy where bovine industries have unprecedented value, the commodification and instrumentalization of the gendered/communalized/casteized *animal other*, and the gendered/communalized/casteized *human other* are interlinked. More starkly in India than elsewhere, the milk-and-beef economy operate as a conjoined continuum: there is no beef economy without a milk economy. Beef, a mere by-product of Indian dairying, alone becomes the focus of ever-increasing vigilantism, aided and abetted by a range of means—emotionally charged propaganda around safeguarding "mothers," covert financial rewards, and sophisticated technology—by the aspirational Hindu state.

In a country that claims to protect the cow *as mother*, both the secular and the Hindu state come together to blur the violence done to the cow, *as mother of her biological calf*, through the celebration of dairying variously as a Hindu, secular nationalist, and development project. What has become a brassy and ostentatious casting of the cow as "mother" of Hindu humans obscures what is really at stake—her milk, a visceral bodily embodiment of motherhood. Hindu women can be understood as what Nira Yuval-Davis calls "cultural transmitters as well as cultural signifiers of the national collectivity,"[26] in this case, of a pure Hindu civilization. So, too, are cows bred by the dairy industry burdened as guardians of Hindu purity. This role as "mothers" of the Hindu civilization is maximally harmful to bovine mothers who are required, through the realities of dairy production, to repeatedly endure the sacrifice of their newborns for the milk-worshipping Hindu nation.

MYTHOLOGIZING MOTHERHOOD FOR THE MOTHER-COW-NATION

In 2016, I attended a national conference on cow protection in Ahmedabad. Its delegates included hundreds of members of Hindu political parties, religious trusts and organizations, and saffron-clad leaders. Large television screens beamed close-ups of panel after panel onstage, where eloquent speeches by Hindu nationalists from all over India were interspersed with Hindu prayers. While some the speeches were in Gujarati which I could not understand, I often caught the word "Pakistan," a clear reference to India's most enduring Islamic "enemy." Outside the large makeshift auditorium, there were stalls ringing the open space. Gaushala dairies peddled butter biscuits, ghee-laden sweets, and kilograms of ghee that they promised to deliver anywhere in India.

Across from these stalls was an enclosed pen-temple where a single cow, a beautiful golden honey-toned native breed Gir cow, stood chained to a tree. A decorated brocade cover was draped over her. Devotees held out bunches of greens to her, which she accepted. After a while, they wandered off to buy milk diverted from other mothers of her species, and the chained cow stood by herself, swishing her tail every now and again to chase off the flies. I sat on the ground next to her, watching the waves of devotion heaped on this one cow, and the mass capitalist production in the name of reverence from the reproductive labor and milk of innumerable faceless, exploited cows in the shops opposite. Was this what "blind faith" looked like?

As I watched a woman and her grown son hold out greens to the cow, a group of men came out of the auditorium. They introduced themselves as gaurakshaks; "we do *goraksha, goseva* [cow protection, cow service]." They were waiting for the arrival of a major Hindu leader who was to speak later that afternoon. I asked them about their motivation for singling out the cow alone as worthy of protection, and the extent to which they'd act "on her behalf."

"*Nothing* will stop me," said a man, clearly the leader of the group. "Nothing." He claimed to have been directly threatened in a phone call by Dawood Ibrahim, one of the foremost terrorists in the world, who is on the "most wanted" list of both the Central Bureau of Investigation in India, and the Federal Bureau of Investigation in the United States. The man continued, "Do you know that this man himself threatened me on the phone, and wanted me to stop *goraksha*?" The terrorist, currently believed to be living in Pakistan, signified the extent of Muslim ruthlessness and threat, both external and internal, to the gentle Hindu cow-nation. "But nothing will stop me," the cow vigilante continued. "I will do *goraksha* until the day I die. I will probably die doing it."

"But why only the cow?" I asked. "Do you feel this strongly about the other animals? After all, they suffer too."

The man impatiently shook his head. "*Haan, haan*, all animals are innocent, all are life," he said. "I will help if I can. But cow is different. Cow is *mata* [mother]. Do you regard any other animal as your *mata*? Is the dog your mother, is the goat your mother, is the buffalo your mother? Only the cow is a mother. For Hindus, the cow is an even more important mother than our own mothers! *Gaumata* comes first for Hindus, even the woman who gave birth to you comes second!"

The objectification of female and feminized "Hindu" bodies as *mothering bodies*, whether human, cow, or the physical and metaphorical landscape of "Mother India," is a crux upon which Hindutva is founded. This erasure of bodily autonomy endured by Hindu female *humans*, becomes mapped onto the "dairy" *cow*, and ultimately onto the concept of *Mother India*. In 2018, the state assembly of Himachal Pradesh proposed a resolution to declare the cow as "rashtra mata" or "mother of the nation." The resolution was advanced, notably, by Congress MLA Anirudh Singh who said, "Cow is not bound to any caste, creed or religion and makes a huge contribution to humanity."[27] However, the frenetic sacral objectification of the cow as "mother" is, of course, emphatically intertwined with India's long history of casteism and, indeed, anthropocentrism, and the casteized bovine mothering body is key to solidifying Hindutva fascism in India.

Against this feminized, multispecies landscape of vulnerable Hindu mothers, Hindutva is driven by a notion of virile masculinity[28] that requires Hindu "mothers, sisters and daughters"—and cows—to be protected from "'the Muslim' who is lecherous and a potential rapist"[29]—and a cow slaughterer. The racialized Muslim beef-eater (and violator of "Hindu" cows) is the same gendered entity as the Muslim rapist (and violator of Hindu women). Mangala Subramaniam writes that women—and indeed, cows—are "endangered" as Hindu men's property,[30] and "instrumentalized as victims,"[31] rather than being recognized as self-governing subjects. In both cases, the women's—and cows'—trauma from violation is less than the trauma that such violation ostensibly presents to the men's sense of honor.

This sense of moral outrage and even emasculation of the Hindu male in the violation of a "Hindu" female—notably, when perpetrated by the Muslim, could not have been more clearly explicated to me than by one of the cow vigilantes at the Ahmedabad conference. After the others had left, he hung back and gestured to me to follow him to a quieter side of the cow pen. We were still in a publicly visible space; I slightly hesitated and walked over to him. "You understand, it is the not the killing I am worried about. It is *not the killing* [emphasis his]." He raised his arm to indicate a sword. "I myself would kill the cow," he said.

This unexpected admission of the cow as killable became viscerally too much. I had to get away. I raised my hand to stop him talking, and started to walk on. He came after me, and insisted on explaining the real problem, "I would kill a cow before allowing Musalmans to kill her.

Being in Hindurashtra, they think they can kill cows, disrespect Hindu dharma. They have to understand, they cannot kill cows."

The concept of "honor" carries with it an established set of violations, where the female compromises or is compromised, typically through "invited" or forced violation of her body, and brings dishonor to the male. During pogroms and riots, Moritz explains that "men are prepared to use violence . . . to defend their reputation as honorable men . . . [and such violence] is institutionalized, regarded as legitimate by the society at large."[32] Hindu male dishonor is a multispecies phenomenon, achieved as much through violating cows as women. As historian Mukul Kesavan explains:

> It isn't a reason; just a belligerent assertion. It goes like this: I am a Hindu, the cow is my mother, and I won't have her killed. What's being invoked here isn't morality or sentimentality or chivalry or economics: this is an assertion . . . that effectively argues that all cows are Hindu women.[33]

If "dairy" cows are equivalent to Hindu women, then their inevitable slaughter for dairy by marginalized Muslims and Dalits who work in the slaughter-end of Indian dairy production becomes framed as a moral offense *to* the milk-consuming Hindus. Such Hindutva outrage is a double-win for the simultaneously milk-loving and cow-worshipping Hindu state, which gets to drink cow milk *and* be outraged about their inevitable slaughter, which can be strategically and neatly displaced as malicious Muslim offense. By framing cows as Hindu "mothers," and their (necessary and inevitable) "assault" in the form of slaughter to sustain the dairy economy as "dishonor" to Hindu men, the millions of exploited and abandoned "dairy" cows may be the most successful vehicle of Hindu ultranationalism yet.

As political totems, female "Hindu" bodies are not exclusively, or in the case of the cows, even at all, mothers to their biological young, but to the Hindu nation-state, who is also a "mother." Women—and cows—are tasked with upholding Hindu culture and identity, and assuaging the anxieties of Hindutva patriarchy about Muslims and Dalits undermining their privilege, "*through their roles as wives and mothers.*"[34] Inherent to motherhood, when instrumentalized *as a sociopolitical and cultural institu-tion*, are social and "economic constraints"[35] for the women, or indeed, other animals politically objectified as "mothers."

The mothering body as a landscape of nationalism and extremism is hardly unique to Hindu patriarchy.[36] However, Indian feminists have long noted that Hindu nationalists use female or feminized bodies stra-tegically—as ""Bharat mata," "matri bhasha" and "gau mata"" (Mother India, Hindi as the mother language, Cow Mother).[37] In the case of women, for instance, this gendered objectification comes at an extremely high cost. Vanaja Dhruvarajan holds that the edification of Hindu women to be ideal *wives* and *mothers* who preserve an ideal Hindu cul-ture and nation is almost singularly responsible for their enduring op-pression and their relegation to the private spaces of the home[38]—or in the case of cows, the dairy farm—as their rightful place. If the defense of motherhood in its most exalted form *as the motherland*, is a righteous duty of the "sons," then upholding the dignity and respect owed to the institution *becomes a patriotic duty of mothers*, and the institution of moth-erhood becomes state or national property. In this way, motherhood it-self becomes a way to politically dominate and subjugate women—and cows.

In the case of Hindu women, Thomas Blom Hansen describes moth-ering as *"patriotic motherhood,"*[39] and identifies three themes around the idea of Hindu motherhood. One, "women are first and foremost moth-ers." To serve the children and her husband is the "supreme duty of any woman." Two, "motherhood is a patriotic duty," as it is the women who uphold Hindu values and culture and pass them to the children. Three, patriotic motherhood does not entail freedom outside the home. Her patriotic duties explicitly lie within the defined threshold of the home. In this construction of a modern and "classicized" culture, where the freedom to engage in the material or external world has been effectively removed, "the woman was constructed as a goddess, and as an upholder of tradition."[40] As custodians of the Hindurashtra, Hindu motherhood encapsulates responsibilities beyond their biological children. That is, women are positioned as *sacrificing mothers* for the Hindu nation itself,[41] an exceptionally charged framing that lends itself easily to violence and hatred in the name of the mother's "protection," whether human or indeed, bovine.

What, however, makes gaurakshaks undertake the filial labor of cow vigilantism? Virtually no study exists that examines the motivations of cow vigilantes or their socioeconomic backgrounds.[42] Cow vigilantes are implicitly and unquestioningly assumed to be inhumane, hate-mongering vehicles of Hindutva, who can, in turn, be conveniently hated back by left-wing liberals. However, the simplistic conclusion that terrorism is produced exclusively by inhumanity is not typically the case,[43] generating an anemic analysis of cow vigilantism in this case, muddying the insidious forces of poverty and social vulnerability that could make many people open to exploitation to perform the labor of vigilantism. Vigilantes who undertake the labor of militant protectionism—chase trucks, lynch and get lynched, and handle animals in dilapidated conditions from the trucks—often work at severe risk to themselves. What sort of vulnerabilities—and, indeed, whose vulnerabilities—do the vigilantes see themselves as protecting?

FILIAL LABOR: VIGILANTE SONS OF MOTHER–COW–NATION

Amar, a gaurakshak in Hyderabad, took me to various gaushalas in the city where he had brought several hundred cows from Telengana and Odisha states, rescued during illicit transportation to slaughterhouses. Amar engaged in all the typical encounters reported in the media—halting trucks, beating up and in turn getting beaten up by the transporters, and often by the police as well. While cow vigilantism in particular has been highlighted in media and populist discourses since 2014, I was surprised to learn that Amar had, in fact, started halting trucks in 1998, in that tense and volatile decade following the destruction of the Babri Masjid and prior to the bloodletting that would occur in the Gujarat pogrom in 2002. In his own words, Amar was already a "well known rowdy and thug," and was being mentored in cow vigilantism by a Hindutva-sympathizing MLA in Andhra Pradesh state at that time.

In 2014, the state split into two, and the new state, Telengana, became a prominent landscape for caste and identity anxieties, I was to learn later during my time in Osmania University. Amar's work as a cow vigilante had also become more established since 2014, and he started to receive an informal salary from a Hindu charitable organization. Amar explained that he had been facing a 14-year imprisonment for multiple murders at the time, but in 2014, as soon as he became a full-time gaurakshak, the charges got "buried" by the new state sympathetic to cow vigilantism.

Amar emphasized to me that he would not tolerate anyone even looking at his "mother" with "bad intentions." In his worldview, the cow herself pleads with her "son" not to exact revenge—i.e., murder—for her assault and dishonor, perpetrated by cow slaughterers who are often Muslim. Rather, he explains, the virtuous mother is willing to wait patiently —*"woh Mussalman khud aayega"*—the Muslim himself will come, to seek her forgiveness and also become her "son":

> I just have one prayer, do not butcher a cow, *do not look at a cow with bad gaze/intention* [emphasis added]. As long as I am alive, I will save gau-vansh [the bovine family] . . . in my heart, there is only one *jasba*, one *junoon*, only one thing—anyone who violates my gaumata [Mother Cow] will be destroyed. Only thing that stops me is the gaumata herself. She says, "son, I am the one enduring it, I am the one getting killed. I am not cursing him [the butcher/Muslim]. You also endure for just a bit longer. A day will come when they bow at my feet and say, "we made a mistake, Ma, please forgive us." You don't take a wrong step.

The emotive grandiloquence of the self-sacrificing, forgiving mother may have worked precisely as intended in arousing self-righteous rage, giving his work a more noble veneer in his eyes or those of Hindutva groups. However, Amar was also motivated by a narrow escape from jail, and a measure of financial security his family had never had thus far, now guaranteed by the Hindu trust. These can be highly compelling reasons to undertake terror work. Terrorism expert Armando Sparato finds two motivations for terrorists which are then exploited in recruitment strategies.[44] The first is a simple, "distorted" religious worldview—"the cow is my mother," for instance—and following on from that, the imperative to liberate her from violence can provide highly meaningful inspiration. The simplicity of such singular and charged rhetoric can provide sufficient reason for terror work, in and of itself. Significantly, Sparato notes that *"practically no importance attaches to the aspiration to liberate specific occupied territories or oppressed peoples* [emphasis added]," even as they make such claims.[45] This anger and insecurity is easily misdirected at the "other," and the outrage against the violation of the tormented "Hindu" cow is invaluable emotive capital for extremist political parties.

Second, the labor of terrorism is usually heavily incentivized financially, in such a way as to "guarantee a future to the family members."[46] Often, the "salary" received for terror work is more reliable than other labor in the informal economy, typically including a pension plan for family members, an otherwise unthinkable package. In an informal economy where opportunities to make money must be quickly exploited, a vigilante in Gujarat told me that the state government offers financial rewards for seized cows. The media, too, intentionally or inadvertently become complicit when they cover only stories about cows rather than buffaloes, goats, sheep, and camels as well,[47] who are also enmeshed in Indian identity politics and the violence of dairying. Explaining the financial inducement to save cows in particular, the vigilante told me:

> The Gujarat government awards Rs 500 [about US$ 8] for each cow progeny to the person filing FIR [first information report] but not for buffaloes. So there is more incentive for the gaurakshaks to save the cows. But also, no media covers news on rescued buffaloes, they are just not interested.

Later I would meet Mohan, another vigilante who worked on the borders of the southeastern states of Andhra and Odisha. Also supported by a "salary" from a Hindu trust, his labor as a gaurakshak became the first time in many years that he had earned a consistent livelihood. The man had three children, whose school fees were covered by the Hindu charity. The shame and frustration of being unemployed and purposeless, and being judged by others, was overturned almost instantaneously by finding meaning in the rescue of an innocent animal *and* safeguarding the Hindu nation. Through gauraksha, it was not only that he lived materially better, he explained; he tried mindfully to *become* a good human being:

> I was a loser, I had no purpose, no meaning, I was lost. I didn't even know how to speak nicely or politely, I would get offended and outraged if someone stared at me or laughed at me, if someone even looked at me, I would beat them. Gaumata broke my arrogance, and took me into her heart. I used to eat meat and fish, I stopped that. I used to be a heavy drinker, I stopped that. I just have a chai and a *gutka* now. I do less of prayers and rituals, and more of *seva* [service] to Gaumata.

However, as I would discover in an unexpectedly distressing encounter, the financial incentivization could also bind the cow vigilantes to the demands of the Hindu political organizations, with no potential pathway out if they did not wish to continue this patriotic service. Recommended by a Hindu political leader in Haryana who I was interviewing, I called a vigilante at his home for an interview from the party's offices itself. The man spoke hesitantly, somewhat monosyllabic as I asked to meet him. Suddenly a woman's voice came on the phone, begging me, "Please don't ask him to do this work! Please leave him!" It was his wife, who thought I was directing him to gauraksha responsibilities, calling as I had from the party office. I quickly reassured her that I was not from the party, that I worked at a university. But she was too upset, and I did not press further.

However, I also found a *third* motivation, at least for some vigilantes—a genuine love and concern for animals, which risked crystallizing into hate for those who Hindutva framed as exclusively responsible for animal suffering. When the politics around animal rights and welfare itself is so disjointed and inconclusive in India as elsewhere, Hindutva often emerges, particularly in the subaltern space, offering the clearest and most definitive mentoring in animal advocacy. In the absence of an understanding that dairying is linked with slaughter, Jeevan, a vigilante I met in Thane city outside Mumbai, rejected the slaughter of all animals for meat. He spoke with a genuine concern for animals; in one sense, these words depict a rejection of human supremacism such that even a poor human being, he claimed, had no right to "plunder" another life. Jeevan told me:

> There is no need to eat meat at all. If you don't have the money, sit in the corner and beg for money if need be, eat dal and rice. There is no need to eat meat, no need at all. Is it necessary to eat flesh and fish? To plunder a life for its own life? If you can't put life into someone, you can't take life away from someone. If you are so poor that you can't afford dal, then how can you afford meat? "Poor" is someone who eats dal chawal, chutney chawal, khatta chawal, dahi chawal [dal rice, chutney rice, spicy rice, curd rice]. Who eats flesh and fish? Flesh and fish are eaten by hi-fi *log* [fancy/wealthy people]. Only they can afford.

Jeevan himself was poor, his life made economically viable by a Hindu political party. Yet, speaking as a Hindu cow vigilante and, indeed, receiving mentorship as such, his words hearkened back to concerns of secular thinkers that Hindutva fascism manifested as vegetarian fascism. Neither Jeevan, nor any of the vigilantes to whom I spoke, were willing to consider that dairy production required slaughter. *"Nahin, doodh se nahin hota hai,"* Jeevan insisted. *No, milk doesn't cause it* [slaughter]. In a manner reminiscent of the justification for beef consumption for health and nutrition, Jeevan went on to say, *"Doodh tho chahiye.* Milk is needed. There is no ailment which milk does not prevent, at any age." While he could not reconcile dairying with the inevitable slaughter of animals, Jeevan nonetheless tried to draw attention to the plight of other animals, including the buffalo, who I had heard many vigilantes reject. The gaurakshak attempted to appeal to a specific Indic secularism that attempted to draw out the universality, indeed, between Hinduism and Islam, in emphasizing compassion for life:

> Even the buffalo is a life. It is not to say that okay, it is a buffalo, do what you like with the buffalo. I must have rescued some 500 buffaloes from all the trucks we have caught so far. We don't say, leave the cows and bulls alone, and take the buffaloes, no! The buffalo is a living breathing creation.

Where is it written . . . nowhere in the Bhagvad Gita or Koran does it say, "Eat flesh and fish. Murder a life."

Another time, I visited a vigilante outside of Ahmedabad city. Her Facebook posts on cow rescues were among the most visceral that I had seen, depicting unfathomable conditions for cows and calves forced into small cars, to be smuggled for slaughter. I went prepared to get straight-away into the logistics of cow smuggling. She was distracted on the day of my arrival, however, by pigeons.

My visit had followed Holi, the colorful festival in March signaling the onset of spring, where thousands of people fly kites. The kites are attached to glass-coated twine so competitors could cut off their oppo-nent's kite; the twine would also shred the wings and bodies of thou-sands of flying birds in the sky. During the week-long festival, this team of gaurakshaks organized a system of triage for the pigeons where the vigilante-volunteer team would drive around the city on motorbikes and cars, and pick up fallen birds all day, responding to phone calls. The birds would be dropped off at the emergency veterinary tent, and the volun-teers would set off again to bring more pigeons, by the hundreds each day. I was expecting to visit gaushalas with her; instead, this vigilante took me to a small shelter that she had constructed for severely injured pigeons in the grounds of a temple. It was time for a mid-day applica-tion of antibiotic cream and she could not miss the inspection time. She carefully lifted several of the pigeons to rub the yellow ointment under their bruised wings and heads. "You know, you really should come back during the festival and see what we do," she said. "One of our best and most efficient rescues. We forget to eat and sleep during that time, it's just rescue, treatment, rescue, treatment."

So too Jeevan's love and care for animals was undeniable as I watched him interact with gentleness with the animals, individually seeking many of them out, when he took me to a gaushala that housed some of his rescued cows. This was quite a contrast to my tours of gaushalas with other vigilantes, who showed no interest in the animals. Jeevan's affec-tion was evident to the animals too, in the way a couple of free-roaming cows in the gaushala came rushing straight for him when they heard his voice, nuzzling, and grooming, and licking him. "Ganga, move! What will my wife say?" he yelled, as I laughed.

Nonetheless, as we walked through the bovines, I noticed a magnificent *goat*, with large impressive curling horns. The goat was young, tightly chained, and had pressed his head against the wall in what seemed like defeat and hopelessness. I asked the gaurakshak what a single (and beautiful) goat was doing in the gaushala. "He is for goat fights!" Jeevan exclaimed with a wide smile. "But you are a gaurakshak!" I couldn't help crying out. "Isn't the goat as capable of suffering as the cows?" Jeevan got a bit irritated. "We don't *kill* the goat," he said. "It's just a bit of fun." The goat was used weekly for fighting, allowing time for recovery before his next fight. Significantly, if the goat was too badly injured to fight again, the gaushala would not rehabilitate him, as they did the cows. "What happens then?" I asked Jeevan. "He will be fine. He will be fine," was all he would say. Jeevan's justification of the use the goat because he wasn't slaughtered was in fact, no different from that of animal welfare campaigns which focus on only selective types of violence to the exploited animal as problematic.

Gradually, I would come to notice an interesting *class* tension in vigilantism. There was a section of the vigilante structure who I started to think of as white-collar vigilantes. They were almost never featured or denounced in the media *as* vigilantes, although they coordinated the administration essential to successful and sustained vigilantism. Hindutva has received enthusiastic support from much of India's Hindu middle class, seduced by the promise of development,[48] often underpinned by technological innovations such as the Smart Cities Mission, for instance, that deploys both nationalism and technology to become a moral *and* "Smart" (Hindu) state.[49] Amar introduced to me one of his mentors from the Hindu charity, an educated English-speaking middle-class man in his thirties with a management degree, working as a businessman. This man, who I will call Bhaskar, was part of a large network of middle and upper-class Hindu citizens who professionalized vigilantism behind the scenes. Bhaskar ran law classes for the vigilantes so they could file charges under the correct penal codes when they caught trucks; he educated the recruits on the institutional structure of the police so they could navigate the system, and he created extensive directories of gaush-alas across the country. Veterinarians might also be part of this network. Bhaskar himself was emphatic about consciously distancing the methods of the Hindu charitable trust from those of the cow vigilantes working for Hindu nationalist parties, to avoid themselves being seen as violent, hateful, or extremist by association. "No, no, these people have actually made things difficult for us, painting us also to be violent like them," Bhaskar said. "We *don't* want to be identified with them, we don't tell our drivers and volunteers to shout '*Jai Shri Ram, Jai Shri Ram*' [glory to Lord Ram] like the gaurakshaks, we don't beat up the butchers, damage the truck and all that."

How was the work of the Hindu religious organization different from Hindu political organizations, then? Bhaskar slipped unselfconsciously into the same reasons as those provided by the vigilantes—rising anxiety about being demographically outnumbered by the Muslims, mixed with apocalyptic prospects for the Hindu civilization, when the cow, symbol-izing precisely such a state, was threatened. "Half of Hyderabad is Paki-stan," Bhaskar told me. "Cow slaughter is everywhere, therefore. The day the cows are finished, Creation itself is finished. And if we Hindus don't do something about that, then only we are responsible." Although his mentees like Amar might engage in violent vigilantism, Bhaskar was careful to emphasize the *civility* with which he himself engaged with the Muslims. "Many prominent Muslim leaders are saying no to cow slaughter during Bakra-Id," he said, referencing the Muslim sacrificial festival. "They realize that we are doing genuine work, not wanting to harm anyone."

Despite wanting to maintain a distance from Hindu political groups, Bhaskar would eventually admit to working cooperatively "when needed," which was often during times of heightened tension like the Bakra-Id, where thousands of camels, goats, and buffaloes—and cows, bulls and calves—are slaughtered in Muslim-dominant areas. The risk to native breed cows arouses even more anger at these times. Muslim malice against Hindu culture was embodied not only through beef con-sumption, but specifically, predation of the flesh of *native* cows who symbolized—indeed, were—Hindu mothers and the nation itself. Amar intriguingly defaulted to the *Islamic* conceptualization of purity and pollution, or *halal* and *haram*, to highlight that these were similar to Hindu understandings of the same notions. But the Muslim used these ideas differently, he pointed out, compared with the Hindu. The native cow was purer, or indeed, *halal*. While her purity made the Hindu revere the cow, this made the Muslim exploit her, for ostensibly purer or *halal* beef, preferring to eat her over the *haram* Jersey. That the *purity* of the native cow was also precisely the rationale used by Hindus to consume the native cow's "purer" dairy over the Jersey's milk, escaped him.

Predictably, against the weaponization of the cow for right-wing Hindutva agenda, she also becomes instrumentalized for resistance movements *against* it, rendering her actual body a warzone. As early as 1920, Mahatma Gandhi had warned in a speech in Bettiah gaushala that cow slaughter (and beef consumption) would be rendered a political act of resistance for Muslims and Dalits by the very Hindu fanatics who claim to love the cow. He said, "If cow-slaughter were for the Muslims a religious duty, like saying namaz, I would have had to tell them that I must fight against them. But it is not a religious duty for them. We have made it one by our attitude to them."[50] The uprising of minorities, such as Dalit political student bodies and Muslim communities retaliating with "beef festivals" becomes a predictable outcome of the Hindutva politicization of beef.[51]

"BEEF! SECRET OF MY ENERGY!": BEEF AS CASTEIST RESISTANCE

In 2015, students from the Dalit-majoritarian Osmania University in Hyderabad announced their intention to hold a "beef festival" on December 10, Human Rights Day, as resistance against the pervasive violence of Hindutva in their lives. The beef festival was seen, as indeed intended, as both resistance and provocation to the Hindu nationalists. In response, "hundreds of policemen in riot gear surrounded the campus and prevented anyone from outside from participating in the beef festival."[52] The students cooked and served beef regardless in their hostels, and posted photos on social media.

I visited Osmania in 2017. Some 97–98 percent of the Osmania student body, the students told me, comprised Dalits, Adivasis, and OBCs. I arrived at the student hostel to meet with some of the youth leaders. My Brahminical identity itself a presence in the room, I quickly explained to the students that I absolutely did not consider the cow to be any sort of relative of mine. The students laughed. One of them said, "If you did, I could not take you seriously," he continued, "because if you claim the cow is your mother, you are actually not connected to the cow at all. You are actually disguising that you have no connection to the cow. If you care for the cow, then why do you need to make such claims?" I felt struck by his response. Merely claiming that the cow was my mother could often be, as historian Mukul Kesavan writes, "an assertion of fictive kinship"[53] that required no accounting of the extensive labor and care that being genuinely responsible for one's mother—and one who is an intensively-bred farmed animal, no less—might involve. As the hot afternoon wore on, a couple of street dogs, who had obviously attached themselves to the hostel students as sources of food, nosed down the corridor a few times and into the room. "That dog is my brother. Even then I feed him!" roared a student, as we laughed.

Shortly after, one of the most popular student leaders arrived in the room and sat with us, the sweetly hospitable Sharath, who went by the ironic sobriquet Sharath Chamar Cobbler to proudly and publicly claim his "untouchable" "cobbler" caste. Sharath rapped as a way of showing resistance. Sharath's spin on the advertising tagline of the dairy malt drink Boost ("Boost! Secret of my energy!") as "Beef! Secret of my energy!" went viral on YouTube. In the afternoon heat, Sharath obligingly rapped out the song for me with its pulsing, rhythmic beat.

In 2017, the caste tensions that brought about the newly formed Telengana state in 2014 remained at the forefront of their political anxieties around identity, manifesting in myriad ways in their personal, professional, and political lives. "I am doing my PhD," said one man studying political science. "I have come this far and still if I go to an upper-caste friend's house, I am asked to sit on the floor. Not everyone, I grant that. But even once is enough to create upset in me." The experience of pointed discrimination in overt and covert ways was intertwined with the fomenting tensions around identity, state, and separatism. The Dalit students felt that the "upper castes" such as the Reddys and the Varmas were pushing their cultural practices to the forefront of a Telengana state identity, which included huge celebrations of Hindu festivals like Diwali, Holi, and Dusshera. At precisely such a time, a routine practice in Dalit social and cultural lives—the consumption of beef—was violently under attack, not just in Telengana, but across the country.

The beef festival became an opportunity for the Hindu right to depict racialized beef eaters—Dalit, Muslim, or Hindu Communists—as uniquely violent and cruel in their treatment of animals. The outpouring of toxic hate on social media by right-wing Hindus in the aftermath of the floods that devastated Communist-ruled Kerala in 2013, for instance, was visceral. One commentator said, "Kerala hindus must stop eating beef. You can't claim you're a hindu and eat beef too. Mother nature will pay back with interest [*sic*]."[54] Another responded with a photo of the Hindu god Shiva devastating the evil-doer, "It seems to be true sir Lord Ayyappa is angry with the Kerala Govt, as whole country knows that Communist & Congressi Workers had publicly slaughtered an innocent Calf in protest of Beef ban, cooked it publicly & feasted on its cooked beef openly on the road! God wouldn't spare [*sic*]."[55]

By holding the beef festival, Osmania students were promptly named as anti-nationalists by Hindu political parties, which infuriated them. The students were struck by the blatant hypocrisy that allowed many common practices around dominant Hindu festivals, which *also* involved slaughtering animals and polluting the environment, to be practiced without challenge. Blowing apart the smokescreen that masked the critical questioning of *Hindu* slaughter of animals, Sudesh, a senior student leader, told me, "Our festivals are actually quite small, even if we slaughter animals, nowhere do we reach those sorts of numbers." The celebration of Hindu festivals, amplified by the wealth of the growing middle and upper classes, are increasingly unprecedented in scale and lavishness, as Sudesh further stated:

Every Hindu *pandga* [festival], Deepawali, Dusshera, Vijayadasami, thousands of animals are being slaughtered. Goats, chickens, buffalo, you name
it, they are being slaughtered. During Diwali, you cannot breathe the air
for a week! Animals and even human beings will die of heart attacks alone,
if they don't get killed by crackers first. How is this okay but if we eat
beef, they call us *desha drohis*? [anti-nationalists, or more accurately, nation-
traitors]. When we had our beef festival, we did not bring a cow to campus
to slaughter. We simply went to the shops, bought the beef which is openly
available, and cooked it. But you have large Hindu festivals where animals
are being slaughtered, who is saying anything about that?

This was a great irony which many of the students mentioned in our
conversations: they bought the beef that was openly available to anyone
in the informal meat markets. In that, their purchase, cooking and consumption of beef did not differ in any respect from that of other customers, including Hindus. As the students spoke, I was reminded of a conversation with informal butchers in Lucknow city earlier in the year. "Do
any Hindus come to buy beef?" I had asked. The butchers roared with
laughter. One man said, "If they stopped, we would have to close down!"
Cow and buffalo beef were sold together in that market, though some
Hindu customers might specifically ask for buffalo beef. What mattered
to Hindu nationalists about the Osmania beef festival was the resistance
suggested by the *openness* of the beef consumption and its geography—
the political spaces of a Dalit university campus.

The curation of beef consumption and cow slaughter alone as morally
outrageous against the prolific bloodletting of all other farmed animals
was perceived as an act subordinating and controlling Dalit cultures
and society. The beef festivals thus became another way of highlighting what was really at stake for Dalits—the restoration of their land,
equal education and employment opportunities, and dignity of labor. In
this, the beef festivals were only one type of protest. After the lynching
of the four Dalit youths who were "caught" skinning a cow in Una in
2015, Gujarat, some 800 Dalit citizens participated the following year
in the Dalit March to Self Liberation, an eighty-one kilometer walk

that traversed the distance from Gujarat's capital city of Ahmedabad to Una.[56] Jignesh Mevani, a Dalit activist and lawyer, compared the 2016 Dalit March to Self Liberation to the "March on Washington for jobs and freedom" organized by Black Americans in 1963. The catch cry of the protest in Gujarati was, "*Marela pashoo tamhe rakho, Amne Jameen Aapo* [keep the dead cows, give us back our land]." Dalit tanners dumped the carcasses of whole cows outside the district collector's [an official of the Indian Administrative Service, responsible for the local district] office, and rallied Dalit communities throughout the nation to do the same.[57]

Far from being a malicious act to provoke "upper caste" Hindus, the task of skinning cows for leather is, in fact, deeply dehumanizing and dangerous work. Mevani explained that the march was a clarion call to Dalits throughout India to boycott the tanning trade. He said that even while the boycott would certainly hurt the livelihoods of the Dalits, they nonetheless swore to abandon the trade as a crucial form of political protest:

> they would renounce, give up in protest the filthy, de-humanising work of lifting dead carcasses, cleaning sewers and gutters and streets, all filthy work designated to them by a rigid and discriminatory caste system, the Hindu caste order. This was a milestone. We hope that this inspires Dalits from all over India. That it has started from Gujarat is historic.[58]

The statement of the protestors read:

> We are demanding alternative employment, dignified occupations. We want to till land, free ourselves from the indignity of carrying dead carcasses of cattle, be they cows or buffaloes, cleaning sewers and gutters and the streets. This is a revolt against the indignities of the caste system dumped on us, for centuries.[59]

The politics of differentiation from not only Hindutva but Hinduism itself, was an emphatic feature of Dalit protests. "We want to pose our own opposition and demand, from all angles. Cultural side, from economy side, religion and politics," said Sudesh.

The beef festival thus cannot be understood as a singular response to the beef ban. The open and defiant consumption of beef was resistance to a *multitude* of factors—untouchability, land rights, dignity of labor, food and cultural identities—that crystallized around cow slaughter in response to Hindutva mobilization of cow protection. The "dairy" cow, subject already to the extractive violence of dairying, was not just part of the dehumanization project of Hindutva; the vulnerable cow, in fact, becomes *necessary* to complete the portrayal of Muslim bodies in particular, as rapists,[60] and now also cow slaughterers.

Inevitably, the realities of what happens to the cows themselves become obscured or rendered irrelevant in these fraught humanist negotiations and oppressions in Indian political discourse. However, where a fascist state has defined and mainstreamed *what* constitutes bovine vulnerabilities, and *who* renders bovines vulnerable, it becomes critical for an animal movement to emerge forthrightly into the political space, and clearly situate its own politics and strategic alliances. In a context where the cow is exploited for dairying, *and* for sectarianism, casteism, and fascism, with devastating implications for people and the bovines, how have various factions of the Indian animal movement responded? What are the implications of these for both animal and subaltern human liberation? How can animal *and* human rights groups find ways to acknowledge human *and* animal vulnerabilities as morally relevant, and work together respectfully?

INDIAN ANIMAL ACTIVISM: DISJOINTED IDENTITY
POLITICS AND SINGLE-ISSUE CAMPAIGNS
The animal movement, such as it is in India, finds similarities with animal justice movements in other parts of the world. It comprises a culturally diverse cohort of activists and supporters—an immense strength that is yet to be maximized; it is relatively nascent as a political formulation; and it is challenged by the need to respond to the multiple ways in which animal bodies are deployed in a casteized and sectarian context. It is often fractional and is not tethered to a unifying politics *for* the animals. And a cohesive Indian animal justice movement, as elsewhere,

perhaps faces one of its most intractable challenges from the animal welfare movement, which purportedly operates in farmed animals' interest, by promoting their breeding and slaughter in "humane" ways, rather than questioning the wholesale exploitation of animals per se. These so-called humane methods ironically compromise real animal wellbeing, best achieved by their liberation from human exploitation altogether, while frequently racializing and vilifying the farming and slaughtering practices of minorities. As exemplified in the case of the cow in India, the animal, whether farmed or wild, might be used as a prominent or peripheral impetus for *other* political activity, and intertwined with different subaltern human motivations. These intersections of the animal and human in politics do not necessarily occur in a way that makes the animal presence meaningful and tangible in their own right, nor is that even a priority.

The killing of a starving pregnant wild elephant in 2020 in Silent Valley nature reserve in Kerala who was allegedly fed a pineapple filled with explosives is a poignant example of what could have been animal-focused advocacy, being hijacked by self-serving vested political interests. The motivation of the offender who had prepared the bomb-laden pineapple was unclear; was the act of cruelty one of pure malice, or due to some desperation (agricultural farmers often use crude bombs to discourage animals from entering their fields)? The elephant stood for four days in agony in a river before collapsing and dying. After initial collective horror at the gruesomeness of the act, the incident quickly deteriorated into communal allegations about her torturer. Although one person was arrested for the act, his religion was not revealed in the public domain, and no convictions have yet been made.[61] However, the Muslim-dominated Mallapuram district where the elephant was tortured featured in the condemnation of several BJP leaders, and Muslims were charged with conducting jihaad against Hindus, weaponizing yet another animal regarded as holy in Hinduism.[62] Muslim citizens were quick to criticize that a similar incident where a pregnant cow was fed with explosives in north India a few months later went unremarked, possibly because it involved a Hindu culprit.[63] The fact of the *animals* experiencing these attacks, and their vulnerability to such devastating *human* violence, becomes lost in political debate which does not yet regard *species*, in their own terms and interests, as also constitutive of identity politics.

There are uneasy slippages between Indian animal activism and right-wing politics that become particularly problematic, and which make parsing out the nuances and stark differences between animal activism and Hindutva politics especially difficult, when high-profile figures blur these lines through their own politics. For instance, one of India's leading animal rights advocates, Mrs. Maneka Gandhi, was also a BJP Union Minister for Women and Child Development between 2014 and 2017. Gandhi broke away early from the Congress party following the death of her husband Congressman Sanjay Gandhi in 1980. In her biographical essay, Dave recounts Gandhi's moment of truth as her eyes "opened" early to the brutal realities of animal lives.[64] Being an animal activist *and* a politician within the BJP regime situates her at the nexus of a constant, politically fraught intersection. Her political platform as a federal minister allows her voice for animals to be amplified, which is no small thing for an animal movement that takes animals' lives and deaths seriously, an imperative that is mostly sidelined in mainstream politics.

However, Gandhi's co-option of communalist rhetoric in the name of animal advocacy risks her being perceived as advancing a Hindutva, rather than an animal justice agenda. Gandhi has frequently accused cow slaughterers of funding terrorist activities,[65] a charge that remains unsubstantiated. Simultaneously, Gandhi has written about the culpability of *all* religious groups in perpetuating gross acts of violence against animals, often in the name of religion itself, and has been unsparing in her condemnation of Hindus as she criticizes their role in the ritual slaughter of animals that is pervasive in Hindu festivals, as the students at Osmania noted. However, coming not only from a BJP leader but also one known to be narrating anti-Muslim rhetoric, Gandhi's animal advocacy politics of itself, is often ignored. Describing the scale of Hindu ritual slaughter in unsparing detail, Gandhi goes on to write,

The only difference between Bakrid and Makara Sankranti is that the Muslims don't bet while they maim and kill animals. The Hindus do. They drink and they gamble on how which animal dies faster. No Hindu pretends that it has a basis in religion. They simply call it Hindu culture, even though some of these massacres have only started a few decades ago.[66]

Indian animal activism, in fact, has a crucial role in unveiling and politicizing the violent exploitation of a myriad of *other* animals, including farmed species, in oppressive identity politics. Less known, for instance, are the ways in which the pig is weaponized to reinforce and solidify caste and sustain nationalisms by producing binary identities. In Bareilly city in Uttar Pradesh, residents celebrate Govardhan festivities (the birth of the cow-loving Lord Krishna) with a deeply cruel cow-pig fight. Four or five bulls are forced to "fight" a lone pig whose legs are tied, and who is then flung in their midst in an enclosed space, surrounded by hundreds of loud, goading humans.[67] The agitated bulls gore the pig to death. This "victory" of the cows over the pig signals the caste ascendancy and triumph of the "upper" caste Hindus over the "untouchables" who often rear pigs.

However, the pig is also weaponized *by* oppressed castes to assert and maintain power in the intricate structures and hierarchies of sub-caste, as a means of humiliating the group that they perceive as "the other." In mid-2017 in Chennai, a hardline Dravida political party, Thanthai Periyar Dravidar Kazhagam, held a protest against Brahminism by making pigs wear the *poonal* or the sacred-thread, a caste marking that Brahmin males wear as a ritual symbol of initiation. The event titled "*Panrikku Poonool podum porattum*" (making pigs wear *poonal*) was held on 7th August outside the Sanskrit College on Avani Avittam day, a sacred day for Brahmins, and the point was to "compare the Brahmins with pigs."[68]

News channels showed the muffled young pigs with the *poonal* being dragged violently through the streets, as a crowd of four to five hundred people jeered, shouted and kicked them.[69] In one piece of footage, a piglet tries frantically to resist, dropping on her knees, and the men drag her through the bitumen regardless. In the end, the police arrested nine men under the Indian Penal Code and the Prevention of Cruelty to Animals

Act 1960.[70] The pigs were brought to the Blue Cross of India animal rescue shelter, where three pigs refused food and died within days. The pigs had no external injuries; presumably shock and trauma led to cardiac arrest. "Pigs really internalize trauma, they know what is going on," manager Dawn William told me. "I think, more than any other animal I have seen, they find it very difficult to recover from shock. These pigs were kicked on the bum to make them move, dragged, and all that shouting, they just could not take it."[71]

In such charged political contexts, the silence of both human *and* animal rights activists in condemning the violence against the subaltern human *and* the subaltern animal becomes notable. This is not unique to India. Racism and speciesism have largely sidestepped each other as mutual concerns in political resistance, remaining separate and less than the sum of their alliance together.[72] Both human and animal advocacy lose the opportunity that comes with understanding that anthropocentrism—a form of oppression that privileges a particular racialized or gendered category of the human (e.g., white, Brahmin, male) above all other humans and excludes other animals—scaffolds violence against the marginalized human *and* the animal in different but connected ways. In her critique of the anthropocentrism that underpins the human rights imagination, Krithika Srinivasan argues: "In today's world, characterised by widespread awareness of the mutual vulnerability of human and nonhuman life . . . it is rendered urgent that the human rights imagination revisit its chauvinistic privileging of just one form of life",[73] that is, only *homo sapiens* life. Hitherto, human rights groups rightfully condemning the Hindutva violence to marginalized human groups have largely failed to reject—or even recognize—the multiple and extreme forms of violence against vulnerable animals in such acts.

By the same token, much animal rights activism in India has often neglected to denounce the ongoing subordination of marginalized human groups, particularly when the use of animals has been at the core of such violence. A major reason for this, as Dave writes, is that the "starting ground is so different" for human social justice movements and the animal rights movement, particularly when the animal movement is "so completely dismissed by other social movements."[74] The pervasive human investment in animal exploitation, the implicit assumption of the human–animal binary in human society and politics, and the unquestioned human supremacy to justify differential ethics for the treatment of animals make it difficult, sometimes impossible, for an animal movement to gain ground. Additionally, the animal movement is constantly confronted, Dave argues, by the "problem of emergency . . . there is so much going on all the time for an animal activist. There is always an emergency. You walk down the street and there are ten things that you could put your attention on, and that make a demand on you."[75] Even compared to human rights activists, animal rights activists can often become particularly depleted in time, resources, and the emotional capacity to engage in intellectual reflection and form strategic intersectional alliances with human rights movements, particularly against the constant dismissal their politics and advocacy, and most importantly, the animals themselves.

Nonetheless, such political affiliation is vital to ensure that Indian human rights *and* animal advocacy distance themselves from right-wing nationalism, that is, as part of the *#notinmyname* movement where concerned Indian citizens wish to separate themselves from objectionable Hindutva activities. When animals are weaponized in communal and caste violence, particularly toward a community that has struggled and fought for centuries to be simply recognized as *also* human and as equal to all humans, it becomes urgent for an animal movement to explicitly extend solidarity to these groups. Mohith, a PhD student active in student politics in Osmania, asked me,

> All the people engaging seriously about animals—how can I understand this? When I am suffering humiliation regarding my food, my clothes, all of my attitudes and practices? That is my first priority, before environmental or animal rights. They never speak for Dalit or Adivasi rights.

In being blinkered or inconsistent in its messaging, particularly in Hindutva-ruled India, animal rights activism risks being seen as one with Hindutva forces, rather than building genuine interspecific alliances with marginalized human groups as a key form of anti-caste *and* anti-anthropocentric resistance. This can negate the immense potential of Dalit animal activism, ironically rendering a Dalit animal politics "inaudible."[76] The Dalit protest march against the Una lynchings led to one of the most evocative demonstrations of some of the real vulnerabilities of India's bovines, elided in Hindutva cow protection rhetoric. As a visually significant part of this march, the Dalit protestors mounted creative challenges to highlight cow death and suffering for which *"upper-caste," upper-class citizens*, as milk consumers, *are also responsible.* The Dalits in Surendranagar, Gujarat, constructed a huge steel cow, eight feet high by seven feet wide. They filled its four stomach compartments with 182 kilograms of plastic, biological, and other toxic waste that the Dalits had collected from the stomachs of dead cows, abandoned on the streets by dairy farmers. As tanners working on cow carcasses, Dalits witness firsthand the evidence of hunger and desperation of these starving sacred "milk" animals. They handed over the steel cow to the district collector and politely sought his advice as to who might be held responsible for the suffering and death of these cows.[77]

The steel cow protest represented a critical opportunity to develop thick, sustained cross-alliances between the Dalit and animal rights movements. Tanning labor is laden with risks to health, reinforces the social abjections of untouchability, and as the Una lynching incident highlighted, is profuse with the peril of inviting Hindutva violence. The dismembering of the bovine reveals in visceral detail the multiple sufferings of the bovine beyond just her slaughter—the destitution of cows who are exploited and then abandoned, their raging starvation that drives them to eat plastic and other lethal waste causing fatal obstructions in their four-chambered stomachs and escalating their suffering manifold—none of which is addressed by Hindutva's cow protectionism. This Dalit–animal alliance illuminates the manifold sufferings and vulnerabilities of both subaltern humans and bovines, and is a critical counter to animal agriculture's single-issue animal welfare campaign strategy that is readily co-opted by Hindutva's one-dimensional account of cow protectionism.

Distinct from animal rights politics that focus on the liberation of the animal from *all* human exploitation, animal welfare is an animal agriculture public relations strategy that is enthusiastically taken up by farms and slaughterhouses to "reassure" the consuming public that violence to the slaughtered and diced individuals in plastic packaging was humanely reduced, or even eliminated. To promote an image of these industries being conscientiously responsive in promoting animal welfare, the animal industry instrumentalizes *single-issue campaigning*—a tactical focus which in India has contributed to the profoundly violent impact on those working at the slaughter-end of the dairy sector.

Cow killing bans in India (which imply that buffaloes, pigs, sheep, chickens, ducks, fish, goat, sheep, and other farmed animals are not worthy candidates of slaughter prohibitions) can be regarded as single-issue campaigning. Single-issue animal welfare campaigns selectively focus the gaze on *one*, often highly cosmetic, aspect of animal abuse[78] in farming and production, which can ostensibly be addressed *in isolation*. Animal welfare focuses only on "exceptionally horrendous acts of exploitation,"[79] posing no challenge to the objectification of animals and the violence inherent therein. Examples include the anti-fur movement (disregarding leather production as equally cruel), or the campaign against battery-cage eggs, or the advocacy for a slight increase in the size of the cages (implying that eggs from slightly larger cages or "free-range" hens are ethical, even though identical issues of cruelty persist, including metabolic starvation of hyper-laying hen breeds, the suffering encoded in their genetics through their selective breeding to hyper-ovulate for egg production,[80] and their sexual, gendered, and reproductive abuse[81]), or the protest against veal crates (that ignores that newborn males used for veal still experience the trauma of mother–child separation, and suffer the cruelty of continuous confinement, albeit now in slightly larger crates[82], and will soon be slaughtered).

The misleading single-issue focus of animal welfare campaigns allows a selective curation of violence *as violence*. It obscures numerous other forms of violence in animal farming to proceed unhindered, rather than acknowledging the *many* severe sufferings that might morally require the cessation of animal agriculture altogether. Animal welfare campaigns can also rely on implicit or explicit racist, casteist, or sectarian discourses, which imply that majoritarian groups are humane to animals, while racialized minorities are not.[83] Animal welfarism is born out of political affiliations and personal investment in consuming animal bodies.

In distilling the idea of cow protection to *one* issue—removal of (only) cow slaughter, implicitly by Muslims and Dalits—"cow politics" is embedded in manifestly humanist power struggles (rather than even weak forms of animal welfare advocacy). It is precisely the muddying of the interlinked human–animal oppressions that enables Hindutva conceptualizations of danger and risk, whereby ideas of "security mask violence in the name of counter-violence, killing in the name of protection."[84] The Hindutva construction of "the Hindu" relies on othering Muslims, and "draws its legitimacy from the representation of 'the Muslim' as a danger to the Hindu body and in turn legitimizes the use of 'any means' to protect and take revenge."[85] The Hindu body, as we have seen, is not only human but also bovine.

The far-right worldwide has been known to both selectively reject or deny, as well as champion environmentalism as per their agenda, by using single-issue animal welfare campaigns from the animal agricultural sector.[86] As the value of Indian bovine industries continues to rise in the global market, problematic far-right political ideologies begin to intersect with equally problematic global environmental concerns. In 2016, vegan Hollywood actor Leonardo di Caprio launched a campaign against the beef industry for contributing to climate change. In the same year, di Caprio, along with Sir Richard Branson, founder of Virgin group and also a vegan, and the nature documentarian David Attenborough, spoke at a high-profile international anti-beef rally in London.[87] The highest echelons of the RSS flew to London to demonstrate allegiance with di Caprio. While the vegan actor was motivated by environmental concerns, the Hindu nationalist RSS party's motivations are sectarianism. Although di Caprio has demonstrated concern for farmed animals and the environmental impact of animal agriculture more broadly, the singular focus on beef at this particular event, presumably centered as a way to attract the support of mainstream meat-eaters who would be unwilling to consider giving up all animal products, unintentionally fueled India's right-wing nationalist agenda.

Despite the powerful possibilities of intersectional alliances, animal rights and human rights politics have largely remained discrete. Reflecting on the entanglements of race and species, Boisseron writes: "[they]

may mutually—or alternately—elide each other, they can empower each other as well by turning this intersectional bond into defiance."[88] Sudesh, the Dalit student at Osmania, says of the animal advocacy movement in India:

> They should also try to communicate with the sufferers of Hindutva. If they are ready to align with the Dalits and Adivasis, they can go fast to achieve their objectives. Otherwise, it will not be possible to achieve their objectives. Green parties have to cooperate with farmers, Dalits, to sustain the Earth as a living space.

In the overall absence thus far of genuine engagements between animal movements, environmental protection groups, and marginalized caste groups in India, beef continues to be decisive as a weapon of resistance.[89] A student at Osmania told me, "Beef is not important for us—it is not important. It has become important. You have made it important, now it has become the most important thing for us. Left alone, beef was no different from chicken or mutton for us." Indeed, beef is so important as a potent Hindutva weapon that many states have made technological investments to penalize beef transporters, thus ostensibly providing "scientific proof" that cow slaughter is a racialized, malevolent act of Muslims and Dalits, rather than a natural stage of dairying.

HINDUTVA FUTURES: BEEFING WITH SCIENTIFIC TECHNOLOGY

Corporation-style statism and technological proficiency are markers of fascism;[90] as chief minister of Gujarat, Modi turned it into "a corporate managerial state with zero degree tolerance for workers' rights and the rights of minorities (especially Muslims) and other marginalised people."[91] Despite a track record of communal violence (and his government also spending less than other states on education and healthcare), Modi won state elections in Gujarat three times through carefully engineering social polarization, and granting enough benefits to the aspirational "neo-middle class" to keep their votes coming.[92] Among these "benefits" was the creation of establishments that seemed scientifically progressive and development-oriented, of great appeal to the middle classes. These institutions would play a key role in helping to solidify a Hindutva state once Modi became the prime minister of India.

One such institution is the National Forensic Sciences University (NFSU, formerly the Gujarat Forensic Sciences University, founded in 2009) in the state capital Gandhinagar, "which aims to create an *army* of Indian forensic science students [emphasis added]" to create intelligence specialists to track and uncover cybercrime, and cyber warfare, and generate expertise in forensic pharmacy, forensic physiology and civil engineering.[93] The aims and mission of the university include a mandate "to carry out Research in the area of Forensic Science, Crime Investigation, Security, Behavioral Science and Criminology."[94] As Jasanoff writes, "the design of technology is . . . seldom accidental; it reflects the imaginative faculties, cultural preferences and economic or political resources of their makers and users."[95]

In less than a decade, this technology was to play a central role in facilitating the lynching of Muslim and Dalit transporters and butchers working at the final stages of dairy production. "Beef anti-nationalism" was to become "scientifically provable" through science, technology, and administrative efficiency when the Gujarat Forensic University started to produce beef-testing kits. The university collaborates with the Gujarat State Directorate of Forensic Science (DFS) "to provide hands-on training" to students; the Directorate, a criminal investigative science laboratory located next to the University campus, even has a "cow-meat testing mobile lab."[96]

Increasingly, mobile forensic testing kits for detecting cow beef in restaurants, vehicles, and even people's homes, are being rolled out by several state governments. In 2017, Amar Immunodiagnostics Private Limited, the laboratory of the Hyderabad-based forensic scientist Jayant Bhanushali, introduced a cow beef detection kit. The kit involves an enzyme-linked immunosorbent assay (ELISA) test, which is used commonly to test for pathogens in foods, to now determine if the flesh seized belongs to a cow or water buffalo.[97]

Soon after, in 2017, Maharashtra provided their state police with mobile beef detection kits to ostensibly manage law and order, and provide evidence for "judicial scrutiny" when cow vigilantes halt trucks and other vehicles suspected of carrying beef.[98] In Jharkhand state, forensic testing was used to confirm that murder victim Alimuddin Ansari (who in turn had a criminal record for killing a child) had stored cow beef in his car.[99] Many states, including Madhya Pradesh and Uttar Pradesh, have stated their intention to buy ELISA beef detection kits.[100] In Haryana, the Gauvansh Sanrakshan and Gausamvardhan Act 2015, which authorizes the police to halt and search vehicles and premises for cows or beef, is facilitated by the growing use of beef detection technologies.

Hindu vigilantes can call on these forensic lab-vehicles anytime they stop a truck or a car filled with beef. At a time when even the *suspicion* of Muslims or Dalits selling beef is enough to provoke extreme violence against them, this public evidence that the meat might conclusively be cow beef is certain to continue and escalate the lynching, rape, and murder of members of Dalit and Muslim communities.

These zones of protection are being formalized at an unprecedented level in the new era of emboldened Hindutva. After the establishment of Modi's government at the center in 2014, the BJP-led Rajasthan state government established the country's first Ministry for Cow Protection in 2015, and intriguingly, Otaram Davasi, who became the first Minister for Cow Protection, was also given the additional portfolio for the Ministry of "Dairy and Devasthan [temples]."[101] In 2020, the BJP-governed state of Madhya Pradesh established a "cow cabinet" bringing together six departments, including animal husbandry, to work on bovine breeding, welfare, and conservation.[102] The Home Minister said, "BJP is the guardian of Indian culture. It believes there are three means of contentment—Gita, Ganga and Gaumata. That inspired the decision to form a 'gau cabinet.'"[103]

When I visited Rajasthan's Ministry for Cow Protection in 2016, it was barely functioning. The *Gau-Palan Mantri* (Cow Protection Minister) was touring, and unavailable for an interview. A state member was seated in the government office, and refused to provide comment, or offer any literature on cow protection—for they had none. He admitted that the Ministry had no staff. In August 2016, government-run Hingonia Gaushala had, in fact, come under fire when it was revealed that more than 8,000 cows had been starved to death since January of that year.[104]

In 2019, Rajasthan's Chief Minister Ashok Gehlot reported that some 74,016 cows had died during the preceding BJP rule in Hingonia.[105] Such apathy, neglect and cruelty underscore the point that remains resolutely unacknowledged in Indian politics—that there is no way to rehabilitate *all* cows from the dairy sector. If they are not slaughtered, they are often starved, including in Hindu spaces of bovine care, or as we have already seen, sold in the underground slaughter market.

Once sold as an ex-dairy resource, whether by commercial or informal dairies, or gaushalas, the "rescue" of cows during transportation at the slaughter-end of dairy production has been, the most publicly visible, violent, and debated aspect of India's cow protection politics. This transport network, operating in the black market or illegal end of the dairy production continuum in India, comprises racially and caste-wise some of the most socially and politically vulnerable and marginalized citizens. An ancient asymmetry of power and powerlessness serves the transport of modern Indian dairying, through caste, religion, and class that relies on Dalit and Muslim labor for the movement of unproductive "dairy" cows, buffaloes, bulls, and calves to their slaughter. Overwhelmingly in popular and political reporting of cow vigilantism, the *animals themselves* continue to remain invisible, as indeed, throughout the dairy production continuum. How do individual cows, calves, buffaloes, and bulls fare during slaughter transportation, and subsequent rescue (albeit, in a minuscule number of cases)?

CHAPTER 6

TRAFFICKING

"EVERYBODY IS IN THIS business, everybody! Everybody uses the cow how they want; you think anyone cares what happens to the cow, *arre*, nobody cares! Hindu, Muslim, everybody is in the game. I hold Hindus most responsible, they are the ones to sell the cow when she stops giving milk, and then enter politics using *goraksha* [cow protection] as an excuse. Then they will make a big noise about *gaumata* [cow mother]. Muslims, what can I say, not a shred of mercy, when you see the animals in the trucks you will not be able to stop weeping. If they have to break legs and bones to fit an animal into a car, they will do it. Cow is just a *jugaad* [a means or a hack] for everyone to get what they want. *Gai ka hi sab jugaad kar dete hein!* [They make *jugaad* out of the cow itself!]"[1]

PROTECTED "DAIRY COW" TO CONTRABAND "BEEF COW"
Tens of thousands of trucks speed the length and breadth of India's national highways each night, crossing state boundaries, winding their way around circuitous back alleys, rural *kachha* roads, past police checkpoints, and through zealously guarded villages that comprise entire sprawling slaughtering regions. They are joined by a legion of other vehicles—large containers, oil tankers, Ashok Leyland lorries, milk trucks, Tata Sumos, tourist buses with darkened windows and hollowed

out without seats, and even 4WDs, auto-rickshaws, and small private cars. All too frequently, two-wheelers like motorbikes join this large battalion, melting more easily into the dark as they race to their undisclosed destinations.

These vehicles carry some of India's most contraband "goods" for trade and commerce—live cows, bulls, buffaloes, and their calves, discarded as waste by the dairy industry—moving them further down the milk production line to slaughterhouses. Sixty, eighty, or even one-hundred-and-fifty animals can be found jammed together in vehicles authorized to carry no more than seven bovines, and most not permitted to carry them at all. Packed tight, occupying every viable inch of space, it is impossible to identify which head and tail belongs to which animal. These dark, airless, hot vehicles contain a large morass of bleeding, dying, suffering animals, whose legs and horns are frequently broken to load them in such a way that packing efficiency is maximized.

These concealed cows, bulls, buffaloes, and their calves are taken to the hundreds of thousands of illegal slaughterhouses throughout rural and urban India, and to the states of Kerala and West Bengal, where there is no prohibition on cow slaughter. In a spirit of cooperative regional relations, the breeding-to-slaughter line of India's milk production is sustained across the national border where the Islamic republic of Bangladesh receives these "dairy waste animals" from milk-loving Hindu-majority India. It is estimated that some 20 million individual ex-dairy cows and bulls are transported annually to Bengal and an additional 15 million cows to Bangladesh,[2] packed into large boats to be taken down the Ichamati River, or even thrown across the international border using cranes and forklifts.[3] While India cannot send slaughter-cows to Nepal, a Hindu-majoritarian republic also bound by cow slaughter prohibitions, it annually sends across thousands of male buffalo calves to be butchered. The Gadhimai festival in Nepal, among the world's largest religious sacrifices of animals, predominantly kills infant buffalo-bulls discarded by Indian dairying.[4] India's "thriving international trade in beef and leather means the continued legacy of starvation, thirst, beatings, broken bones and cruel slaughter for the hundreds of thousands of cattle"[5] sourced from the *dairy* sector.

Live transportation of the animals "as raw materials and labor"[6] from one production site to another is one of the most critical segments of any type of animal farming, including dairying. Without the benefit of transportation constantly moving the animal body through each phase of the production continuum—from breeding farms, to semen centers, to different types of dairy farms, eventually to the slaughterhouses—her fullest economic value will remain untapped. In *Animals and Capital*, Dinesh Wadiwel writes, "The function of transport is fundamentally to realise value; it is the process of transference between one phase of a value chain and another that allows for the realisation of this new use value. . . . Transport thus serves a purpose in transferring and realising value."[7]

States have differential legislation and protections for the bovines. Chhattisgarh, for instance, prohibits the slaughter of all "agricultural cattle" (the entire cow and buffalo family) as well as their transport outside the state.[8] Maharashtra bans the slaughter of any member of the cow/bull family, but conditionally allows buffalo slaughter if certified by a veterinarian.[9] Andhra Pradesh,[10] Gujarat,[11] Karnataka,[12] and Madhya Pradesh[13] ban the slaughter of buffalo calves. Oftentimes these trucks carry smuggled camels, who find themselves, as BJP-governed Rajasthan's "state animal," both protected from slaughter *and* a dairy resource, and therefore increasingly in a similar position to the cow, where camel slaughter is also taken underground.[14] To circumvent the various state laws regulating their transport and slaughter, all these animals are moved in intensely overpacked conditions, though it is the cow who is the persistent landscape of violent identity politics.

In this complex space of cow rescues, both animal activists and cow vigilantes operate, leading sometimes to an acutely problematic and confusing perception of Indian animal activism as right-wing activity. The intricate interlocking together of human and nonhuman animal oppression through cow protectionism has barely begun to be analyzed and addressed as part of human or animal rights discourses. Cow protectionism does offer animal activists a tangible legal hook upon which to criminalize cruelties such as slaughter, which are not covered by the Prevention of Cruelty to Animals Act 1960. It has become commonplace, therefore, for the broader Indian animal advocacy movement to focus on cow protection, as that yields the maximum result of actually being able to remove a farmed animal from spaces of extreme violence.

"There are so few victories for the animals, why shouldn't we take what little is available for them?" I was asked by many frustrated animal activists—frustrated because they saw their unintended complicity in furthering casteism and communalism by using the very tools intended to further them, and indeed, speciesism. Frustrated because they saw themselves—rightly—as caught between a rock and a hard place, when on a daily basis, on the ground, they had to make quick decisions about rescues when confronted with a suffering animal. If the animal in question was a cow, there *were* legal avenues, however problematic, available for their rescue and rehabilitation in most states. It is not only rescues; within the enduring legacy of the special status given to the cow in the Constitution, radical policy and legislative changes can be introduced, despite problems and fierce resistance, in the interests of the cow over other animals. There is sympathy for cow protectionism among a cow-worshipping populace more broadly in India, in stark contrast to mainstream society globally, where such legislative protection for cows is unthinkable. It is an excruciatingly fine moral tightrope for an Indian animal activist to tread.

The gaurakshaks are also a complex group. At least a few of the gaurakshaks I spoke to genuinely loved animals. Some were to show me a number of other species they rescued—buffaloes, donkeys, pigeons, kittens, dogs, snakes—without an agenda to project themselves as secularists. I learned of their rescue work with other species when I met them directly, not via social media posts. Typical of the dangerous confusion and hate politics propelled by animal welfarism—the highly selective focus on *some* forms of violence to *some* animals, followed by the racialization of that violence—many of these rescuers found themselves echoing the shrill and overpowering racist and casteist animal welfare narratives of Hindutva vigilantism, at least when it came to cows.

Over time, I started to notice a pattern emerging in my interviews with this cohort of "protectionists," which became my yardstick to distinguish the cow vigilantes from the animal activists who composed the broader animal justice movement. The mention (or not) of Gaumata (or occasionally Nandi, the mythological bull used by vigilantes to reference native bulls), to explain any motivation or practice became a vital conceptual distinction. The cow as "Mother" was a different beast—and indeed, not even a beast at all—to the cow as an *animal*. Even as animal activists did routinely instrumentalize the special protections for the cow, it was for the cow as an *animal*, in contrast to the cow as a Hindu state. This has often been less than beneficial for the Indian animal advocacy movement though it has benefited individual cows rescued from sites of violence, also a vital moral consideration for an animal activist operating directly on the ground.

If dairying is to be maintained in India, then cow slaughter must be done by stealth, so that government institutions can remain formally "distant" from it. The state thus finds itself in a position of concealing or selectively visibilizing, but not eradicating, the gray activities and spaces of the informal/illegal cow slaughter economy. Formality/informality and legality/illegality do not function as binaries; they work *together* in informal economies as a "continuum."[15] Informal economies are neither legal/white, nor illegal/black, and mostly refer to "gray" activities that have not been formalized or regulated.[16] Urban geographer Oren Yiftachel defines gray spaces as follows:

> developments, enclaves, populations, and transactions positioned between the "lightness" of legality/approval/safety, and the "darkness" of eviction/destruction/death. Gray spaces are neither integrated nor eliminated, forming pseudo-permanent margins of today's urban regions, *which exist partially outside the gaze of state authorities* . . . [emphasis added][17]

These gray activities can involve innovation[18] and criminality.[19] This lack of clarity is important as the transportation of cows per se is not illegal, though the purpose of this movement might be unclear. As economist Arun Kumar writes: "Black income generation requires committing an illegality in a legal activity."[20] Where animals cannot be legally transported from dairies to slaughterhouses, the gray structures of informality—unauthorized transportation, transactions, space use, and infrastructure, involving millions of very small-scale units of labor—interconnect the two spheres. In his analysis of employment in India, Breman explains that the informal economy is characterized by "the minute scale of the work unit, often no more than a single household or even a sole individual."[21] Together, they constitute an informal industrial economy of animal slaughter in the Global South. In India, the gray governance of the secular state is crucial to enable cow slaughter, *and* to reassure the Hindu public and the Hindu Right that it is actively "doing something" to address cow slaughter.

Sonu, a gaurakshak from a village on the Delhi-Haryana border, described the innovations of the informal economy of cow slaughter—the argumentation, agreements, political complicity, and material innovations to conceal cows during their transportation to abattoirs—as *jugaad*. *Jugaad* is a uniquely Indian sociological conception of inventiveness and corruption that helps facilitate activities that may be stymied, slowed, or prohibited by the law. In order to operate a dairying continuum that is celebrated as a national triumph and religious sentiment at the breeding stage, and criminalized as offending these very sentiments at the slaughter stage, creative contracts of *jugaad* are maintained between state institutions, transport networks and slaughterhouses, and diverse racialized, religious, and casteized workers. These contracts maintain "key aspects of a social equilibrium, including beliefs and actions of citizens, organized groups, and state actors,"[22] in this case, sustaining the mythology of a dairy-consuming but non-cow-slaughtering Hindu-majority state.

Violence is certainly not characteristic of all *jugaad*; however, it plays a central role in the *jugaad* of the cow transport economy. Akin to the division of tasks between workers in an industrial slaughterhouse,[23] the large informal industrial complex of India's cow slaughter economy works according to "specializations." Specific productionists (handlers, transporters, butchers) perform particular activities. To keep the conveyor belt of tasks, so to speak, moving from one productionist to another, from one production space to another, physical violence against the animals becomes a necessary and mundane feature of transport throughout the dairy continuum. Together, the activities and contracts facilitate an efficient countrywide network through which ex-dairy animals are moved to slaughter destinations, achieving the crowning *jugaad* of transforming the protected dairy cow into a contraband beef cow.

CROSSING STATE AND NATIONAL BORDERS
It is during transportation that the "white" cow of the dairy economy is first blurred into "gray" as she is transitioned into the "black" end of the production line to become a beef cow. Once a cow or buffalo is sold as an *ex-dairy resource* by the milk farmer and enters the market as a *slaughter resource*, it is rarely the case that they will go through only one transaction in one market.

The bovines are forced to enter and exit a number of markets across three to four state borders, with ostensibly no clear purpose of sale, until their point of origin and destination become untraceable. Middlemen in "cattle markets" facilitate a sophisticated countrywide network of sale and resale of cows from farmer to farmer, state to state, until they can be sold to butchers and slaughterhouses. The slaughter trucks travel within every state, as well as across state boundaries, to unlicensed abattoirs in all metropolitan, urban, regional, and peri-urban areas.

Thousands of bovines, but particularly the cows, might travel the length of one state in a vehicle registered in that state to endure "the death march," as animal activists call it, and cross state borders on foot, to be reloaded into a vehicle registered in the next state. The movement of these animals on foot to their deaths is facilitated by the fact that walking the animals as a means of transport is not illegal.[24] In the northern "cow belt" states of Bihar, Haryana, and Uttar Pradesh, and the eastern state of Orissa, cows walk across hundreds of kilometers to the slaughterhouses of West Bengal, or across the border on foot or boats into Bangladesh. They are almost never fed or watered until they reach the abattoir. Jayasimha Nuggehalli, a leading animal law expert and the director of Humane Society International, India, at the time of our interview in 2017, explained the rationale behind alternating the movement of animals on foot and on trucks:

> [The] Motor Vehicles is a state Act, and we don't want to cross state borders. In Tamil Nadu, you see an Odiya registered truck, the chance of the

police stopping you is much higher. So what they do is that they bring to the border, unload these animals, make them walk across [the state border], the death march, and then they bring them on to another state and load them on again on a vehicle registered to that particular state.

In 2017, I accompanied Rajendran, an activist, to the beautiful hilly tribal area of Araku on the border of Andhra and Odisha states. Araku is a major conduit for the transfer of cows from Odisha into the slaughterhouses of Andhra and Telengana states, or onwards into West Bengal and Bangladesh. A local farmer who had adopted some "temple calves" from VSPCA joined us. The man, who I will call Ramulu, was of the Madiga caste. Ramulu owned some land on which he had eight Jersey calves rehabilitated from Simhachalam. Ramulu looked at me, hesitated, and spoke to Rajendran in Telugu. He requested that I not take any photographs if there were other villagers around. He would let me know if it was safe in a desolate area. The farmer served as an informer to the police and to activists on trafficking activities, and he could not afford to raise the suspicions of the villagers for his own safety. I immediately agreed and he got into the car with us.

Through Rajendran, I asked him about his motivation to adopt the Jersey bulls when the animals, unproductive for milking and traction, might be a financial burden. "I live here," he said. "After a while, you will go mad if you don't do something." I asked if he received a "salary" from the police.

"No," he said. "Sometimes. But there is no support. I only do it because if someone can help, then okay."

We started moving toward Odisha state; we were less than forty kilometers from the border. We could expect to see animals on their "death march" any time now, he said.

About ten minutes into the ride, a pair of large gray *desi* bulls, suddenly emerged round a corner, and almost ran straight into our car. The right hind and front legs of one bull were tied tightly to the left hind and front legs of the other in the manner of an obstacle race. They didn't hit our car; as one, the two tied bulls raced straight past our vehicle. All of us in the car—the activist, the researcher, the local villager, and the driver—were shocked into total silence; the pair ran past without pause and disappeared around the winding roads of the hills. No one needed to tell us; we knew the runaway bulls were already fleeing their slaughter, thousands of kilometers from the slaughterhouse.

The driver started the car again. Within minutes, we saw two handlers running in fury after the bulls with big sticks. I felt sickened at the severity of the beatings the bovines would surely get when they were caught. They would likely be starved for the remainder of the journey to keep them compliant.

Almost immediately after, we found ourselves suddenly surrounded by a large herd of cows and their handlers, from whom the two bulls had clearly broken away. The cows walked row upon row, column on column, all tied tightly together by their legs. As I watched, one transporter raised a big heavy stick, and for no apparent reason, smashed it right on the head of a beautiful, long-lashed, native breed female cow in the middle of the herd. She ducked her head in terror as she tried to walk even more rapidly, stumbling and bumping against her neighbors. As the men continued to hit the rumps and heads of the animals, I nearly cried out in fear myself. I clamped my mouth shut. I could not put the locals accompanying us at risk.

After we drove for a bit longer, we veered off down an unpaved path. Large open fields lay on either side; the farmer pointed to a small forested area at a distance where we could see about five or six cows and bulls grazing on the dry grass. A young man was spraying their rumps with pink or blue paint, to indicate ownership or their intended destination. These animals would soon be joined by others at this collection point, as they were brought by incoming trucks from markets in various states. Once sold by their dairy farmers, the only humans with whom they were familiar, they would constantly encounter strangers, humans, and other animals, throughout the transport–collection–market continuum across different markets and states. Facing repeated transportation, exhaustion, starvation, thirst, and the ever-present threat of beatings, these cows and buffaloes have no stable sense of a family herd, an inordinately stressful phenomenon for these social animals.[25]

This collection area would soon be thickly populated with cows, bulls, buffaloes, and calves of every size, to be loaded into slaughter trucks. It is pertinent to pause and grasp the *jugaad* of packing some fifty or even a hundred bovines, depending on the size of the vehicle, to ensure that the maximum number of animals can fit. Sonu described the cows he rescued from the trucks as tied tight like a round pancake, with their hind legs pulled right up to their heads and wrapped around the neck and then, bound together with the forelegs. He explained that the animals are packed so closely that the floor space between the animals is impossible to see. Many might be dead by the time of arrival, and would enter the supply chain regardless.[26] Amit Chaudhery of People for Animals Gurgaon, describes the loading and packing of animals in markets:

> These trucks are packed tighter than sardine cans. One atop the other, legs broken and tied, groaning from internal and external injuries sustained in loading them. Now that trucks are a giveaway, the traffickers use dumpers and containers. The suffocation, heat and darkness multiply in the new mode of transport. It takes days, weeks really, for the cows to reach from point A to point B. Upon reaching destination, they languish for up to three days in the carriers before the live meat tumbles out (mostly dead or dying) from the vehicles. . . . I have commonly found male calves with legs precisely broken at the joints (they cannot be mended) and rendered immobile so that in the wee hours butchers can lift them into cattle trucks.[27]

I gazed at these animals, so far down death row, and yet so far away from death itself, which could not come soon enough for what they were yet to endure. We got back into the car and started winding slowly down the main road again. A short while later, Ramulu signaled to the driver to stop at a narrow curve near a slightly elevated part of the hill. As we got down, I could see that beyond the view of the road, the elevation sunk down into about a quarter acre of empty muddy space.

"What do you see here?" asked the farmer.

I looked around the fields and hills and greenery and shook my head. Ramulu pointed to the ground; I still couldn't see. He emphatically pointed again. I finally saw two heavy iron rings on either side of the space, joined together with a thick long rope. This was a collection point where cows would be secured along the length of this rope on short leashes, until it was time for them to be loaded into trucks. Some of these trucks might be stopped by vigilantes or activists; almost all the trucks and their load would proceed to slaughterhouses.

Activists and vigilantes had already told me that there are many ways to know when a vehicle is carrying contraband cows. A common way is simply observation. Typically, trucks carrying bovines are lighter than vehicles carrying other heavy goods, and accompanied by a strong smell of dung and urine. Activists or vigilantes would wait at highway checkpoints where vehicles are required to pay toll fees. If suspected of carrying cows, they place themselves in front of the trucks, have them park to the side, and search the vehicles. If a truck contained cows or even buffaloes in overpacked conditions, it would be seized and the animals sent to a gaushala or animal shelter. A first information report may be filed with the police and eventually passed to the courts. In more extreme and violent scenarios, especially in the north and if involving vigilantes, lynching or even killing of those transporting cows may occur.

As a consequence of the heightened vigilantism of Hindu gaurakshaks, and animal activists, the loading and unloading of cows increasingly occurs in concealed "black" spatial zones, away from the "gray" spaces of the animal market. A transporter in a live "cattle" market outside Chennai gave me the number of his "uncle," a polite man whom I will call Deva. Deva belonged to the Vanniyar caste, a sub-section of the scheduled castes (or the former "untouchables"), which was distinct, he emphasized, from the even "lower" Malaivalmakkal or "mountain" castes of Tamil Nadu, who worked as pig butchers. Two of Deva's trucks filled with cows had been seized by animal activists the previous year, and he had now taken the trade entirely underground. Like thousands of other cow transporters, Deva was refining the logistics of the underground slaughter trade—hidden markets and holding places, covert relationships with state institutions including the police, and creative modes of transport.

Deva agreed to meet me in Dindigul, near the industrial city of Coimbatore, Tamil Nadu state's second largest city. Dindigul, located on the Tamil Nadu side of the state border with Kerala, was the last halt for loading and unloading the animals in Tamil Nadu before the trucks crossed into Kerala, one of the final destinations for most ex-dairy bovines from all over India. We met at a *chai* shop that he suggested. Thereafter, Deva got on his motorbike, and asked my driver to follow him through agricultural land. Through a thicket of trees, we came to an open space where cows and buffaloes were tied in two rows. Several trucks were parked to one side, and small groups of transporters and handlers smoked or chatted around the area.

"What you see here, we didn't have this place before. We didn't need it," he told me. "But now we cannot think of doing the trade openly." They would cross the border early the next morning.

Deva started our conversation talking about the recent capture of his trucks, he claimed, by an activist group called People for Cattle India (PCI), causing him financial loss. In a political environment that was increasingly supportive of cow protection, the number of animal activist organizations dedicated specifically to bovines had started to mushroom in order to achieve the tangible returns of rescuing cows. Coopting this strategy for animal liberation had the unfortunate consequence of seeming too closely aligned with, even indistinguishable from, Hindutva cow vigilantism.

It is difficult to quantify the financial burden that the oppressed castes pay to sustain the slaughter segment of the dairy supply chain. Deva had paid anything between Rs 7,000 and 15,000 (US$ 100–200) per bovine, who he would then sell to the slaughterhouse at a small previously agreed profit. Losing fifty cows or bulls per truck—and usually far more would be crammed into the interiors—could mean a loss of some US$ 10,000 from the animals alone. This loss does not include the cost of the truck, fuel, labor, and bail or bribes to reverse the arrest of his labor force, and the bribes he had paid at every police checkpoint up to the point at which he had been halted. It would be impossible to recoup these losses. Deva told me, "I have to pay for petrol, these men, these animals, and then bribe in every check post. This is my job. If I don't fill the truck, none of us will be making any money."

Deva himself turned the conversation to the conditions of overloading that had featured in news reports, along with photos of the suffering animals. Both activists and vigilantes put up photos of animal cruelty during transport or slaughter on social media, but often with different agendas. The photos of the overpacked and severely injured or dead animals can truly defy belief. However, most activists try to highlight the inevitable movement of animals used for dairying to the abattoir when they are no longer productive, and draw attention to the cruelties inherent in such transportation to the bovines and humans. Arun Prasanna, the founder of PCI, had recently become vegan when I met him in 2014, shortly after he started to halt trucks. Pradeep Nath and Dawn William had become vegan more than two decades ago, even before the concept was understood or known as commonly as it is these days. Dawn told me he often worried about the risk of severe back injuries that the transporters, who had no medical insurance or avenues for treatment, took every day as they literally lifted large bovines to throw into trucks. But how did Deva himself perceive the photos? He reflected that he had been so immersed in this world for generations, that the sudden presence of activists highlighting these activities *as violence* abruptly disrupted this normalization:

> I agree what we did was not good. I have been doing this trade since I was sixteen years old. I am forty now. I have myself picked up and flung thousands of animals into trucks. Three or four of us will pick a cow or a bull [with their legs tied] from the ground and throw them inside. I have seen my uncles do it, my father do it, it is what we did. When they [activists] took photos and put it on Facebook and the newspaper, I literally covered my face in shame like this [he pulled a towel over his head as he spoke]. They made us "see" things differently. We don't tie so tight now, don't put so many animals in. And you can see how thickly we have laid the hay [pointing to the truck floors].

The "measures" that he described are an attempt to introduce a degree of "gray" through animal welfare efforts at the "black" end of the Indian dairy production continuum. However, he felt compelled to continue this precarious livelihood, as there was no alternative:

> I would really like to give up this trade, it is nothing but stress now but what can we do? We have no other skills, no education! You tell us what we

can do! We are becoming poorer every day. Today I will leave this if you can get me a job. But let me tell you, even then this trade will not stop. There are thousands and thousands of us in this, you cannot even count.

As Deva said, tens of thousands of workers continue to be involved in blurring the structures of the underground trade. In May 2017, in an attempt to ensure a simpler line of traceability of animals from farm to slaughterhouse, the Ministry of Environment issued the Prevention of Cruelty to Animals (Regulation of Livestock Markets) Rules 2017 (India), which prohibited the transport of bulls, cows, buffaloes, calves, and camels as slaughter resources to *markets*.[28] Of these regulations, Rule 2(b) was particularly controversial. It defined "a market or sale yard [where] animals are exposed to sale or auction," including animals fairs, pounds, and "lairage" where animals are kept prior to slaughter in abattoirs. Immediate outrage erupted against the Rules,[29] particularly in states not governed by the BJP, such as Kerala, Tamil Nadu, and West Bengal,[30] and forced the Ministry subsequently to withdraw the Rules altogether. A watered-down version was eventually reissued in 2018 that prohibited the sale only of unfit and young animals, removed the clause prohibiting sale of the animals for slaughter, and made no mention of interstate transportation of bovines, prohibiting only the crossing of international borders.[31]

These Rules were not, in fact, drafted by Hindutva parties, but by the Humane Society International, India, led by the managing director Jayasimha Nuggehalli with the petitioner Gauri Maulekhi of People for Animals Uttrakhand. People for Animals, which has shelters and branches throughout the country, problematically maintains an indirect association with the BJP, as then BJP Minister Mrs. Maneka Gandhi is its founder. However, both Nuggehalli and Maulekhi (and Maneka Gandhi) have been vegan for several years. The Rules provide yet another classic example of the danger of animal activists drawing on the meta-discourse of cow protectionism and also the tight corner into which Indian animal advocates are pushed in attempting to garner any respite for farmed animals. Nuggehalli told me, "We framed these Rules after having witnessed the cruelties at the markets for years and years;

we have hundreds of hours of footage from our activists documenting what happens."

The Rules were decried on the basis that the inclusion of buffaloes and camels was only to give a secular veneer to the real intended agenda—cow protection. However, Nuggehalli saw the opportunity differently—*to include as many other species as possible* in the cow protection wave. In India, as elsewhere, it is extremely difficult to bring policy or legislative changes for farmed animals. However, depending on the political climate, the plight of large animals like cows might provide an opportunity to bring forth policy change for comparable species. The climate of the BJP-led state, problematic as it was, presented such opportunities. It was worth the attempt.

The cruelties that Nuggehalli was motivated by can be unfathomable. At the end of brutal transport from markets to slaughterhouses, many animals are too severely injured to get up again. Most females might be "downer" animals, disabled by years of milking and pregnancies, as well the conditions of transportation. Once the bovines sit, it is almost impossible to get them to lift themselves. To force the animals to get off the trucks or walk to the kill floor, the transporters stuff their eyes with chilies, tobacco, lemon juice, and ginger (see figure 6.1 and figure 6.2).[32]

An activist showed me a video he took using a hidden camera.[33] A downer cow is beaten on every part of her body by the enraged handler, including her head and genitals to force her to get up. When it is clear that she simply cannot move, the man extricates a bag tucked into his *veshti* [loin-cloth] containing red chili powder, grabs a fistful, and pries open the exhausted cow's eyes to rub it in. The cow jerks violently and trembles, trying to stand, but collapses again immediately, in a fire of pain. Four men then grab her, and fling her onto the dirty, feces-smeared floor of the truck.

These activities had also been part of Deva's role in the dairy production chain, he explained. "Our job was to get an animal from here to there, whatever be the means. Beyond that, it was not our place to think about it."

However, as we walked through the rows of chained cows and buffaloes awaiting loading the next morning, Deva pointed out a few more

FIGURE 6.1: *An exhausted bull in Bagachra market in Bangladesh whose eyes are filled with chili powder to keep him moving or standing. Bangladesh is one of the largest slaughter sites for Indian cows, bulls and calves, due to the slaughter prohibitions in India.*

Source: Christian Faesecke, WeAnimals 2015.

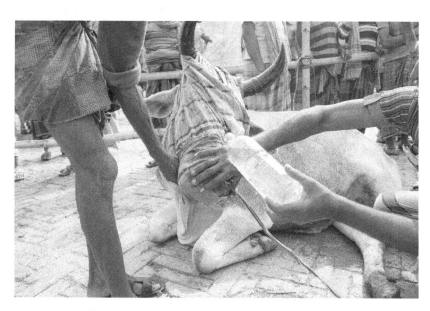

FIGURE 6.2: *Torturous methods to force downed bovines to rise up again include covering the cow's face with water to induce a fear of drowning or suffocating, forcing the terrified animal to get up. A cow from India at the Bagachra market in Bangladesh, downed after an exhausting journey and muzzled.*

Source: Christian Faesecke, WeAnimals 2015.

welfare changes he had incorporated once he had been forced to "see differently." They had small bales of hay in front of them. Previously, the transporter-middleman would not have seen it as his job to feed the animals who were headed to slaughter.

Later, as I thanked Deva and walked back to the car, I asked about the single white cow and her small calf who I had noticed tied on short ropes separate from the other animals, close to a makeshift room where the men slept and stored their belongings. Were they thinking of slaughtering her themselves?

Deva gave me a reply that caught me completely unawares.

Harking back to the platitude invoked to justify the breeding end of dairy production, Deva explained, "She is our *kula daivam* [household goddess]. She is not for slaughter, she is for worship. She is our *gaumata* [cow mother], she is blessing our livelihoods."

"PACKING" COWS IN MARKETS

I realized early on that I would myself have to visit *chandies* (live animal markets) to learn about the sale of the cows and, indeed, witness the animals. The first market that I visited was the Tuni *chandy*, conducted weekly on a Saturday outside of Visakhapatnam; this would be the first of many, across Tamil Nadu, Kerala, and Uttar Pradesh. Once I had confirmed plans to visit Tuni with Malathi, I spent the next two days in a state of acute anxiety, scarcely able to think beyond the horrors of animal abuse that I knew I would soon witness. I also worried about the risks to ourselves as visitors. *Chandies* almost solely comprise members of an extensive transporter–middleman–butcher network. The space was full of hundreds of men. Aside from ourselves, we saw only one woman that day, local to the village, who had come with her son to sell decorative collars and bells for the cows intended to be sold into dairying.

Tuni *chandy*, some 250 kilometers outside the city of Visakhapatnam, is one of the largest "cattle" markets in south India, selling cows and buffaloes for both dairying and slaughter. The bovines are brought from several states, including Andhra Pradesh, neighboring Odisha, Madhya

FIGURE 6.3: *Buffaloes being loaded onto a truck headed towards Kerala for slaughter in an Andhra Pradesh market—the truck will soon be completely filled. Note the buffalo in the far end whose tied head will be raised in this way throughout the interstate transport.*
Source: Photo taken by author.

Pradesh, and Karnataka states, for transport to slaughterhouses in the south in Tamil Nadu and Kerala, and east toward West Bengal and Bangladesh. Trucks and tempos loaded with animals swarmed the place; many animals were also walked on foot into the market. Thick iron rings were semi-buried into the ground throughout the space, where ten or twelve animals would be tied by their face, nose to the ground, allowing them no freedom of movement. They'd spend hours in that position as if in punishment, until each was sold and loaded onto an overpacked truck with other animals (see figure 6.3). Carts of chai, coconuts, and watermelon were dotted around the market, doing brisk sales as the blazing summer sun climbed higher in the Andhra sky. I had been told to expect informal slaughterhouses at the *chandy*, and I was entirely thankful that there weren't any that day. There was no water or hay for the animals, despite the blazing Andhra heat.

The *chandy* seemed to have far more buffaloes than cows, a phenomenon I witnessed across different state markets. I was to learn the reason much later on a visit to a market in Faizabad, near Ayodhya in Uttar Pradesh state, where a male veterinarian had accompanied me. The man explained that in the outer ring of markets, only cows and buffaloes being recirculated as dairy capital and buffaloes intended for slaughter were sold. *Slaughter cows* would be sold in the innermost rings of the market. He flatly refused to take us there; the risks to both of us were real if we dared to go that far.

On that day at Tuni, we stayed at the outer ring witnessing the collection and loading of animals into trucks, among the most visceral experiences of this research. The laws governing the live transportation of bovines are contained in the Prevention of Cruelty to Animals Act 1960. According to Rule 56(c) of the Transport of Animal Rules 1978 under Section 38 of the Act, only six cows may be transported in a single "goods vehicle." These Rules require a certification of origin and destination to be carried by the transporter. However, it is the contraband nature of the "goods," combined with cost efficiency that actually determines the number of animals packed within a single vehicle. Nuggehalli described the economic rationale behind non-compliance:

> If I load six-and-a-half animals, I am still breaking the law, and I have to bribe multiple law enforcement agencies across the route. And if I have to bribe, I would much rather put sixty instead of putting six-and-a-half . . . because it makes economic sense to do so.

The animals are required to be assessed as "fit-for-transport" by authorized veterinarians in all live animal markets though these documents are forged and bought, to transport even young, pregnant, sick, old, or disabled animals. Public health and veterinary officers, who are required to approve or deny permission for their transport, neatly sidestep this responsibility by simply being absent from the markets. Instead, Nuggehalli explains, they pre-sign a stack of certificates, which would then be sold to the transporters at the markets:

In fact, a couple of years ago when I was in Pollachi market [in Tamil Nadu state], you could actually go to a chai shop and buy a fit-for-transport certificate being sold there. It was signed and sealed by the veterinarian, and you could just fill in the number of animals yourself. There was nobody doing inspections.

So too in Tuni, we asked if there was a veterinarian present; there was none. Malathi pointed out how animals were curated, depending on the purpose of sale. The slaughter buffaloes in Tuni were all marked with blue, pink, white, or yellow paint on their bony hips, indicating their ownership by different sellers and purchasers. The cows and buffaloes for dairy would usually be accompanied by a small calf, and have swollen udders. Female calves might be priced at an additional Rs 1,500 (US$ 30); the males, being a liability, were free. It would be the dairy farmer's responsibility to dispose of the little bull, often to a veal trader within the market itself. I went near a cow and her calf tied to a tempo to take a photo; the mother went stiff with fear and anxiety, and ineffectually lowered her head at me and grunted. I retreated quickly, sorry for having frightened her and for having stolen any moments at all from the all-too-brief time that this mother and her baby might have together.

Many cows and buffaloes were heavily pregnant. While the law prohibits the transport of pregnant animals,[34] they are profitable as slaughter resources due to their weight. The loading and unloading can be so traumatizing that pregnant animals sometimes experience spontaneous miscarriages. Much later at the Faizabad *mandi* in Uttar Pradesh, I saw many buffalo mothers with stillborn calves next to them in the saleyard, licking and grooming their dead infants (see figure 6.4). These pregnant mothers had been forced to endure transportation when they were already in the agony of last-stage labor, and had delivered in the market itself, to be loaded for transport again within hours. One buffalo had delivered so recently that red bloody placenta and afterbirth dangled out of her vagina; her tiny newborn lay on the dirt (see figure 6.5). The mother's neck was tied low to a stake on the ground. She shuffled around the tight spot to try and get comfortable, perhaps to relieve her back pain.

FIGURE 6.4: *A mother buffalo near her dead newborn, who was perhaps unable to withstand transport.*

Source: Photo taken by author.

FIGURE 6.5: *A mother buffalo transported during the very final stages of her labor, and she delivered her calf in the market. Her afterbirth is still freshly hanging out of her.*

Source: Photo taken by author.

The buffalo finally lay exhausted, barely able to reach and lick his small newborn head.

Overpacking of animals destined for slaughter is extreme, as compared to the animals sold into dairying. Bovines sold for dairy must arrive at their destinations in good enough shape to continue their lives as milk producers. Bovines at the end of their dairy productivity need make it only to the slaughterhouse as *bodies*, dead or alive. While it may seem commercially counterintuitive to have disabled or downed animals, these supposed losses prove profitable. In his work on the pig industry in the United States, Jan Dutkiewicz describes the PEDv virus that killed record numbers of pigs and piglets in 2014. However, "market logics" thrive on supposed "disadvantage." Due to alarm over shrinking supplies of pig products, the industry experienced its most profitable year in history—not despite but indeed, because of the swine flu.[35] Similarly, dead animals or those injured, disabled, or downed during transport do not lower the profits of the slaughter trade. Indeed, the underground transport network in India *needs* to cause injury or break legs to fit as many animals as possible into vehicles. There is no dearth of low-waged workers to carry or drag dead animals, despite the risk of physical injury and even greater cruelty to downed animals as no attempt is spared to force them to move.

As Malathi and I walked through the market, we saw that many animals had started to be rounded up near trucks, collectively tied to a stake. Near one truck, an exhausted buffalo had managed to lie down, amid the crowd of other buffaloes pressing into her on either side (see Figure 6.6). Her udders dropped limp and shriveled, her head lost among the press of other heads tied to the low stake, hidden by the large bodies standing around her. We paused near her, her tail listlessly flicking, the only sign of life. A young boy, perhaps no more than sixteen years old, saw us watching and came over. Before we understood what he was doing, he grabbed her tail and twisted it violently. She jumped up and stood, and then moved her neck around slowly and wearily, as if it took great effort and energy, to look at her tormentor. She would almost undoubtedly be a downed buffalo by the time she reached her slaughter destination, goaded to the kill floor with more tail twisting or with chilies rubbed in her eyes.

FIGURE 6.6: *An exhausted and tightly tied buffalo lying down in Tuni chandy (market). Moments later, a young worker came and twisted her tail hard until she jumped up again.*
Source: Photo taken by author.

Groups of men, even boys, started to hit each animal hard and repeatedly until they ran into the truck in terror. Nonetheless, perhaps implicitly aware of being pushed further down the slaughter line, or in plain terror of the violent men, every buffalo tried to resist and hold her ground. And even as we were watching, the men grabbed big sticks and pushed them straight into the vagina of each resisting animal who would stumble into the truck in pain. Once inside, each animal was forcibly seated on the floor of the truck. Thick ropes were threaded through the nostrils of the buffaloes closest to the walls of the truck, and they were tied to the upper rims of the truck walls, so their heads would be raised during the long ride. The nasal wall between nostrils, the septum, is extremely sensitive, and ropes or rings strung through it inflict considerable pain and are highly effective modes of control for large animals who may otherwise be quite powerful. Bumpy rides lead to painful or even broken nostrils, and thus discourage them from moving, reducing the risk of alerting anyone on the roads to the fact that the truck contains live animals. These practices in cattle markets were also recorded in a 2014 report by the Germany-based animal welfare organization Animals' Angels, which observed:

> Horrendous loading practices and transport conditions: heavy beating; sticks pushed into animal genitalia; unfit animals are pulled on the trucks with ropes; cows are forced to the ground and tied up; lying on top of each other; unable to move; horns being sawn off.

At this stage, I had not yet seen the *jugaad* involved in the modification of the vehicles that carried and concealed the cows. Vehicular *jugaad* was not unusual in itself; creative examples include "simple tractors turned into large-capacity passenger vehicles, bicycles that are modified to enable them to float on water, improvised pulleys attached to two-wheeler scooters that carry heavy load in the absence of industrial cranes, and portable smokeless stoves."[36] So too, *jugaad* is manifest in the creative manipulation and re-design of trucks, heavy containers, cars and three-wheelers for undercover transport of cows and buffaloes to illegal slaughter.

THE *JUGAAD* OF VEHICULAR TRANSPORTATION
A seized Ashok Leyland truck, which had been filled with concealed cows headed to slaughterhouses in Delhi, stood outside the police station in Bharatpur in Rajasthan, the last police checkpoint in the state before the trucks crossed the border toward Delhi. Originally intended for transporting fragile and expensive white goods like refrigerators and air conditioners, the container was now the favored means to transport cows to slaughter. I walked the length of the truck; a constable pointed out how the standard-length container vehicle had been elongated at the back to fit in more "goods." The truck's registration number plate had been blanked out. About one-hundred-and-thirty bovines had been stuffed into the truck, many already severely injured or dead at the time of rescue. The animals had been moved to a gaushala that had sent over their own transfer trucks and ambulance.

The interiors of trucks are manipulated or disguised so the animals can be forced into spaces unsuitable for bovine bodies. Indistinguishable on the outside from other goods trucks, these re-purposed vehicles are sectioned into two horizontal halves. The roof of the vehicle, visible from the outside, is stacked with vegetables and fruit. The lower section, covered with tarpaulins, conceals cows, bulls, or calves tied tightly together. An activist from the Sanjay Gandhi Animal Hospital in Delhi described his raids on single-purpose vehicles like milk containers, oil tankers, or tourist buses with tinted windows: "They were taking live bulls inside containers meant for milk. Once we even caught a bus, a tourist bus where they had removed the seats and seated fifty-six bulls there."

Animals may be transported to slaughter in 4WDs and private cars carrying just one or two cows. Nath explained that he had caught three-wheeler autos, each carrying one or two male calves who might be only days or weeks old, folded onto the tiny cramped floor or the back seat. The Tata Ace, a mini-truck launched by the Tata group in 2005 to supplement the three-wheeled auto-rickshaw as a means of cheap and efficient transport, is also commonly used. At a length of only 3.8 meters, width of 1.5 meters, and height of 1.86 meters,[37] it was intended to travel short distances with light to medium loads. Dawn William, manager of the Blue Cross of India, Chennai, said:

> I caught a Tata Ace with six live animals inside, three large and three small babies. The vehicle had Tamil Nadu registration. Recently we caught another vehicle with four large animals and five small ones! It is inhumane how they fit them all in.

The response of the state to transgressions or even criminality in the gray or black economy is typically to overlook what is going on through the intentional neglect and under-development of these spaces for long periods of time.[38] Many government departments are ill-equipped to address illegal animal trafficking, have no means to house the tens of thousands of ex-dairy animals transported to their slaughter every day, and thus willingly or unwillingly become complicit in the continuation of these activities. Finally, this segment of the dairy production line conveying the cows to their slaughter is facilitated through "dysfunctional social contracts" among different stakeholders—Hindu and Muslim, productionists and protectionists, and the police, transporters, and handlers. When this is no longer tenable, the state may engage in violent containment, often through informal means, such as their tacit support of cow vigilantism and lynch mobs.[39]

THE BUTCHER-VIGILANTE-POLICE INFORMER NETWORKS

To facilitate the transportation of ex-dairy cows to slaughter—or conversely, to halt these trucks—the cow transporters and the cow vigilantes, respectively, rely on "informers." Cow slaughtering, like any other informal or illegal economy, constitutes a "dense exchange of protection, favors, information, and money that often dictates how state policies are implemented or not implemented."[40] The informers alert transporters to police or activist presence on the route, or alternatively, forewarn vigilantes and activists of trucks expected to pass through particular routes.

To be able to share such confidential information, "informers," by necessity, have "insider" status in the community they are informing about. It came as no surprise then, when my Hindu vigilante respondents explained that most of their informers are recruited from the Muslim butchering community. To buy protection from the dominant Hindu community, they inform on the illegal activities of their own and provide information about the make of the vehicle, its registration number, the number of animals it is carrying, and its expected route. The vigilantes then wait at strategic points along this route, usually on bridges or atop tall structures, so they have a vantage point from which to keep watch.

Informers may also be recruited through social manipulation and coercion, where the recipients of such information may exploit the tensions within the informer community, to force one member to "inform" on the other. Mohan, the gaurakshak in Hyderabad, described how he employs a "divide and rule" strategy to cultivate an informer network among the Muslim butchers, creating a situation where each is pressured to "inform" on the others to protect his business:

> I have some twenty-five informers, they tell me [about the illegal bovine trucks expected to pass certain routes]. The informers come from their own community. Let's say you are a Muslim [butcher], I catch your vehicle, you

will know that one of your own has given this information about you. You
and them would have had a disagreement, this is their revenge. All the
informers are Muslim, I have two to three Hindu informers but the rest are
all Muslims. And we take the opportunity to create more tensions between
them. If I catch someone's vehicles, I will say, "*philana-philana* [so-and-
so] told me about you" and he will automatically get incensed. I only have
one goal, create divisions within them, and save my gaumatas. How do I
achieve this? Say I catch Salim's *gadi* [vehicle], and I will tell him, "*arre*
Asim told me about you," and then he immediately gets angry, "Asim told
you!" and I say, "yes, Asim told me you are taking a vehicle full of cows."
Then I catch Asim's truck and blame it on Salim. Then if these two are
out of the picture, I take Madar's name. To Madar I tell him, Aslam told
me. To Aslam, I take Irfan's name. To Irfan, I take Qureshi's name. So we
create distrust within them, and then do our work. . . . This is how I work,
create divisions with them, and make each an informer against the other.

Correspondingly, the truckers and butchers also have extensive networks of informers, all too frequently from within the community of
Hindu gaurakshaks, and the police, who are typically Hindu. These
groups might "leak" information to the transporters about which routes
to avoid, where the trucks may be halted and seized by waiting vigilantes. In an article in *The Indian Express*, Pati quotes a cow smuggler:

> A cow smuggler, on condition of anonymity, admitted, "We take the help
> of police for the business. During day, we inform the police stations con-
> cerned about the number of trucks or vehicles carrying the animals which
> would pass through [the highways]. As per our plan, a pilot van leads a fleet
> of 10 to 15 cow-laden trucks. It is entrusted to bribe the police officials on
> their way. About Rs 800 to Rs 1,500 is paid per truck to each police station
> depending on the number of cattle head."[41]

Cows themselves are turned into landscapes and weapons of warfare.
Two women in Gurgaon spotted six cows being trucked in an "unhealthy
manner" and started a chase.[42] A cow protection task force in the Sohna
area joined them, and coordinated with their members to put spikes up
in front of the truck. This task force, also known as the Gau Raksha Task

Force, is a special arm of the Haryana state police. Under the Haryana Gauvansh Sanrakshan and Gausamvardhan Act, 2015, their mandate is to prevent cow smuggling and slaughter. The cow truck zoomed over the spikes, and continued to drive despite the tires getting punctured and a rear tire coming off. As the women drew closer, the transporters turned fire on them, and threw a live cow at the car. Three cows died of severe injuries.

Vigilantes and activists usually halt trucks at highway toll points, directly placing themselves in front of the vehicle suspected of carrying contraband animals. If the truck contains cows, a prolonged fight between the activists or vigilantes and the butchers can involve the police, who may seize the trucks. The trucks may be taken to a nearby gaushala, or the shelter may send its own vehicles to convey the animals. If the vehicle contains other species of animals whose slaughter is not prohibited but where the conditions of overpacking are intense, the activists or vigilantes may insist that the transporters call for additional trucks to redistribute the "load."

Knowing that there is an increasing risk of their trucks being halted, the transporters have pilot vehicles that run ahead of the trucks, assessing the highway ahead. The pilot vehicles watch for stationary motorcycles and small cars on the roads, or even one or two persons waiting at a roadside chai shop or restaurant. If deemed clear of suspicious presence, the driver of the pilot vehicle for the transporters will send a message on WhatsApp. Alternatively, if activists or vigilantes are sighted, or if a truck is seized, WhatsApp messaging is used to instruct the other drivers to immediately change routes. There has been a "widespread dissemination of affordable mobile phones" among "Indians of every status."[43] Mobile phones are used to enable crime in India[44] and, in the cow slaughter economy, are used by transporters to circulate information about trucks carrying contraband loads. WhatsApp messaging disadvantages animal activists, who usually live in cities, and may be unfamiliar with the peri-urban regions. A volunteer from the organization PCI, Chennai, said,

These truckers are all on WhatsApp groups—as soon as we catch one truck, the onslaught of trucks stops altogether and that too immediately.

One of these guys must send everyone in the group a message saying we are on the highway, or in this location. After that, the trucks just stop coming immediately, and take different routes, right in the interior areas, we will never be able to guess and chase after them. We don't know these areas; they know them too well.

The cow vigilantes also have pilot vehicles and lookout points along highways, from where they can keep a close eye on suspicious trucks, private cars, or individuals. These surveillance points are a seamless part of the peri-urban landscape. I went on a tour of several gaushalas with two gaurakshaks along a highway point between Ahmedabad and Baroda. We were ravenous by the time we finished; one of the men suggested lunch at their "pilot" café, a roadside restaurant where they often wait for hours before the awaited truck passes through. As we waited for our *thalis*, I observed the other lunchers, workers, and occasionally a holidaying family, stopping for a quick lunch. The restaurant, with its plain ceiling fans, plastic chairs, and faded advertisements for Pepsi and Nestle, was indistinguishable from numerous others, and it served as a direct lookout station to observe both sides of the highway.

Police play a complex role in facilitating transportation. In 2017, the Human Rights Watch released a 104-page report, "Violent Cow Protection in India: Vigilante Groups Attack Minorities," which noted: "In almost all of the cases, the police initially stalled investigations, ignored procedures, or even played a complicit role in the killings and cover-up of crimes. Instead of promptly investigating and arresting suspects, the police filed complaints against victims, their families, and witnesses under laws that ban cow slaughter."[45] As early as 2002, in the volatile year of the Gujarat pogrom, the People's Union for Democratic Rights described the Haryana state police as "highly culpable" in the killing of five Dalit men suspected of cow slaughter in Jhajjar district.[46]

Notably, cow vigilantes also report experiences of police brutality. Angered by a situation that can render an ill-equipped, ill-prepared police officer with no real capacity to respond, the police instead intimidate or threaten the vigilantes, who may be more vulnerable to police violence than educated, urban activists. Mohan described a time when his team caught a truck outside Hyderabad at 12:30 am. Returning with a friend from the raids on cow trucks that they had conducted on the Andhra-Orissa state border, they were sitting in their bus waiting to pass through the Srikakulam tollgate on the highway in Andhra Pradesh. Goods vehicles usually have to pass this checkpoint to enter or exit the state of Andhra Pradesh.

The two men noticed covered trucks smelling faintly of bovine dung and urine at the stop. They got down, placed themselves physically in front of the truck, and found restrained buffaloes inside. While they had initially stopped the trucks on suspicion of transporting cows, the sight of those buffaloes was among the worst instances of overpacking they had seen. They could not let it go. When the single policeman at the gate became visibly nervous at their complaint, Mohan described the frustration that typically leads to violent altercations between the vigilantes and transporters as each then take the law into their own hands:

> We were sitting on the bus at Srikakulam tollgate and then we saw the vehicles covered carrying animals, we could smell them, we know these things. So Amit and I grabbed our bags and got down. We stopped the vehicles, there were buffaloes inside, tied so badly, fitted tight against each other, head and legs tied together, a terrible situation. The policeman would just take 200 rupees and let them go. We called the cop and told him to check, he faltered and said, "I don't know what's in there." I was very angry, I said, "Look at the buffaloes, transported in such a terrible condition, just look! Will you take action, or will we?"

After a protracted fight with the transporters which involved shouting and threats by both parties, the vigilantes reached the police station with the truckers and the truck filled with animals by 2:00 a.m. The police refused to book a case against the transporters until 11:00 a.m. the next day, even as calls from senior officials, politicians, and activists started to fly across the country. Instead, they shifted Mohan and his friend to another police station. Mohan said, "They don't even beat dogs so badly, they beat me worse than a dog. But I will not leave gauraksha, not until I die. They were Hindu police who beat me. They kept saying, 'How dare you catch the trucks, what authority do you have?' I only replied, 'I am a Hindu, I have to catch.'" Eventually the buffaloes were moved to a gaushala, and a case was booked against the transporters, though Mohan suspected that they would buy their way out of litigation.

The Indian police often find themselves both unable and unwilling to address the issue. As an issue of animal cruelty alone, the laws have no teeth; as per the Prevention of Cruelty to Animals Act, 1960, the fine is only Rs 50 (less than US$ 1). However, I learnt from both vigilantes and transporters that the trucks are also a major source of bribes, and often real income, for the police constabulary, who demand kickbacks from both cohorts. Police constables' work is classified as "semi-skilled labor" on the government pay scales, with low wages.[47] The money extorted as bribes supplements insufficiently-funded police budgets, and finances official supplies, petrol for police vehicles, and payments to police informers, particularly in Uttar Pradesh.[48] Bribe resources move both "vertically" and "horizontally," and fund the campaigns of powerful politicians.[49]

Police checkpoints along highways are major bribe collection centers. Heavy vehicles are not allowed within metropolitan city limits after 6:00 a.m. as they cause congestion and up to 70 percent of fatal road accidents.[50] However, transporters and the police set up an agreement for drivers to pay a nominal "fine" when the truck enters the city limits. Once the driver has paid, he has free run of the city to take his contraband load to slaughterhouses. Thus, slaughter transportation can continue largely unchecked through the night and even during the day.

The police in different states, however, were clear that they had been asked to deliver a responsibility for which they had no infrastructural support. A police superintendent at a station outside Lucknow city explained there was a lack of space, funds, and resources to rehome the thousands of ex-dairy animals who were being moved and were often also in need of veterinary treatment. In Bharatpur city, cow smugglers opened fire on the police, injuring a policeman, when their truck carrying twenty-one cows was stopped.[51] When I visited the station, a senior Hindu officer in Bharatpur told me:

> Okay, when I was young, my grandmother used to sell her cows every one
> or two years. We all knew where they were going. Nobody objected. Now

you suddenly have a situation where that is wrong. Okay, fine. But then give us the vehicles we need, give us the constables we need, raise our salaries, give us some proper support. Don't just say, "you are the police, stop cow slaughter." Where do you want me to put the animals? Don't make that a police problem. This is a police station, not a gaushala.

The risk of communal violence and riots is real. A police commissioner in Trivandrum in Kerala told me that they needed almost military level assistance to address the scale of slaughter transportation: "We need cattle terra force [police teams working exclusively on cow trafficking across different states] dedicated to this." The Lucknow superintendent echoed these views. At the time of my interview in 2016, the Lucknow police were preparing for Prime Minister Modi's visit to the city. The official explained that the entire police force of the city would be diverted for Prime Ministerial security duty. During this time, the slaughter trucks would pass unchallenged, ironically taking advantage of the presence of publicly-cow-revering Modi in the city:

> Tomorrow and day after the PM is coming to Lucknow. The whole force is going for PM duty. So the trucks that want to go through will do so—there is nobody to stop them on these days. There is a shortage of police personnel, there is no training for this specific task. The truckers are ruthless, they can force their own truck on to our vehicles, they can cause accidents deliberately. We may have two constables for this, they will have 10-plus people. We don't even have jeeps, we use motorcycles.

The vehicles that get caught, and attract media attention for vigilante attacks on minorities are a small portion of the fleet of vehicles that successfully head to slaughter destinations. While many BJP-controlled states in particular have tried to crack down on illegal slaughterhouses, they will not—and cannot—be removed when dairies keep discarding animals. These laws simply become a means of revenue generation for the state machinery to accept bribes to allow the slaughterhouses to continue, or to mushroom elsewhere. As I made my way further down the dairy production continuum, I found myself, predictably, in slaughterhouses.

CHAPTER 7

SLAUGHTER

THE TREMORS OF AN APPROACHING EARTHQUAKE
I stood in front of a highly modern and mechanized authorized export-
only slaughterhouse for buffaloes, only a few kilometers away from
central Kanpur city. I had arrived at the designated hour, and security
guards opened the gates after a quick phone call inside to confirm that
I was, indeed, an expected visitor. I was immediately amazed at how
pleasant the premises were. In contrast to the city of Kanpur with its
constant fog of toxic industrial pollution, the visible filth in the streets,
and unregulated traffic, what lay before me were green lawns on either
side of the driveway lined with short trees and terracotta pots with flowers. It struck me later that the ambience was unexceptionally agreeable, a
generic sort of neat grassy landscaping that made me feel safe, as if I was
in an orderly space, but with no evocative feature that would linger in
my memory after I had left. I worried that I had not come to the slaughterhouse at all, that perhaps I had been directed instead to the abattoir's
corporate offices. It made sense that the slaughterhouse itself might be
located in the outskirts, or even outside of the city altogether.

It would turn out that I was, indeed, as unprepared as Pachirat had
been during his first visit to an industrial slaughterhouse in Nebraska,
for the extraordinarily inconspicuous *mundanity* of the built architec-
ture of a slaughterhouse, blending seamlessly and unremarkably with the

general ordinariness of the city. *"Nothing in my imagination had prepared me,"* wrote Pachirat, *"for the utter invisibility of slaughter, the banal insidiousness of what hides in plain sight* [emphasis added]."[1]

I walked up to the reception desk at the front, framed by giant potted greens. There was a small fountain near the desk, reminiscent of a hotel lobby. It was very quiet; I could scarcely hear the sounds of the city, its roaring traffic and the incessant honking of vehicles, outside of the slaughterhouse gates. The female receptionist—an agreeably soft and feminized public front—phoned my host to let him know I had arrived. She ushered me into the general manager's office to wait; it was framed by glass walls on three sides. An open office lay on one side where three men sat in front of computers; one had his headphones on. All the other desks were empty. On another side were a number of sectioned cubicles, presumably for the senior managerial and professional staff.

The industrial abattoir was run from this command position; "the front office of the slaughterhouse is indistinguishable from front offices worldwide in which the control of others' lives is directed from a distance, opaquely, without the benefit (or burden) of visceral, direct experience."[2]

My guide walked in, a Muslim meat microbiologist. Their abattoir, I knew, was non-operational at the time as it was undergoing repairs and renovations. We had spoken on the phone earlier and discussed that he would give me a "walking interview"; in other words, quite literally walk me through the carceral and killing operations of a regular working day. However, as we settled in the office, I wondered if the plans had changed, and whether we would just have a normal face-to-face interview.

"Where is the slaughterhouse?" I asked hesitantly. "Is it far?"

"No, this is the slaughterhouse," he said.

My eyes widened. *This?* He walked me past the reception area, outside the building, and we turned left; there, almost immediately round a sharp corner, within seconds, was the lairage or the "waiting" area for the animals.[3] As discreetly blended in with the ordinariness of the city outside, so, too, the heart of the abattoir—the "waiting area" and the directly connected kill floor—could be almost missed even *inside* the walled confines of the industrial slaughterhouse. The lairage where the actual animals would spend their last hours, alive, in states of hyper-vigilance, fear, and in the physical condition (injured, thirsty, hungry, and exhausted) in which they arrived, would be carefully concealed from the civilized space and gaze of the white-collar slaughterhouse bureaucracy itself.

Unlike the operational slaughterhouses I was to visit later, this one was almost spotlessly sterile, free of any signs of animal presence—no pools of blood, coagulated bodily discharges, piles of organs, feces from panicked defecating animals, and indeed, no living animals at all. The only corporeal indication that animals had been killed here was the dull raw smell of carcass that I would come across later, emanating from a single skinned buffalo cadaver hanging in their chill room.

Before we started our tour, I hesitated. Fully expecting him to deny it, I nonetheless had to ask my guide. "Do you think the animals know? Do they know what is coming?"

The man gave me a wry smile. "Of course they know, from the minute they enter here," he said. "When a *bhookhamp* [earthquake] is approaching, the animals know much before us. *Insaan* [human] takes their cue from them. When the *bhookhamp* is coming in their own lives, you think they won't know?"

THE POLITICS OF CURATING COW (AND ANIMAL) SLAUGHTER

The concealed, securitized, and discreetly designed slaughterhouse that I was in, in fact, is not the norm in India. It is the unauthorized, small-scale, backyard abattoir operations, which account overwhelmingly for animal slaughtering in India, and indeed, throughout the Global South, even as most animal rights theory and activism focuses on the devastations and violence of industrial slaughterhouses. Informal or even illegal animal slaughterhouses in the Global South constitute one of the most critical segments of the global dairy and meat supply chains, though it is almost impossible to assess its scale due to its shadowy nature. According to the United States Department of Agriculture (USDA), there are some 3,600 registered slaughterhouses, and some 25,000 unregistered, small-scale retail meat shops in India.[4] We do know that domestic demand for meat in India is so high that, as Jitendra writes in a *Down to Earth* report, "the raw material" has to come from "municipal-run slaughterhouses that do not have APEDA [Agricultural and Processed Food Products Export Development Authority] approval and from illegal small slaughterhouses."[5]

Cow slaughtering in India specifically, however, *needs* to occur almost entirely in the illegal economy—albeit also on an industrial scale—due to the legislative prohibitions on cow killing in most of the country. When inherently unworkable rules are selectively imposed by the state—such as cow slaughter prohibition in a leading dairy nation—it paves the way for innovations in noncompliance and subversive behavior. India's dairy sector almost wholly relies on these unclassified cow slaughterhouses and the precarious, racialized labor enmeshed in them. As Adriaenssens et al. write, "There is no empty set of underground activities in any given modern society. . . ."[6] By continuing to heavily subsidize the breeding of cows for dairy, and providing no adequate system of rehabilitating non-lactating animals—because there is no practical, profitable, and sustainable way to do so—the state effectively creates an environment in which cow slaughter simply goes underground.

Underground cow slaughter is possible because there is no consensus—there are even glaring contradictions—among different Indian laws as to what constitutes a slaughterhouse.[7] This blurring allows immense possibilities for informal, unauthorized, or illegal "workarounds" to emerge in both the scale of slaughter, and in the animals who are killed in different sites. According to the Food Safety and Standards Authority of India (FSSAI) 2011 Food Safety and Standards Regulations, a slaughterhouse is "a food business operator which slaughters large and small animals, including sheep and goat or poultry birds, within the premises of a factory for production of meat/meat products for supply/sale/distribution."[8]

However, this can also encompass the unauthorized, roadside, butcher houses. The Prevention of Cruelty to Animals (Slaughter House) Rules define a slaughterhouse as a site "wherein 10 or more than 10 animals are slaughtered per day." Together, these small operations over-whelmingly constitute cow and buffalo (and other) slaughter, producing meat in industrial-scale volumes comparable with, and perhaps even exceeding, some licensed slaughterhouses. The Dharavi slum in Mumbai, for instance, contains over 20,000 small-scale manufacturing units[9] and is a major hub of abattoirs and tanneries. In 2016, the Mumbai police seized over 6,500 kilograms of beef from an unlicensed slaughterhouse in Dharavi.[10]

The liberalization of the Indian economy in 1991 was to dramatically alter the landscape of animal slaughtering in the country, leading to a proliferation of *authorized*, mechanized abattoirs. India's economy became intricately interlocked with the global economy of open trade, subject to the regulations of the World Trade Organization's (WTO's) General Agreement on Tariffs and Trade (GATT). Indian ecofeminist Vandana Shiva has long been a robust critic of the inherently predatory clauses contained within the GATT and the WTO, which in essence, require that the poorest of the developing world bear a disproportionately heavy burden for cheap trade inflow into Western nations. A 1994 amendment to GATT clauses prohibits the placement of any restriction or prohibition on open trade between importing and exporting parties, allowing a free flow of exploited goods, natural resources, and labor.

This has had an exceptionally "disastrous effect"[11] on farmed animals in India (and elsewhere in the Global South) used as mass products for both an exploding middle class domestically and as profitable commodities of international trade. Shiva writes: "The conflict between animals and humans in global trade is artificial and contrived . . . the real conflict is between the free trade rights of global corporations and the rights of humans and animals."[12] Moreover, as human labor and animal welfare movements become stronger in the West, a raft of exploitative, polluting industries, including slaughterhouses, have been relocated to the developing countries.

Meat—specifically carabeef extracted from buffaloes discarded by the Indian dairy sector—has become a core export product since 1988 when the Department of Animal Husbandry and Dairying started schemes offering 100 percent subsidies and tax exemptions to modernize slaughterhouses. Both the central and state governments contributed 50 percent of the total costs respectively, to establish "carcass utilization centers" and "for building, plant & machinery and effluent treatment plant."[13] The subsidies for the infrastructure would cover expensive and resource-intensive costs such as transport, pre-cooling, water treatment, cold storage, and air freight, as well as product literature, brand publicity, packaging, and quality control.[14] The Ministry of Food Processing Industries (MoFPI) set up several new slaughterhouses in the 2000s and invested heavily in modernizing existing ones to ensure greater compliance with the hygienic slaughter practices, and public health protocols required to send Indian meat to the international market. Mechanized slaughtering also contributed to profits through more efficient use of "by-products" that might be wasted otherwise, such as offal, blood and fetuses from pregnant animals.[15] This strategy was cemented via the Five-Year Plans put in place after 2008–09, with a stated objective of upgrading or establishing 50 new animal abattoirs. In 2018–19, India exported 12,36,638.39 metric tonnes of buffalo flesh, earning US$ 3,608.72 million for that year.[16] Such mechanized, export-only animal slaughtering is authorized by the FSSAI under the Ministry of Health and APEDA, and within the Ministry of Commerce and Industry. Export-only abattoirs have to comply with a range of legislation, including the Export of Raw Meat Rules; FSSAI Act; Pollution Control Board; and some provisions as regards animal welfare in the Prevention of Cruelty to Animals Act 1960, which, given the very nature of killing itself, I was to learn, were purely cosmetic.

The fittest and healthiest of the spent buffaloes from the dairy industry are selected from markets by middlemen to be sent to the "export-only" slaughterhouses. It is two other categories of abattoirs, that is, (1) municipal and Panchayat-run village slaughterhouses; and (2) the unlicensed/illegal slaughterhouses, dispersed throughout cities and regions, that dispose of the unwanted *cows*, as well as the "poor quality" buffaloes—emaciated, diseased, injured, or downed—from India's milk sector.

Municipal and village-level Panchayat slaughterhouses catering to local consumption are overseen by two bodies sitting within two central ministries: (1) APEDA,[17] housed under the Ministry of Commerce and Industry and MoFPI; and (2) the FSSAI within the Ministry of Health. To some extent, the Ministry of Animal Husbandry, Dairying and Fishing (in collaboration with MoFPI) also oversees slaughter regulations and processes, especially for rural slaughterhouses. Most butchers are not on the official payroll of government abattoirs though they perform risky labor on sites where "contraband" animals may be disposed of.

The animal welfare discourse—at its core, an animal agriculture public relations narrative—is significantly responsible for circulating the idea to the meat and dairy consuming public, that industrial, mechanized slaughtering is a "humane" alternative to backyard slaughtering, and also, ostensibly more hygienic. It would be from butchers and slaughterhouse workers themselves, across killing spaces, that I would learn about the banality of classification and curation of geography as humane or inhumane, which makes no difference when confronted with frightened, resisting animals, and which indeed, entrenches racism and casteism in Indian society.

Industrial Slaughter: The Liminal Spaces of the Dying Dead
Back in Kanpur, the meat microbiologist and I stood with our backs to the tall walls, close to eighteen feet high, that fully enclosed the lairage area, well away from the main entrance through which I had entered. "Starting from the beginning," as he had promised me, he led me for over two hours, generous with his time and with exacting attention to detail, through the entirety of the slaughter line. Patient and respectful as I stumbled through inexpert scientific or cultural questions about slaughter, we traced the steps together, from when the living animals are brought in truck after truck through a massive side gate leading directly to the lairage, to the packing section from where the "meat" left the abattoir in refrigerated trucks.

At our feet was a shallow dip carved into the concrete, dry now but usually filled with disinfectant, through which the truck tires must pass to avoid bringing contaminants, as they enter the biosecure area. The primary concern of laws regulating animal slaughter is human health, to ensure that contaminated meat does not enter the "food" supply. Slaughterhouses produce such quantities of toxic pollution in the form of blood and organic material that in India, animal killing is a classified "industrial" (not agricultural) activity.[18]

However, ideas of sanitization around pollution and infection control in slaughterhouses worldwide are interlinked with cultural concepts of hygiene.[19] So too in a Hindu nationalist state, notions of *scientific* and *social* hygiene and pollution intersect. Hindu nationalist discourses invoke the practice of animal sacrifice by Muslims (disregarding that many Hindu communities also ritually kill animals) to frame these practices as disgusting and backward.[20] Through her ethnographic work in Mumbai's Deonar slaughterhouse, Shireen Mirza argues that "the colonial government's scientific ideas of sanitation have been seamlessly blended into the developmental mandate of the Hindu nationalist state that seeks a ban on cow slaughter and the upholding of upper-caste Hindu practices."[21] Mechanized slaughtering becomes another way to "upgrade" the butchering castes, and "remake the whole butcher community's identity as modern, viable and empowering."[22]

The gate directly faced the lairage area. If the animals were to be slaughtered right away, the crush of living buffaloes would be off-loaded onto ramps that led directly into the winding "queues" to the kill floor. Otherwise, the trucks would move toward enclosed sheds next to the lairage, where the animals may wait overnight or even for a few days. It would be later, in an operational slaughterhouse, that I would bear witness to the trauma that *waiting* animals experienced.

I stood at the entry of the lairage and looked ahead. The "corridor" through which every day hundreds of individuals would walk their final steps was more than a hundred meters, winding over and over in sharp zig-zags. I glanced at my companion; he started to walk down this passageway and I followed. It was then that I noticed that the space between the strong permanent metal fencing on either side was extremely constricted. I started to feel claustrophobic.

"It has to be this narrow," he said, "otherwise, they will turn around and try to run, stampede over each other, big mess." Animal resistance impedes the efficiency of any killing system. Consultant for slaughterhouses Temple Grandin uses ethological work to quash resistance in the slaughterhouse, claiming that these methods allow humane slaughtering. Recent work like Sarat Colling's *Animal Resistance in the Global Capitalist Era*, however, provides a detailed and compelling account of how animals, regardless of the "design" of the site, resist the horrendous violence to their bodies that has become banal and normative under capitalism and domestication.[23]

"But even so . . . how *does* a big buffalo get through here?" I wondered. "How is it physically even possible?"

The man assured me that electric prods were very effective. He pointed to the overhead showerheads that, until that moment, I had not noticed. In the last ten meters before the buffaloes are forced *inside* the slaughterhouse, agitation and resistance truly peak. The sounds of the machinery inside are thunderous. The severest beatings might not be sufficient to move a wide-eyed, mouth-foaming buffalo, but the drenching from the showers help to intensify the severity of the shocks from the electric batons. "The water increases the electric shocks—when the skin is dry, they don't respond that well to electric shocks," he explained. "The water and electricity together force them. . . ."

The last step in the lairage, and the first step inside the slaughterhouse, leads the condemned animal directly into the *knocking box*. Even as a member of a species who would *not* be converted into "food," I felt the visceral bodily reaction of pure physical tension, of leaden legs, in taking the step between the "outside" and the "inside" to the heart of the slaughterhouse. That step signaled the demise of any hope. I walked to the "edge" of the queue and looked quickly into the knocking box— and just as quickly looked away again. The microbiologist, wanting to be helpful, encouraged me to step into the box if I wanted to get a sense of the size. I hastily declined, although in hindsight, I wish I had thrown it more than a quick glance.

The knocking box is a deep container, large enough to hold two small buffaloes or one large bovine. As soon as the buffalo steps onto the final edge of the ramp, it gives way beneath her, and she falls into the cavernous box, which immediately seals her, swinging almost 180 degrees. The right side of the box along its width would be open, allowing only her head to stick out. Inside the box, the animal would be on her back with her legs up in the air, a highly stressful position for a buffalo or a cow. Once the animal is restrained, one of two things may happen—the animal may be stunned or not stunned. The APEDA offers a prosaic description of this stage:

> the animals are led to knocking box where the animals to be slaughtered can not see the slaughtered animals in the abattoir. The knocking box could be for an individual animal or for two animals. Knocking box helps in re-straining the animals for slaughter where slaughter is done either by stunning the animals or without stunning as per the requirement of the importing country.[24]

Stunned slaughter or captive-bolt stunning involves "a rigid cast of steel . . . propelled at the skull of the cattle, designed to *concuss but not fracture the skull* [emphasis added]."[25] In his book, Pachirat describes the difficulties with stunning; even with the capacity to move only her head, the cow is likely to continue to frantically resist, and many animals endure their slaughter improperly stunned or unstunned. The use of a stun gun is not mandatory in mechanized slaughterhouses in India as this may affect the demand for exports; as the APEDA Executive Manual states, "Animals are slaughtered by being stunned and slaughtered mostly by the Halal method in all the export-oriented units. For some countries stunning is mandatory, whereas for other countries stunning is not allowed."[26]

The ethics and logistics of stunned or unstunned slaughter are heavily debated in animal welfare discourses, as though killing occurs in a vacuum removed from the realities of the human workers who operate in these exhausting, dangerous, and fraught spaces. The workers in the *actual killing spaces* of the slaughterhouse where stunning takes place (or not) constantly experience the enormous physical and psychological toll of slaughtering, sometimes resulting in aggression toward their families, and indeed, the animals.[27] In *Slaughterhouse*, Gail Eisnitz describes the aggression that can occur in workers caused by the sensory overload, especially the smell of blood, and by exhaustion. One worker told her, "You get an attitude that if that hog kicks at me, I'm going to get even.

You're already going to kill the hog, but that's not enough. It has to suffer."[28] Others have described how the act of killing does not even register after a while, and "evaporates into a routinized, almost hallucinatory blur."[29] Pachirat writes, "By the end of the day . . . it hardly matters what is being cut, shorn, sliced, shredded, hung, or washed: all that matters is that the day is once again, finally coming to a close."[30]

The origins of stunned slaughter lie, in fact, in human welfare. Slaughterhouses produce high rates of injury and death of human workers while trying to manage large frightened animals like bovines and pigs in a risky environment with slippery floors and machinery explicitly designed to kill. U.S. slaughterhouses, for instance, have at least seventeen "severe" accidents a month, resulting in "hospitalizations, amputations or loss of an eye" for the workers.[31] The velocity of slaughter is so fast that amputations, typically the arms, hands, fingers, and toes of human workers occur at least twice a week.[32]

The issue of "stunned slaughter," as opposed to "conscious slaughter" as per halal practices, globally constitutes perhaps one of the most prominent issues of animal welfare that is couched explicitly in binary terms—Western versus Islamic; science versus religion; modern versus backward; and above all, *humane and compassionate* versus *inhumane and cruel*.[33] Offended specifically by "cultural practices" (but not other practices) involving "cruelty" to animals, Galgut argues that "religious or cultural rituals . . . does not count as a sufficiently good reason to harm or kill animals."[34] Slaughtering animals in the name of science (such as in university research labs), or using "scientific" methods in abattoirs, is morally acceptable, however. To negotiate the violence of halal slaughter while also allowing Muslims freedom of religious expression, Anna Joseph recommends that animals must be stunned after *forty seconds* if still conscious after they are cut[35]—disregarding the impossibility of such timing in a system where such large numbers of animals are killed that slaughter, in reality, occurs *every twelve seconds*.[36]

The banning of only halal or kosher slaughter in Scandinavian countries, for instance, rather than all animal butchery, is precisely an example of race politics exploiting animal welfare to demarcate who does—and does not, in this case—belong to the Scandinavian national and cultural identity. It also suggests that the violent methods inflicted on animals by majoritarian white groups are morally acceptable. European parties like the English Defence League, write Will Kymlicka and Sue Donaldson:

> have jumped on the issue of the cruelty of ritual slaughter, solely as a way of telling Muslims they are not welcome and do not belong. . . . These parties have no track record of concern for animals, and in many cases, they only picked up the animal issue when other options for provoking Muslims had proven a dead end (e.g., when attempts at banning burqas or minarets were ruled unconstitutional).[37]

Framed in such reductionist terms, the debate continues to circle the kinds of *racialized* violence that may be perpetrated on animals, rather than questioning the infliction of *any* violence on other animals. The narrow scope of discussion disregards that the animal *is conscious* up to a *very specific moment* in the continuum of killing, which micro-instance alone is selectively—racially—problematized. The racist discourses around stunned slaughter disregard what ethnographic and activist work globally has repeatedly revealed—that fundamentally, it means little, if anything, to the animal who is desperately resisting her killing in a myriad different ways.[38]

In India, as my guide explained to me in Kanpur, once enclosed and immobilized in the knocking box, and with only her neck sticking out of the box, the jugular and carotid veins of the buffalo are cut with a knife. During any slaughter—halal or stunned, formal or informal— there is a stage of *being alive, being dead*, and *a liminal space for dying* between life and death.[39] This space is when an animal dies, *piece by piece*, as the conveyor belt inches forward.[40] However, in most industrial and halal slaughter, this moment of the "cut" is when the animal is *conceptually* dead.

Back in the knocking box, the "cut" animal would slide out, bleeding but still alive, as the box swung back 180 degrees and opened to release the buffalo. The drains underneath the flooring around the knocking box would begin collecting a continual river of gushing blood. Three or four buffaloes might jerk around in a fire of pain on this floor at the same time, as the knocking box would continually dump animals.

"Sometimes a buffalo manages to get up and run before its leg is winched," the man said.

Profusely bleeding with a sliced neck, running in extreme panic, sliding and slipping on the bloody floor, the liminally dead buffalo also puts the workers at risk. Animals become terrified by the smell of blood and other bodily material, the sight of the hanging bodies of their herd off the conveyor belt above,[41] and the sound of machinery. "It is so loud inside, we have to literally shout at the top of our voices to each other, our ears are always in pain," said the microbiologist.

Once the still-alive-not-yet-dead buffalo is winched, she will be hoisted up to the "first floor" near the ceiling, where some forty to sixty butchers would labor, each responsible for dismembering a particular part of her. The first butchers would hack off her forelegs to avoid human injury; as the animal is often still alive and thrashing around, the physical risk to humans is high.

At each of these stages, as the microbiologist continued to walk me through, I kept asking him, "So would the animal be dead here?" He would shake his head. "Not yet," he'd reply.

At one point, my companion showed me the spot where the butcher would apply an electric shock to the hanging tongue of the animal to ensure a "final shake" to remove the blood. "Would the buffalo be dead here?" I asked.

"You could say," he said, "but conclusively it is dead only once the head is removed. That is the next step."

"How long would that be since the cut in the knocking box?" I asked.

He paused, calculating the minutes between each stage. "Maybe seventeen minutes," he said, "but this is also when the slaughter starts. Once slaughter is on properly, it can even take longer." Sometimes machinery needs to be briefly stopped, or resisting animals need to be caught again, all causing delays.

"What does halal or humane mean here, then, when the animal is alive and enduring so much?" I asked my guide.

"Halal is only till the neck is cut," explained the man. "Once its neck is cut, it is no longer an animal. The *qurbani* [sacrifice] has happened, now it is [conceptually] *qurbani* and not an animal."

The use of metaphor in ritual—in this case slaughter, in an attempt to cleanly splinter a moment of life from a moment of death in the hope of bypassing the liminal space of *dying*—is a primordial human impulse itself. Anthropologists of religion and secularity note that the state of liminality—the unknown or the uncertain—can be uncomfortable, necessitating the need for clear boundaries.[42] The minutes following the "cut" or the "stunning," where the animal is not-quite-alive-and-not-quite-dead, are emotionally, intellectually, and legislatively difficult to address. In moments where sentience, blood, flesh, and life itself are wildly wavering, it becomes important to draw metaphorical lines. If such conceptual muddling is necessary to slaughter the buffaloes, cow slaughter in India requires even greater depths of concealment, euphemism, and systemic racial and communal violence, ghettoization, and ongoing impoverishment of these human communities to sustain it.

Municipal Slaughter
At 2 pm, in the glaring desert sunshine of the early afternoon, Manil, an Animal Welfare Board of India (AWBI) certified animal welfare officer, and I walked through the gates of the municipal slaughterhouse of a major city in Rajasthan. It was a non-operational time of day; the killing would not begin until the evening, and Manil was there to conduct an inspection of the facilities. Truck after truck had already begun arriving, carrying hundreds of lambs, bleating incessantly, presumably starving and anxious for their mothers who were likely also lactating. I watched workers unloading the lambs roughly, throwing them down, their bleating and crying reverberating through the hot enclosed area. The lambs huddled against each other, leaping back in terror if a human approached too close.

Manil photographed the lambs; the water troughs, black, thick, and stinking, with a bloated decomposed dead frog afloat; dead goats and lambs stacked atop one another in a room, also containing workers' clothes and personal items. A female goat was tied separately outside the lairage, and she had pressed her head against the wall, her eyes closed, seeming in great agony.

Manil asked to be shown the bovines. Within minutes, a group of men materialized, seemingly out of nowhere. Manil and the men started arguing in Rajasthani, and at one point, three men roughly pushed him against the wall. I quickly walked to his side, my face frozen into a rictus smile at the men.

Manil outwardly remained utterly calm and collected, but started chain-smoking rapidly, the only sign of his extreme stress. "Where is the vet?" he asked. "Call the vet."

"Vet *nahin hai*!" snapped one of the men. The vet is not here! He would come in the evening. However, I knew that slaughterhouses are required to have a vet on the premises throughout the day and night, as their duties included tending to sick or injured animals.

Slaughterhouse veterinarians in different parts of the country had told me they were not allowed to work safely. One vet in Kerala told me that he was not even allowed to assess an animal as "fit-for-slaughter." All farmed animals can be legally slaughtered in India only upon the provision of a veterinarian-issued "fit-for-slaughter" certificate, so a sick or injured animal needs to be brought *back* to full health so she can be killed. However, "spies" in the slaughterhouse would immediately contact their superiors, and the vet would get a phone call, straightaway, from the local political party backing the gangs. "Doctor, back off." Municipal slaughterhouses are also deliberately under-staffed with veterinarians. In this Kerala municipal slaughterhouse, only two vets were employed. The vet stated their eagerness to "start something," take some initiative, even to clean up the place; however, all "improvements" were stymied by strategic under-provisioning of resources and labor. He told me:

> The vet is supposed to be present during slaughter. But here there is only one vet each for each large slaughterhouse. Realistically how can one vet be present morning and evening? We are supposed to work from 3:00 a.m. to 8:00 a.m. in the morning. Yesterday from 10:00 a.m. to 5:00 p.m. we were in the office. The thing is, if we started something, everything will be done by you. It's all you actually. We don't have anybody to process your paperwork, do the clerical work. The scientific part, slaughterhouse work, paperwork, everything is the sum total responsibility of one vet and we have no support at all. And if I choose not to do any work, nothing is going to happen to me. I can sit back and relax and nothing is going to happen to me.

Back in Rajasthan, the idea of a vet accompanying us had been briefly reassuring but then I became steadily nervous; it looked like neither Manil, nor the men were willing to back down, though we were outnumbered. Ultimately, we had to leave; Manil had little doubt that their hostility was because the bovine section, authorized only to kill buffaloes, likely also contained cows. These suspicions are not unwarranted. In 2019, T. N. Chandrani, a State Animal Welfare Officer for the AWBI in Hyderabad city stated that they were planning to lodge a case with the Telengana High Court, accusing the police, the Greater Hyderabad Municipal Corporation, and the animal husbandry department of failing to halt the illegal transport and slaughter of "cows, calves and other cattle" during Bakra-Id (festival of sacrifice).[43] The Delhi-based Gau Gyan Foundation also lodged a case with the Telengana High Court about the illegal transport of thousands of animals, including cows, calves, bulls, bullocks, buffaloes, and camels, arriving in Hyderabad ahead of Bakra-Id.[44]

Such court appeals, often filed during the Islamic festival, exemplify the fraught intertwining of cow protectionism, and communal, racist, and casteist animal welfarism. *All* religious slaughter is intertwined with the cold economic logistics of disposal inherent to animal production per se. More than 70 percent of the animals slaughtered at Gadhimai, the large Hindu animal sacrifice festival in Nepal, are "spent" or "unproductive" goats and buffaloes from Indian dairying.[45] By putting only cow slaughter in the spotlight, slaughterhouses become sites of micro-resistance for marginalized human groups, and animal bodies themselves become landscapes of communal warfare. However, conducting raids or inspections in cow-slaughtering abattoirs are among the few legal avenues available to Indian animal activists to conduct rescues that might actually result in a meaningful outcome for a farmed animal, leading potentially to their conflation by some with Hindutva extremists. Animal activist raids and inspections in slaughterhouses are not without profuse risks, where they are unarmed and the sites of butchery, by virtue of the trade itself, are heavily weaponized sites. Usually located in Muslim dominated areas, small teams of activists can often be outnumbered quickly, as I was to witness, leading to an enduring situation of threat and risk for local activists (and their families) who live alongside the butchers in the same city. Raids on slaughterhouses therefore tend to occur less frequently than halting of trucks, whether by activists or vigilantes.

In 2017, there were an estimated 1,176 municipal slaughterhouses in India.[46] Largely unmechanized, with hardly any refrigeration facilities, these slaughterhouses cater to domestic consumption.[47] In regional India, slaughter is managed by Panchayats or village-level governance, which maintain the lowest standards for hygiene and pollution control as they are under-resourced.[48] These spaces tend to be heavily controlled by corrupt state institutions or political parties, according to the accounts of both activists and slaughterhouse vets throughout the country who may be intimidated by them, as I would later witness.

One such encounter was recounted to me by Malathi after she had observed and kept watch on a municipal slaughterhouse in Andhra Pradesh for a week. Speaking to distressed households in poor slums immediately around the slaughterhouse, Malathi found out that hundreds of cows and calves—whose slaughter was prohibited in the state—were brought in and killed each weekend. She managed to circle the slaughterhouse precinct, taking photos of the decomposing organic matter and calf skeletons in the open drains around the abattoir. On the next Saturday night, she gathered a mixed team of outraged citizens—two other activists, twelve dairy farmers, and two police constables—to raid the abattoir.

"*Dairy farmers?*" I asked.

Some of the local dairy farmers were furious about the slaughter of their animals who they had abandoned in the Simhachalam temple, Malathi explained. It is ingrained in many poor dairy farmers that wealthy temples could afford to look after their unproductive animals—or they may have hitherto chosen to turn a blind eye. The sale of these calves, widely reported in the media, made their real fates an undeniable reality.

"The farmers are giving Devasthanam [referring to the Simhachalam temple-authorities] calves, they are angry about the slaughter, they all agreed to come with me, 'we will come with you, support you, fight with you.'" she said.

This team arrived after 10:00 p.m. at night and banged on the door. Every window of the abattoir crashed shut and the butchers initially refused to open the doors until they realized that the police were also present. Malathi said:

> Before we raided, five animals had already been slaughtered, calves, and their skins had been hanging on the windows. And we could hear *taka-taka-taka* meat cutting in the next room, we could hear that some butchers are in the slaughterhouse. Some twenty men were there, all butchers. Some animals are inside, they are seeing the cutting in front of them. The animals are shivering [*sic*]. . . . Then we are all entering the slaughterhouse, the policemen are shouting "get out, get out," all the butchers are coming out. Inside [the abattoir] only our staff, the farmers and the policemen. "Immediately leave, don't cut another animal." I threatened them [the butchers].

Once inside the large cavernous hall of the slaughterhouse, the team found several calves, all male, shaking violently in pools of the spilled blood of the dead animals. A large wooden table at the end of the hall held large knives and blocks for chopping through bones and muscle.

"The butchers were requesting, 'okay take the animals but at least give me the meat' but I didn't let them have one hair also," recounted Malathi. "I said, 'I won't give you one calf hair. Just get out.' They hung around waiting for the meat."

The butchers narrowly escaped heavy sentencing, for on that night, there was no female cow killed or awaiting slaughter on the premises. Malathi told me, "That day it so happened, all male calves were being slaughtered. They [the butchers] were lucky fellows that day—if there had been a cow there, they would have had to face a very big punishment."

None of the butchers were formally employed by the municipality though they worked on municipal premises. They received no benefits of stable employment and instead, faced the full dangers of butchering some of the most politically risky animals. Indeed, according to the V. V. Giri National Labour Institute, "Occupations related to slaughterhouses and tanneries remain a last resort for the extreme poor when they fail to get any other work."[49]

The animals were removed to a local animal shelter. In the end, however, the raids culminated in no change. The constables made no arrest—presumably they were bought off; the municipal administration remained resolutely uncontactable; journalists promised to come and never showed up. After close to twenty-four hours of repeated phone calls, the chief veterinary officer finally arrived later the next day, and a journalist and a cameraman from a local television channel came as well.

However, Malathi said, "They took interviews, they printed nothing, showed nothing. I was a very big fool to have believed the media that day."

Everyone had been bought off or silenced. The next weekend, Malathi returned on her own to the slaughterhouse at night. The "cutting" had resumed. This time, no one came to her aid.

"There is no point, just come back, you are a lady, there will be problems," she was told by the police and the farmers.

"I don't come back!" she roared. "I am not a lady! I don't come back!"

Malathi kept vigil outside the municipal slaughterhouse, on her own, all night. Ultimately, everyone had backed off, even from making arrests, for also one other simple reason—there was nowhere to keep the animals. Every shelter and gaushala in the state, indeed the country, was full.

Malathi told me, "I can do rescues, okay. I have the numbers of many police officials, okay. But what will we do with the animals? No place to keep them. Every day I see the long containers on the road on the highway, full of cattle, my heart races. 'Help them, help them, please God, help them,' I pray. 'Help them, God.'"

Malathi had tried to intervene in a municipal slaughterhouse in Andhra Pradesh where cow slaughter was indeed banned, and failed. Later I would bear witness in a Kerala slaughterhouse, one of the few states where authorized cow slaughterhouses operate. In Kerala, there was no legislative hook, however tenuous, for rescue, as there was in Andhra Pradesh. However, many animal activists possess certified animal welfare officer cards issued by the AWBI, which authorizes them to visit slaughterhouses. I made contact with a team which was to conduct an inspection of a municipal slaughterhouse to check if other rules, such as the use of stun guns, were being followed. We quickly formulated a plan; I would join them. Together, we would travel toward the final extremity of the dairy production line.

The activist team showed their letter of authorization to conduct the inspection at the door and within minutes, we were inside the long hall. I noticed a small pile of hooves against the wall—a pile that would grow into a mountain over the night. My mind went into hyper-drive; I could feel my legs shake. I started aiming the camera at the skinned bovines, the piles of flesh, and the rivers of blood on the floor. I would find the next day that every single photo was blurry, my hands had been shaking so much.

The speed of slaughter, even in unmechanized spaces, is rapid. The workers have to constantly keep the animals moving onto the kill floor as the large team of butchers inside work with equal speed to disembowel the dead animals. The violence, as the animals are forced to stay and move in line, was incessant—they were hit hard on the head, their rumps, rods pushed into their vaginas and anuses as they were made to run into the slaughterhouse. It is impossible for animals not to see, hear, smell, and sense others of their herd being killed all around them. A veterinarian from another Kerala slaughterhouse told me later, "The animal definitely knows when the other animal is being slaughtered. Why not! Saturday is mad, it's the busiest day, 250 animals, fourteen booths are there." In Samata's eyewitness account of a city corporation slaughterhouse in Calcutta, he writes:

> At the municipal slaughterhouses in Kolkata, workers, including small children, violently push and drag the animals to the slaughter floor, where they are made to lie in a pool of blood and guts removed from their dead brethren. The animals are then made to watch their companions die while they wait for their turn, their eyes wide with tears and terror![50]

At the far end of the long hall, we could see two bulls, one brown Jersey and one white bull, still standing. As we continued to walk and look, I kept glancing at the pair from the corner of my eye. The brown bull was completely docile and broken; the white one grunted and bellowed, hooves stamping wildly. Within seconds, the men flung ropes around the white bull's four legs, and pulled them together in a single knot; the white bull, wide-eyed in shock, fell on his side with a thud, four legs tied tight together. I looked away.

As one of the activists asked questions of the workers, we learned that about 350 animals would be killed that night, their flesh distributed to hotels, roadside restaurants, and meat shops within hours. As an activist in Kerala, she could only focus on what was illegal about the slaughtering methods, rather than the species of animals being slaughtered. *Why were they not using stun guns?* she asked. The licensed slaughterhouse had none. *Why were they killing on the floor? That is not allowed.* The halal method, motivated by hygiene concerns, prohibits "cutting" on the floor.

The men shrugged. *This is how it has always been done.* Shortly afterward, a group of men claiming to be party workers from a Hindu nationalist party would arrive, menacing and intimidating, and throw one of the male activists against the wall. Calls had been surreptitiously made to bring in reinforcements against the unarmed activists. *Why are you here? Get out unless you want to go the halal way as well.* Later the activists would repeatedly marvel and shake their heads. *But those guys are supposedly sympathetic to cows! What happened to their gauraksha?* It was a reminder of the power of state politics and culture over the attempt of Hindu nationalists in north India to homogenize Hindutva as a national politics. Hindu nationalism is considerably weaker in the South, and in Communist-ruled Kerala, beef was one of the most consumed meats, the local cultural preferences and business interests trumping Hindutva's aspirations at the center.

In the meantime, the brown bull was next. My mind whirred as I looked at him, absolutely still except an alertly flicking tail. Should I stroke him? I felt certain in my bones that I would want a gentle, strong hand to hold me in my final minutes. But what would this bull want— an animal who had likely experienced violence from humans, even in the most routine contexts? Would my touch, my presence, be a comfort when I was a member of the species who was the cause of his death? Courage failed me. I turned my back on him and walked back to the middle of the hall toward the dead bodies mutilated beyond recognition now, pieces of ex-dairy animals already being sectioned into salable commodities as beef, bone char, raw skin, or disposed of as waste.

When I felt it might have been over, I hesitantly turned around. I could see the brown Jersey bull was on the floor, head almost but not entirely severed from his body, resting on the tray, blood gushing out of his neck. I walked back slowly, and bent down to him. Death had claimed all of his life only seconds before, his beautiful bovine eyes now vacant and unseeing.

Shadowy, Underground Cow Slaughtering
It is in underground, shadowy abattoirs, that the buffaloes, cows, bulls, and calves are overwhelmingly slaughtered in India. The scale and size of these illegal slaughterhouses vary widely, butchering anywhere between one or two animals to several hundred a day, together comprising an industrial scale of slaughter. These butcher houses are a critical part of the global animal production supply chain for "raw material" such as rawhide, which is collected by middlemen and forwarded to tanning factories. Domestically, the illegal slaughterhouses are among the most important suppliers of meat. A slaughterhouse vet described his surprise at finding out that Dindigul, which does *not* have a licensed abattoir, is a key source of beef for both Kerala and Tamil Nadu:

> Dindigul where slaughter happens . . . all the offal, etc., comes by the tonne from Dindigul. I asked, is there a slaughterhouse in Dindigul? No, it just comes from a hall like this. This [volume] is from one hall, there are many others. Some of this meat arrives in a chilled truck, maybe it is going to Chennai and some parts may be coming to Kerala. Here in Kerala, people want to buy fresh meat, blood dripping.

In fact, butchers, he told me, want authorized slaughterhouses to be closed altogether. In Kerala, cow slaughter prohibition was not the issue; rather, it was the fact that no rules or regulations need be followed at all in informal sites. Even as municipal slaughterhouses are protected by local gangs and their political connections, they are not entirely safe from occasional government inspections. The vet told me:

> Even the municipal slaughterhouse, they want to shut it down. They can slaughter anyway, without the inspection of the veterinarian and all that

hassle. When we went there, there was just tonnes and tonnes of dung. When I first went there, there was almost two feet of dung. Animal was lying and sitting on the dung. 36 truckloads of dung were taken away. The same animal would be taken for slaughter and there would be dung everywhere.

It is to unauthorized slaughterhouses that the dilapidated animals are sent. My host at the mechanized slaughterhouse at Kanpur had told me that they instruct their middlemen to only bring them animals who seemed healthy, and more importantly, had no obvious physical impairments from "cattle" markets as export-only slaughterhouses have to be scrupulously careful about the law's "fit-for-slaughter" mandate. If an animal was disabled or diseased but "treatable," she would be "treated" until deemed fit enough for killing. If they were, as my companion told me, "hopeless" in terms of the minimum "recovery" required for mechanized slaughtering, those animals were returned to the middlemen, who would send them to the illegal slaughterhouses.

These bovines are often downed, with prolapsed uteruses, or severely disabled with laminitis from years of exploitation in dairying or traction. However, even incapacitated animals try to resist their killing and therefore endure truly horrific violence at human hands that try and make them move at any cost. In *A Life for Animals*, Christine Townend describes walking into an illegal slaughterhouse in Rajasthan where a downed buffalo was being violently subdued.[51] His tail had been broken in so many places that it resembled a pulpy bloody rag—and still he continued to resist and fight. Amit Chaudhery also describes the extremities of the violence inflicted on resisting animals in some of these slaughterhouses in his eyewitness accounts:

> The kine [cows] who wait outside the sheds for their turn are forced to run towards the killing sheds by iron rods inserted into anuses and vaginas, chili powder rubbed in, eyes gouged out, fires lit under them. They are beaten, kicked and dragged with ears, udders, penises, horns ripped.

Illegal slaughtering often takes place in enclosed spaces[52] in poor, segregated neighborhoods, or on the fringes of cities. This is not dissimilar from other informal work such as agrarian production (including but not limited to cotton, sugar, and tanning operations), which might grow on "the edges of secondary or tertiary urban nuclei, whose workers come partly from surrounding villages."[53] The over-representation of poor Muslims and Dalits at the slaughter-end of dairy production is far from coincidental. In the United States, it is the poor ethnic minorities who typically work in slaughterhouses.[54] So too in India, writes Breman: "Workers for the most humble and miserable forms of informal sector work, people who roam the streets and open-air workplaces, are mostly recruited from the lowest ranks of the social hierarchy. They belong to tribal and *dalit* communities."[55] The Maharashtra beef bans in 2015 led to Dalit protests as "thousands of Dalits work in slaughter houses, tanneries and leather factories."[56] Similarly, "India's leather sector is still almost exclusively reliant on Muslims and Dalits for the 'dirty work' of skinning and tanning."[57]

Underground slaughterhouses can thus become sites of sectarian, communal, and casteist volatility. By the accounts of activists and vigilantes alike, butcher areas can sometimes comprise entire villages, even regions, as they necessarily have to be concentrated and fortified against any intervention. These peripheries can become borderlands, demarcating illegal/legal, Hindu/Muslim, and even India/Pakistan. One cow vigilante who ran a well-maintained gaushala on rented land in Haryana, told me, "All around Delhi are butcher villages, if you go there, it is likely you won't even return. Don't go there. Consider these places mini-Pakistan. When we go there, we leave our lives here and go with faith only."

Butchers too have to become creative as a way of sustaining livelihoods, and indeed, their own lives in these spaces of killing, and many become informers for the Hindu nationalists as a result of these pressures. A Hindu vigilante in Ahmedabad introduced me to their Muslim informer in Godhra city, Gujarat. In 2002, Godhra was the site of a planned pogrom against Muslims when Narendra Modi was the state's chief minister, an event that contributed to the growing muscularity of Hindutva. The Muslim was a former butcher; he now made money through cash bribes from Hindu vigilantes by "informing" on the activities of his butcher colleagues. This was an extremely risky business; discovery by his fellow Muslims could get him killed.

When I asked him about his motivations, he said, "*Main nahin manta* [I don't agree (with the killing)]. It is very difficult, seeing the animals suffering, crying. I have stopped completely, I don't do any *kaasai kaam* [butcher work] now." He was also angry and worried that the butchers were putting the rest of the Muslim community at risk, and wanted to safeguard at least his own by becoming an informer.

These racialized sites of animal butchery are severely degraded environments as slaughtering is a high-polluting activity. A 2017 Central Pollution Control Board (CPCB) report notes that even in recently modernized and government-subsidized abattoirs, "compliance with discharge standards is very poor."[58] Human workers in small and unauthorized abattoirs are maximally vulnerable to pollution and disease. The waste from slaughterhouses is a prolific breeding ground for diseases, and the report highlighted that "solid wastes from abattoirs attract 'vermin'" ("flies, dogs, birds" causing "public nuisance") and constitute a "breeding ground for pathogenic micro-organisms." The toxic waste from blood, organs, and other bodily matter is particularly polluting and sourced from both municipal and unlicensed slaughterhouses. The CPCB warned, "The most significant environmental impact resulting from slaughterhouses is the effluent. . . . Municipal sewer will be choked or over loaded if wastes from slaughterhouses are discharged without basic treatment."[59]

The sheer concentration of such toxic degradation was highly evident when I visited Tangra's cow slaughterhouses in Kolkata. Built during British colonial times, it is one of Asia's oldest formal slaughterhouses. With permission from the municipal offices, I asked to visit after operational hours. Though heavily dilapidated, the old colonial balustrades could still be seen. *This should be a memorial museum*, I thought, *a sobering reminder of how things had once been.* Opposite the old cow abattoir is the mechanized Al-Nazar slaughterhouse, which slaughters buffaloes for export only.

Throughout Tangra, there are innumerable backyard abattoirs, each slaughtering about ten or more animals daily. These slaughterhouses are surrounded by a canal, which is ringed by slums. Mounds of decaying bodily matter, together with plastic and other rubbish, was piled high along and in the canal, with the most terrible smell emanating from the site. As I got talking to a small shop owner dealing in tires outside the slaughterhouse, the man, a scheduled caste resident, told me:

> There is no high-drain, and during rains or Bakra-Id [when ritual sacrifice is performed by residents on the road], the whole place is like a *nali* [small river or drain] and flowing with blood, and even corpses left lying around. The smell is terrible. Pollution is strong in this area but we have learned to live with it, our family has been living here for seventy-five years, many generations.

The holding area for the backyard slaughterhouses is the public commons of Tangra itself—the roads, street corners, shop fronts, and practically every scrap of available land is turned into makeshift stockyards made of dried palms and bamboo. They are makeshift only as regards the construction material—these have been holding spaces for decades. The unwritten agreement between handlers, slaughterhouse, public, and owners of shops and homes (many of whom work in slaughterhouses) is as strong, if not stronger, than any formal agreement.

Informal agreements across not only different production units, but also race, caste, and religious groups are necessary to scaffold the underground slaughter economy. On the way to a "cattle" market in rural Tamil Nadu, my driver and I pulled up outside a ramshackle illegal slaughterhouse in the peri-urban outskirts of Chennai city. This backyard abattoir was openly promoting itself; a large advertising billboard towered over the slaughterhouse. A semi-naked muscular white man dressed in cow leather posed on the hoarding, presumably an aspirational figure for the brown races who could become racially, politically, and sexually powerful like him by consuming emaciated cows and buffaloes. The abattoir was a semi-informal structure of thatched roofs with three small sections segregated by three rough brick walls, used respectively as a "holding" pen for live bovines, the "kill floor," and the "front" area where the corpse would be sectioned and sold.

As I approached, I could see movement through a very small window on a wall on my left; a quick peek revealed two small, thin bulls, ribs protruding, tied to stakes with a paltry amount of dirty hay on the floor. Small slaughterhouses typically work without basic facilities like lights, water supply, drainage, etc. In the front section, a man chopped into muscle and tissue; a pile of fresh black buffalo skin lay on the floor by his table. A multireligious panoply of frames—Radha and Krishna, Jesus, and the white Islamic crescent against green—hung over the thick wooden slab that served as both a counter and a chopping board.

"We are all in this together," the owner explained when I asked about his multireligious pantheon.

The owner of this slaughterhouse was a "low" caste Hindu but his butcher was Muslim. The owner said that while he selected and transported the animals from the market, the *bhai* [a colloquial reference to Muslims]—and emphatically not himself—would perform the actual slaughter.

Recognizing the irony, he smiled slightly as he asked me, "Do you think I have no *pasam* [compassion]?"

When I probed his idea of *pasam*, he said he was not involved in subduing the resistance shown by the animal in her very last minutes.

"I don't drag and tie their legs—I am not the one bringing the knife that close to their face and eyes. I am not the last face they see and curse," he said. At the same time, his words were inflected with self-deprecation and sarcasm; he knew his complicity well, of course.

The man was friendly and happy to run me through the logistics of their work. "How do you slaughter?" I asked, wanting to quickly get the question out of the way.

The man laughed, clearly a bit embarrassed. "You ask him, he is the expert!" he said, pointing to a sixteen-year-old boy who was sitting on the low steps at the entryway. The two nodded at each other and the young man returned with a large iron hammer. I asked to hold the hammer; it was not terribly heavy. "*Pottu addipom*," said the man. *We beat them black and blue.*

"How long does it take?" I asked, not quite being able to imagine the repeated blows on the thick skull of the bovine until it finally smashed. "Big cow, easily it can take thirty minutes," he said. "If it is a calf, much quicker."

The beatings would begin around midnight, explained the man. "We have to be blind drunk for this job." "Why?" I asked. "For courage," he explained. "You cannot do this without drink."

In her work on the Gond, an Adivasi community in Chhattisgarh, Naila Kabeer and others note the role that alcohol plays in allowing men to endure the trauma of their labor as landless farm workers, and the escalated violence against women and children of the community as a result of male alcoholism.[60] The violent impact of alcoholism on the animals entangled in their lives has hardly begun to be understood in critical feminist or animal studies. Perceived untrammeled alcoholism contributes to the view of "low" caste communities as unrefined or lacking in self-control, or in other words, as "wild" or "uncivilized."[61]. However, the very nature of their labor as butchers requires them, as the man put it, to be "blind drunk."

BEARING WITNESS: "WAITING" ANIMALS AND THE ABSTRACTION OF ANIMAL DEATH

I had, from the outset of this research, most dreaded bearing witness at slaughterhouses, worrying about seeing the actual act of killing an individual. A fuller comprehension of the slaughter economy in India increased my despair. The illegal economy of underground cow slaughter was far from marginal or incidental. An industrial if not *industrialized* scale of contraband cow slaughter was *required* to scaffold Indian dairying, through a precarious racialized and casteized labor force who are then violently penalized for this work. And almost always, in the debates around violent casteism and sectarianism that characterize animal slaughter in India as elsewhere, the reality of the *animal* is almost all but abstracted, the focus pinpointed microscopically—and exclusively—on racial contestations around animal killing.

Countering the racism (and casteism and classism) to which slaughtering and agricultural communities are subject is an urgent task analysis against their vilification by the Hindu right and the broader society that wishes to distance itself from the violence from which it profits. To this end, many liberal scholars conclude that *intentional* human violence upon other animals, whether for slaughtering or "sport," is an ethically fraught endeavor that does not automatically equate with animal cruelty. Seeking to offer "an alternative discursive and material repertoire through which to understand the violence of slaughter," Shaheed Tayob argues that it is possible to understand "violence towards animals [such that it] does not demand accusations of cruelty."[62] Muslims (like other groups), he argues, have developed socio-cultural protocols that allow extreme and fatal violence to animals to be morally acceptable. In a similar way, in her analysis of the bullock racing in Maharashtra that was banned by the Supreme Court of India in 2016 for its cruelty to animals, Aarthi Sethi suggests that "the ritual imagines animals not as rights-bearing species, but as members of the agricultural community. [Therefore] [t]he rite does not disavow violence."[63]

This refusal to see animals as politically meaningful, rights-bearing citizens in multispecies landscapes is not fundamentally different from Hindutva rationalizations and defense of *their* ways of exploiting the animals and subjecting them to violence as uniquely ethical. Justifications of fatal violence against animals are not just present in vulnerable human communities; "conscious omnivorism" in many wealthy Western societies, for instance, endorses people "humanely" slaughtering the animals they have raised.[64] These exonerations are, ultimately, mundane *human* ways of developing mythologies and traditions that ennoble cruelty and violence to animals, which are then given sanctified status in our moral imaginations. The justification of willful violence against other animals, and the refusal to take it seriously *as such*, particularly when advanced by scholars of the liberal left, is an unselfconsciously duplicitous departure from parallel analyses of human-to-human perpetration of violence, where the concern and empathy is for the *victims* of violence. Presumably, these scholars would not explain the perpetration of extreme and fatal violence against vulnerable *humans* as ethically fraught or regrettable but ultimately acceptable as part of the social, cultural, and sporting life of privileged groups as long as these elites acknowledged or grieved the suffering that they intentionally caused.

Attending to the emotional lives of the perpetrators of violence, however marginalized, while deliberately disregarding the emotional

and physical suffering of the victims—other animals in this instance—
is non-innocent. Scholar of Christian theology and animal liberation
Nekeisha Alayna Alexis argues: "As a tactic of evasion, emphasizing affect [of the slaughterer] also masks how conscious omnivores perpetuate
the dominant human–animal binary. The result is a circular ill-logic in
which killers are allowed or encouraged to kill so long *as they are troubled
by their killing* [emphasis added]."[65] These justifications are particularly
questionable when advanced by middle- and upper-class scholars who
might be exploiting the animal *and* his human slaughterer to justify
their own consumption of animal products that rely upon such cruelty
and suffering. "Intimate, lethal violence against other animals," writes
Alexis, "is an act of power within a system of power."[66] And legitimating
this violence allows us—even as we purport not to do so—to minimize
the physical, psychological and emotional harms to humans who are engaging in labor that by its very nature constitutes brutality, and overlook
its implications, even for human society.

Imagining only humans as "right-bearing subjects" to justify human
violence against other animals becomes inconsistent when the *suffering*
of abjected human beings is perhaps *the* central motivation to become
political on their behalf. However, the suffering of another animal, even
and especially when caused by deliberate human action, becomes easy
to disregard, when it is this very suffering that makes animal torture
itself a form of entertainment. The casual bypassing of animals' suffering *because animals' protests and resistance are not recognized in their
own terms* destabilizes the integrity of the intent and spirit of such liberal outrage that it is reserved exclusively for human beings. The respect for human rights is not just about protecting the fundamental
entitlements of life but also demands that we "*force ourselves* to respect
and protect that which is alien, different, vulnerable, indefensible and
speechless [emphasis added]."[67] It actively requires us humans not to
abstract and diminish those who are so vulnerable to our abstraction
and diminishment.

The totalizing nature of the abstraction of the individual animal along
the slaughter spectrum of milk production was brought home to me in a
visceral encounter for which I was utterly unprepared. My companions at

the Kerala municipal slaughterhouse asked to see, and were taken to the waiting animals. The sight of *waiting* animals in a slaughterhouse—with mere minutes, hours, or days left on the death row, inches away from the knife, with the smell of fresh blood and the deaths of their family members thick in the air—was one of the most confronting of my research. It was a witnessing that was as unexpected and primeval as the milking hour at the Visakhapatnam dairy farm.

We turned right outside the killing hall. It was dark but for a pale moon and the throwaway light from the killing hall; it took a few seconds for me to register the hundreds of *waiting* ex-dairy buffaloes, cows, and bulls—still, alert, silent. A white cow was tied closest to where I stood, glowing softly among the hundreds of bovine silhouettes in the moonlight. She was utterly still, watchful, ears erect, and eyes wide. She and the others stood like statues. It would be an hour before these individuals were moved to a more brightly lit waiting shed on the left of the hall, where death would be much closer.

The singular bodily alertness was unlike any I had ever seen, which can perhaps only come from not just a sense of approaching death, but one's death by *killing*. I was reminded of what the meat microbiologist at the Kanpur slaughterhouse had told me at the very start of this stage of the research—*they know*. Emotions are experienced as bodily reactions across species including humans; risks and dangers to animals can manifest as "adrenaline release, increased heart rate, and muscular changes."[68] Hyper-anxiety can be embodied as the manic frenzy of a female buffalo who was further ahead in the slaughter line, or the deathly still, motionless hyper-vigilance and alertness I witnessed in these bovines.

We didn't spend too long looking at these faces of death; we quickly walked over to the left side. In this section, huge white bulls stood still, all tied to short ropes. On the ground were small hard droppings, akin to pellets of goat feces, unlike the generous mounds of healthy cow dung, pointing to the dehydration and starvation of these animals who had had no food or water since they were loaded onto slaughter trucks days or even a week before.

We asked for some hay; we would feed the animals what we could before they were led off. A man brought a small thin bundle—all that was available—and went to a nearby bull, chained on a short rope, and crouched on the side as he threw some at the animal. Even minutes from death, the beautiful young bull had an innate power and dignity. He and the nearby bulls fell upon the straw ravenously; it disappeared in seconds. Near them, a she-buffalo paced the length of her short rope in escalating agitation; the sight was unbearable. I prayed for their quick deaths, the buffalo especially. I knew that resisting animals often endure some of the most horrific cruelty in any kill-line.

I would repeatedly find that slaughterhouse workers—unlike consumers of meat and dairy—fully accept that the animals have an intuition of their oncoming death, and that they *resist* in many forms—bellowing, howling, charging, brokenness, even begging for mercy. In a large municipal slaughterhouse in Maharashtra, a young worker accompanied me as we walked through huge sections of the lairage area, where hundreds of buffaloes, goat, and sheep were on death row. It was a Sunday, a non-operational day; their killing would commence early the next morning. The piercing wail of a mother goat with bleating kids waiting to be slaughtered, I learnt that day, was indistinguishable from the screams of a distressed woman. The cries continuously rose and reverberated through the lairage. Many kids and lambs curled up against each other, huddled so tightly together that I could not imagine their distress when torn apart on the slaughter line. Some of the goats kept pushing their horns against the locks of the gate, seeming to knowing exactly what kept them trapped.

The young man nodded, "They know as soon as they come here. In the *gaon* [village], they are all skipping around, as soon as they get here, they droop. They know straightaway."

Outside the lairage, we could see a single buffalo at some distance tied to a stake, possibly just brought in by a farmer. As soon as the buffalo saw me—out of the hundreds of workers and farmers moving around in that space—he started bellowing, walking the short length of his rope in agitation. I felt without a doubt at that moment that he was specifically begging me for help.

The slaughterhouse worker with me almost choked up a bit. "He is calling to you, he knows if anyone can get him out of here, it will be you. You are his last hope."

As we drew closer, the buffalo's cries escalated. I walked to him and tried to pat him. He frantically nuzzled and paced against me. I was overwhelmed with grief and self-loathing as I tried to figure out what to do. I had arrived in Mumbai the day before, my first time in twenty years. I was yet to meet any activist who I could call for help. And I worried about his quality of life, even if he were rescued from slaughter; intensive or overcrowded confinement of animals is typical in many Indian shelters. In the end, I turned my back on this desperate buffalo.

As I walked away, I looked back to see the buffalo had turned his head, and was looking at me. I could not be more certain of the shock and betrayal all over his face. I think of him every day, a haunting reminder of the abject failure of not only me, but our human species as a whole.

CHAPTER 8

ENVISIONING POST-DAIRY FUTURES

I WAS BORN and raised vegetarian based on a cultural, caste and religious inheritance of a food tradition. I did not grow up thinking about the ethics, or cultural or environmental politics of what I ate. Although my father's spin on a school prayer, emphatic that I should "thank the *farmer*"—not God—"for the food I ate," always stayed with me. If I had thought more, I might have felt some smugness that my diet did not involve the one thing that *seemed* to distinguish the vegetarian's diet from a meat-eater's—animal slaughter. The inescapable evidence of the animal in a meat diet was constantly around—emaciated chickens trussed up, hanging upside down off the side of motorcycles as they were sped on their way to slaughter; roadside chicken butchers and fish shops; the sharp smell of drying fish in coastal cities; goat kids and lambs tied to poles, awaiting slaughter. The lives and deaths of animals who composed a *vegetarian* diet were less palpable, as such. These individuals, encountered fleetingly, nonetheless became a normative part of the foodscape. Even then, I intuitively knew not to look too closely. I learned to be indifferent.

Much later, I would, painfully, unlearn indifference, when confronted with the almost unfathomable scale of suffering, misery and terror that animals condemned to be food experienced, routinely, as a consequence of such indifference. There is nothing natural about such indifference, I started to realize. Indifference to other species is a concerted outcome of human society's effort to ensure that, reduced and reframed as different to humans/not-human/non-human, and above all *animal*, other animals can remain steadfastly outside of our fundamental moral, political, and legal consideration. This is due, however problematically, to the human species alone.

In the era of liberalization in the 1990s in India, with a growing number of middle- and upper-class Indians starting to travel abroad and returning with stories of eating hamburgers, steak and shepherd's pie, I often felt among the minority of even the Brahmin community I grew up in, because I did not take to eating meat. It feels difficult to emphasize how little—if even at all—the *animal*, including the cow, seemed to feature as a subject of moral consideration in society. While we might have occasionally seen cows brought to temples for worship, they did not—and could not—register in our minds as also their own sentient beings, when we saw them objectified as gods and goddesses. The immigrant or foreign-returned beef- or meat-consuming Brahmin was largely simply undertaking a rite of passage into becoming part of Western society. I remember, as a young PhD student and research assistant to a senior professor in Australia, I was given responsibility to organize catering for a workshop which included a lunch BBQ. Two days later, a member of the administrative staff called me in panic, apologizing for the "cultural insensitivity" in asking me to organize a lunch involving dead cows. I reassured her that it had not even crossed my mind to be offended, and indeed, it had not. I was, if anything, mildly annoyed at being stereotyped as a cow-worshipping Hindu.

Nonetheless, it came as a profound shock to learn that my diet was no more innocent of animal slaughter than a meat-eater's, and specifically, that one of the largest areas of animal slaughter in India (and globally) occurs for *dairy* (and eggs), products that are routinely present in vegetarian diets. Through the years of this research, to learn, undeniably, about these farmed animals' *individual* personalities, their profoundly rich and advanced emotional lives, and to viscerally witness their suffering, misery, and terror in being reduced to, and objectified as a "food" animal, was almost debilitatingly traumatic. And I think this resonates with most people in an intuitive, shared *animal* empathy. "I could not do what you do," I'd be told over and over by meat-eaters and vegetarians alike. "I could not see what you see." And then to realize at far greater depth than I could have envisaged, the pernicious configurations of sustained, violent exploitations of systemically marginalized, abjected human communities that scaffolded dairying, further immobilized me.

How best does one respond? In a fraught context like India, where the consumption of animals (or not) is a deeply polarized, casteized, and racialized political battle, and where the livelihoods of farmers is at stake, how might less exploitative and less precarious futures be enacted? What would this require of us, as multicaste, multiracial, and multireligious human communities and as a species, both in our obligations to each other as humans and our accountability to members of other species? It is when we no longer weaponize animals for our politics, or objectify them as food, that we humans also have an opportunity to stand more nakedly in front of each other, *as* humans. In India, a post-dairy society is perhaps the foundation of the fullest extent of an anti-Hindutva politics, i.e., an anti-anthropocentric anti-Hindutva resistance. Our very humanity, I believe, might depend on post-dairy (and post-meat) futures.

THE LEFT'S FOOD SOLIDARITY: (BUT) WHAT OF THE ANIMALS?

Food is a highly political dimension of human existence, raising complex questions and provocations around health, environment, and the cultural dimensions of what, and increasingly, *who* we eat. Anxieties around food—product, smell, cultural notions of its purity, even cooking methods—have been used to oppress, legitimize, or dehumanize some cultures, castes, races, religious traditions, or genders over others. What or *who* we eat, builds, nourishes, or pollutes and sickens the nation itself.

Illustrating these complexities, in 2020, the National Democratic Progressive Party in Nagaland, affiliated with the BJP, banned dog meat in the state. In contrast to the outrage against cow beef, the debate around dog meat, notes anthropologist of Nagaland Dolly Kikon, "does not centre around religion but on a civilisational logic."[1] Kikon writes, "If ban on cow slaughter became a legitimising move to persecute religious minorities, the dog meat ban represents a moment of civilising savages, one where animalistic tribals are being taught about clean and safe food." Dog meat in fact does not feature centrally in the Naga diet, and is consumed by a small tribal community. The live trade of dogs for meat, notes Kikon, is also not hidden; transactions occur openly in marketplaces, where dogs are sold next to commonly slaughtered animals like chickens. However, as eating dogs, per se, is seen as unique to Nagaland, dogs become a handy weapon to provoke "violence, hate and racism" against the "collective Naga identity itself" such that the dog and the dog-eating Naga have become inseparable in "mainland" Indian imagination.[2] Notably, it is not flesh foods alone that are racially weaponized. While cooking and processing all types of food may generate particular smells, Kikon writes at length about how the Naga process of fermenting plant foods such as soya is also regarded with disgust because the aroma thus produced is regarded as "revolting."[3]

Against this backdrop, vegetarianism in India has been politically problematic due to its fascist associations in the making of a "hyperbolic vegetarian" Hindutva state.[4] In a caste system, where a significantly vegetarian community sees itself as at the top of the social scale—and "pure" as a result—it emboldens the fascist use of vegetarianism to strengthen this perceived distinction. These fraught political complexities are located against a vast historical and contemporary landscape of horrific and ongoing brutality against other animals in the name of food, fashion, medical and scientific experimentation, among others. The rage and outrage against the violence to (other) animals often crystallizes into misanthropy—more specifically, a racialized misanthropy. Aryanic fascism, both Germanic and Hindutva, have regarded for instance, the Semitic religions—Christianity, Islam and Judaism—as sanctioning violence against animals, and consider non-Semitic ideologies of care toward animals—Nazism or Hindutva—as their civilizing distinction.[5]

However, as this book has demonstrated throughout, Hindu practices of reverencing nature can be as profusely violent, extractive, and
anthropocentric, particularly if nature is valuable economic and political
capital. The perception of Hinduism as a "nature religion," as ecologically
friendly, in harmony with the environment, and as a protector of Mother
Earth is not straightforward. Bron Taylor describes nature religion as
"an umbrella term to mean religious perceptions and practices that are
characterized by a reverence for nature and that consider its destruction
a desecrating act."[6] However by no means are nature religions or various
forms of such religiosity—*"natural religion, nature worship, nature mys-
ticism,* and *earth religion"*[7] uniformly or universally benevolent in their
attitudes and approaches toward nature; they can also be unequivocally
violent in their treatment and exploitation of nature, especially animals,
in the name of worship and piety. Scholar of nature and religion Catherine Albanese makes a crucial distinction between nature as sacred and
nature as a *sacred resource*; in the latter case, the value of nature based on
its *utility* can drive violence against nature.[8] Domination of nature can
be an inherent part of the religious practices of what can be regarded as
nature religions.

The resurgence of Hindutva's perpetuation of violence against Muslims and Dalits for being "beef-eaters" is only the most recent manifestation of fascist vegetarianism, against a long historical backdrop of Hindu
"upper-caste" injuries to Dalits and Muslims by weaponizing meat to
convey contempt and superiority. How can those of us from privileged
communities genuinely and meaningfully disassociate ourselves from
such historical narrow-mindedness and violence? How can we best demonstrate that such fascist vegetarianism is *#notinmyname?*

The response of the progressive, liberal left to such fascism, can *also*
be reactionary, often unselfconsciously so, as the immediate response,
understandably, might be to empathize with oppressed humans. To show
solidarity with the subaltern targets of Hindutva fascism, Hindu intellectual progressives often start to consume beef or pork (as yet, we do
not know of "upper-caste" scholars of the liberal left eating dogs!) An
"upper-caste" female Hindu scholar told me with pride that while she

never used to eat beef before, she was now an avid and enthusiastic consumer to show "solidarity" with the human targets of Hindutva extremism. In her reflections on Indian dietary politics, Naisargi Dave recounts
being told at lunch with young Indian human rights activists that there
would be no vegetarian option available as "vegetarianism is a tool of the
right wing. It's coercive, and it's oppressive, and it's elitist dietary politics."[9] Demonstrating the same lack of imagination that sees a (Muslim)
beef-eater as a threat to the Hindu civilization, in the worldview of many
of the Indian left, the vegetarian can only be a Hindu fascist. "I would be
hard-pressed to think of [another] place," continues Dave, "where being
progressive precisely means militantly eating animals, whether you want
to or not."[10] Ironically, Dalit groups themselves by no means demand
beef consumption by other groups as solidarity—quite the contrary. I
recall Sudesh the Dalit student leader in Osmania explaining the central
politics of the beef festival: "Don't eat it if it makes you uncomfortable.
We are not asking anyone else to eat, we don't want to force anyone—if
we did, how would we be different from those forcing food choices on
us?"

This singular framing of vegetarianism as fascist blurs the reality
of the sentient, suffering animal who is rendered object *and* abject as
unworthy of consideration, and does not, in fact, constitute the most
meaningful form of solidarity with marginalized human groups. The
liberal "upper-caste" who eats beef to show solidarity with Muslims and
Dalits, has missed the point, and in fact, has negated the real problem
even more, because *beef is not the problem.* As Dave writes, "What this
high caste person doesn't understand is that *people aren't subject to violence
because they eat beef. They are subject to violence because they are Muslims
or Dalits* [emphasis added]."[11] The liberal left eating beef as resistance
to Hindutva, or in solidarity with Muslims and Dalits, is emphatically
neither resistance, nor solidarity; it is in fact, a dangerously misguided
reinforcement and validation of the political symbolism of beef and the
cow as key differentiators of Hindutva politics.[12] By eating beef, notes
Dave, privileged progressives "are not rejecting the use of the cow as a
violent symbol; it's appropriating it, and not appropriating it in a way

that undoes the problem. It's more of a wholesale adoption of an ideology than an appropriation, actually."[13]

Differential treatment of Hindus and Muslims around the same issues is often pervasive in India. In April 2020, Muslims were charged with conducting "Corona Jihad" against Hindus, and spreading coronavirus in India, when the Tablighi Jamaat gathering of Sunni Muslims in New Delhi emerged as one of the early super-spreaders. All too predictably, lynching against Muslims resumed; a Muslim man on a motorbike near Delhi was almost strangulated to death by Hindu mob looking for a "scapegoat."[14] A week earlier however, in late March, on the very first day of the nationwide lockdown, Uttar Pradesh Chief Minister Yogi Adityanath attended a Ram Navami event at the controversial Ram Janmabhoomi Temple at Ayodhya.[15] In January 2021, despite India having the second largest COVID-19 caseload in the world, and against the looming threat of the rapid spread of the Delta variant of the virus, tens of thousands of Hindu pilgrims attended the annual week-long Kumbh Mela festivities in Allahabad, with organizers expecting over a million devotees.[16] The most catastrophic, mega super-spreader was to come in April 2021, as close to *nine million* devotees congregated for the month-long Kumbh Mela celebrations,[17] leading to the devastating second-wave of the coronavirus that is estimated to have claimed about 5 million lives in India.[18] Ashish Jha, dean of the School of Public Health at Brown University, called the Kumbh Mela "the biggest superspreader event in the history of the pandemic."[19]

In another instance of misplaced solidarity as resistance to Hindutva's cow protectionism, in 2017 Delhi-based photographer Sujatro Ghosh created a provocative visual project depicting Indian women in assorted spaces—on the road, in a classroom, on trains, and their bedroom—wearing cow masks. Ghosh explained that his intention was to protest the violence perpetrated by Hindu cow vigilantes upon Muslims and Dalits in the name of cow protection, while disregarding gendered crimes against women, especially rape.[20] This well-intentioned project, which sought to challenge violent patriarchy, is emblematic of the cognitive dissonance of humans, wherein sexually violated females of one species are caricatured and mocked to protest the sexual violence against the females of another, that is, ours. In one unselfconscious depiction, a woman is wearing a cow mask as she is waiting to make her purchase outside a meat shop. This is only possible when the toxic cocktail of humanism, anthropocentrism, and speciesism negates a spectrum of extreme violence, including sexual violence against other animals in the name of farming, *as violence*, thereby allowing animal farming to occur without inconvenient moral earthquakes.

The real, more difficult question that gets elided in all this frantic beef consumption is: how can privileged progressives genuinely show solidarity with marginalized groups in a manner that honors and values them as equal, safe and rightful citizens in India?

The reduction of the animal as a mere fetish to be bullied, terrorized, and exploited at will—and the complicity of the liberal left in perpetuating this violence—is out of character with their own claims in advocating for the marginalized, the subaltern, the invisibilized. As Kymlicka and Donaldson note, "The vast majority of the Left—whether feminist, postcolonial multiculturalist, critical race theory, disability, cosmopolitan, and queer—*continues to view human violence against animals with complete indifference* [emphasis added]."[21] The sentient animal is reduced to a warscape upon whom humans wage their bloody battles, and a bargaining tool in negotiating compromises between conflicting human groups. Using animals as pawns or diplomatic objects to negotiate and compromise on intra-humanist strife can be a craven strategy that effectively shields humans from being properly accountable for their role in causing social injustice, inequality, and exploitation in humanist realms. Ultimately, this means that the real issues that cause suffering in diverse human communities remain unresolved.

Compassion for other animals has no place in fascist vegetarianism, where the *animal*, per se, is not even conceptually a concern. The issue is certainly one of race, caste, and religion, but not *exclusively* one of race, caste, and religion. When political analyses focus only on one type of hierarchy (human majority over human minority), rather than also human domination over other animals, only half the story is revealed, Claire Kim argues.[22] In the process, she writes, "Racial and cultural meanings are denaturalized and deconstructed but species meaning—what it means to be human, what it means to be animal—are naturalized once again."[23]

(Other) animal bodies—like human animal bodies—are in fact simultaneously *casteized, racialized, and animalized.* Ultimately, an exclusive focus on humanism that negates all other animals is as dangerously blinkered and violent as, for example, a narrow focus on the inherent worth of Brahmins or whiteness or maleness to the exclusion of everyone else. Seen another way, a continued affirmation of humanism in what is, and always has been, a multispecies political landscape is *also* intolerance, conservatism, and illiberalism.

We need a radical rethinking of *humanity* and *animality* as means of relatedness. Humanity refers to ways of relating to humans of any race, tribe, color or gender empathetically. In its absolute focus on members of our species alone, the idea of humanity narrows the showing of goodwill, mercy, inclusivity, empathy, and generosity to animals of our own kind only. Our ideas of humaneness have come to exclude relating with unconditional respect to other animals. To acknowledge and reclaim our own animality—not as savage, an understanding of animality that is racist and anthropocentric but rather, as the fullest expression of our humanity as *also* members of a *species*—would be foundational, then, to relating to other animals, as the Constitution of India asks, with "compassion."

Asking us to cross the ethical limitations of solely intra-humanist politics and go beyond into multispecies-inclusive politics of justice, Kim calls on us to engage "a practice of *multi-optic vision*, a way of seeing that takes disparate justice claims seriously without privileging any one presumptively."[24] In other words, rather than dismissing the distress of the "other" as "not relevant" to one's politics or interests, Kim asks instead for "a reorientation towards an *ethics of mutual avowal*, or respectful acknowledgment of other struggles."[25]

Animals suffer immensely as racialized and casteized beings, when they are weaponized and militarized in nationalist politics. These violences are doubled when their bodies are additionally violable as "food." And yet, can we begin and dare to imagine an alternative that extends the fullest possibilities and personal freedoms of democratic, inclusive politics to species other than our own? The embracing of animal rights as *also* a core and fundamental part of progressive politics would, write Kymlicka and Donaldson, require majority *and* minority communities "to give some ethical justification for their treatment of animals. And it is clear that minorities, as much as majorities, are reluctant to do so."[26] Minorities' treatment of animals are easy racialized targets, and in response, "the minority's reaction is typically to point out the arbitrariness and double standards involved."[27] However, the default positionality in either case—the majority or the minority community—becomes an avoidance of focused discussion of accountability for the condition, suffering and vulnerability of the *animal*.

Against this fraught racial and sectarian landscape of identity politics, a significant and notable political philosophy, practice, and movement—veganism—is slowly but steadily emergent in India and elsewhere. The Vegan Society defines veganism as a way of living that rejects:

> all forms of exploitation of, and cruelty to, animals for food, clothing or any other purpose; and by extension, promotes the development and use of animal-free alternatives for the benefit of animals, humans and the environment. In dietary terms it denotes the practice of dispensing with all products derived wholly or partly from animals.[28]

Veganism is not a form of extreme Brahminism. Quite the contrary; Brahminic ritual, as we have seen throughout this book, relies on dairy products, a primary cause of cow slaughter in India. In contrast, veganism eschews the use of *all* animal-derived products, including dairy. Veganism is perhaps the ultimate democratic food politics that asks *all* identity groups to re-evaluate their commodification of animals, regardless of how meaningful such violence is to their cultural, religious, caste, or ethnic identities. In *Veganism*, Eva Haifa Giraud writes, "in order to grasp veganism's distinctiveness as a form of food culture it is, paradoxically, necessary to understand it as *more than a diet*."[29] Rather than being merely about food choices, veganism, she argues, is fundamentally a political examination of human–animal relationships themselves. Bringing (other) animals into political landscapes as *also* stakeholders, veganism asks that human-to-animal relationships across species be politicized. This re-imagining of human relations with other animals is most critical in the case of species objectified as food—human–chicken; human–fish; human–buffalo; human–cow; human–goat, among many others. At the same time, writes Giraud, "to grasp the tensions that surround vegan practice, it needs to be situated as something that is in constant negotiation with markets, specific social formations and institutions, and particular discourses about non-human animals, which attempt to reduce veganism to *just a diet*."[30]

This is no easy task when farmed animals are so thoroughly objectified that they are only seen as resources and about as worthy of compassion and empathy as an inanimate chair or a table. The animal agriculture industry has managed to infiltrate almost all aspects of the commercial and cultural lives of humans, to the extent that it is almost "difficult to envision an alternative" because the absence of these bodies will be seen as a "scarcity."[31] Additionally, a "scientific" or a "rational" objection to veganism that is often raised, specifically in India, is the ostensible environmental case *against it*, because in India, the poor rely on animals for their livelihoods. However, the environmental costs of animal agriculture are so catastrophically high—and the health and ecological benefits so immense—that ironically it is the poor who will bear the immediate and enduring burden of not seriously exploring pathways to a vegan food economy.

THE QUESTION OF ANIMAL-BASED LIVELIHOODS:
A GENUINE ATTEMPT TO EXPLORE AND SUSTAIN
ALTERNATIVES

The environmental case for veganism, in fact, is definitive. A team of researchers led by Marco Springmann at the University of Oxford published a now widely publicized study in the *Lancet Planetary Health* about the multiple benefits to planetary and human health in following a vegan diet.[32] Not only did nutrient levels improve and premature mortality decline, but it "markedly reduced environmental impacts globally": greenhouse gas emissions reduced by as much as 87 percent in some cases; nitrogen-enhancement of the soil, phosphorus application, and use of croplands and freshwater all showed sustained reduction.[33] More than 80 percent of the Earth's farmland is used for animal farming; if retrieved, we would only need 4 percent of this land for plant-based agriculture, and 76 percent could be used for rewilding projects to save species from the sixth mass extinction.[34] In an article in 2018, leading environmentalist George Monbiot wrote: "We can cut our consumption of everything else almost to zero and still we will drive living systems to collapse, unless we change our diets. All the evidence now points in one direction: the crucial shift is from an animal to a plant-based diet."[35]

India has a significant global and national obligation to take accountability for, and reverse the impacts of its animal farming, especially dairying. Dairy economists Smita Sirohi and Axel Michaelowa had noted in 2007 that "India emerged as the largest contributor to the livestock methane budget, simply because of its enormous livestock population."[36] In another study, Sirohi et al. further confirm: "Of the various livestock enterprises, dairying is most popular in the country and dairy animals, which comprise of the majority of the livestock, account for nearly 60% of these enteric emissions."[37] A study led by scientists from the Indian Institute of Technology, Delhi, revealed that the rise in global surface temperatures caused by methane emissions from Indian "livestock" is about 14 percent of the emissions caused by farmed animals globally.[38]

However, the reality of India's methane contributions to global climate change—and the environmental realities of farming animals in particular—is dismissed not just by right-wing politicians but astonishingly, by leading Indian environmentalists. In 2019, in a series of articles damning cow vigilantism because of the real concerns for farmers' livelihoods, Sunita Narain, the editor of India's leading environmental magazine *Down to Earth*, asserted her right as an "Indian environmentalist" to argue *against* a transition to a vegan or even a vegetarian development model because this would destroy the livelihoods of poor Indian farmers.[39] The end of animal farming would "kill" farmers' income, she argues, where animals are their "insurance policy" against "bad times, made worse today because of climate change-induced variables and extreme weather."[40] Narain charges Western models of industrial farming

as responsible for environmental damage, disregarding the fact that Indian animal farming, in toto, is also on a mega-industrial, albeit informal, scale,[41] and is in fact, actively contributing to water scarcity and
desertification. Calling out the "false dichotomy" of the harms of small-
scale versus the industrial factory farm, Gillespie writes: "Less widely
acknowledged, but no less relevant, are the deleterious environmental
impacts of *small-scale* animal agriculture, the unjust labor relations even
on many small farms, and the foundational harm to the animal built into
farming animals at any scale."[42]

In a country ravaged by malnutrition, the heavy over-investment in
animal agriculture severely aggravates the problem. According to the
United Nation's *State of Food Security and Nutrition in the World 2020*
report, India is home to some 14 percent of the world's malnourished,
that is, 189.2 million malnourished people.[43] If that was not devastating
enough, the report further notes that *more than a third*—34.7 percent—of
Indian children suffer from stunting as well as wasting, when they are
severely underweight in proportion to their height.[44] Despite this, large
amounts of arable land are diverted to grow feed for animals, causing
enormous waste of nutrition. As Tony Weis writes in *The Ecological Hoofprint*, this represents "one of the most fundamental imbalances in the
distribution of the world's food supply, as cycling humanly edible grains
and oilseeds through animals to produce flesh, eggs, and milk destroys
much more protein and other usable plant nutrition than it contributes
to human societies."[45] Indian animal farming traditionally used only
waste and by-products from agriculture, as well as "grasses, weeds and
tree leaves gathered from cultivated and uncultivated lands"—and indeed,
plastic and toxins—and "feed has always remained short of normative
requirement."[46] India is now the world's largest producer of raw, semi-
processed, and processed and concentrated animal feed in the world.[47]
The notion that an *avowal* of other animals must mean the *disavowal* of
some humans,[48] or that the end of dairying means negating the interests
of dairy farmers who rely on animals for their livelihoods, then, is hardly
straightforward.

The *avowal of animals* can also be intertwined with the *avowal of
humans*, and, indeed, the *disavowal of animals* can interlace with the

disavowal of some humans. If the end of animal dairying, for instance, means the end of a certain type of livelihood, it can also mean the flourishing of *other* under-invested possibilities in the agricultural sector, such as vegan dairying. State investment through research and development in plant-based dairying can remake livelihoods and labor conditions for poor and exploited farmers, and encourage former dairy farmers to transition to more profitable agriculture. The polluting tanning industry could be replaced with unprecedented opportunities in vegan leather, including but not limited to raw and biodegradable materials such as mushroom, pineapple, coffee, tea, grass, recycled paper, yeast, coconut, and apple "leather."

The fact is that research and development on the potential of vegan production in addressing food insecurity, poverty alleviation, and environmental sustainability are as yet vastly untapped. This is devastating against the fact that India registers the highest rates of farmer suicides in the world, caused by an *under-investment* in agriculture and irrigation, the pressure to grow cash over food crops, and poor credit and trade opportunities.[49]

In contrast, animals are profitable *as* resources because animal industries are heavily state-subsidized globally. India is, in fact, hemorrhaging money it can ill-afford on keeping dairying afloat, and the dairy sector has *not* alleviated poverty in India. It only *appears* to do so, sustained by constant subsidization. In 2018–19, just two Indian states, Gujarat and Maharashtra, invested US$ 72.78 million in dairy subsidies to aid dairy exports, against a heavily over-supplied domestic market.[50] However, "[e]ven after the subsidy, dairies will be losing money on the exports," said Devendra Shah, chairman of Parag Milk Foods, a dairy firm based in the western state of Maharashtra.[51]

Instead of throwing their weight behind a plant-based food production system and seeking solutions to end animal farming *and* abject poverty, scientists in India and elsewhere are looking to modify animal bodies. At the time of writing, medical experiments are being conducted on tens of thousands of bovines in laboratories to reduce the amount of methane they produce through their flatulence.[52] These efforts acknowledge the deleterious effects of animal agriculture on the environment, but instead of questioning the system itself, they rely on invasive and painful techno-fixes as a "solution" that disciplines animal bodies to make *them* climate compliant, rather than human behavior or the food production system itself.

These are devastating solutions for India. It is, in fact, an extreme human rights violation to be diverting precious financial resources away from chronic hunger, homelessness, disease, and poverty, toward animal farming. Hristov et al. write, "In addition, increasing animal production in the developing world may be a costly and long-term process because it will require both genetic improvements and improvements in animal nutrition."[53] And this further absolves humans of taking responsibility for the perversity of causing anthropogenic climate change by breeding cows and buffaloes, who will then also be made responsible for the resultant global warming.

DECOLONIZING AND PROVINCIALIZING VEGANISM

As I pondered the question of how a transition from animal dairying might be facilitated at the level of state institutions, I had intuitively started to think in terms of "product replacement" and the possibilities of vegan dairying, and its potential benefits for livelihoods, climate change, and, of course, the end to animal exploitation. Even in the seven years since I had become vegan, I had witnessed a huge growth in the quantity *and* quality of vegan dairy products, which in some cases were almost indistinguishable from the "real" thing. However, it soon became clear that thinking only in terms of product replacement was an inadequate and superficial way of addressing complex and deeply entrenched social, political, economic, and food security issues.

The core focus of vegan production was not meat or dairy product replacement; it *should be*, I realized, sustaining the farmers' livelihoods, and provincializing veganism through local food and nutrition. Vegan food production *also* had to be decolonized and provincialized to truly meet the farmers' needs, as global food and agricultural systems had become some of the most violent structures of oppression under capitalism, in their ongoing takeover of land, water, genetic and seed material, environment, and local knowledge.

Businesses oriented toward social enterprise and empowerment—whether vegan, fair trade, child-labor free, slave free—now operate in a neoliberalized era wherein "solutions" to persistent social justice problems have become privatized and consumer focused; wherein individuals are encouraged to be good citizens by being good consumers. Want to save the environment? Buy carbon-offsets for flights! Buy water-saving washing machines! Buy solar paneling for your private home! Buy fair trade! Buy organic! Buy! Buy! The message is unrelentingly consumerist—one has to *buy* the salvation of our planet and its living beings through the very consumption focused behavior that has pushed the Earth to the edge in the first place.

In a capitalist system, the thrust of vegan enterprises, and the farmed animal movement more broadly, has so far been on effecting individual, rather than institutional change. This involves asking individuals to make different consumer choices, i.e., to *choose* to buy vegan. As regards animal justice, a strategy that focuses on encouraging different individual choices alone is doomed. As Delon writes, "(a)ttitudinal change in a context of deeply entrenched anthropocentrism has rather low tractability."[54] Social change must be driven by states and enterprises or business rather than by individuals. In the case of the farmed animal movement, Reece argues, "The standard message, 'Go vegan,' is typically targeted at individuals. A corresponding message within the institutional approach would be, 'End animal farming.'"[55]

Under capitalism, like any food production, the challenges for vegan food policy are the industrialization of food, and the exclusion or exploitation of poor food producers. In her article *Fake Meat, Fake Foods* questioning the production of cellular meat, Vandana Shiva lambastes vegan corporations for homogenizing food—in this case, meat—and removing its production from the hands of subsistence farmers.[56] Shiva misses the point when she says, "I had thought that the plant-based diet was for vegans and vegetarians, not meat lovers." Vegans *are* overwhelmingly former meat-lovers and vegetarians who may enjoy the taste of animal products, but want the suffering of sentient animals to be removed from the food production chain. However, she is correct in her outrage that "Fake food is thus building on a century and a half of food imperialism and food colonisation of our diverse food knowledges and food cultures." "Fake food" of any description can cause multiple types of impoverishment—of peoples, environment, cultures, and histories.

Their producers are often non-vegan conglomerates, regarding vegan food production as merely another means to profit. Sofit and Soy Milky, for instance, are some of the leading purveyors of soya milk in India. Their parent companies are the American dairy conglomerate Hershey's and the Australian vegan conglomerate Life Health Foods respectively. Hershey's foray into vegan dairy products is a strategic expansion of profitable avenues; and vegan companies are just as liable to functioning as capitalist corporations. As Arvidsson argues, "corporations always look to create new consumer markets . . . there is nothing inherently ethical in that."[57] While the investment in vegan products by corporations is often celebrated by vegans as a mainstreaming of veganism in society, plant-based capitalism carries the real risk of trivializing veganism's radical political potential.[58] Veganism's popularization through capitalism can reduce the politics to "'just' a diet" through the commodification of vegan food, dulling the critique of dominant human–animal relations, as well as veganism's intersectional potential with "other social justice issues."[59]

Shiva also has a second major objection to vegan replacements which is wholly surprising for a leading environmentalist. She claims that plant-based food production is environmentally unsustainable because of its "reliance" on soy, widely acknowledged as responsible for severe global deforestation, and intensive water reliance. However, Shiva negates the fact that soy is overwhelmingly used for *animal farming*. The Norwegian Rainforest Foundation's report *The Avoidable Crisis*, details the "reckless" quantities of industrial soy grown in developing countries to feed pigs and cows worldwide.[60] As Monbiot dryly notes, "if you want to eat less soya, then you should eat soya: 93% of the soya we consume, which drives the destruction of forest, savannah and marshland, is embedded in meat, dairy, eggs and fish, and most of it is lost in conversion."[61] Further, in taking to heart Shiva's own recommendation to support diverse and indigenous food cultures, soy would only occupy a peripheral role in Indian vegan diets.

A transformative transition to a national vegan food policy must be creatively and simultaneously provincialized and globalized. To this end, investing in animal product replacement (or vegan food that mimics animal products) must be carefully mediated. On the one hand, vegan replacements are seen as necessary to transition to a plant-based diet,[62] particularly important perhaps in a high meat- and dairy-consuming culture such as India. The vast human potential for creativity in veganizing animal-based foods can be a vital driver of vegan entrepreneurship, mostly in astonishingly cheap *and* healthful ways—the use of flax or chia seeds, or chickpea flour as egg replacements, for instance. A form of globalized veganism could also be a critical support to farmers of ingredients used in vegan dairying such as nuts, pulses, lentils, and oats. Indian cashew farmers, for instance, experience extreme poverty (earning less than US$ 1.90 a day), and experience physical and psychological violence as part of cashew production.[63] With state subsidization of cashew, peanut, and oat farming, and addressing entrenched human rights violations in this sector, vegan dairying could provide livelihoods in this sector with an unprecedented boost. Jackfruit farmers in Kerala experienced precisely such an improvement in sales via exports, thanks to the growing use of jackfruit as a substitute for pork in the West.[64] Easily and abundantly grown, "tonnes of it went to waste every year" until recently, causing farmers enormous losses.[65]

In the main, Indian vegan food practices must be robustly provincial and local, drawing on and strengthening indigenous diets that enrich the environment and human health through locally grown, ecologically sustainable plant protein such as indigenous pulses and legumes. Shiva is correct that the homogenization of any food through industrialized or corporate production—including vegan foods—can destroy "the diversity of cultures that have used a diversity of plants in their diets." "Real food," as Shiva describes it, "gives us a chance to rejuvenate the earth, our food economies, food sovereignty and food cultures. Through real food we can decolonise our food cultures and our consciousness." Shiva adds that "real" food is "living"; however, a truly expansive decolonial approach to "our food cultures and our consciousness"—an *anti-anthropocentric* one, in other words—must remove sentient, cognitive animals from the human food consumption chain.

In removing the animal as a resource from the production chain and replacing him with vegan resources, an older battle—of which both Narain herself and ecofeminists like Vandana Shiva have been long advocates—must continue. This is the liberation of the Indian agricultural farmer from the developmental colonialism of global institutions like the World Bank, the International Monetary Fund, and the state. Vegan farming for dairying and other products should adhere to a more socialist model which reinforces rather than undermines grassroots democracy, empowering the farmer through cooperatives that advocate their interests. The elimination of the extractive middleman was vital to emancipation via dairying, as the farmer retained control and a stake in turning raw milk into capital. It would be the farmers' cooperative that would be in charge of the entire spectrum of dairy production.

There is, now, technological know-how for the production of dairy and meat from plant sources. And India has something even better—a bespoke blueprint for dairy management and poverty alleviation, customized to the economic, and socio-political conditions of India, created by "India's First Milkman."

THE LEGACY OF "INDIA'S FIRST MILKMAN": FLOODS OF VEGAN MILK

Verghese Kurien, the widely regarded father of India's White Revolution, was not a dairy farmer. Kurien's legacy was the professionalization and management of a democratic grassroots rural cooperative, based on an unwavering commitment to advance empowerment and self-determination for poor Indian farmers. The fundamental genius of Kurien was astute management skills, combined with a burning desire for social justice. The role of the Kaira Cooperative, the first dairy cooperative that Kurien started, was, above all, poverty alleviation. It was so successful as a grassroots empowerment program that it launched the blueprint for rural enterprise and management, and subsequently, the largest rural poverty alleviation program in the world, replicated throughout countries in the Global South. Cow and buffalo milk was merely a conduit and a resource to cement grassroots enterprise; to this end, an astute management plan, *and* creating a demand for the product were necessary.

What lessons can vegan dairying in India and elsewhere glean from the lessons of India's First Milkman? Kurien's primary driver—and this simply cannot be emphasized enough—was social justice, and his outrage at the condition of India's poorest, the disenfranchized farmers. Kurien's focus was to give the power to create, grow, and flourish into the hands of the farmers.

Kurien thus focused on making sure heavy state subsidies for animal dairying kept the welfare of the farmer paramount, while at the same time ensuring that the "product" was salable. He achieved both. For instance, Kurien lobbied for cuts on imported butter, and with the help of the then-minister of commerce TT Krishnamachari, increased the reduction in butter imports from 25 percent to 67.5 percent, eventually succeeding in placing a complete ban on butter imports.[66] The dairying federation developed by Kurien never refused to buy the milk that was produced, unlike the dairying model in place in developed dairying nations like New Zealand, Denmark, Holland and the United States.[67] As a heavily state-subsidized enterprise, Kurien describes what was possible for poverty alleviation:

> We had one clear advantage in that, unlike private companies impatient to make profits, to sell, to show the shareholders and bosses that they were doing well, we were very patient. It would be a slow and steady progress for us. We kept our sights clearly on the target—the producers must get their due. In our case, the producer was a farmer, mostly a marginal farmer. The challenge was to see that the farmers' interests continued to remain paramount.[68]

Kurien was acutely aware of the pitfalls of privatization in entrenching poverty for the farmers. Kurien was emphatic that subsidies to guarantee farmers' income are even more vital for agricultural farming in Indian climate conditions. He explains: "Since our agricultural production is so dependent on the monsoons, it cannot be finely tuned and planned, and such variations are inevitable."[69] Subsidies remain crucial in an era of neoliberalism and climate change, as agricultural farming is impacted by the slightest seasonal variations in weather. Subsidies are crucial to guarantee both an assured minimum income for farmers and motivation to generate *more* produce, where the state acts as a guarantor by buying all the harvest. State subsidies also insure agricultural farmers against cheap imports.

Can such a model work for vegan farming and dairying? It was none other than Kurien himself who also demonstrated the success of this model for plant-based farmers' cooperatives. In 1977, Kurien was asked by India's then-finance minister H.M. Patel if he could replicate the animal milk cooperative model in the case of vegetable oil, which the country was heavily importing at the time. Kurien unhesitatingly replied in the affirmative—the result was Dhara cooking oil, made from groundnuts and sunflower seeds. Kurien's customized farmers' cooperative model would be adopted for the vegan enterprise, as it had been for the dairy sector. The National Dairy Development model would serve the groundnut farmers in the same way that it did the buffalo and cow farmers—it would buy the raw material unconditionally from the farmers, eliminate exploitative middlemen from the production chain, and "buy both oilseeds and oil, as it deemed appropriate, store these, mill the oilseeds and market the oil."[70] Kurien writes:

> Following the Anand pattern meant the procuring, processing and marketing of vegetable oil would have to be transferred to the hands of those who produced the oilseeds. The oilseed farmers would have to own and command the system and in the process eliminate the *telia rajahs* [oil kings] who interposed themselves between the producers of the seeds and the consumer of the oil. Only this could help us bring to the producer a greater share of the consumer's rupee.[71]

It is possible to argue that there simply won't be wide customer demand for vegan dairy products. As any undergraduate in business management can tell us, however, the opportunity is in *creating one*. An enduring major lesson from Kurien's success in animal dairying is the extent to which he focused on creating a demand on a scale that simply did not exist previously by evoking nostalgia, memories and tradition, sentiment, *and* high-quality products. As Kurien wrote: "But we knew that even while we kept our farmers firmly in focus, we had to make these products as attractive as possible to the market. We sought help from advertising professionals."[72] In creating an advertising meta-narrative that blended bovine lactate with nationalism, wholesomeness, tradition, and the idea of family, Operation Flood could not have been more successful. Its largest cooperative, Amul, has cemented itself over the last five decades as the "Taste of India," the nostalgia of Indian childhood itself.

Fifty years is but a blip in the history of the planetary collective. At the turn of the decade, against a sharp rise in the popularity of right-wing extremism the world over, we are also witnessing an extraordinary assertion of social justice movements in India—the Dalit Lives Matter movement, inspired by the Black Lives Matter movement; farmers' resistance movements; #*notinmyname* in India rejecting Hindutva violence against minorities; the LGBTQI++ resistance that led to the removal of Article 377 of the Constitution which criminalized homosexuality; and, indeed, the comparatively small but nonetheless steady growth of the animal movement as a civil justice movement such as India Against Speciesism. As a planetary collective and as individuals, we are perhaps more ready than ever to forge new traditions and rituals that profoundly reflect our deepest values and outrage against injustice and our compassion, including for animals of other species.

The Constitution of India, acclaimed by many as one of the finest national codes in seeking to uphold ideas of social justice and democracy, is the first in the world to explicitly state that human beings must relate with *compassion for other animals.* Article 51A(g) declares that every Indian citizen has a fundamental duty "to protect and improve the natural environment including forests, lakes, rivers and wild life, and *to have compassion for living creatures* [emphasis added]." The etymological root of "compassion," I learned, was co-suffering. The Constitution of India asks us to *co-suffer* with other animals as a fundamental mandate of good human citizenship itself. If one is to co-suffer, can one possibly cause intentional harm? Through the years of witnessing, and then writing this book, I have thought many times about this beautiful passage from the *Dhammapada.*[73]

All beings tremble before violence.
All fear death.
All love life.
See yourself in others.
Then whom can you hurt?
What harm can you do?

I needed no more convincing that dairying was founded upon perhaps some of the most visceral suffering that is possible for any sentient, living creature to experience—the loss of the relationship between
a mother and her newborn. In moments of real integrity when we allow
ourselves to think about it—*and we must*—we humans can hardly claim
to be unaware of the extreme suffering of mothers, fathers, and their infants, throughout the dairy production chain. As Jessica Eisen says "we
are not without resources for understanding [bovine] lives . . . [we know]
we harm them and their calves when we separate them."[74] Knowing this,
we are obliged to take cognizance of "a new account of truth."[75]

FARM TO FREEDOM: THE COWS OF BHARATPUR FOREST

Toward the end of my research, I finished my interviews early at the
police commissioner's office at Bharatpur, which had the last police
checkpoint in the state of Rajasthan before "cattle" trucks crossed the
state border toward slaughterhouses in Delhi and Uttar Pradesh. After
a quick meal at one of the numerous roadside *dhabas* along the national
highway, I decided to take the time to visit the Bharatpur Bird Sanctuary, one of India's most well-known avifauna nature reserves that is
home to hundreds of resident avian species as well migratory wetland
and dryland birds.

As I paid for my ticket, the man at the counter told me that I would
not see a huge variety of species at this time of year. In February, many
birds like the Sarus Cranes, Eastern Greylag Goose and the Comb
Ducks would have departed for their long journey over the Himalayas
to Central Asia, but the incoming migrants like the Asian Open Bill,
Indian Cormorant, and Purple Herons would not yet have arrived. "That
is okay," I said. After these hard years of witnessing every facet of animal

bodies, lives, and habitats micro-controlled by humans, I simply wanted to take some joy in watching any truly free animals thriving in their natural habitats, seasonally, naturally. This little trip felt like a pilgrimage. I was not there to watch a spectacle; I wanted a glimpse of what the simplicity and purity of true freedom for other animals might look like.

Then the man told me something that stunned me. "Watch out for the *junglee gais*," he said. "If you see them, don't go near."

Junglee gais? The reference was not just to cows who lived in the jungle, but *wild* cows, even feral cows. "What do you mean?" I asked.

The man explained that a few herds of *junglee gais* lived in the Bharatpur forest. They weren't owned, they weren't farmed; they were possibly abandoned as "waste" from the dairy industry, and now, incredibly, were fortunate enough to unexpectedly form free familial herds in the jungle. At least one group of cows lived not too far from the borders of the protected world heritage reserve. On the other side of the fencing was the ticket counter, the forest reserve's parking lot, and the highway that carried thousands of cows, buffaloes, and other animals to their death each night.

"There are some calves in the herd right now," he explained. "We think maybe six or seven new calves, but not sure. But if there is even one calf in the herd, you should not go near. The mothers are very fierce, and the bulls even more so. They will gore you so keep far."

I went with my waiting guide on the three-wheeler rickshaw provided by the sanctuary: motor vehicles were not allowed inside the protected reserve. With his practiced eye, he pointed out several beautiful species of birds on branches and emerging from tree holes that I would otherwise have surely missed. I laughed in happiness when he showed me a dusky horned owl, the largest among the nine species of owls who lived in the reserve, who had, unbeknownst to me, been directly fixing her observant gaze on my every move.

Then he pointed out a sight that showed me what freedom for billions of animals incarcerated worldwide in "farms" might perhaps look like.

Past the narrow trail where we were, far across the marshy wetlands and tree thickets was an open space where we could just about glimpse a herd of about twenty-five of the *junglee gais*. Many of them were white or gray cows, some possibly of the native Rajasthani Kankrej breed, some perhaps abandoned Jerseys, but we were too far to tell. Not even the zoom function on the camera could capture this beautiful large family, and that was as it should be. In the dusky afternoon sun, they evoked *go-dhooli*, the kicking of dust by Krishna's beloved cows in the forest, but perhaps even better, for the cows of Bharatpur forest lived their own lives, in free bodies, on their land.

ACKNOWLEDGMENTS

Vivid images, profuse with color, squawks, shrieks, cries, barks, bellows, and silence, inflect my memories of the multispecies beings who animated the making of this book. In setting out to focus on a particular species of animal, my mind—and heart—was blown open as never before to the myriad and intricately intersectional nature of many lives and worlds. Deep and unfathomable suffering, but also resilience and moments of pure joy, formed a constant backdrop to this work. Five rescued "astrology" parrots, brought hastily to a gaushala in Visakhapatnam where I was interviewing, still cramped in their tiny cages with clipped wings, and then, their unimaginable excitement at the plate of fresh chopped tomatoes they were offered when released into a sectioned area. An activist at a local shelter, exhausted from fights and pleas at a "cattle market," at the end of the day, unable to contain his grief when two men dropped off a healthy frightened "nuisance" cat who they didn't want in their neighborhood. Next to the cow pen in another shelter, a "mad" mother donkey rescued from illegal sand mining, demonstrating severe stereotypic psychosis as she raced round and round her pen, ramming her head hard into a tree at the end of every circle. Her infant foal stood shell-shocked at the center.

Against this backdrop of relentless multispecies witnessing over the seven years it took to complete this research, I was fortunate that this book was nourished in a forest of oaks. I am equally and profoundly grateful to Pradeep Kumar Nath, Dawn William, Katie Gillespie, and my husband Lambert Brau.

It is difficult to convey or overstate the work of frontline soldiers as activists that Pradeep and Dawn perform every day, or the sheer dogged courage it takes to do it. Their logistical, intellectual, and emotional support for this book was unfailing, finding ways to help me undertake the most difficult of field research, even when the demand on their own time was acute. I am honored to count Pradeep and Dawn among my friends and teachers in the world of animal activism and politics.

Katie's support of this book—intellectual, emotional, critical, and even logistical through cross-continental real-time witnessing of my field sites in India—is quite simply impossible to describe. In her care for the various individual animals who were part of this work through the years, combined with brilliant and sustained critique of this work through endless readings—and ultimately, naming this book—Katie is, indeed, this work's fairy godmother. Bearing every unfiltered experience and thought, to virtually thousands of cooked meals, to reading endless shabby drafts—as a soil microbiologist—my loving husband Lambert is this book's third parent. In enabling our backyard to become a micro-sanctuary for chickens liberated from egg farms, Lambert's exceptional care for them makes our shared hen-human home a space of multispecies joy, and acute learning about the reproductive exploitations imposed upon farmed females of another species, this time, for eggs.

The book has benefited from the keen insight of many friends and colleagues. I am especially grateful to Kama Maclean, Dinesh Wadiwel, Dolly Kikon, Fiona Probyn Rapsey, Krithika Srinivasan, Priya Chacko, and Naisargi Dave (who also helped name the "Breeding Bovine Caste" chapter). Special thanks to Robert Horvath for being pivotal in enabling this research to occur.

My teachers, like the disciple Dattatreya's, also come from nonhuman worlds. Our elderly cat, the late Kato Brau (2000–2018) stunned me with the sheer force of his individuality, ensuring that I could never again look at any animal and fail to perceive the *individual*. Each of our eight ISA brown hens—"commercial egg breeds" who have lived, flourished, and some of whom have now died in our care—have startled me with the depth of chicken individuality and uniqueness. Sultam, Rani, Rooibus, Lila, Rhea, Miller, Popper, and Charlum have each shown me the sheer zest that chickens have for truly enjoying their lives, an extraordinary inspiration that most humans rarely get to perceive.

My warmest thanks to Thomas Blom Hansen, series editor of the "South Asia in Motion" series at Stanford University Press, for providing this book with a home. I could not be more grateful to the two anonymous reviewers of this book for steadfastly meeting the book on its own terms, while raising the most insightful critiques and suggestions for its improvement. Their time and investment have markedly improved this book. I am very grateful to the press editors Dylan Kyung-lim White, Kate Wahl, and Marcela Cristina Maxfield for seeing this book through at various stages. I am also thankful to Sunna Juhn, Sarah Campbell, Erin Ivy, Emily Smith, and Tiffany Mok for overseeing various aspects of production and copyediting, Kapani Celeste Kirkland (marketing), and to Jason Anscomb for rendering such a moving cover.

Across India, I have been readily helped by a wide spectrum of interlocutors: animal activists, dairy farmers, workers in the informal economy, political workers, and industry and government officials and workers in state after state. In their willingness to invite me into their worlds by revealing and accompanying me to critical local field sites, oftentimes over several long days, enabling an ongoing shared sense of these worlds by regularly sending me WhatsApp updates and receiving me back into their lives year after year, they have allowed me a more vividly kaleidoscopic immersion in India's cow politics than I could have imagined. In particular, I owe thanks to Jayasimha Nuggehalli, Shreya Paropkari, Sumanth Bindumadhav, and Preethi Sreevalsan. In naming the people who enabled this research, I am acutely mindful that this is scarcely half the story. I am profoundly grateful to the many willing participants of this research, the nature of whose work, affiliations, and stakes—or sheer vulnerability in socio-political worlds—makes it impossible for me to identify and thank, but without whom, this story could not be even partially told.

I owe a debt of gratitude to Eliza Waters and Esther Alloun respectively for outstanding research assistance through the first four years of this project and its final two years. At various stages, the project has benefitted from the contributions of Gonzalo Villaneuva, Paula Arcari and Katherine Calvert.

I am grateful for the support that I have received at my home institution, the Alfred Deakin Institute for Citizenship and Globalization at Deakin University, that has provided a sustained and supportive home for the intellectual work of this book and friendship and mentorship. In particular, I thank Fethi Mansouri, Emma Kowal, Anita Harris, Melinda Hinkson, Andrew Singleton, and Shahram Akbarzadeh. For administrative support, my thanks to Yvonne Williams, Arlene Pacheco, and Helen Andrew. Special thanks to the Deakin South Asia office in New Delhi, especially Kanika Chauhan, for exceptional on-ground, logistical support throughout this research, which brought so much ease to difficult research conditions. I thank the Australian Research Council for a Discovery Early Career Researcher Award (DECRA) that supported this research.

I acknowledge permissions for using parts of previously published work: "Animals and urban informality in sacred spaces: Bull-calf trafficking in Simhachalam Temple, Vishakapatnam," in *Religion and Urbanism: Reconceptualising Sustainable Cities for South Asia*, ed. Yamini Narayanan, London: Routledge, 143-161, 2016; "Animating caste: Visceral geographies of pigs, caste and violent nationalisms in Chennai city," *Urban Geography*, https://doi.org/10.1080/02723638.2021.1890954, 2021; "*Jugaad* and informality as drivers of India's cow slaughter economy," *Environment and Planning A: Economy and Space* 51 (7), 1516-1535, 2019; "'Cow is a mother, mothers can do anything for their children!' Gaushalas as landscapes of anthropatriarchy and Hindu patriarchy," *Hypatia: A Journal of Feminist Philosophy* 34 (2), 195-221, 2019; "'Cow protection' as 'casteised speciesism': sacralisation, commercialisation and politicisation," *South Asia: Journal of South Asian Studies* 41(2), 331-351, 2018.

My thanks for the opportunity to speak about this book through the years to Fiona Probyn Rapsey, Rivke Jaffe, Raf de Bont, Maneesha Deckha, Will Kymlicka, Sue Donaldson, Jishnu Guha-Mazumdar, Don Kulick, Paula Arcari, Richard Twine, Lori Gruen, Katie Gillespie, Jonathan Dickstein, Barbara Hodrege, Assa Doron, Amitabh Mattoo, and Barbara Creed.

For friendship, "life" conversations, and cocktails through the years: Emma Kowal, Crystal Legacy, Robert Horvath, Eugenia Demuro, Margaret Raven, Kama Maclean, Poornima Mohan, Priya Chacko, Maree Pardy, Elizabeth Grant Suttie, Aleisja Henry, and Sam Balaton-Chrimes. I am deeply grateful to Jennifer Wolch for bearing witness to multispecies realities with me in India, and for her unstinting support and compassion for animals and animal researchers enmeshed in these worlds. My gratitude to Ashima Obhan for pivotal help in this book coming to fruition. I am thankful to Fizzah Shah for taking Rafi ("Beloved of God"), a "stray" kitten who I rescued in Mumbai. Allowing me to rescue an individual in field sites through which I was fleetingly passing, and taking on their lifetime care, is a gift.

Many more-than-human others who sustained this work through the years are now no more. Bandoo, the sweet street dog who was a fixture through many visits to Simhachalam, died before the end of this research. Each of the sixteen hens, chicks and one frightened rooster I rescued from a Visakhapatnam "poultry" market died in the ensuing months despite medical care. Sultam, our top hen in our rescue flock in Melbourne (and my favorite girl) who ran a tight flock for six years after liberation, died of a cardiac arrest. My love to Marley, a sweet and extremely sick puppy who I rescued from a Jaisalmer slum, who died barely two weeks later. My thanks to Stray Assist for providing him with end-of-life care. And virtually all the individual buffaloes, cows, bulls and calves—and goats, sheep, lambs, camels, chickens and pigs—I witnessed through the years in various field sites, many of whom I think of daily, sometimes hourly, can be presumed to be no more.

Closer to home, our now ageing liberated hens Ranum Brau, Ruber Brau and Charlum Brau, and our cats Bas, Bean, and Ruder who people my every day. The native Australian ring-tailed possums, rainbow lorikeets, magpies, and bats who come to our backyard for figs and persimmons, and on whose native land, territory, and habitat this work has unfolded. The non-native Indian mynas, rock pigeons, and Eurasian collard doves who are among the millions of racialized multispecies beings persecuted as "pests," leading precarious lives in settler colonies, some of whom share our worlds (and the chickens' food). My enduring gratitude and respect for the learned elders and traditional owners, the Wurundjeri People of the Kulin Nations on whose land in Naarm/Melbourne I have lived and worked through most of this research.

Above all, Goddess Saraswati, from the beyond-human realms, for holding vigil over my quest for learning and knowledge.

NOTES

INTRODUCTION

1. *Independent.* 2019. "Inside India's Plastic Cows: How Sacred Animals Are Left to Line Their Stomachs with Polythene," 24 February. Retrieved 16 May, 2019, from https://www.independent.co.uk/news/world/asia/india-delhi-plastic-cows-shelters -bjp-modi-gaushala-a8794756.html.

2. Patnaik, Prabhat. 1993. "Fascism of Our Times." *Social Scientist* 21 (3/4): 69–77.

3. *India Today.* 2016a. Muslim Couple Beaten Up in Madhya Pradesh Over Beef Rumours," 15 January. Retrieved 14 November, 2019, from https://www.indiatoday.in/ india/madhya-pradesh/story/muslim-couple-beaten-up-in-madhya-pradesh-over-beef -rumours-303965-2016-01-15.

4. Shinde, R. 2016. "The Most Powerful Weapon of the Gujarat Dalit Revolt." *Huffington Post*, 29 July. Retrieved 7 February, 2022, from https://www.huffpost.com/ archive/in/entry/the-most-powerful-weapon-of-the-gujarat-dalit-revolt_a_21441261.

5. BBC. 2016. India Protests Continue After Cow Protectors Assault Dalits in Gujarat." 20 July. Retrieved 31 July, 2016, from http://www.bbc.com/news/world-asia-india -36844782.

6. Shinde, 2016.

7. Human Rights Watch. 2019a. *Violent Cow Protection in India: Vigilante Groups Attack Minorities.* Retrieved 7 August, 2019, from https://www.hrw.org/sites/default/files/ report_pdf/india0219_web3.pdf.

8. *The Hindu.* 2019a. Rajasthan High Court Quashes Cattle Smuggling Case Against Pehlu Khan, His Two Sons and Driver," 30 October. Retrieved 7 February, 2022, fromhttps://www.thehindu.com/news/national/rajasthan-hc-quashes-cattle -smuggling-case-against-pehlu-khan-his-two-sons-and-driver/article29832749.ece.

9. Tomlinson, H. 2016. "Woman and Cousin, 14, 'Gang-Raped for Eating Beef.'" *The Times*, 13 September. Retrieved 28 July, 2021, from https://www.thetimes.co.uk/ article/woman-and-cousin-14-gang-raped-for-eating-beef-pwrz3w87h.

10. NDTV. 2016. "'Minimal': That's How Minister Describes Beating of Women Over Beef Rumours," 28 July. Retrieved 7 July, 2022, from https://www.ndtv.com/india-news/ minimal-thats-how-minister-describes-beating-of-women-over-beef-rumours-1437406.

11. NDTV, 2016.

12. NDTV, 2016.

13. Human Rights Watch, 2019a.

14. Human Rights Watch, 2019a, 15.

15. NDTV. 2018a. "Under Modi Government, VIP Hate Speech Skyrockets—by 500%," 19 April. Retrieved 21 December, 2019, from https://www.ndtv.com/india-news/under-narendra-modi-government-vip-hate-speech-skyrockets-by-500-1838925.

16. NDTV. 2018b. "In New Hate Speech, BJP Lawmaker Says 'Hindustan is for Hindus.'" 2 January. Retrieved 21 December, 2019, from https://www.ndtv.com/india-news/in-new-hate-speech-bjp-lawmaker-vikram-saini-says-hindustan-is-for-hindus-1794689.

17. NDTV. 2018c. "'Smuggle, Slaughter Cows, You'll Be Killed,' Warns Rajasthan BJP Lawmaker," 25 December. Retrieved 21 December, 2019, from https://www.ndtv.com/india-news/smuggle-slaughter-cows-youll-be-killed-warns-rajasthan-bjp-lawmakergyan-dev-ahuja-1791811.

18. NDTV, 2018b.

19. Narayanan, Y. 2019a. "'Cow is a Mother, Mothers Can Do Anything for Their Children!' Gaushalas as Landscapes of Anthropatriarchy and Hindu Patriarchy." *Hypatia: A Journal of Feminist Philosophy* 34 (2): 195–221.

20. Iliah, K. 2004. *Buffalo Nationalism: A Critique of Spiritual Fascism*. New Delhi: Sage.

21. Hardy, K. C. 2019. "Provincialising the Cow: Buffalo–Human Relationships." *South Asia: Journal of South Asian Studies* 42 (6): 1156–1172. doi: 10.1080/00856401.2019.1680484.

22. Wilson, H. H. (ed. and trans.). 1840. *The Vishnu Purana: A System of Hindu Mythology and Tradition*. London: John Murray, 151.

23. Hardy, 2019, 17.

24. Iliah, 2004, xv.

25. Iliah, 2004, vi.

26. Pachirat, T. 2012. *Every Twelve Seconds: Industrialized Slaughter and the Politics of Sight*. New Haven, CT: Yale University Press, 14.

27. Adams, C. J. 2010. "Why Feminist-Vegan Now?" *Feminism and Psychology* 20 (3): 302–317.

28. Baber, Z. 2004. "'Race,' Religion and Riots: The 'Racialization' Of Communal Identity and Conflict in India." *Sociology* 38 (4): 701–718: 703.

29. Natrajan, B. 2021. "Racialization and Ethnicization: Hindutva Hegemony and Caste." *Ethnic and Racial Studies* 45 (2): 298–318. https://doi.org/10.1080/01419870.2021.1951318.

30. Natrajan, 2021.

31. Thapar, R. 1996. "The Theory of Aryan Race and India: History and Politics." *Social Scientist* 24 (1–3): 3–29.

32. Hansen, T., Blom. (1994). "Controlled Emancipation: Women and Hindu Nationalism." *The European Journal of Development Research*, 6 (2): 82–94; Subramaniam, M. (2014). "Resisting Gendered Religious Nationalism: The Case of Religious-Based Violence in Gujarat, India." *Gendered Perspectives on Conflict and Violence*, 18B: 73–98; Gupta, Charu. 2001. "The Icon of Mother in Late Colonial North India: 'Bharat Mata,' 'Matri Bhasha' and 'Gau Mata.'" *Economic and Political Weekly* 36 (45): 4291–4299.

33. NDDB. (2017). *Facts at a Glance: Summary of Operation Flood Achievements.* Retrieved 22 December, 2019, from https://www.nddb.coop/about/genesis/significant/facts.

34. Twine, Richard. 2010. Intersectional Disgust? Animals and (Eco)Feminism. *Feminism and Psychology* 20 (3): 397–406, 400.

35. Srinivasan, Krithika. 2016. "Towards a Political Animal Geography?" *Political Geography* 50: 76–78, 76.

36. Deckha, Maneesha. 2015. Vulnerability, Equality, and Animals. *Canadian Journal of Women and the Law* 27 (1): 47–70.

37. Probyn-Rapsey, F. 2018. "Anthropocentrism." In *Critical Terms for Animal Studies*, ed. L. Gruen, 47–63. Chicago: University of Chicago Press, 47.

38. Calarco, Matthew. 2016. Reorienting Strategies for Animal Justice. In *Philosophy and the Politics of Animal Liberation*, ed. Paola Cavalieri, 45–69. New York: Palgrave Macmillan, 54–55.

39. United Nations. n.d. *Universal Declaration of Human Rights.* Retrieved 12 July, 2021, from https://www.un.org/en/about-us/universal-declaration-of-human-rights.

40. Farmer, P. 2003. *Pathologies of Power: Health, Human Rights, and the New War on the Poor.* Berkeley, CA: University of California Press.

41. Yamin, A. E. 2016. *Power, Suffering, and the Struggle for Dignity: Human Rights Frameworks for Health and Why They Matter.* Philadelphia, PA: University of Pennsylvania Press, 4, 21.

42. Cochrane, A. 2013. "From Human Rights to Sentient Rights." *Critical Review of International Social and Political Philosophy* 16 (5): 655–675, 655.

43. Srinivasan, K. 2015. "The Human Rights Imagination and Nonhuman Life in the Age of Developmentality." *Journal of the National Human Rights Commission* 14: 289–309, 290.

44. Cochrane, 2013.

45. Elwood, S. and Lawson, V. 2018. "Introduction: (Un)thinkable Poverty Politics." In *Relational Poverty Politics: Forms, Struggles, and Possibilities*, ed. V. Lawson and S. Elwood, 1–24. Athens, GA: University of Georgia Press, 3.

46. Haraway, D. 2016. *Staying with the Trouble: Making Kin in the Chthulucene.* Durham, NC and London: Duke University Press.

47. Butler, J. 2009. *Frames of War: When is Life Grievable?* London and New York: Verso.

48. DAHD. 2019c. *20th Livestock Census: 2019 All India Report.* Animal Husbandry and Dairying Statistics Division, Ministry of Fisheries, Animal Husbandry and Dairying. New Delhi: Government of India. https://dahd.nic.in/sites/default/filess/20th%20Livestock%20census-2019%20All%20India%20Report_0.pdf. Notably, in response to a query, the U.S. Department of Agriculture (USDA) estimated the 2021 figures for total cattle "beginning stocks" for India at 305,500 million, and 2022 at 306,700 million (USDA, n.d., b).

49. Gillespie, Kathryn. 2018. *The Cow with Ear Tag #1389.* Chicago: University of Chicago Press, 146.

50. Gillespie, 2018, 145.

51. Down to Earth. 2018. "India Witnesses One of the Highest Female Infanticide Incidents in the World: Study," 8 July. [Press release]. Retrieved 16 June, 2020, from https://www.downtoearth.org.in/news/health/india-witnesses-one-of-the-highest-female-infanticide-incidents-in-the-world-54803.

52. Gillespie, 2018.

53. Gillespie, 2018, 21.

54. Walby, Sylvia. 1986. *Patriarchy at Work*. Minneapolis: University of Minnesota Press, 51.

55. Narayanan, 2019a.

56. Gillespie 2018, 21.

57. Twine, R. 2014. "Vegan Killjoys at the Table: Contesting Happiness and Negotiating Relationships with Food Practices." *Societies* 4: 623–639.

58. Potter, Will. 2011. *Green is the New Red: An Insider's Account of a Social Movement Under Siege*. San Francisco, CA: City Lights Books.

59. mowson, lynn. 2019. "Making and Unmaking Mammalian Bodies." In *Animaladies*, ed. L. Gruen and F. Probyn-Rapsey, 25–46. New York: Bloomsbury.

60. Gillespie, Kathryn 2019a. "The Loneliness and Madness of Witnessing: Reflections from a Vegan Feminist Killjoy." In *Animaladies*, ed. L. Gruen and F. Probyn-Rapsey, 77–88. New York: Bloomsbury.

61. Valent, P. 2002. "Diagnosis and Treatment of Helper Stresses, Traumas, and Illnesses." In *Treating Compassion Fatigue*, ed. C. R. Figley, 1–17. New York: Taylor and Francis, 19.

62. jones, p. 2007. *Aftershock: Confronting Trauma in a Violent World: A Guide for Activists and Their Allies*. New York: Lantern Books, 90.

63. Gruen, Lori, and Probyn-Rapsey, Fiona. 2019. "Distillations." In *Animaladies*, ed. L. Gruen and F. Probyn, 1–10. New York: Bloomsbury, 2.

64. Gruen and Probyn-Rapsey, 2019, 3.

65. Gruen and Probyn-Rapsey, 2019, 2.

66. Potter, Will. 2009. "The Green Scare." *Vermont Law Review* 33 (4): 672–673, in Gillespie, 2018, 40, emphasis in original.

67. "In 2019, the Australian Government advanced the Criminal Code Amendment (Agricultural Protection) Bill 2019, which would deem the presence of animal activists on farmland as 'trespass' and place them at risk of criminal prosecution. In 2019, Queensland state also introduce heavy on-spot fines for any activists found 'trespassing' on the purported basis of violating biosecurity." Voiceless. 2019. "The Co-Founder of the Animal Defenders Office on Australia's Impending Ag-Gag Laws." 29 July. Retrieved 21 December, 2019, from https://www.voiceless.org.au/content/co-founder-animal-defenders-office-australias-impending-ag-gag-laws.

68. Govindrajan, R. 2018. *Animal Intimacies: Interspecies Relatedness in India's Central Himalayas*. Chicago: University of Chicago Press, 177.

69. Tayob, S. 2019. "Disgust as Embodied Critique: Being Middle Class and Muslim in Mumbai." *South Asia: Journal of South Asian Studies* 42 (6): 1192–1209, 1208.

70. Govindrajan, 2018, 177.

71. Dave, N. N. 2014. "Witness: Humans, Animals, and the Politics of Becoming." *Cultural Anthropology* 29 (3): 433–456, 434.

72. Pachirat, 2012, 236.

73. Dutkiewicz, Jan. 2018. "Transparency and the Factory Farm: Agritourism and Counter-Activism at Fair Oaks Farms." *Gastronomica: The Journal of Critical Food Studies* 18 (2): 19–32, 27.

74. Dutkiewicz, 2018, 30.

75. Kasturirangan et al. 2014. "Dark and Dairy: The Sorry Tale of the Milch Animals." *The Hindu*, 8 November. Retrieved 8 December, 2015, from http://www.thehindu .com/opinion/open-page/the-sorry-tale-of-the-milch-animals/article6578663.ece.

76. Narayanan, Y. 2015a. *Religion, Heritage and the Sustainable City: Hinduism and Urbanisation in Jaipur*. Oxford: Routledge.

77. Hobson, Kersty. 2007. "Political Animals? On Animals as Subjects in an Enlarged Political Geography." *Political Geography* 26: 250–267, 250.

78. Landes et al. 2016. *From Where the Buffalo Roam: India's Beef Exports*. USDA Economic Research Service. Retrieved 16 June, 2020, from https://www.ers.usda.gov/ webdocs/outlooks/37672/59707_ldpm-264-01.pdf?v=4082.5.

79. Kirksey, E. S., and Helmreich, S. 2010. "The Emergence of Multispecies Ethnography." *Cultural Anthropology* 25 (4):545–576.

80. Hamilton, Lindsay, and Taylor, Nik. 2017. *Ethnography After Humanism: Power, Politics and Method in Multi-Species Research*. London: Palgrave Macmillan, 7.

81. Kim, C. J. 2015. *Dangerous Crossings: Race, Species, and Nature in a Multicultural Age*. Cambridge: Cambridge University Press.

82. Gillespie, Kathryn 2019b. "For a Politicized Multispecies Ethnography: Reflections on a Feminist Geographic Pedagogical Experiment." *Politics and Animals* 5: 1–16, 1.

83. Hamilton and Taylor, 2017, 7.

84. Gillespie, 2019b.

85. Hamilton and Taylor, 2017, 10.

86. Haraway, Donna. 2008. *When Species Meet*. Minneapolis: University of Minnesota Press, 21.

87. Alloun, Esther. 2020. "Veganwashing Israel's Dirty Laundry? Animal Politics and Nationalism in Palestine-Israel." *Journal of Intercultural Studies* 41 (1): 24–41, 34. Alloun emphasizes the importance of deeply listening to the "other" "*on their own terms*" (emphasis in original). "Listening", writes Alloun, "is not an objective, neutral or unemotional process. Particularly in densely fraught contexts of caste hierarchies, listening requires self-restraint and discomfort on the listener's part, so that the speaker is not rendered 'inaudible.'" (Alloun, 2020, 34).

88. "In 2015, news emerged of a Dalit woman being forcibly stripped and fed urine by an 'upper' caste couple in Chatarpur district in Madhya Pradesh" [*The Times of India*. 2015a. "Dalit Woman Stripped, Forced to Consume Urine in MP," 2 September. Retrieved 7 February, 2022, from https://m.timesofindia.com/videos/news/Dalit-woman -stripped-forced-to-consume-urine-in-MP/videoshow/48776050.cms?mobile=no].

Forcing members of the Dalit communities to drink urine is often used as a way of humiliating them. In 2020, a Dalit man in Roda village, Uttar Pradesh, was allegedly beaten and forced to drink urine when he complained against an "influential man" [Nisar, Naqshab. 2020. "Forced to Drink Urine: 65-yr-old Dalit Thrashed for Complaining Against 'Influential Man' in UP," 13 October. Retrieved 7 February, 2022, from https://www.ibtimes.co.in/forced-drink-urine-65-yr-old-dalit-thrashed-complaining-against-influential-man-829249].

In 2022, a 25-year-old Dalit man was abducted by eight men and forced to drink urine in Churu district, Rajasthan. The man reported that the accused used "casteist slurs and other derogatory terms saying the Dalits would be taught a lesson for confronting them as all of them belonged to an 'influential' community." [*East Mojo*. 2022. Rajasthan: 8 Booked for Forcing Dalit Man to Consume Urine, 2 Held," 30 January. Retrieved 7 February, 2022, from https://www.eastmojo.com/national-news/2022/01/30/rajasthan-8-booked-for-forcing-dalit-man-to-consume-urine-2-held/.]

89. Yengde, S. 2022. "Global Castes." *Ethnic and Racial Studies* 45(2): 340-360, 340 doi: 10.1080/01419870.2021.1924394.

90. Yengde, 2022, 340.

91. Mosse, D. 2018. "Caste and Development: Contemporary Perspectives on a Structure of Discrimination and Advantage." *World Development* 110: 422–436.

92. Jodhka, S. S. 2014. *Caste in Contemporary India*. London: Taylor and Francis, 16.

93. Berg, D.-E. 2017. "Race as a Political Frontier Against Caste: WCAR, Dalits and India's Foreign Policy." *Journal of International Relations and Development* 21 (4): 990–1013.

94. Yengde, 2022, 356.

95. Cháirez-Garza, J. F. 2021. Moving Untouched: B. R. Ambedkar and the Racialization of Untouchability. *Ethnic and Racial Studies*, 45(2), 216–234. doi: 10.1080/01419870.2021.1924393, 216.

96. Cháirez-Garza, 2022.

97. Narayanan, Y. 2021a. "Animating Caste: Visceral Geographies of Pigs, Caste and Violent Nationalisms in Chennai City." *Urban Geography*. doi: 10.1080/02723638.2021.1890954.

98. Boisseron, Benedicte. 2018. *Afro-Dog: Blackness and the Animal Question*. New York: Columbia University Press.

99. Doniger, W. 2009. *The Hindus: An Alternative History*. New York: Penguin, 200.

100. In my subsequent work, I would learn of how both the Hindu Right and Dalit Right are invested in using the pig to erect and strengthen binary framings of Hindu/Dalit, and, indeed, cow/pig hierarchies as also on a spectrum (Narayanan, 2021a). In a different way, the camel was also used by the Hindu Right in Rajasthan as an assimilating symbol, and also a strategy of erasure. [Narayanan, Y. 2021b. "'A Pilgrimage of Camels': Dairy Capitalism, Nomadic Pastoralism, and Subnational Hindutva Statism in Rajasthan." *Environment and Planning E*. DOI: 10.1177/25148486211062005].

101. Banerjee, Dwaipayan. 2020. "Anthropology's Reckoning with Radical Humanism." *Anthropology Now* 12 (3): 50–55, 50.

102. Banerjee, 2020, 50–51.

103. Cibney, E. 2016. "When the Human in Humanism Isn't Enough." *Humanist* 76 (2): 12–17.

104. Boisseron, 2018, xxv.

105. Banerjee, 2020, 51.

106. Deckha, Maneesha. 2012. "Toward a Postcolonial, Posthumanist Feminist Theory: Centralizing Race and Culture in Feminist Work on Nonhuman Animals." *Hypatia* 27 (3): 527–545, 530.

107. Collard, R.-C., and Gillespie, K. 2015. "Doing Critical Animal Geographies: Future Directions." In *Critical Animal Geographies: Politics, Intersections and Hierarchies in a Multispecies World*, ed. K. Gillespie and R.-C. Collard, 1–16. Abingdon, UK and New York: Routledge, 13.

108. NDDB. n.d., b. *Milk Production by States*. Retrieved 14 November, 2019, from https://www.nddb.coop/information/stats/milkprodstate.

109. *The News Minute*. 2017. "Meat is Dear to Kerala, State Tops in Cattle Slaughter," 19 April. Retrieved 14 November, 2019, from https://www.thenewsminute.com/article/meat-dear-kerala-state-tops-cattle-slaughter-60581.

110. *India Today*. 2019. "Cattle Smuggling: BSF Recovers Cows Tied with IEDs in West Bengal Rivers," 25 July. Retrieved 14 November, 2019, from https://www.indiatoday.in/india/story/cattle-smuggling-bsf-recovers-cows-tied-with-ieds-in-west-bengal-rivers-1573641-2019-07-25.

111. Victor, R., and Bhatt, K. 2017. "Misconception, Misinformation, Misdirection and Misplaced Aggression: A Case Study of a Murdered Macqueen's Bustard." *International Journal of Environmental Studies* 74 (2): 183–191.

112. *The Tribune*. 2016a. "Money from Cow Smuggling Being Used in Terrorism: Police," 29 August. Retrieved 27 July, 2021, from https://www.tribuneindia.com/news/archive/features/money-from-cow-smuggling-being-used-in-terrorism-police-287198.

113. Sur, Malini. 2020. "Time at its Margins: Cattle Smuggling across the India–Bangladesh Border." *Cultural Anthropology* 534 (4): 546–574.

114. Ghosh, Sahana. 2019. "Chor, Police and Cattle: The Political Economies of Bovine Value in the India–Bangladesh Borderlands." *South Asia: Journal of South Asian Studies* 42 (6): 1108–1124, 1109.

115. Collard and Gillespie, 2015, 206.

116. Alger, J. M., and Alger, S. F. 2003. *Cat Culture: The Social World of a Cat Shelter*. Philadelphia, PA: Temple University Press, 38.

117. Pachirat, 2011, 354.

118. *DNA India*. 2015. "Cattle Trafficking: Supreme Court Wants Suggestions from Centre, Uttar Pradesh, Uttarakhand," 21 November. Retrieved 5 August, 2016, from http://www.dnaindia.com/india/report-cattle-trafficking-supreme-court-wants-suggestions-from-centre-uttar-pradesh-uttarakhand-2049907; *The Hindu*. 2013. "77 Heads of Cattle Seized Near Chennai," 30 June. Retrieved 9 October, 2018, from https://www.thehindu.com/news/national/tamil-nadu/77-heads-of-cattle-seized-near-chennai/article4866685.ece.

119. Tittensor, David. 2016. Doing Political Ethnography in a Difficult Climate: A Turkish Case Study. *Ethnography* 17 (2): 213–228.

CHAPTER 1

1. DAHD. 2002a. "Chapter III—Administration of Cattle Laws." In *Report of the National Commission on Cattle.* Retrieved 2 April, 2020, from https://dahd.nic.in/node/86828; Ahmad, Tariq. 2015. "FALQs: Beef Bans in India," 10 November, 22 [online]. Law Library of Congress. Retrieved 18 May, 2016, from http://blogs.loc.gov/law/2015/11/falqs-beef-bans-in-india/; Mandhani, Apoorva. 2017. "Sikkim State Assembly Passes Bill Prohibiting Cow Slaughter." LiveLaw, 30 August. Retrieved 6 October, 2018, from https://livelaw.in/sikkim-state-assembly-passes-bill-prohibiting-cow-slaughter/.

2. Maharashtra Animal Preservation Act. 1976. Amended March 2015. http://bw cindia.org/Web/Info&Action/Legislation/MaharashtraAnimalPreservationAct1976 (AmendedMarch2015).pdf.

3. Gujarat Animal Preservation (Amendment) Act 2017. https://lpd.gujarat.gov.in/assets/downloads/acts_12042017.pdf.

4. USDA Foreign Agricultural Services. 2017. *India: Livestock and Products Annual.* Retrieved 4 July, 2022, from https://apps.fas.usda.gov/newgainapi/api/report/downlo adreportbyfilename?filename=Livestock%20and%20Products%20Annual_New%20 Delhi_India_9-1-2017.pdf.

5. USDA, 2017.

6. Meat & Livestock Australia. 2018a. "Indian Carabeef Exports Set to Increase in 2018," [press release]. Retrieved 5 March, 2018, from https://www.mla.com.au/news-and-events/industry-news/indian-carabeef-exports-set-to-increase-in-2018/.

7. Chilkoti, A. and Crabtree, J. 2014. "India's Beef Battleground Sizzles Ahead of Election." *Financial Times,* 2 January. Retrieved 4 July, 2022, from https://www.ft.com/content/033680fa-027d-11e3-880d-00144feab7de ; ; Joshipura, Poorva. 2015. "India's High Beef Exports Are Linked to its Milk Consumption." *Huffington Post,* 5 July. Retrieved 18 August, 2019, from https://www.huffingtonpost.in/poorva-joshipura/holy -cow-milk-consumption_b_8087156.html.

8. *The Times of India.* 2015b. "Government to Set Up Labs at Ports to Check Illegal Cow Meat Export," 7 October. Retrieved 5 January, 2018, from https://timesofindia.in diatimes.com/india/Government-to-set-up-labs-at-ports-to-check-illegal-cow-meat -export/articleshow/49245226.cms.

9. USDA Economic Research Service. 2017. "India Remains the World's Largest Dairy Producer," [press release]. Retrieved 21 January, 2018, fromhttps://www.ers.usda .gov/data-products/chart-gallery/gallery/chart-detail/?chartId=82987.

10. DAHD. 2002b. "Chapter II—Executive Summary." *Report of the National Commission on Cattle,* Retrieved 12February, 2020 from https://dahd.nic.in/hi/node/86810.

11. DAHD, 2002a, Section 11.

12. Sen, Amartya. 1990. "More Than 100 Million Women Are Missing." *New York Review of Books* 20: 61–66.

13. See: Torres, B. 2007. *Making a Killing: The Political Economy of Animal Rights.* Oakland, CA: AK Press, 44; Williams, R. E. 1997. *The Political Economy of the Common Market in Milk and Dairy Products in the European Union.* FAO Economic and Social Development Paper 142. Rome: FAO Economic and Social Department, 59.

14. Statista. 2022. "Number of Milk Cows Worldwide in 2021, by Country." Retrieved 7 February, 2022, from https://www.statista.com/statistics/869885/global-number-milk-cows-by-country/.

15. APEDA. 2022. "Exports from India of Dairy Products." Retrieved 28 January 2022, from

https://agriexchange.apeda.gov.in/indexp/Product_description_32headChart
.aspx?gcode=0407.

16. DAHD, 2019c f.

17. Bazzoli et al. 2014. "Factors Associated with Age at Slaughter and Carcass Weight, Price, and Value of Dairy Cull Cows." *Journal of Dairy Science* 97 (2): 1082–1091, 1082.

18. Landes et al., 2016.

19. Gupta et al. 2014. "Dairy Animals." In *Encyclopedia of Agriculture and Food Systems*, Vol. 2, ed. N. K. Van Alfen, 419–434. London: Academic Press, 420.

20. Phillips, Clive J. C. 2010. *Principles of Cattle Production*, 2nd Edition. Wallingford, UK: CABI, 59.

21. Herring, A. D. 2014. "Beef Cattle." In *Encyclopedia of Agriculture and Food* Systems, Vol. 2, ed. N. K. Van Alfen, 1–20. London: Academic Press, 14.

22. Fiems, Leo O. 2012. "Double Muscling in Cattle: Genes, Husbandry, Carcasses and Meat." *Animals* 2: 472–506, 473. doi:10.3390/ani2030472.

23. Taylor, Sunaura. 2017. *Beasts of Burden: Animal and Disability Liberation.* New York: The New Press. Human manipulation of animal bodies to serve "production" commoditizes and capitalizes on what are their carefully designed and produced bodily impairments, such that these impairments themselves become a crucial, foundational resource of animal agriculture; for instance, the Jersey-breed cows who produce vastly excessive amounts of milk for human consumption and undergo agonizing mastitis; the double-muscled "meat" breed chickens, pigs, and bovines who experience lifelong arthritis and have trouble even standing or walking; or the super-ovulating "laying" chickens who experience fatal reproductive problems. In *Beasts of Burden*, Sunaura Taylor writes: "The more I looked, the more I found that the disabled body is everywhere in animal industries" (xiv).

24. Meat and Livestock Australia. 2017. "Market Supplier Snapshot Beef: India." Retrieved 14 November, 2019, from https://www.mla.com.au/globalassets/mla-corporate/prices--markets/documents/os-markets/red-meat-market-snapshots/mla-ms_india_-snapshot-2017_r2.pdf.

25. Dutkiewicz, Jan. 2015. "Uncertain Hog Futures (Or, Two Bacon Shortages and the Financial Life of the Capitalist Pig)." Paper presented at the University of Chicago Animal Studies Workshop, Chicago, IL, November 18.

26. Gillespie, 2018, 59.

27. *Beef Magazine.* 2019. "Why Does the U.S. Both Import and Export Beef?" Retrieved 27 January, 2021, from https://www.beefmagazine.com/cowcalfweekly/0611 -why-does-us-import-export-beef.

28. Meat and Livestock Australia. 2018. "Market Snapshot—Beef—North America (US, Canada, Mexico)." Retrieved 12 February 2022, from https://www.mla.com.au/globalassets/mla-corporate/prices--markets/documents/os-markets/red-meat-market -snapshots/2018-mla-ms_north-america_beef.pdf.

29. De, Rohit. 2013. "Who Moved My Beef?" Retrieved 12 November, 2018, from https://www.thehindubusinessline.com/opinion/who-moved-my-beef/article22995192 .ece.

30. Aggarwal, M. 2017. "CPCB Says India's Slaughterhouses Need to Upgrade to Check Pollution." *Live Mint.* Retrieved 19 September, 2019, from https://www.livemint .com/Politics/7SDlidlFCvE7ds3gCkheiI/CPCB-says-Indias-slaughterhouses-need-to -upgrade-to-check-p.html.

31. Gandhi, Maneka. 1999. "Factory Farming and the Meat Industry in India." In *The Meat Business: Devouring a Hungry Planet*, ed. Geoff Tansy and Joyce D'Silva, 92–102. London: Earthscan Publications Ltd, 93.

32. Gillespie, 2018, 56–57.

33. USDA Foreign Agricultural Services. 2020. "EU-28: Livestock and Products Annual." https://apps.fas.usda.gov/newgainapi/api/Report/DownloadReportByFileNam e?fileName=Livestock%20and%20Products%20Annual_The%20Hague_European%20 Union_09-09-2020.

34. Part IV of the Constitution of India contains the Directive Principles of State Policy. As per Article 37 of the Constitution, "it shall be the duty of the State to apply these principles in making laws."

35. Weis, Lael K. 2017. "Constitutional Directive Principles." *Oxford Journal of Legal Studies* 37 (4): 916–945, 920.

36. Constitution of India. 2022. "Article 48: Organisation of Agriculture and Animal Husbandry." Retrieved 12 February, 2022, fromhttps://www.constitutionofindia .net/constitution_of_india/directive_principles_of_state_policy/articles/Article%2048.

37. Ambedkar, B. R. 1948. *The Untouchables: Who Were They and Why They Became Untouchables?* New Delhi: Amrit Book Co, 29–30.

38. Ambedkar, B. R. (2015). *Did Hindus Never Eat Beef?* Retrieved 16 July, 2019, from https://www.countercurrents.org/ambedkar050315.htm.

39. Ambedkar, 1948, 92–93.

40. Copland, Ian. 2017. "Cows, Congress and the Constitution: Jawaharlal Nehru and the Making of Article 48." *South Asia: Journal of South Asian Studies* 40 (4): 723–743.

41. Chigateri, Shraddha. 2011. "Negotiating the 'Sacred' Cow: Cow Slaughter and the Regulation of Difference in India." In *Democracy, Religious Pluralism and the Liberal Dilemma of Accommodation*, ed. Monica Mookherjee, 137–159. Dordrecht: Springer, 142,

42. Mazumdar, S. 1995. "Women on the March: Right-wing Mobilization in Contemporary India." *Feminist Review* 49: 1–28.; Thapar, R. 1996. "The Theory of Aryan Race and India: History and Politics." *Social Scientist* 24 (1–3): 3–29.

43. Mazumdar, 1995: 1.

44. Banaji, J. (ed.). 2013. *Fascism: Essays on Europe and India*. Gurgaon: Three Essays Collective, ix.

45. Banaji, 2013,8.

46. Savarkar, V. D. [1923] 1969. *Hindutva—Who is a Hindu?* 5th ed. Bombay: Veer Savarkar Prakashan, 115. https://archive.org/details/hindutva-vinayak-damodar-savarkar-pdf/page/n1/mode/2up/search/first+discernible+source.

47. Savarkar, 1969, 116.

48. van der Veer, Peter. 1999. "Hindus: A Superior Race." *Nations and Nationalism* 5 (3): 421.

49. Truschke, Audrey. 2018. "Anti-Semitism of Hindu Nationalists Made Me a Target of Their Attacks." *India Abroad*, 5 November. https://www.indiaabroad.com/opinion/anti-semitism-of-hindu-nationalists-made-me-a-target-of/article_2c6b47be-e15a-11e8-b1f2-4b62626ebf78.html. American historian of India Audrey Truschke writes, "Speaking in 1939 in Calcutta, V. D. Savarkar, the ideological godfather of Hindu nationalism, identified Indian Muslims as a potential traitorous people not to be trusted, 'like the Jews in Germany.' In the same year, M. S. Golwalkar, an RSS leader, wrote that Germany's 'purging the country of the semitic Race—the Jews' was 'a good lesson for us in Hindusthan to learn and profit by.'"]

50. Egorova, Y. 2018. *Jews and Muslims in South Asia: Reflections on difference, religion and race*. Oxford University Press: New York, 29–30.

51. The ongoing pursuit of Hindu nationalist parties to exclude or render Muslims vulnerable in the Indian state emerged again in the heavily controversial Citizenship (Amendment) Act, 2019, that was passed by the parliament of India in December 2019. The Act allows the fast-tracking of Indian citizenship to non-Muslim religious minorities such as Hindus, Christians, Sikhs, Buddhists, Zoroastrian and Jains from Muslim-dominated states (Pakistan, Bangladesh and Afghanistan), but excludes Muslims. This is the first time in the history of independent India that religion has been used officially as a determinant of Indian citizenship. The BJP government has also excluded Muslims from protection in other ways, such as the deportation of Rohingya Muslims back to Myanmar. Human Rights Watch (2019b) reports, "BJP politicians have also demonized Muslim immigrants and asylum seekers, including calling them 'infiltrators,' to gain electoral support." [Human Rights Watch. 2019b. "India: Citizenship Bill Discriminates Against Muslims." Retrieved 7 February, 2022, from https://www.hrw.org/news/2019/12/11/india-citizenship-bill-discriminates-against-muslims.]

52. Lorimer, Jamie, and Driessen, Clemens. 2016. "From 'Nazi Cows' to Cosmopolitan 'Ecological Engineers': Specifying Rewilding Through a History of Heck Cattle." *Annals of the American Association of Geographers* 106 (3): 631–652.

53. Lorimer and Driessen, 2016, 5.

54. Thapar, 1996, 7.

55. Jha, D. N. 2002. *The Myth of the Holy Cow*. London: Verso, 146.

56. Freitag, Sandria B. 1989. *Collective Action and Community: Public Arenas and the Emergence of Communalism in North India*. Berkeley, CA: University of California Press, 151.

57. Lodrick, Deryck O. 1981. *Sacred Cows, Sacred Places: Origins and Survival of Animal Homes in India*. Berkeley, CA: University of California Press.

58. Rao, Anupama. 2009. *The Caste Question: Dalits and the Politics of Modern India*. Berkeley, CA: University of California Press, 40.

59. Jha, 2002, 115.

60. Jha, 2002, 115.

61. Lodrick, 1981, 59.

62. Morrison, K. D. 2014. "Conceiving Ecology and Stopping the Clock: Narratives of Balance, Loss, and Degradation." In *Shifting Ground: People, Animals, and Mobility in India's Environmental History*, ed. M. Rangarajan and K. Sivaramakrishnan, 39–64. New Delhi: Oxford University Press, 59.

63. Morrison, 2014, 59.

64. Morrison, 2014, 44.

65. Copland, 2017.

66. Snow et al. 2013. "Social Movements, Framing Processes, and Cultural Revitalization and Fabrication." *Mobilization: An International Quarterly* 18 (3):225–242; Nauriya, A. 2015. "M K Gandhi and the Founders of the African National Congress." *Mainstream* 53 (41)., Retrieved 4 July, 2022, from http://www.mainstreamweekly.net/article5982.html.

67. Ghosal, A. K. 1959. "Sarvodaya Gandhian Philosophy and Way of Life." *The Indian Journal of Political Science* 20 (1): 23–30.

68. Indian National Congress. 2010. "Constitution & Rules of the Indian National Congress." Retrieved 12 February, 2022, from https://cdn.inc.in/constitutions/inc_constitution_files/000/000/001/original/Congress-Constitution.pdf?1505640610.

69. Gould, William. 2004. *Hindu Nationalism and the Language of Politics in Late Colonial India*. Cambridge: Cambridge University Press, 7.

70. Gould, 2004, 1.

71. Gould, 2004, 7.

72. Brown, Theodore M., and Fee, E. 2008. "Spinning for India's Independence." *American Journal of Public Health* 98 (1): 39.

73. Wiley, A. S. 2014. *Cultures of Milk: The Biology and Meaning of Dairy Products in the United States and India*. Cambridge, MA: Harvard University Press, 111–112.

74. Wiley, 2014, 95.

75. Fundamental duties are "duties of individual citizens" (*Surya v Union of India*, AIR 1982 Raj 1, [19]), though they "are not themselves enforceable in the Courts nor their violation, as such, punishable.".

76. Gould, 2004.

77. Larson, Gerald. 1995. *India's Agony Over Religion*. Albany, NY: State University of New York Press.

78. Vij, S. 2016. "New symbol of Hindutva project: Is Gau Raksha the new Ram Mandir?" *Hindustan Times*. Retrieved 21 September, 2016, from http://www.hindustan times.com/india-news/the-new-symbol-of-hindutva-project-is-gau-raksha-the-new -ram-mandir/story-fPqg5TL2XBE16PooS4kZeM.html.

79. De, 2013.

80. Kurien, Verghese. 2005. *I Too Had a Dream*. New Delhi: Roli Books, 183.

81. Basu, Pratyusha. 2009. *Villages, Women and the Success of Dairy Cooperatives in India*. Amherst, MA: Cambria Press, 59.

82. Basu, 2009, 59.

83. Scholten, Bruce A. 2010. *India's White Revolution: Operation Flood, Food Aid and Development*. New York: Tauris Academic Studies, 2–3.

84. Siegel, Benjamin Robert. 2018. *Hungry Nation: Food, Famine, and the Making of Modern India*. Cambridge: Cambridge University Press.

85. Kudaisya, Medha. 2008. "'A Mighty Adventure': Institutionalising the Idea of Planning in Post-colonial India, 1947–60." *Modern Asian Studies* 43 (4): 939–978, 939.

86. Siegel, Benjamin. 2016. "'Self-Help which Ennobles a Nation': Development, Citizenship, and the Obligations of Eating in India's Austerity Years." *Modern Asian Studies* 50 (3): 975–1018.

87. Siegel, 2016, 1018.

88. Siegel, 2016, 975.

89. See Shiva, V. 1991. *The Violence of the Green Revolution: Third World Agriculture, Ecology, and Politics*. London: Zed Books; and Shiva, V. 1993. *Monocultures of the Mind: Perspectives on Biodiversity and Biotechnology*. London: Zed Books.

90. Scholten, 2010, 3.

91. Cunningham, K. 2009. *Rural and Urban Linkages: Operation Flood's Role in India's Dairy Development*. International Food Policy Research Institute (IFPRI) Discussion Paper 00924. Washington DC: IFPRI. Retrieved 4 July, 2022, from https://ebrary .ifpri.org/utils/getfile/collection/p15738coll2/id/28869/filename/28870.pdf.

92. Kurien, 2005, 77.

93. Kurien, 2005, 80.

94. Kurien, 2005, 183.

95. Kurien, 2005, 184.

96. Kurien, 2005, 185.

97. Kurien, 2005, 35, 200–201.

98. DAHD. 2015b. "Estimated Livestock Population Breed Wise: Based on Breed Survey 2013." Animal Husbandry Statistics Division. New Delhi: Department of Animal Husbandry, Dairying and Fisheries, 15. Retrieved 4 July, 2022, from: http:// dahd.nic.in/sites/default/filess/Breeding%20Survey%20Book%20-%20Corrected .pdf.

99. Govindrajan, 2018; Narayanan, Yamini. 2018a. "'Cow Protection' as 'Casteised Speciesism': Sacralisation, Commercialisation and Politicisation." South Asia: Journal of South Asian Studies, 41 (2): 331–351.

100. Hardy, K. C. 2019. "Provincialising the Cow: Buffalo–Human Relationships" *South Asia: Journal of South Asian Studies* 42 (6): 1156–1172,1158 doi: 10.1080/00856401.2019 .1680484.

101. Shukin, Nicole. 2009. *Animal Capital: Rendering Life in Biopolitical Times*. Minneapolis: University of Minnesota Press, 13.

102. Gandhi, M. K. n.d. "Cow slaughter and Cow-protection" Centre for Study of Society and Secularism Retrieved 12 February, 2022, from https://www.mkgandhi .org/g_communal/chap14.htm.

103. Gandhi, M. K. 1917. Speech on Cow Protection (delivered in Bettiah), 9 October. Retrieved 5 July, 2022, from https://www.sabhlokcity.com/2022/03/gandhi-on -voluntary-cow-protection-he-disliked-coercion-or-laws/.

104. Chapple, Christopher Key. 1993. *Nonviolence to Animals, Earth, and Self in Asian Traditions.* Albany, NY: State University of New York Press, xiii.

105. Gandhi, M. K. 2018. *An Autobiography or the Story of My Experiments with Truth.* New Haven, CT: Yale University Press, 699.

106. Gandhi, M. K. 2017 [1920]. "Gandhiji on Cow Protection – Various Articles." Extracted from *Navajivan*, 8 August 1920. Retrieved 5 July, 2022, from https://shrishri71. wordpress.com/.

107. Gandhi, M. K. 1927. "Conditions of Cow Protection." *Young India*, 31 March 1927. Retrieved from internet archives of *Young India*, 5 July, 2022, from https://archive .org/stream/HindSwaraj.yi.10973.33464/yi.10973.33464_djvu.txt.

108. Kurien, 2005, 33.

109. Kurien, 2005, 128.

110. Kurien, 2005, 80.

111. See also Siegel's *Hungry Nation* (2018).

112. Kurien, 2005, 147.

113. Scholten, 2010, 10.

114. Scholten, 2010, 216–217.

115. Kurien, 2005, 112.

116. Kurien, 2005, 187.

117. Kurien, 2005, 139.

118. NDDB. n.d. *National Dairy Plan.* Retrieved 28 January, 2022, from https:// www.nddb.coop/ndpi/about/brief. See also World Bank. 2012. "Project Signing: Government of India and World Bank Sign US$ 352 Million Agreement for National Dairy Support Project," [press release]. Retrieved 12 December, 2020, from https:// www.worldbank.org/en/news/press-release/2012/04/13/project-signing-government -of-india-and-world-bank-sign-us-352-million-agreement-for-national-dairy-support-project. The World Bank released its evaluation of the project in 2020 (NDDB. (National Dairy Development Board). 2020b. *Implementation Completion and Results Report (Document of the World Bank).* Retrieved 5 July, from https://www.nddb .coop/sites/default/files/pdfs/ndpi/NDPI_World_Bank_Evaluation_Report_(ICRR) .pdf.).

119. APEDA. 2017b. *Dairy Products.* Retrieved 6 January, 2018, from http://www .apeda.gov.in/apedawebsite/SubHead_Products/Dairy_Products.htm.

120. APEDA. n.d., a. "Indian Production of Milk." Retrieved 7 January, 2022, from https://agriexchange.apeda.gov.in/India%20Production/AgriIndia_Productions .aspx?productcode=1023.

121. Gillespie, 2018.

122. Hennelly, William. 2015. "100,000-Cow-Power Dairy Farm in China to Feed Russian Market." Retrieved 12 February, 2022, from https://www.farmland grab.org/post/view/25115-100-000-cow-power-dairy-farm-in-china-to-feed-russian -market.

123. Punjabi, Meeta. n.d. "India: Increasing Demand Challenges the Dairy Sector." Food and Agriculture Organization. Retrieved 12 February, 2022, from https://www .fao.org/3/i0588e/i0588e05.htm.

124. Shapiro, Ken. 2010. "Big Numbers." Message posted to the Animals and Society Institute website (ASI Diary, 25 January). Retrieved 5 July, 2022, from http://www .all-creatures.org/articles/ar-finitude.html.

125. Gillespie, Kathryn. 2014. "Sexualized violence and the gendered commodification of the animal body in Pacific Northwest US dairy production." *Gender, Place and Culture: A Journal of Feminist Geography* 21 (10): 1321-1337, 1321.

CHAPTER 2

1. Padalino et al. 2014. "Could Dromedary Camels Develop Stereotypy? The First Description of Stereotypical Behaviour in Housed Male Dromedary Camels and How It Is Affected by Different Management Systems." *Plos One* 9 (2): 1–7, 1, 3.

2. Wiley, 2014, 87.

3. Biardeau, Madeleine. 1993. "Kamadhenu: The Religious Cow, Symbol of Prosperity." In *Asian Mythologies*, ed. Yves Bonnefoy. Chicago: University of Chicago Press, 99.

4. Wiley, 2014, 87.

5. Sastri, D. B. and Ramaswami, K. S. 1945. "The Religion and Romance of Cow-Worship in India." *Kalyana Kalpataru* 11 (1): 67.

6. Patel, Deven M. 2008. "Kāmadhenu." In *Encyclopedia of Hinduism*, ed. Denise Cush, Catherine Robinson and Michael York. London: Routledge, 403.

7. Wiley, 2014, 96; Williams, George M. 2003. *Handbook of Hindu Mythology*. Santa Barbara, CA: ABC-Clio.

8. Goa Government. 2016. *Kamdhenu Scheme (Sudharit)*. Retrieved 17 July, 2019, from https://www.goa.gov.in/wp-content/uploads/2016/12/1.-KAMDHENU-SCHEME -SUDHARIT-2016-17.Form_.pdf.

9. Caton, B. P. 2014. "The Imperial Ambition of Science and Its Discontents." In *Shifting Ground: People, Animals, and Mobility in India's Environmental History*, ed. M. Rangarajan and K. Sivaramakrishnan, 132–154. New Delhi: Oxford University Press, 133–134.

10. Smith-Howard, K. 2017. *Pure and Modern Milk*. New York: Oxford University Press, 8.

11. Stockler, R. 2015. "Heifer Development: From Weaning to Calving." In *Bovine Reproduction*, ed. R. M. Hopper, 272–275. Oxford: Wiley Blackwell, 655.

12. Gordon, I. 2004. *Reproductive Technologies in Farm Animals*. Oxford: CABI Publishing, 51.

13. Gupta et al., 2014, 420.

14. SAG (Sabarmati Ashram Gaushala). 2013. *Annual Report 2012–13: Sabarmati Ashram Gaushala Bidaj.* Bidaj Farm, Kheda, Gujarat: Sabarmati Ashram Gaushala, 6.

15. SAG, 2013, 10.

16. Phillips, 2010, 60.

17. Phillips, 2010, 61.

18. Shiva, Vandana. 1999. "Penalizing the Poor: GATT, WTO and the Developing World." In *The Meat Business: Devouring a Hungry Planet*, ed. G. Tansy and J. D'Silva, 198–213. London: Earthscan Publications Ltd., 201.

19. Gandhi, 1917.

20. SAG, 2013, 4.

21. SAG, 2013, 6.

22. Chenoweth, P. J. 1983. "Sexual Behaviour of the Bull: A Review." *Journal of Dairy Science* 66: 173–179.

23. Hall, Stephen J. G. 2002. "Cattle Behaviour." In *Ethology of Domestic Animals: An Introductory Text*, ed. Per Jensen, 131–143. Wallingford, UK: CABI (Centre for Agriculture and Bioscience International); Chenoweth, 1983, 173–179.

24. Chenoweth, 1983.

25. Chenoweth, 1983, 174.

26. *Waikato Times.* 2022. "Genetics firm plans to breed non-gassy cows," 4 April. Retrieved 1 August, 2022, from https://www.pressreader.com/new-zealand/waikato-times/20220404/281857237055839.

27. Morell, V. 2014. *Animal Wise: The Thoughts and Emotions of our Fellow Creatures.* Collingwood, Melbourne: Black Inc., 1. Morell further argues that it is precisely the rich, wide and sophisticated spectrum of emotions displayed by animals that precisely make them attractive as "pets" or companion animals. Morell writes: "my pets' behaviours, activities and facial expressions all suggest thoughts and emotions. Isn't that . . . perhaps the main reason, we have pets in our homes? In short, we want to be around something more than pet rocks" (2).

28. King, Barbara J. 2018. "Emotion." In *Critical Terms for Animal Studies*, ed. L. Gruen, 125–140). Chicago: University of Chicago Press, 136, emphasis added.

29. King, 2018, 38.

30. Chenoweth, 1983, 175. Electroejaculation is used even more widely in bulls reared for beef as they tend to be less sexually active than bulls bred for milk.)

31. Rouge, M., and Bowen, R. 2002. *Semen Collection*. Retrieved 15 November, 2019, from http://www.vivo.colostate.edu/hbooks/pathphys/reprod/semeneval/collection.html.

32. Hendry, W. F. 1994. "Treatment for Loss of Ejaculation after Para-Aortic Lymphadenectomy." In *Germ Cell Tumours III: Proceedings of the Third Germ Cell Tumour Conference*, ed. W. G. Jones, P. Harnden, I. Appleyard, 353–358. Held in Leeds, UK, on 8–10 September 1993. Oxford: Pergamon.

33. *India Times.* 2017. "1,500 kg Super Buffalo Yuvraj Is Worth Rs 9.25 Crore and He Makes Rs 50 Lakh a Year Selling Semen!" Retrieved 22 July, 2019, from https://www.indiatimes.com/news/india/1-500-kg-super-buffalo-yuvraj-is-worth-rs-9-25-crore-and-he-makes-rs-50-lakh-a-year-selling-semen-272372.html.

34. *India Times*, 2017.

35. Biswas, Soutik. 2015. "The Bull Whose Semen Is Worth $3,000." *BBC*. Retrieved 8 December, 2018, from http://www.bbc.com/news/magazine-31107115.

36. *India Times*, 2017; Biswas, 2015.

37. Crichton, J. S., and Lishman, A.W. 1988. "Factors Influencing Sexual Behaviour of Young Bos Indicus Bulls Under Pen and Pasture Mating Conditions." *Applied Animal Behaviour Science* 21 (4): 281–292, 281.

38. Crichton and Lishman, 1988, 281.

39. Mosse, D. 2020. "The Modernity of Caste and the Market Economy." *Modern Asian Studies* 54 (4): 1225–1271.

40. Mosse, 2020.

41. Collard, Rosemary-Claire, and Dempsey, Jessica. 2017. "Capitalist Natures in Five Orientations." *Capitalism Nature Socialism* 28 (1): 78–97, 78.

42. Collard and Dempsey, 2017, 78.

43. Gillespie, Kathryn. 2020. "The Afterlives of the Lively Commodity: Life-Worlds, Death-Worlds, Rotting-Worlds." *Environment and Planning A: Economy and Space*, 1–16, 3. doi: 10.1177/0308518X20944417.

44. Krishna, Nanditha. 2010. *Sacred Animals of India*. New Delhi: Penguin Books Ltd.

45. Srila Krsnadasa Kaviraja Gosvami (trans. Advaita Dasa). 2000. *Sri Govinda Lilamrta*. Vrindavan: Rashbihari Lal & Sons, Text 31–34.

46. Krishna, 2010, 60.

47. Krishna, 2010, 61.

48. Wilson, Horace Hayman (ed. and trans.). 1840. *The Vishnu Purana: A System of Hindu Mythology and Tradition*. London: John Murray, 311.

49. Swami Vijñanananda. 2010 [1922]. *The S'rimad Devi Bhâgawatam*, Book VII, Chapter XXVII, 686. Kindle Edition.

50. Wood, Ernest, and Subrahmanyam, S. V. (eds and trans.). 1911. *The Garuda Purana*, Chapter 5. Allahabad: Sudhindra Natha Vasu.

51. Wood and Subrahmanyam, 1911, 38.

52. Wood and Subrahmanyam, 1911, 39.

53. Pintchman, Tracy. 2001. "The Goddess as Fount of the Universe: Shared Visions and Negotiated Allegiances in Puranic Accounts of Cosmogenesis." In *Seeking Mahadevi: Constructing the Identities of the Hindu Great Goddess*, ed. Tracy Pintchman, 77-92. New York: State University of New York Press.

54. Gupta, Dipankar. 2000. *Interrogating Caste: Understanding Hierarchy and Difference in Indian Society*. New Delhi: Penguin Books India, 25.

55. Singh, Hira. 2008. "The Real World of Caste in India." *Journal of Peasant Studies* 35 (1): 119–132.

56. Sharpes, Donald K. 2006. *Sacred Bull, Holy Cow: A Cultural Study of Civilization's Most Important Animal*. New York: Peter Lang; Simoons, Frederick J. 1974. "The Purificatory Role of the Five Products of the Cow in Hinduism." *Ecology of Food and Nutrition* 3 (1): 21.

57. Adcock, Cassie. 2020. "'Preserving and Improving the Breeds': Cow Protection's Animal-Husbandry Connection." *South Asia: Journal of South Asian Studies.* doi: 10.1080/00856401.2019.1681680.

58. Adcock, 2020, 1.

59. Adcock, 2020, 3.

60. Boisseron, 2018, 43.

61. Kesavan, Mukul. 2015. "Ghoulish Game—The Morality of Protecting the Indian Cow." *Telegraph India*, 12 October. Retrieved 10 February, 2018, from https://www.tele graphindia.com/opinion/ghoulish-game/cid/1436205.

62. Narayanan, Yamini. 2018a. "'Cow Protection' as 'Casteised Speciesism': Sacralisation, Commercialisation and Politicisation." *South Asia: Journal of South Asian Studies* 41 (2): 331–351.

63. Nussbaum, Martha. 1995. "Objectification." *Philosophy and Public Affairs* 24 (2): 249–291.

64. Jewitt, Sarah. 2011. "Geographies of Shit: Spatial and Temporal Variations in Attitudes Towards Human Waste." *Progress in Human Geography* 35 (5): 608–626, 611.

65. Hardy, 2019, 5.

66. Jha, 2002.

67. Jha, 2002.

68. Jha, 2002.

69. Wood and Subrahmanyam, 1911, 21.

70. Kipling, J. L. 1904. *Beast & Man in India*. New Delhi: Inter-India Publications, 157.

71. Kipling, 1904, 154–155.

72. Wilson, 1840, 333.

73. Anant, Santoksh S. 1970. "Caste Prejudice and Its Perception by Harijans." *Journal of Social Psychology* 82 (2): 165–172, 167.

74. Lal, Deepak. 2005. *The Hindu Equilibrium: India c. 1500 B.C.–2000 A.D.* Oxford: Oxford University Press.

75. Wiley, 2014, 95.

76. Oltenacu, P. A., and Broom, D. M. 2010. "The Impact of Genetic Selection for Increased Milk Yield on the Welfare of Dairy Cows." *Animal Welfare* 19 (1): 39–49.

77. The Dairy Site. 2007. *Blackleg in Cattle.* Retrieved 16 November, 2019, from http://www.thedairysite.com/articles/843/blackleg-in-cattle/. Black quarter or blackleg disease is extremely common in farmed animals who are confined to the same production area over successive generations, leading to clostridium bacteria being present in the soil. When animals graze on such land, they ingest these bacteria. Once they contract the infection, their limbs get severely infected. The animal cannot graze, limbs swell and become painful, and death follows quickly.

78. Franklin Vets. 2017. *Theileria.* Retrieved 16 November, 2019, from https://franklinvets.co.nz/dairy/disease-management/theleiria/. Theileriosis is a tick-infection, and widespread in farmed cows. It can lead to severe anemia and death. Newly delivered mothers, and their newborns are at maximum risk of Theileriosis.

79. New South Wales Government (Department of Primary Industries). 2015. "Cancer Eye in Cattle." Retrieved 13 February, from https://www.dpi.nsw.gov.au/__data/assets/pdf_file/0009/584226/cancer-eye-in-cattle.pdf.

80. O'Dea, L., and Woodle, D. E. 1972. "India's Approach to Cattle Development: Heifer Project as Catalyst in India's White Revolution." *Iowa State University Veterinarian* 34 (2): 102–106.

81. Collard, Rosemary-Claire, and Dempsey, Jessica. 2013. "Life for sale? The Politics of Lively Commodities." *Environment and Planning A: Economy and Space* 45 (11): 2682–2699. Rosemary Collard and Jessica Dempsey theorize the *lively commodity* as "live commodities whose capitalist value is derived from their *status as living beings*" (2684, original emphasis).

82. Torres, 2007, 40.

83. Das, Bireshwar. 2021. "Why Liquid Nitrogen Is Critical to the Indian Animal Husbandry Sector." *Times of India*, 21 October. Retrieved 7 February, 2022, from https://timesofindia.indiatimes.com/blogs/voices/why-liquid-nitrogen-is-critical-to-the-indian-animal-husbandry-sector/.

84. DAHD. 2015a. "Guidelines for Export/Import of Bovine Germplasm (Revised May 2015)." Retrieved 13 February, 2018, from https://dahd.nic.in/sites/default/filess/Guidelines%20for%20Export%20or%20Import%20of%20Bovine%20Germplasm%20revised%20may%202015.pdf02.pdf.

85. DAHD, 2015a.

86. NDDB. 2020a. *NDDB Annual Report 2019–20.* Retrieved 7 February, 2020, from https://www.nddb.coop/sites/default/files/pdfs/NDDB_Annual_Report_2019_20_Eng.pdf, 76.

87. NDDB, 2020, 76.

88. Gordon, I. 2004. *Reproductive Technologies in Farm Animals.* Oxford: CABI Publishing, 81.

89. DAHD. 2019a. Chapter VII: Breed Improvement and Preservation. Retrieved 15 November, 2019, from http://dahd.nic.in/hi/node/86833.

90. Verma, Kanika, and Singh, A. P. 2021. "Catalysing India's Bovine Population Through Technology Intervention." *Invest India.* Retrieved 13 February, 2022, from https://www.investindia.gov.in/team-india-blogs/catalysing-indias-bovine-population-through-technology-intervention.

91. Verma and Singh, 2021.

92. Hasler et al. 1983. "Superovulatory Responses of Holstein Cows." *Theriogenology* 19 (1): 83–99.; Jaton et al. 2016. "Genetic Analysis of Superovulatory Response of Holstein Cows in Canada." *Journal of Dairy Science* 99 (5): 3612–3623.

93. Gordon, 2004, 103.

94. Boyde, M. 2018. "The Dairy Issue: 'Practicing the Art of War.'" *Animal Studies Journal* 7 (2): 9–24.

CHAPTER 3

1. Thesaurus. 2022. Milk (tap/exploit). Retrieved 8 July, 2022, from https://www.the saurus.com/browse/milk.

2. Whittier et al. 2009. "Calving Emergencies in Beef Cattle: Identification and Prevention." Retrieved 13 February, from https://vtechworks.lib.vt.edu/bitstream/handle/10919/50696/400-018.pdf?sequence=1&isAllowed=y.

3. Whittier et al., 2009.

4. Extension Animal Science Program. n.d. "Recognizing and Handling Calving Problems." *Texas A&M Agrilife Extension*. Retrieved 6 January, 2021, from https://agril ifeextension.tamu.edu/library/ranching/recognizing-and-handling-calving-problems/.

5. March of Dimes. 2021. "Maternal Death and Pregnancy-Related Death." Retrieved 20 August, 2021, from https://www.marchofdimes.org/complications/pregnancy-related-death-maternal-death-and-maternal-mortality.aspx.

6. Cohen, Mathilde. 2017. "Animal Colonialism: The Case of Milk." *American Journal of International Law Unbound* 111: 267–271, 270.Available at SSRN: https://ssrn.com/abstract=3039747.

7. Pick, A. 2018. "Vulnerability." In *Critical Terms for Animal Studies*, ed. L. Gruen, 410–423. Chicago: University of Chicago Press, 411.

8. Deckha, M. 2015. "Vulnerability, Equality, and Animals." *Canadian Journal of Women and the Law* 27 (1): 47–70. Postcolonial and law scholar Maneesha Deckha advocates for species-specific *vulnerabilities* to replace equalities in juridical interventions on behalf of animals, for instance, in order to understand the full spectrum of injustices that animals face in human hands.

9. Pick, 2018, 410.

10. Pick, 2018, 410.

11. Gaard, G. 2013. "Toward a Feminist Postcolonial Milk Studies." *American Quarterly* 65 (3): 595–618, 613.

12. Srivastava, M. C. P. 1979. *Mother Goddess in Indian Art, Archaeology and Literature*. Delhi: Agam Kala Prakashan, 726.

13. Srivastava, 1979, 231.

14. Srivastava, 1979, 605.

15. Srivastava, 1979, 223.

16. Korom, F. J. 2000. "Holy Cow! The Apotheosis of Zebu, or Why the Cow Is Sacred in Hinduism." *Asian Folklore Studies* 59 (2): 181–203.

17. Gaard, 2013, 613.

18. Flower, F. C., and Weary, D. M. 2001. "Effects of Early Separation on the Dairy Cow and Calf: Separation at 1 Day and 2 Weeks After Birth." *Applied Animal Behaviour Science* 70: 275–284, 281.

19. Hudson, S. J., and Mullord, M. M. (1977). "Investigations of Maternal Bonding in Dairy Cattle." *Applied Animal Behaviour Science* 3: 271–276.

20. Flower and Weary, 2001; Johnsen et al. 2015. "The Effect of Nursing on the Cow–Calf Bond." *Applied Animal Behaviour Science* 163: 50–57.

21. Flower and Weary, 2001.

22. Flower and Weary, 2001, 281.

23. Australian Breastfeeding Association. 2019a. *Weaning*. Retrieved 25December, 2019, from https://www.breastfeeding.asn.au/bf-info/weaning-and-introducing-solids/weaning

24. Lewis, D. 2016. "New Way to Wean Calves Leaves Them Happier and Healthier." *The Smithsonian*, 25 January. Retrieved from: https://www.smithsonianmag.com/smart-news/new-way-wean-calves-leaves-them-happier-healthier-180957919/#R3KKijx6jegSCRjP.99.

25. Phillips, C. 2002. *Cattle Behaviour and Welfare*. 2nd Ed. Oxford: Blackwell Science, 33.

26. *The Times of India*. 2010. "Dead Calf Used to Milk Cows in Surat." Retrieved 14 November, 2019, from https://timesofindia.indiatimes.com/city/surat/Dead-calf-used-to-milk-cows-in-Surat/articleshow/6290067.cms.

27. Chaudhery, Amit. 2014. "The Force of Falsity." Retrieved 13 February, 2021, from https://vosd.in/the-force-of-falsity-by-amit-chaudhery/.

28. Gillespie, 2018.

29. Hale, C. R. (ed.). 2008. *Engaging Contradictions: Theory, Politics, and Methods of Activist Scholarship*. Berkley, CA: UCLA Press.

30. Hale, 2008, 21.

31. Johnsen et al, 2015, 51.

32. Ballard, O., and Morrow, A. L. 2013. "Human Milk Composition: Nutrients and Bioactive Factors." *Pediatric Clinics of North America* 60 (1): 49–74. doi:10.1016/j.pcl.2012.10.002.

33. Nissen et al. 2017. "Colostrum and Milk Protein Rankings and Ratios of Importance to Neonatal Calf Health Using a Proteomics Approach." *Journal of Dairy Science* 100 (4): 2711–2728.

34. Ballard and Morrow, 2013, 2.

35. Godden, S. 2008. "Colostrum Management for Dairy Calves." *Veterinary Clinics of North America: Food Animal Practice* 24 (1): 19–39, 19.

36. Godden, 2008, 34; Jasper and Weary, 2002.

37. Johnsen et al., 2015.

38. Johnsen et al., 2015, 56.

39. Johnsen et al., 2015.

40. Johnsen et al., 2015.

41. Johnsen et al., 2015.

42. Johnsen et al., 2015.

43. Phillips, 2002, 33, citing Reinhardt and Reinhardt, 1981.

44. Scheduled castes (and scheduled tribes) are classified as such, and recognized by the Constitution of India as "among the most disadvantaged socio-economic groups in India," and are recipients of affirmative discrimination in recognition of their historically severely oppressed status. (UN in India, n.d. "Scheduled Castes and Scheduled Tribes," accessed 21 July 2022 from: https://in.one.un.org/task-teams/scheduled-castes-and-scheduled-tribes/)

45. Whittier et al., n.d.

46. Kurien, 2005, 71.

47. Kurien, 2005, 71.

48. Kurien, 2005, 80.

49. Compassion in World Farming. 2019. "'Standard Intensive Milk Production' Food Business, Good Dairy Award." Retrieved 16 August, 2022, from https://www .compassioninfoodbusiness.com/awards/good-dairy-award/standard-intenstive-milk -production/.

50. Oltenacu, P. A., and Broom, D. M. 2010. "The Impact of Genetic Selection for Increased Milk Yield on the Welfare of Dairy Cows." Animal Welfare 19 (1): 39-49. Oltenacu and Broom cite: Webster J. 1993. Understanding the Dairy Cow, 2nd Edition. Oxford: Blackwell.

51. Oltenacu and Broom, 2010, 42.

52. Animals Australia. 2021. "The Reality of Dairy: Killing Calves," 21 December. Retrieved 13 February, 2022, from https://animalsaustralia.org/latest-news/what -happens-to-dairy-calves/.

53. SAG (Sabarmati Ashram Gaushala), 2013, 10.

54. Gillespie, 2018.

55. Animals Australia, 2021.

56. Compassion in World Farming. 2012. "The Life of Dairy Cows." Retrieved 20 August, 2021, from https://www.ciwf.org.uk/media/5235185/the-life-of-dairy-cows.pdf; Knaus, W. 2009. "Dairy Cows Trapped Between Performance Demands and Adaptability." *Journal of the Science of Food and Agriculture* 89: 1107–1114.

57. Phillips, 2002, 10.

58. Australian Breastfeeding Association. 2019b. *Mastitis.* Retrieved 25 December, 2019, from https://www.breastfeeding.asn.au/bf-info/common-concerns–mum/mastitis. Common reasons that can predispose a human female to mastitis include swollen breasts due to missed or delayed feed; tight bras; uncomfortable sleeping positions; tight seatbelts, and reactions to nipple creams.

59. Phillips, 2002, 147.

60. Gillespie, 2018.

61. Amir, Lisa Helen, and Lumley, Judith. 2006. "Women's Experience of Lactational Mastitis: 'I Have Never Felt Worse.'" *Australian Family Physician* 35 (9): 745–747, 746.

62. Khan et al. 2016. "Invited Review: Transitioning from Milk to Solid Feed in Dairy Heifers." *Journal of Dairy Science* 99 (2): 885–902, 885. doi: 10.3168/jds.2015-9975.

63. FAO (Food and Agriculture Organization). 2017. *Zero-Grazing of Improved Cattle Breeds Using Drought-Tolerant Fodder in Uganda.* Retrieved 6 January, 2021, from http://www.fao.org/3/CA2565EN/ca2565en.pdf.

64. FAO, 2017.

65. Tiwari et al. 2007. "Buffalo Calf Health Care in Commercial Dairy Farms: A Field Study in Uttar Pradesh (India)." *Livestock Research for Rural Development* 19 (3):1–8, 1.

66. Chaudhuri, Una. 2017. *The Stage Lives of Animals: Zooesis and Performance.* Abingdon, UK: Routledge, 162.

67. Tiwari et al., 2007, 1.

68. FAO. 2003. *Working with Local Institutions to Support Sustainable Livelihoods.* Retrieved 13 February, 2022, from https://www.fao.org/3/y5083e/y5083e.pdf; George, S. 1985. "Operation Flood and Rural India: Vested and Divested Interests.", *Economic and Political Weekly* 20 (49): 2163–2170.

69. Poonia et al. 2014. "Management Issues and Prospects of Dairy Industry in Varanasi District Of Uttar Pradesh, India." *Asian Journal of Dairy and Food Research* 33 (3): 161–162.

70. FAO, 2003; George, S. 1985. "Operation Flood and Rural India: Vested and Divested interests" *Economic and Political Weekly,* 20 (49): 2163–2170.

71. Dohmwirth, Carla, and Hanisch, Markus. 2019. "Women's Active Participation and Gender Homogeneity: Evidence from the South Indian Dairy Cooperative Sector." *Journal of Rural Studies* 72: 125–135, 130. Similarly, they note a study by Shah et al. (2006) which found that "in 47 per cent of the villages in their sample, Dalits were not allowed to sell milk to a cooperative because of norms of untouchability. Moreover, non-Dalit women seem to enforce norms of untouchability more rigidly than men, as women are perceived as being responsible for upholding caste purity for their household." (Shah et al., 2006, 119, in, Dohmwirth and Hanisch, 2019, 130–131).

72. FAO, 2003.

73. FAO, 2003.

74. Kumar et al. 2013. "Do Dairy Co-operatives Enhance Milk Production, Productivity and Quality? Evidence from the Indo-Gangetic Plain of India." *Indian Journal of Agricultural Economics* 68(3, 457–468

75. Santos, Jose Eduardo P. 2011. "Nutritional Management of Lactating Dairy Cows." In *Dairy Production Medicine,* ed. Carlos Risco and Pedro Mendelez, 33–72 [e-book]. John Wiley and Sons. https://doi.org/10.1002/9780470960554.ch5

76. Edwards, R. and Kellett, R. 2000. *Life in Plastic: The Impact of Plastic on India.* Goa: Other India Press.

77. Doron, Assa, and Jeffrey, Robin. 2018. *Waste of a Nation: Garbage and Growth in India.* Cambridge, MA: Harvard University Press, 45.

78. Doron and Jeffrey, 2018, 45.

79. Ahmad, N. 2011. "Acid Attacks on Women: An Appraisal of the Indian Legal Response." *Asia Pacific Journal on Human Rights and the Law* 12 (2): 55–72.

80. Ahmad, 2011.

81. Ahmad, 2011.

82. Kennedy et al. 2018. "The Sheltering of Unwanted Cattle: Experiences in India and Implications for Cattle Industries Elsewhere." *Animals: An Open Access Journal from MDPI* 8 (5): 64.

83. Animals Legal and Historical Centre. 2022. "The Prevention of Cruelty to Animals Act, 1960." Retrieved 13th February, 2022, from https://www.animallaw.info/statute/cruelty-prevention-cruelty-animals-act-1960. The Prevention of Cruelty to

Animals Act 1960 allows humane euthanasia for suffering animals in some cases. However, Article 30 of the Act presumes guilt in the euthanasia of animals, including cows, unless proven otherwise. "If any person is charged with the offence of killing a goat, cow or its progeny contrary to the provisions of clause (l) of sub-section (1) of section 11 [injection of strychnine], and it is proved that such person had in his possession, at the time the offence is alleged to have been committed, the skin of any such animal as is referred to in this section with any part of the skin of the head attached thereto, it shall be presumed until the contrary is proved that such animal was killed in a cruel manner." Some state legislations allow for the euthanasia of cows if it is in the "public interest" (if the cow is suffering from a transferable zoonotic disease), or if it is suffering from "intolerable pain." (Uttarakhand Protection of Cow Progeny Act 2007).

84. Fischer, W. J., Schilter, B., Tritscher, A. M., and Stadler, R.H. 2011. "Contaminants of Milk and Dairy Products: Contamination Resulting from Farm and Dairy Practices." In *Encyclopedia of Dairy Sciences*, Second Edition, ed. John W. Fuquay, 887–897 [e-book]. Academic Press.

85. Fischer et al., 2011, 893.

86. Pullakhandam et al. 2014. "Effect of Oxytocin Injection to Milching Buffalo on its Content and Stability in Milk." *Indian Journal of Medical Research* 39 (6): 933–939. Studies are inconclusive as to whether oxytocin contamination has an impact on human health but conclude that the results of research point away from there being adverse health effects.

87. Tiwari et al., 2007.

88. Bakshi et al. 2010. "Nutritional Status of Animals in Peri-Urban Dairy Complexes in Punjab, India." *The Indian Journal of Animal Sciences* 80 (8): 52.

89. Lammoglia et al. 2016. "Behavior Affected by Routine Oxytocin Injection in Crossbred Cows in the Tropics." *Revista Brasileira de Zootecnia* 45 (8), 478-482.

90. Lammoglia et al., 2016. Of late, oxytocin is even used in plant industries to increase the size of "pumpkins, watermelons, brinjals, gourds and cucumbers."

91. *Reuters*. 2018. "India Bans Imports of Hormone Oxytocin to Halt Misuse in Livestock Industry," 27 June. Retrieved 16 August, 2022, from https://www.reuters.com/article/india-oxytocin-ban-idINKCN1HD14J.

92. The Times of India. 2018a. "Oxytocin Ban to Come into Effect from July 1," 27 June. Retrieved 7 September, 2020, from http://timesofindia.indiatimes.com/articleshow/64769427.cms?utm_source=contentofinterest&utm_medium=text&utm_campaign=cppst.

93. The Times of India. 2018b. "Oxytocin Ban Put on Hold till September. Retrieved 25 December, 2019, from https://timesofindia.indiatimes.com/india/oxytocin-ban-put-on-hold-till-september/articleshow/64830926.cms.

94. Hegde, Narayan G. 2014. "Forage Resource Development in India." *Indian Journal of Animal Sciences* 84 (7): 715–722; Singh et al. 2021. "Availability of Feed Sources and Nutritional Status of Hariana Cattle in Different Seasons in the Breeding Tract." *Biological Rhythm Research* 52 (6): 862–868doi: 10.1080/09291016.2019.1607222.

95. National Commission for Backward Classes. 2015. *Central List of OBCs*. Retrieved 8 July, 2022, from: http://www.ncbc.nic.in/user_panel/GazetteResolution.aspx?Value=mPICjsLiaLv3iHvqDjLo2b6bRBzpX69AoP2QYNS1c%2bG5fYPaeM7PeVC ET3GMjhgG.

96. Pick, 2014, 422.

97. Pachirat, 2011, 252.

CHAPTER 4

1. Burgat, Florence. 2004. "Non-Violence Towards Animals in the Thinking of Gandhi: The Problem of Animal Husbandry." *Journal of Agricultural and Environmental Ethics* 17 (3): 223–248.

2. According to a survey conducted in 1956, "there were 1,020 organized gaushalas in 21 states of India which maintained 130,000 cattle, and 1,400 breeding bulls and produced 11.2 million kg of milk. . . ." Makhijani, H. J. 1956. *Gaushalas and Pinjrapoles in India*. New Delhi: Central Council of Gosamvardhana.

3. Mohan, C. Madan. 1989. *Dairy Management in India: A Study in Andhra Pradesh*. Delhi: Mittal Publications.

4. *The Times of India*. 2016a. "Cry for Holy Cows Fails to Draw Funds for Gaushalas." Retrieved 28 May, 2017, from http://timesofindia.indiatimes.com/india/Cry-for-holy-cows-fails-to-draw-funds-for-gaushalas/articleshow/52921244.cms.

5. Gruen, L. (ed.). 2014. *The Ethics of Captivity*. New York: Oxford University Press.

6. Donaldson, S., and Kymlicka, W. 2015. "Farmed Animal Sanctuaries: The Heart of the Movement? A Socio-Political Perspective." *Politics and Animals* 1 (1): 50–74, 51.

7. The Physicians Committee for Responsible Medicine writes: "The most healthful calcium sources are green leafy vegetables and legumes, or 'greens and beans' for short. Broccoli, Brussels sprouts, collards, kale, mustard greens, and other greens are loaded with highly absorbable calcium and a host of other healthful nutrients." It goes on to note that dairy contains perhaps the most harmful source of calcium, as "it is accompanied by animal proteins, lactose sugar, animal growth factors, occasional drugs and contaminants, and a substantial amount of fat and cholesterol in all but the defatted versions." [Physicians Committee for Responsible Medicine. 2022. *Calcium and Strong Bones*. Retrieved 16 August, 2022, from https://www.pcrm.org/good-nutrition/nutrition-information/health-concerns-about-dairy/calcium-and-strong-bones.] A Harvard study notes, "Milk is actually only one of many sources of calcium—dark leafy green vegetables and some types of legumes are among the other sources—and there are some important reasons why milk may not be the best source for everyone." The study associated dairy with increased risk of ovarian cancer for women, and prostate cancer for men. [Harvard School of Public Health. 2019. "Calcium: What's Best for your bones and health?" *The Nutrition Source*. Retrieved 18 September, 2020, from: https://www.hsph.harvard.edu/nutritionsource/what-should-you-eat/calcium-and-milk/calcium-full-story/#calcium-from-milk.] Another study published by Ludwig and Willcett notes: "Humans have no nutritional requirement for animal milk, an evolutionarily recent

addition to diet. Anatomically modern humans presumably achieved adequate nutrition for millennia before domestication of dairy animals, and many populations throughout the world today consume little or no milk for biological reasons (lactase deficiency), lack of availability, or cultural preferences. Adequate dietary calcium for bone health, often cited as the primary rationale for high intakes of milk, can be obtained from many other sources. Indeed, the recommended levels of calcium intake in the United States, based predominately on balance studies of 3 weeks or less, likely overestimate actual requirements and greatly exceed recommended intakes in the United Kingdom. Throughout the world, bone fracture rates tend to be lower in countries that do not consume milk compared with those that do. Moreover, milk consumption does not protect against fracture in adults, according to a recent meta-analysis." [Ludwig, D.S., and Willett, W.C. 2013. "Three Daily Servings of Reduced-Fat Milk: An Evidence-Based Recommendation?" *Journal of the American Medical Association of Pediatrics.* 167 (9):788–789.]

8. Gaard, 2013.

9. Jagga, R. 2014. "Over 1.5 Lakh Litre Extra Milk Consumed on Mahashivratri." *The Indian Express.* Retrieved 31 August, 2020, from https://indianexpress.com/article/cities/ludhiana/over-1-5-lakh-litre-extra-milk-consumed-on-mahashivratri/.

10. Malhotra, Pratishtha. 2016. "Rajinikanth Fans, Can We Stop Wasting Milk Please?" *The Quint,* 26 July. Retrieved 13 February, 2019, from https://www.thequint.com/entertainment/why-we-should-do-away-with-the-practice-of-immersing-rajinikanths-cut-out-in-milk-every-year.

11. Archana, K. C. 2020. "Instead Of Wasting Milk Offered by Devotees, Temple Feeds It to Stray Dogs and Wins Hearts." *India Times.* Retrieved 31 August, 2020, from https://www.indiatimes.com/trending/human-interest/temple-uses-milk-offered-to-gods-to-feed-strays-519537.html.

12. Francione, Gary. 2010. "Animal Welfare and the Moral Status of Nonhuman Animals." *Law, Culture and the Humanities* 6 (1): 24–36.

13. Lodrick, 1981.

14. Lodrick, 1981.

15. Sharpes, 2006, 215.

16. *The Hans India.* 2015. "South India's Biggest Goshala at Shamshabad." Retrieved 15 May, 2019, from https://www.thehansindia.com/posts/index/Hyderabad/2015-01-18/South-Indias-biggest-goshala-at-Shamshabad/126532.

17. *The Hindu.* 2010. "ISKCON's Largest 'Goshala' Coming Up." Retrieved 16 May, 2019, from https://www.thehindu.com/news/national/andhra-pradesh/ISKCONs-largest-Goshala-coming-up/article15906492.ece.

18. Lodrick, 1981.

19. Animal People Online. (2004). "Why cattle 'offerings' prevail where cow slaughter is illegal." Retrieved 26 December, 2014, from http://www.animalpeoplenews.org/04/5/cattleOfferings5.04.html

20. Krishnan, Anantha P. 2007. "The Calves of Simhachalam." *ISKCON News.* Retrieved 15 December, 2014, from http://iskconnews.org/the-calves-of-simhachalam,293/.

21. *The New Indian Express*. 2013. "100 Cows Starve to Death at Simhachalam Temple," 15 May. Retrieved 26 December, 2015, from http://www.newindianexpress.com/states/andhra_pradesh/100-cows-starve-to-death-at-Simhachalam-Temple/2013/05/15/article1590412.ece.

22. VSPCA (Visakha Society for the Protection and Care of Animals). 2013. "Simhachalam Calves: 2013 Update—12 Months of Liberation for Thousands of Male Calves." Retrieved 13 February, 2015, from https://vspca.org/portfolio/simhachalam-calves/.

23. VSPCA, 2013.

24. Kumar, Anshuman. 2019. "Tensions Among Farmers in Uttar Pradesh on the Rise ss Stray Cows Run Amok." *The Economic Times*, 2 January. Retrieved 16 August, 2022, from https://economictimes.indiatimes.com/news/politics-and-nation/tensions-among-farmers-in-uttar-pradesh-on-the-rise-as-stray-cows-run-amok/articleshow/67343354.cms?from=mdr.

25. Srinivasulu, K. 2002. "Caste, Class and Social Articulation in Andhra Pradesh: Mapping Differential Regional Trajectories." Retrieved 13 February, 2021, from https://cdn.odi.org/media/documents/2692.pdf.

26. Tayob, Shaheed. 2019. "Disgust as Embodied Critique: Being Middle Class and Muslim in Mumbai." *South Asia: Journal of South Asian Studies* 42 (6): 1192–1209, 1208.

27. Wadiwel, Dinesh. 2018. "Chicken Harvesting Machine: Animal Labor, Resistance, and the Time of Production." *The South Atlantic Quarterly* 117 (3):527–549, 540.

28. Sethi, Aarti. 2019. "Mahadev's Gift: Men, Bullocks and the Community of Cultivation in Central India." South Asia: Journal of South Asian Studies 42 (6): 1173–1191.

29. Giraud, E. H. 2019. *What Comes after Entanglement? Activism, Anthropocentrism, and an Ethics of Exclusion*. Durham, NC: Duke University Press, 2–3.

30. Narayanan, Y. 2018b. "Animal Ethics and Hinduism's Milking, Mothering Legends: Analysing Krishna the Butter Thief and the Ocean of Milk." *Sophia: International Journal of Philosophy and Traditions* 57 (1): 133–149.

31. Narayanan, 2018b.

32. Debroy, Bibek (trans.) 2016. *Harivamsha*. Chapter 69. (Kindle edition). Penguin Books, India.

33. Hurn, Samantha. 2017. "Animals as Producers, Consumers and Consumed: The Complexities of Trans-Species Sustenance in a Multi-Faith Community." *Ethnos: Journal of Anthropology* 82 (2): 213–231, 221.

34. Hawley, J. S. 1983. *Krishna: The Butter Thief.* Princeton, NJ: Princeton University Press, 10.

35. Grillo, R. 2016. *Farm to Fable: The Fictions of our Animal-Consuming Culture*. Danvers, MA: Vegan Publishers, 24–25.

36. Maan Mandir Gaushala. n.d. *Maan Mandir Gaushala*. Retrieved 6 October, 2017, from http://maanmandir.org/gaushala/

37. Ganguli, Kisari Mohan (trans.). 1896. *The Mahabharata of Krishna-Dwaipayana Vyasa*. http://www.sacred-texts.com/hin/maha/index.htm, 117.

38. Jain, P. 2014. "Bovine Dharma: Nonhuman Animals and the Swadhyaya Parivar." In *Asian Perspectives on Animal Ethics: Rethinking the Nonhuman*, ed. N. Dalal and C. Taylor, 169–178). New York: Taylor and Francis, 172.

39. Jain, 2014, 171–72.

40. McKenzie, Linda. 2018. "Comparing Cows to Mothers and Children Does Not Work as a Justification for Exploiting Them for 'Ahimsa Milk': Part 8 of a Response to Sivarama Swami." *Vox Vegan*, 15 February. Retrieved 28 February, 2018, from https://vox vegan.com/2018/02/15/comparing-cows-to-mothers-and-children-does-not-work-as-a -justification-for-exploiting-them-for-ahimsa-milk-part-8-in-a-response-to-sivarama -swami/.

41. FAO. 2002. *Livestock Diversity: Keepers' Rights, Shared Benefits and Pro-Poor Policies*. Retrieved 22 January, 2018, from http://www.fao.org/3/a-x6104e.pdf.

42. Yarris, Kimberley. 2017. "A2 Milk Facts." Retrieved 13 February, 2019, from https://cdrf.org/a2-milk-facts/.

43. Jianqin et al. 2016. "Effects of Milk Containing Only A2 Beta Casein Versus Milk Containing Both A1 and A2 Beta Casein Proteins on Gastrointestinal Physiology, Symptoms of Discomfort, and Cognitive Behavior of People with Self-reported Intolerance to Traditional Cows' Milk." *Nutrition Journal* 15 (35): 1–16.

44. Yarris, 2017.

45. Yarris, 2017.

46. *The Hindu*. 2017. "Make Cow a National Animal: Justice Sharma." Retrieved 3 September, 2019, from https://www.thehindu.com/todays-paper/tp-national/make -cow-a-national-animal-justice-sharma/article18685210.ece.

47. *The Hindu*. 2019b. "Cow Is the Only Animal That Exhales Oxygen, Says Uttarakhand CM." Retrieved 2 October, 2019, from https://www.thehindu.com/news/ national/other-states/cow-only-animal-that-exhales-oxygen-says-uttarakhand-cm/ article28718605.ece?homepage=true&fbclid=IwARomP8NJ3rYIZ5XdkQGPrZb6OVcI EXWZRloeNyr4326miP9ZZskA_atXv9E.

48. RSPCA (Royal Society for the Prevention of Cruelty to Animals). 2022. "What Are the Animal Welfare Issues with Sow Stalls and Farrowing Crates?" Retrieved 14 February, 2022, from https://kb.rspca.org.au/knowledge-base/what-are-the-animal -welfare-issues-with-sow-stalls-and-farrowing-crates/. A similar justification is also used for confining mother pigs in farrowing crates. Even more intensive than the confinement of gestation crates, female pigs in farrowing crates are confined in smaller and narrower cages "a week before farrowing (giving birth) and [are] kept there until the piglets are weaned at about 3–4 weeks of age." The mother pig does not even have the space to turn around, and can only take a step forward or backwards. The industry's justification is that the severe restraint prevents the mother from crushing her piglets or attacking other sows, as pregnancy and delivery can be high-stress events, amplified by the overcrowding and lack of opportunities to engage in natural foraging and nesting behaviors.]

49. Dave, Naisargi N. 2017. "Something, Everything, Nothing; or, Cows, Dogs, and Maggots." *Social Text*, 35 (1): 37–57, 48.

50. Dave, 2017, 48.

51. *Hindustan Times.* 2016. "Holy or Not: Decade of Loving Deserted Cows," 27 June. Retrieved 4 June, 2018, from https://www.hindustantimes.com/delhi-news/ holy-or-not-decade-of-loving-deserted-cows/story-ywRwaSZa1rV6xWImBy9KZM .html.

52. *Hindustan Times.* 2017. "Muslim Man Donates Land for Construction of 'Gaushala' in Uttar Pradesh," 3 May. Retrieved 4 June, 2018, from https://www.hindustantimes .com/india-news/muslim-man-donates-land-for-construction-of-gaushala-in-uttar -pradesh/story-ShgNDClfhTEYfGWZcuhQOL.html.

53. *The Times of India.* 2015c. "Aligarh's Largest Gaushala Survives on Hindu, Muslim Largesse." Retrieved 4 June, 2018, from https://timesofindia.indiatimes.com/city/ agra/Aligarhs-largest-gaushala-survives-on-Hindu-Muslim-largesse/articleshow/ 49705256.cms.

54. *The Times of India.* 2016a. "Cry for Holy Cows Fails to Draw Funds for Gaushalas." Retrieved 28 May, 2017, from http://timesofindia.indiatimes.com/india/Cry-for -holy-cows-fails-to-draw-funds-for-gaushalas/articleshow/52921244.cms.

55. *The Indian Express.* 2017a. "Muslim Man in Ahmedabad to Sit on Fast to Spread Message of Cow Protection." Retrieved 4 June, 2018, from http://indianexpress.com/ article/india/muslim-man-in-ahmedabad-to-sit-on-fast-to-spread-message-of-cow -protection-4744673/.

56. *Common Cause v Union of India.* 2000. Unreported, Delhi High Court, Singh and Sodhi J. J., 3 November, para 1–2.

57. Burgat, 2004, 238.

58. Karpagavinayagam, M. 2004. *Jaigopal Garodia Foundations v. T. R. Srinivasan.* 2004. *Criminal Law Journal,* 2420 (April 1). Retrieved 12 July 2022 from: https:// indiankanoon.org/doc/805722/?type=print

59. Karpagavinayagam, M. 2004. *Jaigopal Garodia Foundations v. T. R. Srinivasan,* 2004, paras. 17–18.

60. *The Tribune.* 2016b. "8,122 Cows Died Since Jan at Hingonia Gaushala: Rajasthan Govt," 6 August. Retrieved 8 February, 2022, from https://www.tribuneindia.com/ news/archive/8-122-cows-died-since-jan-at-hingonia-gaushala-rajasthan-govt-276859.

61. *India Today.* 2016b. "Beef Market in Rampur, UP Exposed." YouTube. Retrieved 11 January, 2018, from https://www.youtube.com/watch?v=Idv8vbMqgzw.

62. Mishra, Ritesh. 2017. "200 Cows Die of Starvation at a Shelter Run by BJP Leader in Chhattisgarh." *The Hindustan Times,* 18 August. Retrieved 16 August, 2022, from https://www.hindustantimes.com/india-news/200-cows-die-of-starvation-at-a -shelter-run-by-bjp-leader-in-chhattisgarh/story-C1fxj4Pj4DgOcGAtmbBdTN.html.

63. *India Today.* 2017. "Haryana: 25 Cows Die at Government-Run Shelter Due to Improper Facilities, Lack of Food," 7 July. Retrieved 29, August, 2020, from https:// www.indiatoday.in/india/story/haryana-25-cows-die-at-government-run-shelter- 1023044-2017-07-07.

64. Singh Rawat, Virendra. 2019. "UP Tops Up Rs 600 Crore Cow Protection Budget with Special Corpus." *Business Standard,* 29 May 2019. Available from: https://

www.business-standard.com/article/current-affairs/up-tops-up-rs-600-crore-cow-pro
tection-budget-with-special-corpus-119052900825_1.html

65. Chari, Mridula. 2019. "Hindutva Paranoia About Cow Slaughter Has Given India a Stray Cattle Problem That's Here to Stay." accessed 14th February. https://scroll
.in/article/908702/the-cow-and-bull-story-as-farmers-vent-anger-indias-stray-cattle
-problem-is-here-to-stay.

66. Kumar, Anshuman 2019. "Tensions Among Farmers in Uttar Pradesh on the rise as Stray Cows Run Amok," *The Economic Times*, 2 January. Retrieved 16 August, 2022, from https://economictimes.indiatimes.com/news/politics-and-nation/tensions-among
-farmers-in-uttar-pradesh-on-the-rise-as-stray-cows-run-amok/articleshow/67343354
.cms?from=mdr.

67. Gupta, 2001.

68. People's Union for Democratic Rights. 2003. "Dalit Lynching at Dulina: Cow-Protection, Caste and Communalism." Retrieved 8 February, 2020, from https://pudr
.org/sites/default/files/2019-02/jhajhar_dalit_lynching.pdf.

CHAPTER 5

1. Naqvi et al. 2013. "In Lawless Uttar Pradesh It's Rule of the Gun." *Hindustan Times*. Retrieved 4 January, 2021, from https://www.hindustantimes.com/india/in-law
less-uttar-pradesh-it-s-rule-of-the-gun/story-WKpeNkUjsBqRUKHLQB05KI.html.

2. Naqvi et al., 2013.

3. Chaurasi Devataon-wali Gai. 2020. Stock Photo—Alamy: Chaurasi Devataon-wali Gai. Retrieved 16 August, 2022, from https://www.alamy.com/chaurasi-devataon
-wali-gai-image446736351.html.

4. Gupta, 2001, 4296.

5. Hindu Janajagruti Samiti. 2014. "Heinous Act of Cow slaughtering." Retrieved 10 February, 2019, from https://www.hindujagruti.org/hindu-issues/cow-slaughter/
heinous-act-of-cow-slaughtering.

6. Struggle for Hindu Existence. 2016. "Five Muslims Held for Slaughtering Cows in Maharashtra," 29 August. Retrieved 16 August, 2022 from https://hinduexistence
.org/2016/08/29/five-muslims-held-for-slaughtering-cows-in-maharashtra/save-cow
-save-nation-2/.

7. NMVG (Namo Mission Vande Gaumathram). n.d. "Namo Mission Vande Gaumathram." Retrieved 9 February, 2022, from https://namomissionvandegaumath
aram.com/.

8. Newar, Sanjay. 2016. *A Hindu's Fight for Mother Cow*. Retrieved 3 January, 2020, from http://agniveer.com/books/a-hindus-fight-for-mother-cow/.

9. Anderson, Edward, and Longkumer, Arkotong. 2018. "'Neo-Hindutva': Evolving Forms, Spaces, and Expressions of Hindu Nationalism." *Contemporary South Asia* 26 (4): 371–377.

10. Jaffrelot, C. 2015a. "The Modi-centric BJP 2014 Election Campaign: New Techniques and Old Tactics." *Contemporary South Asia*. 23(2): 151–166, 160.

11. Jaffrelot, 2015a, 160.

12. Varadarajan, Siddharth. 2015. "The Pink Revolution is Marching On." *The Wire*. Retrieved 8 February, 2022, from https://thewire.in/communalism/the-pink-revolution -is-marching-on.

13. Balchand, V. 2014. "Modi Fears a 'Pink Revolution.'" *The Hindu*. Retrieved 8 February, 2022 https://www.thehindu.com/news/national/other-states/modi-fears-a -pink-revolution/article5864109.ece.

14. Jaffrelot, 2015a, 160.

15. Freeman, Andrea. 2017. "Milk, a Symbol of Neo-Nazi Hate." *The Conversation*. 31 August. Retrieved 7 December, 2017, from https://theconversation.com/milk-a -symbol-of-neo-nazi-hate-83292.

16. Freeman, 2017.

17. Gambert, Iselin, and Linne, Tobias. 2018. "From Rice Eaters to Soy Boys: Race, Gender, and Tropes of 'Plant food Masculinity.'" *Animal Studies Journal* 7 (2): 131–182.

18. Gupta, 2001, 4296.

19. Modi, Narendra. 2012. "Janmashtami—the Protector of Cows, Lord Krishna's Birthday." *Narendra Modi's Blog*, 10 August. Retrieved 10 August, 2018, from https:// timesofindia.indiatimes.com/blogs/narendra-modis-blog/janmashtami-the-protector -of-cows-lord-krishna-s-birthday/.

20. *First Post*. 2017. "To Teach Muslims 'Save the Cow' Message, RSS to Organise Iftar with Only Cow Milk Products." Retrieved 28 May, 2017, from http://www.first post.com/india/to-teach-muslims-save-the-cow-message-rss-to-organise-iftar-with -only-cow-milk-products-3462918.html.

21. *The Asian Age*. 2017. "RSS Plans 'Cow Milk Only' Iftar." Retrieved 8 April, 2019, from https://www.asianage.com/india/all-india/230517/rss-plans-cow-milk-only-iftar .html.

22. *The Wire*. 2021. "In Syllabus for National Exam on Cows, Rastriya Kamdhenu Aayog Unleashes Half-Truths." *The Wire*. Retrieved 7 January, 2021, from https:// thewire.in/government/cows-rastriya-kamdhenu-aayog-exam-gau-seva.

23. Rashtriya Kamadhenu Aayog. 2021. "RKA Syllabus." Retrieved 7 January, 2022, from https://www.scribd.com/document/489869645/RKA-syllabus#from_embed, 9.

24. Rashtriya Kamadhenu Aayog, 2021, 10.

25. Rashtriya Kamadhenu Aayog, 2021, 12.

26. Yuval-Davis, Nira. 1993. "Gender and Nation." *Ethnic and Racial Studies* 16 (4): 621–632.

27. *The Times of India*. 2018c. "Himachal Govt Wants Cow to Be Made 'Mother of Nation.'" Retrieved 7 December, 2019, from https://timesofindia.indiatimes .com/city/shimla/himachal-govt-wants-cow-to-be-made-mother-of-nation/ articleshow/67084492.cms?fbclid=IwAR2fD7Na2G4HwTdrnnzrhrhDd-q8Zpki5xY -oTza565iq2xhjh-eoA2-Xas.

28. Hansen, 1994.

29. Anand, D. 2007. "The Violence of Security: Hindu Nationalism and the Politics of Representing 'the Muslim' as a Danger." *The Round Table: The Commonwealth Journal of International Affairs* 94 (379): 203–215, 209.

30. Subramaniam, M. 2014. "Resisting Gendered Religious Nationalism: The Case of Religious-Based Violence in Gujarat, India." *Gendered Perspectives on Conflict and Violence* 18B: 73–98, 76.

31. Subramaniam, 2014, 93.

32. Moritz, M. 2008. "A Critical Examination of Honour Cultures and Herding Societies in Africa." *African Studies Review* 51 (2):99–117, 101.

33. Kesavan, 2015.

34. Basu, Amrita. 1998. "Appropriating Gender." In *Appropriating Gender: Women's Activism and Politicized Religion in South Asia*, ed. Patricia Jeffery and Amrita Basu. New York, NY: Routledge, 7.

35. Maroney, Heather Jon. 1985. "Embracing Motherhood: New Feminist Theory." *Canadian Journal of Political and Social Theory* 11 (1–2): 40–64, 40.

36. Basu, A. 1999. "Women's Activism and the Vicissitudes of Hindu Nationalism." *Journal of Women's History* 10 (4): 104–124.

37. Gupta, Charu. 2001. "The Icon of Mother in Late Colonial North India: 'Bharat Mata,' 'Matri Bhasha' and 'Gau Mata.'" *Economic and Political Weekly* 36 (45): 4291–4299.

38. Dhruvarajan, V. 1990. "Religious Ideology, Hindu Women, and Development in India." *Journal of Social Issues* 46 (3): 57–70.

39. Hansen, T. B. 1994. "Controlled Emancipation: Women and Hindu Nationalism." *The European Journal of Development Research* 6 (2): 82–94, 93, emphasis in original.

40. Hansen, 1994, 87.

41. Hansen, 1994.

42. Hörnqvist, Magnus and Flyghed, Janne. 2012. "Exclusion or Culture? The Rise and the Ambiguity of the Radicalization Debate." *Critical Studies on Terrorism* 5 (3): 319–334; Dalgaard-Nielsen, Anja. 2010. "Violent Radicalization in Europe: What We Know and What We Do Not Know." *Studies in Conflict and Terrorism* 33 (9): 797–781; Yusuf, Hakeem O. 2013. "Harvest of Violence: The Neglect of Basic Rights and the Boko Haram Insurgency in Nigeria." *Critical Studies on Terrorism* 6 (3): 371–391. Security and terrorist studies debate the role of ideology vs. the experience of structural violence (especially in the form of socio-economic marginalization) in recruiting the poor, especially youth to radicalization. Hörnqvist and Flyghed (319) consider both perspectives to be influential in reality. In Dalgaard-Nielsen's review of terrorist radicalization in Europe, he points to "classical sociological factors such as socioeconomic marginalization, lack of education, and/or neighborhood solidarity and peer pressure . . . to explain the radicalization of individuals from Europe's lower social strata" (799). Likewise, Nigeria's "governance gap" is believed to have "created fertile breeding grounds for the recruitment of disillusioned youths who are easily mobilized to violence" (Yusuf, 371).

43. Spataro, Armando. 2008. "Why Do People Become Terrorists? A Prosecutor's Experiences." *Journal of International Criminal Justice* 6: 507–524.

44. Spataro, 2008.

45. Sparato, 2008, 519.

46. Spataro, 2008, 519.

47. Narayanan, Yamini. 2021b. "'A pilgrimage of camels': Dairy capitalism, nomadic pastoralism, and subnational Hindutva statism in Rajasthan." *Environment and Planning E: Nature and Space.* https://doi.org/10.1177/2514848621106 2005.

48. Jaffrelot, C. 2015b. "What 'Gujarat Model'? Growth Without Development—and with Socio-Political Polarisation." *South Asia: Journal of South Asian Studies* 38 (4): 820–838.

49. Datta, Ayona. 2019. "Postcolonial Urban Futures: Imagining and Governing India's Smart Urban Age." *Environment and Planning D* 37 (3): 393–410, 393.

50. Gandhi, M. K. 1920. Speech at Bettiah Goshala (December 8). *Mahadevbhaini Diary,* Vol. V. Ahmedabad: Navajivan Publishing House.

51. Kapoor, Mugdha. 2015. "'Beef Festivals' to Fight Against #BeefBan. How's That for a Protest?" *India Times.* Retrieved 8February, 2022, from https://www.india times.com/news/india/beef-festivals-to-fight-against-beefban-hows-that-for-a-protest -231355.html.

52. *The Indian Express.* 2015. "Osmania 'Beef Festival' Row: Police Raid Hostels, Detain 30 Students, BJP MLA Raja Singh." Retrieved 4 September, 2019, from https://indianexpress.com/article/india/india-news-india/beef-festival-row-bjp-mla-arrested -8-organisers-detained/.

53. Kesavan, 2015.

54. *News18.* 2018. "'God Punished You for Eating Beef': Ugly Responses to Kerala Floods Prove Bigotry is Alive and Kicking." *News18.* Retrieved 2 August, 2021, from https://www.news18.com/news/buzz/god-punished-you-for-eating-beef-responses-to -kerala-floods-prove-how-bigotry-is-alive-and-kicking-in-india-1849169.html.

55. *News18,* 2018.

56. *Sabrang India.* 2016. "If the Cow is Your Mother, You Bury Her: Gujarat Dalits Cry Liberation." Retrieved 21 January, 2019, from https://sabrangindia.in/interview/ if-cow-your-mother-you-bury-her-gujarat-dalits-cry-liberation.

57. *Scroll.* 2016. "'Your Mother, You Take Care of It': Meet the Dalits Behind Gujarat's Stirring Cow Carcass Protests." *Scroll.* Retrieved 21 January, 2019, from https:// scroll.in/article/812329/your-mother-you-take-care-of-it-meet-the-dalits-behind-gujar ats-stirring-cow-carcass-protests.

58. Sabrang India, 2016.

59. Sabrang India, 2016.

60. *India Times.* 2015. "RSS Says Killing or Smuggling a Cow Equivalent to Rape of a Hindu Girl." Retrieved 8 February, 2022, from https://www.indiatimes.com/news/ india/rss-says-killing-or-smuggling-a-cow-=-raping-a-hindu-girl-234350.html; Human Rights Watch. 2017. "India: 'Cow Protection' Spurs Vigilante Violence." 27 April. Retrieved 8 February, 2022, from https://www.hrw.org/news/2017/04/27/india-cow-protec tion-spurs-vigilante-violence. The rape of Hindu women, and the slaughter of cows are frequently equated in the statements of Hindu nationalist party workers. Jishnu Basu, an RSS worker in West Bengal, said, "Killing or smuggling a cow is equivalent to raping a Hindu girl or destroying a Hindu temple" (*India Times,* 2015). [Human Rights Watch notes: "BJP leaders have attempted to portray the majority Hindu population as victims,

whipping up fear of Muslim men who they say kidnap, rape, or lure Hindu women into relationships as part of a plot to make India into a Muslim-majority country."

61. *First Post.* 2020. "Kerala Elephant Death: Police Make First Arrest; No Evidence Locals 'Fed' Pachyderm Pineapple Stuffed with Firecrackers, Claim Officials." Retrieved 8 February, 2021, from https://www.firstpost.com/india/kerala-elephant -death-police-make-first-arrest-no-evidence-locals-fed-pachyderm-pineapple-stuffed -with-firecrackers-claim-officials-8451501.html.

62. Sikandar, Zainab. 2020. "Elephant or Cow, Hindutva Doesn't Give Two Hoots About Animal Welfare. Deaths Are Political." *The Print.* Retrieved 22 July, 2021, from https://theprint.in/opinion/elephant-cow-hindutva-give-two-hoots-about-animal-wel fare-deaths-political/437520/.

63. Sikandar, 2020.

64. Dave, 2014, 433.

65. Singh, Akhilesh. 2014. "Funds from Cow Slaughter Racket Being Pumped into Terror: Maneka Gandhi." *Struggle for Hindu Existence*, 16 September. Retrieved 22 July, 2021, from https://hinduexistence.org/2014/09/16/illegal-cow-slaughter-rackets-en hance-islamic-terrorism-hindu-muslims-both-are-guilty/

66. Gandhi, M. Sanjay. 2017. "The Many Faces of Cruelty." *Mathrubhumi.* Retrieved 22 July, 2021, from https://english.mathrubhumi.com/news/columns/faunaforum/ the-many-faces-of-cruelty-maneka-gandhi-1.1661360

67. *The Times of India.* 2016b. "Administration Stops Cruel Cow-Pig Fight to Mark Govardhan Puja Celebrations." Retrieved 14 February, 2022, from https://timesofindia .indiatimes.com/city/bareilly/admin-stops-cruel-cow-pig-fight-to-mark-govardhan -puja-celebrations/articleshow/55165592.cms

68. *OneIndia.* 2017. "Pigs to Flaunt Sacred Thread to Mark Protest Against Brahminism, BJP in Tamil Nadu." Retrieved 27 August, 2020, from https://www.oneindia .com/india/pigs-flaunt-sacred-thread-mark-protest-against-brahminism-b-2504733 .html

69. YouTube. 2017. "Periyarites Arrested While on Their Way to a Janeu Ceremony for Pigs." Retrieved 30 October, 2020, from https://www.youtube.com/watch? v=rfyFW5phlpQ.

70. *DT Next.* 2017. "9 TPDK Members Held for Animal Cruelty." Retrieved 27 August, 2020, from https://www.dtnext.in/News/City/2017/08/08023607/1041057/9 -TPDK-members-held-for-animal-cruelty.vpf.

71. Narayanan, Y. 2021a. "Animating Caste: Visceral Geographies of Pigs, Caste and Violent Nationalisms in Chennai City." *Urban Geography.* doi: 10.1080/02723638.2021.1890954. This section on pigs is partly extracted from my article.

72. Boisseron, 2018; Kim, 2015.

73. Srinivasan, 2015, 305.

74. Dave, Naisargi. 2019. "The Tyranny of Consistency." In *Messy Eating*, ed. S. King, S. R. Carey, I. Macquarrie, V. N. Millious, E. M. Power, and C. Wolfe, 68–83. New York: Fordham University Press, 75.

75. Dave, 2019, 76.

76. Alloun, 2020, 24. Alloun's work on vegan washing as a means of advancing the politics of the exclusionary Zionist Israeli nation, and establishing Jewish Israeli belonging and Palestinian unbelonging is a model in showing how the narratives "paradoxically rendered them [Jewish Israelis] inaudible."

77. Civil Society. 2015. "Give Cows Pastures Not Plastic, Say Dalits." Retrieved 21 January, 2019, from https://www.civilsocietyonline.com/protest/give-cows-pastures-not -plastic-say-dalit-protesters/

78. Francione, 2010.

79. Wrenn, C. Lee, and Johnson, R. 2013. "A Critique of Single-Issue Campaigning and the Importance of Comprehensive Abolitionist Vegan Advocacy." *Food, Culture and Society* 16 (4): 651–668.

80. Narayanan, Yamini. (forthcoming). An Ecofeminist Politics of Chicken Ovulation: A Socio-Capitalist Model of Ability as Farmed Animal Impairment. *Hypatia: A Journal of Feminist Philosophy.*

81. Davis, 2019.

82. Anomaly, J. 2015. "What's Wrong with Factory Farming?" *Public Health Ethics* 8 (3): 246–254.

83. Kim, 2015; Kymlicka, W., and Donaldson, S. 2014. "Animal Rights, Multiculturalism, and the Left." *Journal of Social Philosophy* 45 (1): 116–135.

84. Anand, 2007, 212.

85. Anand 2007, 209.

86. Forchtner, B. 2019. "Climate Change and the Far Right." *Wiley Interdisciplinary Reviews–Climate Change* 10 (5): 1–11; Hurd, M., and Werther, S. 2013. "Nature, the Volk and the Heimat." *Baltic Worlds* 6 (2): 13–19; Forchtner, B. (ed.). 2020. *The Far Right and the Environment: Politics, Discourse and Communication.* Abingdon, UK; New York, NY: Routledge; Lockwood, Matthew. 2018 "Right-Wing Populism and the Climate Change Agenda: Exploring the Linkages" *Environmental Politics* 27 (4): 712–732.

87. *The Express Tribune.* 2016. "Leonardo DiCaprio Joins Hands with Hindu Nationalist Group to Ban Beef. Retrieved 28 October, 2019, from https://tribune.com.pk/story/ 1130516/leonardo-dicaprio-joins-hands-hindu-nationalist-group-ban-beef/.

88. Boisseron, 2008, xix.

89. Staples, James. 2017. "Beef and Beyond: Exploring the Meat Consumption Practices of Christians in India." *Ethnos: Journal of Anthropology* 82 (2): 232–251.

90. Boggs, Carl. 2018. *Fascism Old and New: American Politics at the Crossroads.* New York: Routledge.

91. Jal, M. (2015). "Rethinking Secularism in India in the Age of Triumphant Fascism." *Critique* 43 (3–4): 521–549, 522.

92. Jaffrelot, 2015b.

93. *The Economic Times.* 2015. "Gujarat Forensic Sciences University: Creating an Army of Indian Forensic Students." Retrieved 22 January, 2019, from https://economic times.indiatimes.com/industry/services/education/gujarat-forensic-sciences-university -creating-an-army-of-indian-forensic-students/articleshow/46486887.cms.

94. NFSU (National Forensic Sciences University). 2019. "Vision & Mission." Retrieved 14 February, 2020, from https://www.nfsu.ac.in/vision-&-mission.

95. Jasanoff, Sheila. 2004. "Ordering Knowledge, Ordering Society." *States of Knowledge: The Co-Production of Science and Social Order*, edited by Shiela Jasanoff,1–12. London: Routledge, p.16.

96. *The Economic Times*, 2015.

97. *Bangalore Mirror*. 2017. "Meet the Vegetarian Scientist Who Devised the Maharashtra Government's Cow-Meat Detection Kit." Retrieved 22 January, 2019, from http://bangaloremirror.indiatimes.com/columns/sunday-read/meet-the-vegetarian-scientist-who-devised-the-maharashtra-governments-cow-meat-detection-kit/articleshow/59716738.cms.

98. *DNA India*. 2017. "Maharashtra: Portable Cow Meat Detection Kits to be Rolled Out This Month." Retrieved 22 January, 2019, from https://www.dnaindia.com/mumbai/report-portable-cow-meat-detection-kits-to-be-rolled-out-this-month-2493385.

99. *News18*. 2017. "Forensic Test Reveals Lynch Victim Was Carrying Beef: Police." Retrieved 22 January, 2019, from https://www.news18.com/news/india/forensic-test-reveals-lynch-victim-was-carrying-beef-police-1455783.html.

100. Fazal, Imran. 2017. "UP, MP May Buy Maha's Instant Beef-Testing Kits." *DNA India*. Retrieved 9 April, 2020, from https://www.dnaindia.com/mumbai/report-up-mp-may-buy-maha-s-instant-beef-testing-kits-2531209.

101. Deshmane, Akshay. 2015. "Meet India's First Cow Minister Otaram Devasi Who Likes to Address Himself As 'Gaupalan Mantri.'" *Economic Times*. Retrieved 14 February, 2021, from https://economictimes.indiatimes.com/news/politics-and-nation/meet-indias-first-cow-minister-otaram-devasi-who-likes-to-address-himself-as-gaupalan-mantri/articleshow/45815837.cms. The Ministry was renamed as a department when its establishment met a Constitutional prohibition that states could not inaugurate their own ministries.

102. *The Times of India*. 2020. "MP Sets Up Country's First 'Cow Cabinet.'" Retrieved 14 February, 2022, from https://timesofindia.indiatimes.com/india/mp-sets-up-countrys-first-cow-cabinet/articleshow/79293785.cms.

103. *The Times of India*, 2020.

104. *The Tribune*. 2016b. "8,122 Cows Died Since Jan at Hingonia Gaushala: Rajasthan Govt." Retrieved 8 February, 2022, from https://www.tribuneindia.com/news/archive/nation/8-122-cows-died-since-jan-at-hingonia-gaushala-rajasthan-govt-276859.

105. *The Hindu*. 2019c. "More Than 70,000 Cows Died in a Gaushala During BJP Rule." Retrieved 8 February, 2022, from https://www.thehindu.com/news/national/other-states/more-than-70000-cows-died-in-a-gaushala-during-bjp-rule/article26072773.ece.

CHAPTER 6

1. Interview with Sonu, independent Hindu cow vigilante, 2016.

2. *The Indian Express*. 2018. "Seeking to Curb Illegal Slaughter of Cows, Central Committee to Visit Bengal." Retrieved 14 February, 2020, from https://indianexpress

.com/article/cities/kolkata/seeking-to-curb-illegal-slaughter-of-cows-central-commit tee-to-visit-bengal-5307267/.

3. Sandhu, Kamaljit Kaur. 2016. "Hung from the Neck and Dropped Across the Fence: Viral Video Shows Cruel Side of Cattle Smuggling in Bangladesh." *India Today*, 26 September. Retrieved 20 January, 2021, from https://www.indiatoday.in/india/story/ viral-video-cattle-smuggling-bangladesh-343203-2016-09-26.

4. Narayanan, Yamini. 2015b. "Sperm to Slaughter: The Shocking Abuse of Bulls in Dairy Farming." *Huffington Post*. Retrieved 14 February, 2018, from https://www.huff post.com/archive/in/entry/sperm-to-slaughter-the-sh_b_7516454/amp.

5. Samanta, S. 2006. "Calcutta Slaughterhouse: Colonial and Post-Colonial Experiences." *Economic and Political Weekly* 41 (20): 1999–2007, 2005.

6. Wadiwel, D. Joseph. (forthcoming). *Animals and Capital*. Edinburgh, UK: University of Edinburgh Press.

7. Wadiwel, forthcoming.

8. The Chhattisgarh Agricultural Cattle Preservation Act, 2004.Retrieved from http://www.lawsofindia.org/statelaw/2874/TheChhattisgarhAgriculturalCattlePreservationAct2004.html. The Act describes "Agricultural cattle" as: Cows of all ages; calves of cows and of she-buffaloes; bulls; bullocks, and male and female buffaloes. The bans in this Act include the slaughter of these animals, transport outside state boundaries, and beef consumption.

9. Maharashtra Animal Preservation (Amendment) Act, 1995, Maharashtra Act No. V of 2015. Retrieved from http://www.bwcindia.org/Web/Info&Action/Legislation/ Maharashtra%20Animal%20Preservation%20Act%201976%20(amended%20March %202015).pdf

10. The Andhra Pradesh Prohibition of Cow Slaughter and Animal Preservation Act, 1977. Retrieved from http://tgahd.nic.in/awelfare/4.Animal%20Welfare%20Acts. pdf (p.21–22).

11. The Bombay Animal Preservation Act, 1954 (applies to Gujarat). Retrieved from http://www.bareactslive.com/Guj/guj012.htm.

12. The Karnataka Prevention of Cow Slaughter and Cattle Preservation Act, 1964. Retrieved from http://www.lawsofindia.org/statelaw/2358/TheKarnatakaPreventionof-CowSlaughterandCattlePreservationAct1964.html.

13. The Madhya Pradesh Agricultural Cattle Preservation Act, 1959. Retrieved from http://www.bareactslive.com/MP/MP044.HTM.

14. Holding both the mundane status of a "dairy" animal, as well as the "state animal" of Rajasthan, camel transport outside of the state is prohibited. Male camels are trafficked outside of the state and slaughtered underground.

15. Guha-Khasnobis et al. 2006. "Beyond Formality and Informality." In *Linking the Formal and Informal Economy: Concepts and Policies*, ed. Basudeb Guha-Khasnobis, Ravi Kanbur and Elinor Ostrom, 1–21. Oxford: Oxford University Press, 7.

16. Roy, Ananya. 2011. "Slumdog Cities: Rethinking Subaltern Urbanism." *International Journal of Urban and Regional Research* 35 (2): 223–238.

17. Yiftachel, Oren. 2012. "Critical Theory and 'Gray Space': Mobilization of the Colonized." In *Cities for People, Not for Profit: Critical Urban Theory and The Right to the City*, ed. N. Brenner, P. Marcuse and M. Mayer, 150–170. Oxford and New York: Routledge, 153.

18. Holston, J., and Caldeira, T. 2008. "Urban Peripheries and the Invention of Citizenship." *Harvard Design Magazine* 28: 19–23.

19. Kudva, Neema. 2009. "The Everyday and the Episodic: The Spatial and Political Impacts of Urban Informality." *Environment and Planning A* 41: 1614–1628.

20. Kumar, Arun. 2016. "Estimation of the Size of the Black Economy in India, 1996–2012." *Economic and Political Weekly*, 51(48):36–42.

21. Breman, Jan. 1999. "Industrial Labour in Post-Colonial India II: Employment in the Informal-Sector Economy." *International Review of Social History* 44: 451–483.

22. Perry et al. 2007. *Informality: Exit and Exclusion*. Washington, D.C.: World Bank Publications.

23. Pachirat, 2012.

24. In fact, the state explicitly sanctions the foot-march by drafting some rules. The Prevention of Cruelty to Animals (Transport of Animals on Foot) Rules 2001 require each animal to be certified by a veterinarian as "fit to travel"—old or very young, pregnant, diseased or sick, and crippled animals are not "fit" for travel. The Rules make it mandatory to provide the bovines with fodder and water, and also carry "adequate reserve . . . to last during the journey" (Rule 54). If animals are transported on foot, then the rest interval stipulated for cattle is: "At every 2 hours for drinking and at every 4 hrs for feeding" (Rule 12).

25. Gillespie, 2018.

26. Slaughterhouse veterinarian, Cochin, interview 2016. The veterinarian also told me that the methods of cooking in India such as the use of high-temperatures and pressure cooking meant that technically, even rotten meat could be safely consumed as it was being cooked in sterile conditions. It is common for even offal to be transported over two to three days without refrigeration.

27. Chaudhery, 2014.

28. *The Indian Express*. 2017b. "New Animal Market Rules Ban Sale of Cattle for Slaughter." Retrieved 6 November, 2017, from http://indianexpress.com/article/india/cow-slaughter-ban-new-animal-market-rules-ban-sale-of-cattle-beef-ban-4675382/.

29. Sebastian, Manu. 2017. "Rule Banning Cattle Sale for Slaughter Contradicts the Act Permitting Slaughter of Animals for Food." *Outlook India*. Retrieved 9 October, 2020, from https://www.outlookindia.com/website/story/why-prevention-of-cruelty-to-animals-regulation-of-livestock-markets-rules-2017-/299119.

30. Human Rights Watch, 2019a, 17.

31. Sharma, Nidhi. 2018. "Government Dilutes Rules on Cattle Sale in Animal Market." *Economic Times*. Retrieved 9 October, 2020, from https://economictimes.indiatimes.com/news/politics-and-nation/government-dilutes-rules-on-cattle-sale-in-animal-market/articleshow/63690408.cms.

32. *The Times of India.* 2013. "Traffickers Use Chili Paste to Torture Animals Taken to Slaughterhouses." Retrieved 12 November, 2018, from https://timesofindia.indiatimes .com/city/chennai/Traffickers-use-chilli-paste-to-torture-animals-taken-to-slaughter houses/articleshow/24788706.cms.

33. YouTube. 2016. "The Barbaric Transports of Cattle in Kerala (India)." Retrieved 27 November, 2019, from https://www.youtube.com/watch?v=IRpOMUAuQc4.

34. FSSAI (Food Safety and Standards Authority of India). 2011. *Food Safety and Standards (Licensing and Registration of Food Businesses), Regulations 2011.* Part IV, Section A,100–101. Retrieved 16 April, 2020, from https://fssai.gov.in/upload/uploadfiles/ files/Licensing_Regulations.pdf.

35. Dutkiewicz, 2015.

36. Kaur, Ravinder. 2016. "The Innovative Indian: Common Man and the Politics of Jugaad Culture." *Contemporary South Asia* 24 (3): 313–327, 314.

37. TATA. 2017. "Tata Ace HT." Retrieved 6 January, 2018, from http://ace.tatamo tors.com/tata-trucks/tata-ace-ht/specifications/tata-ace-ht-specifications.aspx.

38. Avni, N. and Yiftachel, O. 2013. "The New Divided City? Planning and 'Gray Space' Between Global Northwest and South-East." In *The Routledge Handbook on Cities of the Global South*, ed. S. Parnell and S. Oldfield, 487–505.London and New York: Routledge, 490.

39. Human Rights Watch, 2019, 17. In 2017, People's Union for Democratic Rights noted that since Haryana implemented the cow protection law in 2015, for instance, "there has been an increase in the number of gaurakshaks [cow protectors] who act as 'eyes and ears' of the administration and also as enforcers of law and dispensers of 'lynch justice.'" (People's Union for Democratic Rights A year earlier in 2016, it was reported that "Over 1,900 people have responded to a call from the state's Department of Animal Husbandry to serve as 'eyes to monitor the beef ban.'" These voluntary posts are supposed to be endorsed by a registered animal welfare body "which can vouch for the applicant's integrity." The police can be made accountable to respond to calls from such volunteers. (Nair, Smita. 2016. "Over 1,900 People Line Up to Become 'Eyes' for Maharashtra's Animal Husbandry Dept to Monitor Beef Ban." *The Indian Express*. Retrieved 8 February, 2019, from https://indianexpress.com/article/india/india-news-india/over -1900-people-line-up-to-become-eyes-for-maharashtras-animal-husbandry-dept-to -monitor-beef-ban-2939458/).

40. Gandhi, Ajay. 2011. "'Informal Moral Economies' and Urban Governance in India." In *Urban Informalities*, ed. Colin McFarlane and Michael Waibel. Farnham, UK; Burlington, VT: Ashgate, 52.

41. Pati, A. 2015. "Jajpur NH Roads, A Safe Corridor for Cattle Smuggling." *The New Indian Express*, 28 March. Retrieved 5 August, 2016, from http://www.newindian express.com/states/odisha/Jajpur-NH-Roads-A-Safe-Corridor-for-Cattle-Smuggling/ 2015/03/28/article2734651.ece.

42. Pati, Ipsita. 2017. "NRI, Friend Claim They Were Targeted by 'Cattle Smugglers' in Gurgaon." *Hindustan Times*, 26 September. Retrieved 14 February, 2021, from https://

www.hindustantimes.com/gurgaon/nri-friend-claim-they-were-targeted-by-cattle
-smugglers-in-gurgaon/story-TCeJuZBzzJVnuaIygoeNnK.html.

43. Doron, Assa, and Jeffrey, Robin. 2013. *The Great Indian Phone Book: How the Cheap Cell Phone Changes Business, Politics, and Daily Life.* Cambridge, MA: Harvard University Press, 2–3.

44. Doron and Jeffrey, 2013, 2–3.

45. Human Rights Watch, 2019, 2.

46. People's Union for Democratic Rights. 2003. "Dalit Lynching at Dulina: Cow-Protection, Caste and Communalism." Retrieved 8 February, 2020, from https://pudr.org/sites/default/files/2019-02/jhajhar_dalit_lynching.pdf, 7.

47. Burke, Jason. 2011. "The Problem with Crime Against Women in Delhi." *The Guardian*, 22 February. Retrieved 22 February, 2018, from https://www.theguardian.com/commentisfree/2011/feb/22/problem-crime-against-women-delhi.

48. Jauregui, Beatrice. 2016. "Provisional Agency in India: Jugaad and the Legitimisation of Corruption." *American Ethnologist* 41 (1): 76–91.

49. Jauregui, 2016.

50. Mohan, Dinesh. 2002. "Traffic Safety and Health in Indian Cities." *Journal of Transport & Infrastructure* 9 (1): 79–92.

51. *The New Indian Express*. 2018. "Rajasthan: Cow Smugglers Open Fire at Police, Policeman Injured," 4 June. Retrieved 6 December, 2019, from https://www.newindianexpress.com/nation/2018/jun/04/rajasthan-cow-smugglers-open-fire-at-police-policeman-injured-1823553.html?fbclid=IwARoDWs16EMUOQOPaToxlhOTHqsD2lSFhgQG8-HSY8fzES4xKW_gslVJsSxo.

CHAPTER 7

1. Pachirat, 2012, 23.

2. Pachirat, 2012, 28.

3. As Pachirat described the abattoir in Omaha, so too in Kanpur: "No direct route connects the kill floor and the front office. The quickest way to move from one to the other is to leave the building and walk around the perimeter." (38).

4. USDA Foreign Agricultural Service. 2017. "India, Livestock and Products Annual," 4–5. Retrieved 20 January, 2020, from https://apps.fas.usda.gov/newgainapi/api/report/downloadreportbyfilename?filename=Livestock%20and%20Products%20Annual_New%20Delhi_India_9-1-2017.pdf.

5. Jitendra, Rajat Ghai. 2016. "Cattle Economy: How Cow Became the Mother of Demigods," 20 July. *Down to Earth*. Retrieved 8 January, 2019, from https://www.downtoearth.org.in/coverage/agriculture/cattle-economy-54972.

6. Adriaenssens et al. 2015. "Lineland and the Underground Economy: The Multidimensionality of Informal Work by Secondary Education Students." In *Sociologies of Formality and Informality*, ed. Adriana Mica, Jan Winczorek and Rafal Wiśniewski, 75–102. New York: Peter Lang, 75.

7. Jitendra, I. K. 2017. "Meat Matters." *Down to Earth.* Retrieved 26 January, 2021, from https://www.downtoearth.org.in/coverage/agriculture/meat-matters-57633.

8. FSSAI, 2011, 97.

9. Assainar, Raina. 2014. "At the Heart of Dharavi Are 20,000 Mini-Factories." *The Guardian*, 25 November. Retrieved 25 November, 2019, fromhttps://www.theguardian .com/cities/2014/nov/25/dharavi-mumbai-mini-factories-slum.

10. *Deccan Chronicle*. 2016. "6,500 kg of Beef Seized from a Processing Unit in Mumbai's Dharavi." 9 April. Retrieved 22 December, 2019, from https://www.deccanchron icle.com/amp/nation/in-other-news/090416/6-500-kg-of-beef-seized-from-a-proces sing-unit-in-mumbai-s-dharavi.html.

11. Stevenson, Peter. 1999. "Trade Rules, Animal Welfare and the European Union." In *The Meat Business: Devouring a Hungry Planet*, ed. Geoff Tansy and Joyce D'Silva, 187–197. London: Earthscan Publications Ltd., 188.

12. Shiva, 1999, 198.

13. DAHD. 2019b. *Assistance for Modernization of Slaughter Houses and Carcass Utilization Plants*. Retrieved 27 January, 2021, from https://dahd.nic.in/related-links/ assistance-modernization-slaughter-houses-and-carcass-utilization-plants.

14. Shiva, 1999, 203.

15. Ministry of Food Processing Industries. 2013. "Operational Guidelines for the Scheme for Setting Up/Modernization of Abattoirs." Government of India. Retrieved 29 January, 2020, fromhttps://mofpi.nic.in/sites/default/files/Revised_12PLan_Abat toir_Guidelines_251113.pdf_0.pdf.

16. APEDA. 2019. "Buffalo Meat Profile." Ministry of Commerce and Industry, Government of India. Retrieved 20 January, 2020, from https://apeda.gov.in/apedaweb site/SubHead_Products/Buffalo_Meat.htm.

17. APEDA, 2019; USDA Foreign Agricultural Service, 2017; APEDA, n.d., b. In total, under APEDA, there are seventy-seven slaughterhouses, of which eleven are kill-only sites in Maharashtra, Uttar Pradesh, Andhra Pradesh and Telengana states. The remaining abattoirs are integrated with "meat processing" facilities for these dead animals, located in Uttar Pradesh, Punjab, Maharashtra, Bihar, Andhra Pradesh, Haryana, and Kerala. There are an additional thirty-two meat-processing-only facilities (APEDA 2019; USDA 2017), with highly sophisticated meat chilling, processing, storing, and refrigerated transport facilities. APEDA's main role is to grow India's animal meat industry worldwide; thus, adhering to international standards for sanitation and hygiene for "meat processing," maintaining a careful system for documenting cross contamination, upholding biosecurity security measures, and having standard designs for slaughterhouses to hold and track animals (APEDA, n.d. b) are vital.

18. Central Statistical Organisation. 2008. "National Industrial Classification." Ministry of Statistics and Programme Implementation, 9 April. Retrieved 20 November, 2018, from http://mospi.nic.in/sites/default/files/main_menu/national_industrial _classification/nic_2008_17apr09.pdf.

19. Kim, 2015. In *Dangerous Crossings*, Claire Kim describes the framing of live chicken markets and slaughterhouses in San Francisco's Chinatown as backward, un-clean, and *un-American*, in contrast to industrial chicken slaughterhouses, which are conveniently located out of sight.

20. Ghassem-Fachandi, Parvis. 2012. *Pogrom in Gujarat: Hindu Nationalism and Anti-Muslim Violence in India.* Princeton, NJ: Princeton University Press, 12–20.

21. Mirza, Shireen. 2019. "Cow Politics: Spatial Shifts in the Location of Slaughterhouses in Mumbai City." *South Asia: Journal of South Asian Studies* 42 (5): 861–879, 878.

22. Mirza, 2019, 878.

23. Colling, Sarat. 2020. *Animal Resistance in the Global Capitalist Era.* Ann Arbor, MI: Michigan State University Press.

24. APEDA. 2020. *Indian Meat Industry: Red Meat Manual,* 3rd ed. Ed. Tarun Bajaj and S. K. Ranjhan, 20. Retrieved 20 January, 2020, from https://apeda.gov.in/aped awebsite/Announcements/RED_MEAT_MANUAL_.pdf.

25. Probyn-Rapsey, F. 2013. "Stunning Australia." *Humanimalia: A Journal of Human/Animal Interface Studies* 4 (2): 84–100, 85.

26. APEDA, n. d., b, 13.

27. Silbergeld, Ellen, K. 2016. *Chickenizing Farms and Food: How Industrial Meat Production Endangers Workers, Animals, and Consumers.* Baltimore, MD: Johns Hopkins University Press; Eisnitz, Gail A. 2009. *Slaughterhouse: The Shocking Story of Greed, Neglect, and Inhumane Treatment Inside the U.S. Meat Industry.* [e-book] New York: Prometheus.

28. Eisnitz, 2009, 87.

29. Pachirat, 2012, 138.

30. Pachirat, 2012, 138.

31. Wasley et al. 2018. "Two Amputations a Week: The Cost of Working in a US Meat Plant." *The Guardian,* 5 July. Retrieved 2 August, 2020, from https://www.theguardian .com/environment/2018/jul/05/amputations-serious-injuries-us-meat-industry-plant.

32. Wasley et al., 2018.

33. Miele, Mara. 2016. "Killing Animals for Food: How Science, Religion and Technologies Affect the Public Debate About Religious Slaughter." *Food Ethics* 1: 47–60.

34. Galgut, Elisa. 2019. "A Critique of the Cultural Defense of Animal Cruelty." *Journal of Animal Ethics* 9 (2): 184–198.

35. Joseph, Anna. 2016. "Going Dutch: A Model for Reconciling Animal Slaughter Reform with the Religious Freedom Restoration Act." *Journal of Animal Ethics* 6 (2): 135–152.

36. Pachirat, 2012.

37. Kymlicka and Donaldson, 2014, 124.

38. Pachirat, 2012; Eisnitz, 2009; Ribas, Vanessa. 2015. *On the Line: Slaughterhouse Lives and the Making of the New South.* Berkeley, CA: University of California Press.

39. Pachirat, 2012, 60–61.

40. Pachirat, 2012, 60–61.

41. Pachirat, 2012.

42. Trubshaw, Bob. 1995. "The Metaphors and Rituals of Place and Time—An Introduction to Liminality." Retrieved 4 January, from http://www.indigogroup.co.uk/ foamycustard/fco09.htm.

43. *The Hans India.* 2019. "Animal Welfare Board to File Contempt of Court Plea." Retrieved 21 January, 2020, from https://www.thehansindia.com/telangana/

animal-welfare-board-to-file-contempt-of-court-plea-554409?fromNewsdog=1&utm _source=NewsDog&utm_medium=referral.

44. *Deccan Chronicle.* 2019. "Violate Rules, Get Cattle Seized: Telangana High Court." 9 August. Retrieved 21 January, 2021, from https://www.deccanchronicle.com/ nation/in-other-news/090819/violate-rules-get-cattle-seized-telangana-high-court .html.

45. Humane Society International. 2014. "Supreme Court of India Intervenes to Save Thousands of Animals from Nepal's Brutal Gadhimai Festival Sacrifice," 20 October. Retrieved 8 February, 2020, from https://www.hsi.org/news-media/ india-supreme-court-gadhimai-ruling-102014/.

46. CPCB (Central Pollution Control Board). 2017. "Revised Comprehensive Industry Document on Slaughter Houses." Ministry of Environment, Forest and Climate Change, Government of India. Retrieved 29 January, 2020, from http://www.indiaenvi ronmentportal.org.in/files/file/slaughter_house.pdf.

47. A slaughterhouse vet in Kerala explained that the health regulations in slaughterhouses catering for domestic consumption were not necessarily more "lax." Rather, this difference was cultural, he said. Indian cooking typically involves pressure-cooking meat at very high temperatures that could be understood as sterile. Western cooking methods involve cooking temperatures of 50 to 60 degrees Celsius, where the consumed meat might be raw in places, and require refrigeration.

48. CPCB, 2017.

49. Cited in Anand, Mina. 2020. "Why We Should Ban Meat Exports." *The New Indian Express,* 15 January. Retrieved 26 January, 2021, from https://www.newindianex press.com/opinions/2020/jan/15/why-we-should-ban-meat-exports-2089635.html.

50. Samanta, 2006, 2006.

51. Townend, Christine. 2017. *A Life for Animals.* Sydney: Sydney University Press.

52. Breman, 1999, 458.

53. Breman, 1999, 459.

54. Striffler, Steve. 2005. *Chicken: The Dangerous Transformation of America's Favorite Food.* New Haven, CT: Yale University Press; Pachirat, 2012.

55. Breman, 1999, 456.

56. World Watch Monitor. 2015. "Indian Beef Ban Hits 'Untouchable' Dalits Hardest." 3 March. Retrieved 8 February, 2020, from https://www.worldwatchmonitor .org/2015/03/indian-beef-ban-hits-untouchable-dalits-hardest/.

57. Prabhu, Maya. 2016. "India's Dalit Cattle Skinners Share Stories of Abuse." Aljazeera, 25 August. Retrieved 8 February, from https://www.aljazeera.com/ features/2016/8/25/indias-dalit-cattle-skinners-share-stories-of-abuse.

58. CPCB, 2017, 44.

59. CPCB, 2017, 14.

60. Kabeer et al. 2019. "Group Rights and Gender Justice: Exploring Tensions Within an Indigenous Community in India." Retrieved 27 January, 2021, from http:// eprints.lse.ac.uk/101873/.

61. Narayanan, 2021a.

62. Tayob, 2019, 1208.

63. Sethi, 2019, 1173.

64. Alexis, Nekeisha Alayna. 2019. "There's Something About the Blood . . .: Tactics of Evasion Within Narratives of Violence." In *Animaladies*, ed. Lori Gruen and Fiona Probyn-Rapsey, 47–64. New York: Bloomsbury.

65. Alexis, 2019, 52.

66. Alexis, 2019, 51.

67. Mendieta, E. 2011. "Interspecies Cosmopolitanism: Towards a Discourse Ethics Grounding of Animal Rights." *Logos* 10 (1). http://www.logosjournal.com/interspecies -cosmopolitanism.php

68. King, 2018, 130.

CHAPTER 8

1. Kikon, Dolly. 2020. "The Politics of Dog Meat Ban in Nagaland." *Frontline*. Retrieved 13 January, 2021, from https://frontline.thehindu.com/the-nation/the-politics -of-dog-meat-ban-in-nagaland/article32082833.ece.

2. Kikon, 2020.

3. Kikon, Dolly. 2015. "Fermenting Modernity: Putting Akhuni on the Nation's Table in India." *South Asia: Journal of South Asian Studies* 38 (2): 320–335.

4. Ghassem-Fachandi, Parvis. 2009. "The Hyberbolic Vegetarian: Notes on a Fragile Subject in Gujarat." In *Being There: The Fieldwork Encounter and the Making of Truth*, ed. John Borneman and Abdellah Hammoudi, 77–112. Berkeley, CA: University of California Press.

5. Goodrick-Clarke, Nicholas. 1998. *Hitler's Priestess: Savitri Devi, the Hindu-Aryan Myth, and Neo-Nazism*. New York: New York University Press.

6. Taylor, Bron. 2010. *Dark Green Religion*. Berkeley, CA: University of California Press, 5.

7. Taylor, 2010, 5, emphasis in original.

8. Albanese, Catherine L. 1990. *Nature Religion in America: From the Algonkian Indians to the New Age*. Chicago: University of Chicago Press.

9. Dave, 2019, 71.

10. Dave, 2019, 72.

11. Dave, 2019, 73.

12. Dave, 2019, 73.

13. Dave, 2019, 73.

14. Slater, Joanna, and Masih, Niha. 2020. "As the World Looks for Coronavirus Scapegoats, Muslims Are Blamed in India." *Washington Post*, 22 April. Retrieved 15 January, fromhttps://www.washingtonpost.com/world/asia_pacific/as-world-looks-for -coronavirus-scapegoats-india-pins-blame-on-muslims/2020/04/22/3cb43430-7f3f-11ea -84c2-0792d8591911_story.html.

15. *The Wire*. 2020. "On First Day of Nationwide Lockdown, Adityanath Attends Ram Navami Event in Ayodhya.". Retrieved 15 January, 2021, from https://thewire.in/ politics/coronavirus-yogi-adityanath-lockdown-ram-navami-ayodhya.

16. Davies, Guy. 2021. "Huge Religious Festival of Kumbh Mela Goes Ahead Despite Coronavirus Pandemic." *ABC News*. Retrieved 15 January, 2022, from https://abc news.go.com/International/huge-religious-festival-kumbh-mela-ahead-coronavirus -pandemic/story?id=75246169.

17. Ellis-Petersen, Hannah, and Hassan, Aakash. 2021. "Kumbh Mela: How a Superspreader Festival Seeded Covid Across India." *The Guardian*, 30 May. Retrieved 10 August, 2021, from https://www.theguardian.com/world/2021/may/30/kumbh -mela-how-a-superspreader-festival-seeded-covid-across-india.

18. Pradhan, Bibhudutta, and Chaudhary, Archana. 2021. "Covid May Have Claimed as Many as 5 Million Lives in India." *Bloomberg*, 21 July. Retrieved 10 August, 2021, from https://www.bloomberg.com/news/features/2021-07-21/covid-19 -may-have-claimed-as-many-as-5-million-lives-in-india.

19. Ellis-Petersen and Hassan, 2021.

20. BBC. 2017. "Why Are Indian Women Wearing Cow Masks?" Retrieved 28 May, 2018, from http://www.bbc.com/news/world-asia-india-40404102.

21. Kymlicka and Donaldson, 2014, 117.

22. Kim, 2015, 12.

23. Kim, 2015, 12.

24. Kim, 2015, 19.

25. Kim, 2015, 20.

26. Kymlicka and Donaldson, 2014, 127.

27. Kymlicka and Donaldson, 2014, 128.

28. The Vegan Society. 2020. "The Vegan Society." Retrieved 13 January, 2021, from https://www.vegansociety.com/go-vegan/definition-veganism.

29. Giraud, Eva Haifa. 2021. *Veganism: Politics, Practice, and Theory*. London: Bloomsbury, 2, emphasis in original.

30. Giraud, 2021, 2.

31. Rosales, Jon. 2008. "Economic Growth, Climate Change, Biodiversity Loss: Distributive Justice for the Global North and South." *Conservation Biology* 22 (6): 1409– 1417, 1410.

32. Springmann et al. 2018. "Health and Nutritional Aspects of Sustainable Diet Strategies and Their Association with Environmental Impacts: A Global Modelling Analysis with Country-Level Detail." *Lancet Planetary Health* 2: e451–61. Further, FAO's *Livestock's Long Shadow* argues that livestock production casts a long shadow that is mostly unacknowledged. The report argues:

The livestock sector emerges as one of the top two or three most significant contributors to the most serious environmental problems, at every scale from local to global. The findings of this report suggest that it should be a major policy focus when dealing with problems of land degradation, climate change and air pollution, water shortage and water pollution and loss of biodiversity.

(FAO. 2007. *Livestock's Long Shadow: Environmental Issues and Options*. Retrieved 28 August, 2020, from http://www.fao.org/3/a-a0701e.pdf.)

33. Springmann et al., 2018.

34. Watkins, Stuart. 2018. "The Economic Consequences of Veganism." *Money Week*. Retrieved 13 January, 2021, from https://moneyweek.com/499842/the-economic -consequences-of-veganism.

35. Monbiot, George. 2018. "The Best Way to Save the Planet? Drop Meat and Dairy." *The Guardian*, 8 June. Retrieved 13 January, 2021, from https://www.theguardian.com/commentisfree/2018/jun/08/save-planet-meat-dairy-livestock-food-free-range -steak.

36. Sirohi, Smita, and Michaelowa, Axel. 2007. "Sufferer and Cause: Indian Livestock and Climate Change." *Climatic Change* 85 (3): 285–298, 293.

37. Sirohi et al. 2007. "Mitigation Options for Enteric Methane Emissions from Dairy Animals: An Evaluation for Potential CDM Projects in India." *Mitigation and Adaption Strategies for Global Change* 12: 259–274, 260.

38. Kumari et al. 2018. "Climate Change Impact of Livestock CH_4 Emission in India: Global Temperature Change Potential (GTP) and Surface Temperature Response." *Ecotoxicology and Environmental Safety* 147: 516–522.

39. Narain, Sunita. 2019. "India's Cow Crisis Part 3: Brutal to Kill India's Ancient Uber Economy." *Down to Earth*. Retrieved 3 April, 2020, from https://www.downtoearth.org .in/news/agriculture/india-s-cow-crisis-part-3-brutal-to-kill-india-s-ancient-uber-econ omy-62752?utm_source=Mailer&utm_medium=Email&utm_campaign=Down%20 To%20Earth-2760.

40. Narain et al., 2019.

41. Köhler-Rollefson, Ilse. 2018. "Purdah, Purse and Patriarchy: The Position of Women in the Raika Shepherd Community in Rajasthan (India)." *Journal of Arid Environments* 149: 30–39. Far from being a marginal activity, Indian sheep pastoralism in Rajasthan, for instance, is on such an industrial scale that it contributes to India being among the world's leading exporters of sheep meat and wool.

42. Gillespie, Kathryn. 2021. "An Unthinkable Politics for Multispecies Flourishing within and beyond Colonial-Capitalist Ruins." *Annals of the Association of American Geographers*. doi: https://doi.org/10.1080/24694452.2021.1956297.

43. United Nations. 2020. *The State of Food Security and Nutrition in the World 2020*. Retrieved 25 January, 2021, from https://sustainabledevelopment.un.org/index.php?pa ge=view&type=20000&nr=6909&menu=2993; Shepon et al. 2018. "The Opportunity Cost of Animal Based Diets Exceeds All Food Losses." *Proceedings of the National Academy of Sciences* 115 (15): 3804–3809. https://www.pnas.org/content/115/15/3804 A study by Shepon et al. reports, "Replacing all animal-based items with plant-based replacement diets can add enough food to feed 350 million additional people, more than the expected benefits of eliminating all supply chain food loss"

44. United Nations, 2020.

45. Weis, Tony. 2013. *The Ecological Hoofprint: The Global Burden of Industrial Livestock*. London: Zed Books, 111.

46. Dikshita, A. K., and Birthalb, P. S. 2010. "India's Livestock Feed Demand: Estimates and Projections." *Agricultural Economics Research Review* 23: 15–28.

47. IMARC. 2019. "Indian Animal Feed Market: Industry Trends, Share, Size, Growth, Opportunity and Forecast 2020–2025." Retrieved 25 January, 2020, from https://www.imarcgroup.com/indian-animal-feed-market.

48. Govindrajan, 2018.

49. Merriott, Dominic. 2016. "Factors Associated with the Farmer Suicide Crisis in India." *Journal of Epidemiology and Global Health* 6 (4): 217–227.

50. Farm Policy Exports. 2019. "Subsidy Spotlight: India." Retrieved 15 January, 2020, from https://www.farmpolicyfacts.org/2018/10/subsidy-spotlight-india-2/.

51. Jadhav, Rajendra. 2018. "India's Milk Powder Exports to Surge on Subsidies, Dampen Global Prices." *Reuters.* Retrieved 15 January, from https://www.reuters.com/article/us-india-milk-exports-exclusive/exclusive-indias-milk-powder-exports-to-surge-on-subsidies-dampen-global-prices-idUSKBN1KH0GQ.

52. Patra, A. K. 2016. "Recent Advances in Measurement and Dietary Mitigation of Enteric Methane Emissions in Ruminants." *Frontiers in Veterinary Science* 3, Article 39; Newby et al. 2014. "An Investigation of the Effects of Ketoprofen Following Rumen Fistulation Surgery in Lactating Dairy Cows." *The Canadian Veterinary Journal* 55 (5): 442–448.

53. Hristov et al. 2013. "Mitigation Of Greenhouse Gas Emissions in Livestock Production: A Review of Technical Options for Non-CO2 Emissions." FAO. Retrieved 2 August, 2016, from http://www.fao.org/3/a-i3288e.pdf, 119.

54. Delon, Nicolas. 2018. "Social Norms and Farm Animal Protection." *Palgrave Communications* 4: 139–145, 140.

55. Reese, Jacy. 2020. "Institutional Change and the Limitations of Consumer Activism." *Palgrave Communications* 6 (26): 1-8, 2.

56. Shiva, Vandana. 2019. "Fake Food, Fake Meat: Big Food's Desperate Attempt to Further the Industrialisation of Food." *Independent Science News*. Retrieved 19 December, 2020, from https://www.independentsciencenews.org/health/fake-food-fake-meat-big-foods-desperate-attempt-to-further-industrialisation-food/.

57. Arvidsson, Matilda. 2017. "DIY Plant Milk: A Recipe-Manifesto and Method of Ethical Relations, Care, and Resistance." In *Making Milk: The Past, Present and Future of Our Primary Food*, ed. Mathilde Cohen, 247–251. London and New York: Bloomsbury, 249.

58. Giraud, 2021.

59. Giraud, 2021, 10.

60. Yousefi et al. 2018. "The Avoidable Crisis." Retrieved 13 January, 2021, from https://www.fern.org/fileadmin/uploads/fern/Documents/TheAvoidableCrisisPDF.pdf, 4.

61. Monbiot, 2018.

62. Asano, Yuki M., and Biermann, Gesa. 2019. "Rising Adoption and Retention of Meat-Free Diets in Online Recipe Data." *Nature Sustainability* 2: 621–627.

63. Turner, Emily. 2019. "Poverty Among Workers in the Cashew Industry." Retrieved 21 March, 2020, from https://borgenproject.org/poverty-among-workers-in-the-cashew-industry/.

64. *The New Indian Express*. 2020. "Kerala-Grown 'Superfood' Jackfruit Goes Global as a Meat Substitute," 18 May. Retrieved 13 January, 2021, from https://www.newindian express.com/world/2020/may/18/kerala-grown-superfood-jackfruit-goes-global-as-a -meat-substitute-2144909.html.

65. *The New Indian Express*, 2020.

66. Kurien, 2005, 64.

67. Kurien, 2005, 99.

68. Kurien, 2005, 75.

69. Kurien, 2005, 170.

70. Kurien, 2005, 169.

71. Kurien, 2005, 168.

72. Kurien, 2005, 75.

73. Kornfield, Jack. 2020. *Harmlessness* (trans. Thomas Byrom from the *Dhamma-pada*). Retrieved 2 April, 2020, from https://jackkornfield.com/harmlessness/.

74. Eisen, Jessica. 2017. "Milk and Meaning: Puzzles in Posthumanist Method." In *Making Milk: The Past, Present and Future of Our Primary Food*, ed. Mathilde Cohen and Yoriko Otomo, 237–247. New York: Bloomsbury, 244.

75. Eisen, 2017, 245–46.

BIBLIOGRAPHY

Adams, C. J. 2010. "Why Feminist-Vegan Now?" *Feminism and Psychology* 20 (3): 302–317.

Adcock, Cassie. 2020. "'Preserving and Improving the Breeds': Cow Protection's Animal-Husbandry Connection." *South Asia: Journal of South Asian Studies*. doi: 10.1080/00856401.2019.1681680.

Adriaenssens, S., Verhaest, D., and Hendrickx, J. 2015. "Lineland and the Underground Economy: The Multidimensionality of Informal Work by Secondary Education Students." In *Sociologies of Formality and Informality*, ed. Adriana Mica, Jan Winczorek and Rafal Wiśniewski, 75–102. New York: Peter Lang.

Aggarwal, Mayank. 2017. "CPCB Says India's Slaughterhouses Need to Upgrade to Check Pollution." *Live Mint*, 25 October. Retrieved 19 September, 2019, from https://www.livemint.com/Politics/7SDlidlFCvE7ds3gCkheiI/CPCB-says-Indias-slaughterhouses-need-to-upgrade-to-check-p.html.

Ahmad, Nehalludin. 2011. "Acid Attacks on Women: An Appraisal of the Indian Legal Response." *Asia Pacific Journal on Human Rights and the Law* 12 (2): 55–72.

Ahmad, Tariq. 2015. "FALQs: Beef Bans in India," 10 November [online]. Law Library of Congress. Retrieved 18 May, 2016, from http://blogs.loc.gov/law/2015/11/falqs-beef-bans-in-india/.

Albanese, Catherine L. 1990. *Nature Religion in America: From the Algonkian Indians to the New Age*. Chicago: University of Chicago Press.

Alexis, Nekeisha Alayna. 2019. "There's Something About the Blood . . .: Tactics of Evasion Within Narratives of Violence." In *Animaladies*, ed. Lori Gruen and Fiona Probyn-Rapsey, 47–64. New York: Bloomsbury.

Alger, Janet M., and Alger, Steven F. 2003. *Cat Culture: The Social World of a Cat Shelter*. Philadelphia, PA: Temple University Press.

Alloun, Esther. 2020. "Veganwashing Israel's Dirty Laundry? Animal Politics and Nationalism in Palestine-Israel." *Journal of Intercultural Studies* 41 (1): 24–41.

Ambedkar, B. R. 1948. *The Untouchables: Who Were They and Why They Became Untouchables?* New Delhi: Amrit Book Co.

Ambedkar, B. R. 2015. "Did Hindus Never Eat Beef?" Retrieved 16 July, 2019, from https://www.countercurrents.org/ambedkar050315.htm.

Amir, Lisa Helen, and Lumley, Judith. 2006. Women's Experience of Lactational Mastitis: "I Have Never Felt Worse." *Australian Family Physician* 35 (9): 745–7.

Anand, Dibyesh. 2007. "The Violence of Security: Hindu Nationalism and the Politics of Representing 'the Muslim' as a Danger." *The Round Table: The Commonwealth Journal of International Affairs* 94 (379): 203–215.

Anand, Mina. 2020. "Why We Should Ban Meat Exports." *The New Indian Express*, 15 January. Retrieved 26 January, 2021, from https://www.newindianexpress.com/opinions/2020/jan/15/why-we-should-ban-meat-exports-2089635.html.

Anant, Santoksh S. 1970. "Caste Prejudice and Its Perception by Harijans." *Journal of Social Psychology* 82 (2): 165–172.

Anderson, Edward, and Longkumer, Arkotong. 2018. "'Neo-Hindutva': Evolving Forms, Spaces, and Expressions of Hindu Nationalism." *Contemporary South Asia* 26 (4):3 71–377.

Animals Australia. 2021. "The Reality of Dairy: Killing Calves," 21 December. Retrieved 13 February, 2022, from https://animalsaustralia.org/latest-news/what-happens-to-dairy-calves/#:~:text='Milked'%20dry&text=Producing%20large%20quantities%20of%20milk,be%20associated%20with%20significant%20pain.

Animals Legal and Historical Centre. 2022. "The Prevention of Cruelty to Animals Act, 1960." Retrieved 13 February, 2022, from https://www.animallaw.info/statute/cruelty-prevention-cruelty-animals-act-1960.

Animal People Online. (2004). "Why cattle 'offerings' prevail where cow slaughter is illegal." Retrieved 26 December, 2014, from http://www.animalpeoplenews.org/04/5/cattleOfferings5.04.html

Anomaly, Jonathan. 2015. "What's Wrong with Factory Farming?" *Public Health Ethics* 8 (3): 246–254.

APEDA. n.d., a. "Indian Production of Milk." Retrieved 7 January, 2022, from https://agriexchange.apeda.gov.in/India%20Production/AgriIndia_Productions.aspx?productcode=1023.

APEDA. n.d., b. "Sanitary and Phyto-Sanitary Requirements in Export Oriented Meat Processing Plants." In *APEDA Executive Manual*, Vol. 2, Ministry of Commerce and Industry, Government of India. Retrieved 20 January, 2020, from http://apeda.gov.in/apedawebsite/Announcements/SANITATION_STANDARD_OPERATING_PROCEDURE.pdf.

APEDA. 2017a. "Exports from India of Dairy Products." Retrieved 6 January, 2018, from http://agriexchange.apeda.gov.in/product_profile/exp_f_india.aspx?categorycode=0407.

APEDA. 2017b. *Dairy Products*. Retrieved 6 January, 2018, from http://www.apeda.gov.in/apedawebsite/SubHead_Products/Dairy_Products.htm.

APEDA 2019. "Buffalo Meat Profile." Ministry of Commerce and Industry, Government of India. Retrieved 20 January, 2020, from https://apeda.gov.in/apedawebsite/SubHead_Products/Buffalo_Meat.htm.

APEDA. 2020. *Indian Meat Industry: Red Meat Manual*, 3rd ed. Ed. Tarun Bajaj and S. K. Ranjhan. Retrieved 20 January, 2020, from https://apeda.gov.in/apedawebsite/Announcements/RED_MEAT_MANUAL_.pdf.

APEDA. 2022. "Exports from India of Dairy Products." Retrieved 28 January, 2022, from https://agriexchange.apeda.gov.in/indexp/Product_description_32headChart.aspx? gcode=0407.

Archana, K. C. 2020. "Instead of Wasting Milk Offered by Devotees, Temple Feeds It to Stray Dogs and Wins Hearts." *India Times*. Retrieved 31 August, 2020, from https://www.indiatimes.com/trending/human-interest/temple-uses-milk-offered -to-gods-to-feed-strays-519537.html.

Arvidsson, Matilda. 2017. "DIY Plant Milk: A Recipe-Manifesto and Method of Ethical Relations, Care, and Resistance." In *Making Milk: The Past, Present and Future of Our Primary Food*, ed. Mathilde Cohen, 247–251. London and New York: Bloomsbury.

Asano, Yuki M., and Biermann, Gesa. 2019. "Rising Adoption and Retention of Meat-Free Diets in Online Recipe Data." *Nature Sustainability* 2: 621–627.

Assainar, Raina. 2014. "At the Heart of Dharavi Are 20,000 Mini-Factories." *The Guardian*, 25 November. Retrieved 25 November, 2019, from https://www.theguard ian.com/cities/2014/nov/25/dharavi-mumbai-mini-factories-slum.

Australian Breastfeeding Association. 2019a. *Weaning*. Retrieved 25 December, 2019, from https://www.breastfeeding.asn.au/bf-info/weaning-and-introducing-solids/ weaning.

Australian Breastfeeding Association. 2019b. *Mastitis*. Retrieved 25 December, 2019, from https://www.breastfeeding.asn.au/bf-info/common-concerns–mum/ mastitis.

Avni, N. and Yiftachel, O. 2013. "The New Divided City? Planning and 'Gray Space' Between Global Northwest and South-East." In *The Routledge Handbook on Cities of the Global South*, ed. S. Parnell and S. Oldfield, 487–505. London and New York: Routledge.

Baber, Z. 2004. "'Race,' Religion and Riots: The 'Racialization' of Communal Identity and Conflict in India." *Sociology* 38 (4):701–718.

Bakshi, M. P., Wadhwa, S. M., and Hundal, J. S. 2010. "Nutritional Status of Animals in Peri-Urban Dairy Complexes in Punjab, India." *The Indian Journal of Animal Sciences* 80 (8): 52.

Balchand, V. 2014. "Modi Fears a 'Pink Revolution.'" *The Hindu*. Retrieved 8 February, 2022, from https://www.thehindu.com/news/national/other-states/modi-fears-a -pink-revolution/article5864109.ece.

Ballard, O., and Morrow, A. L. 2013. "Human Milk Composition: Nutrients and Bioactive Factors." *Pediatric Clinics of North America* 60 (1): 49–74. doi:10.1016/j .pcl.2012.10.002.

Banaji, Jairus (ed.). 2013. *Fascism: Essays on Europe and India*. Gurgaon: Three Essays Collective.

Bangalore Mirror. 2017. "Meet the Vegetarian Scientist Who Devised the Maharashtra Government's Cow-Meat Detection Kit." Retrieved 22 January, 2019, from http:// bangaloremirror.indiatimes.com/columns/sunday-read/meet-the-vegetarian-scien

tist-who-devised-the-maharashtra-governments-cow-meat-detection-kit/article
show/59716738.cms.

Banerjee, Dwaipayan. 2020. "Anthropology's Reckoning with Radical Humanism." *Anthropology Now* 12 (3): 50–55.

Basu, Amrita. 1998. "Appropriating Gender." In *Appropriating Gender: Women's Activism and Politicized Religion in South Asia*, ed. Patricia Jeffery and Amrita Basu, 3–14. Taylor & Francis.

Basu, Amrita. 1999. "Women's Activism and the Vicissitudes of Hindu Nationalism." *Journal of Women's History* 10 (4): 104–124.

Basu, Pratyusha. 2009. *Villages, Women and the Success of Dairy Cooperatives in India.* Amherst, MA: Cambria Press.

Bazzoli, I., De Marchi, M., Cecchinato, A., Berry, D. P., and Bittante, G. 2014. "Factors Associated with Age at Slaughter and Carcass Weight, Price, and Value of Dairy Cull Cows." *Journal of Dairy Science* 97 (2): 1082–1091.

BBC. 2016. "India Protests Continue After Cow Protectors Assault Dalits in Gujarat." 20 July. Retrieved 31 July, 2016, from http://www.bbc.com/news/world-asia-india-36844782.

BBC. 2017. "Why Are Indian Women Wearing Cow Masks?" Retrieved 28 May, 2018, from http://www.bbc.com/news/world-asia-india-40404102.

Beef Magazine. 2019. "Why Does the U.S. Both Import and Export Beef?" Retrieved 27 January, 2021, from https://www.beefmagazine.com/cowcalfweekly/0611-why-does-us-import-export-beef.

Berg, Dag-Erik. 2017. "Race as a political frontier against caste: WCAR, Dalits and India's foreign policy." *Journal of International Relations and Development* 21 (4):990–1013.

Biardeau, Madeleine. 1993. "Kamadhenu: The Religious Cow, Symbol of Prosperity." In *Asian Mythologies*, ed. Yves Bonnefoy. University of Chicago Press: Chicago.

Biswas, Soutik. 2015. "The Bull Whose Semen Is Worth $3,000." *BBC.* Retrieved 8 December, 2018, from http://www.bbc.com/news/magazine-31107115.

Boggs, Carl. 2018. *Fascism Old and New: American Politics at the Crossroads.* New York: Routledge.

Boisseron, Benedicte. 2018. *Afro-Dog: Blackness and the Animal Question.* New York: Columbia University Press.

Boyde, Melissa. 2018. "The Dairy Issue: 'Practicing the Art of War.'" *Animal Studies Journal* 7 (2): 9–24.

Breman, Jan. 1999. "Industrial Labour in Post-Colonial India II: Employment in the Informal-Sector Economy." *International Review of Social History* 44: 451–483.

Brown, Theodore M., and Fee, Elizabeth. 2008. "Spinning for India's Independence." *American Journal of Public Health* 98 (1): 39.

Burke, Jason. 2011. "The Problem with Crime Against Women in Delhi," *The Guardian,* 22 February. Retrieved 22 February, 2018, from https://www.theguardian.com/commentisfree/2011/feb/22/problem-crime-against-women-delhi.

Burgat, Florence. 2004. "Non-Violence Towards Animals in the Thinking of Gandhi: The Problem of Animal Husbandry." *Journal of Agricultural and Environmental Ethics* 17 (3): 223–48.

Butler, Judith. 2009. *Frames of War: When is Life Grievable?* London, New York: Verso.

Calarco, Matthew. 2016. "Reorienting Strategies for Animal Justice." In *Philosophy and the Politics of Animal Liberation*, ed. Paola Cavalieri, 45–69. New York: Palgrave McMillan.

Caton, Brian P. 2014. "The Imperial Ambition of Science and Its Discontents." In *Shifting Ground: People, Animals, and Mobility in India's Environmental History*, ed. Mahesh Rangarajan and K. Sivaramakrishnan, 132–154. New Delhi: Oxford University Press.

Central Statistical Organisation. 2008. "National Industrial Classification." *Ministry of Statistics and Programme Implementation*. 9 April. Retrieved 20 November, 2018, from https://mospi.gov.in/documents/213904/0/nic_2008_17apr09.pdf .

Cháirez-Garza, Jesús F. 2021. "Moving Untouched: B. R. Ambedkar and the Racialization of Untouchability." *Ethnic and Racial Studies*, 1–19. doi: 10.1080/01419870.2021.1924393.

Chapple, Christopher Key. 1993. *Nonviolence to Animals, Earth, and Self in Asian Traditions*. Albany, NY: State University of New York Press.

Chari, Mridula. 2019. "Hindutva Paranoia About Cow Slaughter Has Given India a Stray Cattle Problem That's Here to Stay." *The Scroll*, 13 January. Retrieved 14 February, 2020, from https://scroll.in/article/908702/the-cow-and-bull-story-as-farmers-vent-anger-indias-stray-cattle-problem-is-here-to-stay.

Chaudhery, Amit 2014. "The Force of Falsity." Retrieved 13 February, 2021, from https://vosd.in/the-force-of-falsity-by-amit-chaudhery/.

Chaudhuri, Una. 2017. *The Stage Lives of Animals: Zooesis and Performance*. Abingdon, UK: Routledge.

Chaurasi Devataon-wali Gai. 2020. Stock Photo—Alamy: Chaurasi Devataon-wali Gai. Retrieved 16 August, 2022, from https://www.alamy.com/chaurasi-devataon-wali-gai-image446736351.html.

Chenoweth, P. J. 1983. "Sexual Behaviour of the Bull: A Review." *Journal of Dairy Science* 66: 173–179.

Chigateri, Shraddha. 2011. "Negotiating the 'Sacred' Cow: Cow Slaughter and the Regulation of Difference in India." In *Democracy, Religious Pluralism and the Liberal Dilemma of Accommodation*, ed. Monica Mookherjee, Dordrecht: Springer.

Chilkoti, A., and Crabtree, J. 2014. "India's Beef Battleground Sizzles Ahead of Election." Retrieved 4 July, 2022, from https://www.ft.com/content/033680fa-027d-11e3-880d-00144feab7de.

Cibney, Ed. 2016. "When the Human in Humanism Isn't Enough." *Humanist* 76 (2): 12–17.

Civil Society. 2015. "Give Cows Pastures Not Plastic, Say Dalits." Retrieved 21 January, 2019, from https://www.civilsocietyonline.com/protest/give-cows-pastures-not-plastic-say-dalit-protesters/.

Cochrane, Alasdair. 2013. "From Human Rights to Sentient Rights." *Critical Review of International Social and Political Philosophy* 16 (5): 655–675.

Cohen, Mathilde. 2017. "Animal Colonialism: The Case of Milk." *American Journal of International Law Unbound* 111: 267–271. Available at SSRN: https://ssrn.com/abstract=3039747.

Collard, Rosemary-Claire, and Dempsey, Jessica. 2013. "Life for sale? The Politics of Lively Commodities." *Environment and Planning A: Economy and Space* 45 (11): 2682–2699.

Collard, Rosemary-Claire, and Dempsey, Jessica. 2017. "Capitalist Natures in Five Orientations." *Capitalism Nature Socialism* 28 (1): 78–97.

Collard, Rosemary, and Gillespie, Kathryn. 2015. "Doing Critical Animal Geographies: Future Directions." In *Critical Animal Geographies: Intersections and Hierarchies in a Multispecies World*, ed. Kathryn Gillespie and Rosemary Collard, 1–16. New York: Routledge.

Colling, Sarat. 2020. *Animal Resistance in the Global Capitalist Era*. Ann Arbor, MI: Michigan State University Press.

Compassion in World Farming. 2012. "The Life of Dairy Cows." Retrieved 20 August, 2021, from https://www.ciwf.org.uk/media/5235185/the-life-of-dairy-cows.pdf.

Common Cause v Union of India. 2000. Unreported, Delhi High Court, Singh and Sodhi J. J., 3 November, para 1–2.

Constitution of India. 2022. "Article 48: Organisation of Agriculture and Animal Husbandry." Retrieved 12 February, 2022, from https://www.constitutionofindia.net/constitution_of_india/directive_principles_of_state_policy/articles/Article%2048.

Copland, Ian. 2017. "Cows, Congress and the Constitution: Jawaharlal Nehru and the Making of Article 48." *South Asia: Journal of South Asian Studies* 40 (4): 723–743.

CPCB (Central Pollution Control Board). 2017. "Revised Comprehensive Industry Document on Slaughter Houses." Ministry of Environment, Forest and Climate Change, Government of India. Retrieved 29 January, 2020, from http://www.indiaenvironmentportal.org.in/files/file/slaughter_house.pdf.

Crichton, J. S., and Lishman, A.W. 1988. "Factors Influencing Sexual Behaviour of Young Bos Indicus Bulls Under Pen and Pasture Mating Conditions." *Applied Animal Behaviour Science* 21 (4): 281–292.

Cunningham, K. 2009. *Rural and Urban Linkages: Operation Flood's Role in India's Dairy Development*. International Food Policy Research Institute (IFPRI) Discussion Paper 00924. Washington DC: IFPRI. Retrieved 4 July, 2022, from https://ebrary.ifpri.org/utils/getfile/collection/p15738coll2/id/28869/filename/28870.pdf.

Cusack, C., M. 2013. "Feminism and Husbandry: Drawing the Fine Line Between Mine and Bovine." *Journal for Critical Animal Studies* 11(1): 24–44.

DAHD. 2002a. "Chapter III—Administration of Cattle Laws." In *Report of the National Commission on Cattle*. Retrieved 2 April, 2020, from https://dahd.nic.in/node/86828.

DAHD. 2002b. "Chapter II—Executive Summary." *Report of the National Commission on Cattle*. Retrieved 12 February, 2022, from https://dahd.nic.in/hi/node/86810.

DAHD. 2015a. "Guidelines for Export/Import of Bovine Germplasm (Revised May 2015)." Retrieved 13 February, 2022, from https://dahd.nic.in/sites/default/files/Guidelines%20for%20Export%20or%20Import%20of%20Bovine%20Germ plasm%20revised%20may%202015.pdf02.pdf.

DAHD. 2015b. "Estimated Livestock Population Breed Wise: Based on Breed Survey 2013." Animal Husbandry Statistics Division. New Delhi: Department of Animal Husbandry, Dairying and Fisheries, 15. Retrieved 4 July, 2022, from: http://dahd.nic .in/sites/default/files/Breeding%20Survey%20Book%20-%20Corrected.pdf.

DAHD. 2019a. "Chapter VII: Breed Improvement and Preservation." Retrieved 15 November, 2019, from http://dahd.nic.in/hi/node/86833.

DAHD. 2019b. *Assistance for Modernization of Slaughter Houses and Carcass Utilization Plants*. Retrieved 27 January, 2021, from https://dahd.nic.in/related-links/assistance-modernization-slaughter-houses-and-carcass-utilization-plants.

DAHD. 2019c. *20th Livestock Census: 2019 All India Report*. Animal Husbandry and Dairying Statistics Division, Ministry of Fisheries, Animal Husbandry and Dairying. New Delhi: Government of India. https://dahd.nic.in/sites/default/files/20th%20Livestock%20census-2019%20All%20India%20Report_o.pdf.

Dalgaard-Nielsen, Anja 2010. "Violent Radicalization in Europe: What We Know and What We Do Not Know." *Studies in Conflict and Terrorism* 33 (9): 797–781.

Das, Bireshwar. 2021. "Why Liquid Nitrogen Is Critical to the Indian Animal Husbandry Sector." *Times of India*. Retrieved 7 February, 2022, from https://times ofindia.indiatimes.com/blogs/voices/why-liquid-nitrogen-is-critical-to-the-indian -animal-husbandry-sector/.

Datta, Ayona. 2019. "Postcolonial Urban Futures: Imagining and Governing India's Smart Urban Age." *Environment and Planning D* 37 (3): 393–410.

Dave, Naisargi N. 2014. "Witness: Humans, Animals, and the Politics of Becoming." *Cultural Anthropology* 29 (3):433–456.

Dave, Naisargi N. 2017. "Something, Everything, Nothing; or, Cows, Dogs, and Maggots." *Social Text* 35 (1):37–57.

Dave, Naisargi. 2019. "The Tyranny of Consistency." In *Messy Eating*, ed. S. King, S. R. Carey, I. Macquarrie, V. N. Millious, E. M. Power, and C. Wolfe, 68–83. New York: Fordham University Press.

Davis, Karen. 2019. *For the Birds: From Exploitation to Liberation*. New York: Lantern.

Davies, Guy. 2021. "Huge Religious Festival of Kumbh Mela Goes Ahead Despite Coronavirus Pandemic." *ABC News*. Retrieved 15 January, 2022, from https://abcnews.go.com/ International/huge-religious-festival-kumbh-mela-ahead-coronavirus-pandemic/ story?id=75246169.

De, Rohit. 2013. "Who Moved My Beef?" Retrieved 12 November, 2018, from https:// www.thehindubusinessline.com/opinion/who-moved-my-beef/article22995192.ece.

Debroy, Bibek (trans.). (2016). *Harivamsha* (Kindle edition). India: Penguin Books.

Deccan Chronicle. 2016. "6,500 kg of Beef Seized from a Processing Unit in Mumbai's Dharavi," 9 April. Retrieved 22 December, 2019, from https://www.

deccanchronicle.com/amp/nation/in-other-news/090416/6-500-kg-of-beef-seized-from-a-processing-unit-in-mumbai-s-dharavi.html.

Deccan Chronicle. 2019. "Violate Rules, Get Cattle Seized: Telangana High Court," 9 August. Retrieved 21 January, 2021, from https://www.deccanchronicle.com/nation/in-other-news/090819/violate-rules-get-cattle-seized-telangana-high-court.html.

Deckha, Maneesha. 2012. "Toward a Postcolonial, Posthumanist Feminist Theory: Centralizing Race and Culture in Feminist Work on Nonhuman Animals." *Hypatia* 27 (3): 527–545.

Deckha, Maneesha. 2015. "Vulnerability, Equality, and Animals." *Canadian Journal of Women and the Law* 27 (1): 47–70.

Delon, Nicolas. 2018. "Social Norms and Farm Animal Protection." *Palgrave Communications* 4: 139–145.

Deshmane, Akshay. 2015. "Meet India's First Cow Minister Otaram Devasi Who Likes to Address Himself as 'Gaupalan Mantri.'" *Economic Times.* Retrieved 14 February, 2021, from https://economictimes.indiatimes.com/news/politics-and-nation/meet-indias-first-cow-minister-otaram-devasi-who-likes-to-address-himself-as-gaupalan-mantri/articleshow/45815837.cms.

Dhruvarajan, V. 1990. "Religious Ideology, Hindu Women, and Development in India." *Journal of Social Issues* 46 (3): 57–70.

Dikshita, A. K., and Birthalb, P. S. 2010. "India's Livestock Feed Demand: Estimates and Projections." *Agricultural Economics Research Review* 23: 15–28.

DNA India. 2015. "Cattle Trafficking: Supreme Court Wants Suggestions from Centre, Uttar Pradesh, Uttarakhand," 21 November. Retrieved 5 August, 2016, from http://www.dnaindia.com/india/report-cattle-trafficking-supreme-court-wants-suggestions-from-centre-uttar-pradesh-uttarakhand-2049907.

DNA India. 2017. "Maharashtra: Portable Cow Meat Detection Kits to be Rolled Out This Month." Retrieved 22 January, 2019, from https://www.dnaindia.com/mumbai/report-portable-cow-meat-detection-kits-to-be-rolled-out-this-month-2493385.

Dohmwirth, Carla, and Hanisch, Markus. 2019. "Women's Active Participation and Gender Homogeneity: Evidence from the South Indian Dairy Cooperative Sector." *Journal of Rural Studies* 72: 125–135.

Donaldson, Sue, and Kymlicka, Will. 2015. "Farmed Animal Sanctuaries: The Heart of the Movement? A Socio-Political Perspective." *Politics and Animals* 1 (1): 50–74.

Doniger, Wendy. 2009. *The Hindus: An Alternative History.* New York: Penguin.

Doron, Assa, and Jeffrey, Robin. 2013. *The Great Indian Phone Book: How the Cheap Cell Phone Changes Business, Politics, and Daily Life.* Cambridge, MA: Harvard University Press.

Doron, Assa, and Robin Jeffrey. 2018. *Waste of a Nation: Garbage and Growth in India.* Cambridge, MA: Harvard University Press.

Down to Earth. 2018. "India Witnesses One of the Highest Female Infanticide Incidents in the World: Study" [press release]. 8 July. Retrieved 16 June, 2020, from https://www.downtoearth.org.in/news/health/india-witnesses-one-of-the-highest-female-infanticide-incidents-in-the-world-54803.

DT Next. 2017. "9 TPDK Members Held for Animal Cruelty." Retrieved 27 August, 2020, from https://www.dtnext.in/News/City/2017/08/08023607/1041057/9-TPDK -members-held-for-animal-cruelty.vpf.

Dutkiewicz, Jan. 2015. "Uncertain Hog Futures (or, Two Bacon Shortages and the Financial Life of the Capitalist Pig)." Paper presented at the University of Chicago Animal Studies Workshop. Chicago, IL. November 18.

Dutkiewicz, Jan. 2018. "Transparency and the Factory Farm: Agritourism and Counter-Activism at Fair Oaks Farms." *Gastronomica: The Journal of Critical Food Studies* 18 (2): 19–32.

East Mojo. 2022. "Rajasthan: 8 Booked for Forcing Dalit Man to Consume Urine, 2 Held," 30 January. Retrieved 7 February, 2022, from https://www.eastmojo.com/ national-news/2022/01/30/rajasthan-8-booked-for-forcing-dalit-man-to-consume -urine-2-held/.

Edwards, R., and Kellett, R. 2000. *Life in Plastic: The Impact of Plastic on India*. Goa: Other India Press.

Egorova, Y. 2018. *Jews and Muslims in South Asia: Reflections on difference, religion and race*. Oxford University Press: New York.

Eisen, Jessica. 2017. "Milk and Meaning: Puzzles in Posthumanist Method." In *Making Milk: The Past, Present and Future of Our Primary Food*, ed. Mathilde Cohen and Yoriko Otomo, 237–247. New York: Bloomsbury.

Eisnitz, Gail A. 2009. *Slaughterhouse: The Shocking Story of Greed, Neglect, and Inhumane Treatment Inside the U.S. Meat Industry*. New York: Prometheus.

Ellis-Petersen, Hannah, and Hassan, Aakash. 2021. "Kumbh Mela: How a Superspreader Festival Seeded Covid Across India." *The Guardian*, 30 May. Retrieved 10 August, 2021, from https://www.theguardian.com/world/2021/may/30/ kumbh-mela-how-a-superspreader-festival-seeded-covid-across-india.

Elwood, S. and Lawson, V. 2018. "Introduction: (Un)Thinkable Poverty Politics." In *Relational Poverty Politics: Forms, Struggles, and Possibilities*, ed. V. Lawson and S. Elwood, 1–24. Athens, GA: University of Georgia Press.

Extension Animal Science Program. n.d. Recognizing and Handling Calving Problems. *Texas A&M Agrilife Extension*. Retrieved 6 January, 2021, from https:// agrilifeextension.tamu.edu/library/ranching/recognizing-and-handling-calving -problems/.

Farm Policy Exports. 2019. "Subsidy Spotlight: India." Retrieved 15 January, 2020, from https://www.farmpolicyfacts.org/2018/10/subsidy-spotlight-india-2/.

Farmer, Paul. 2003. *Pathologies of Power: Health, Human Rights, and the New War on the Poor*. Berkeley: University of California Press, 6.

FAO (Food and Agriculture Organization). 2002. *Livestock Diversity: Keepers' Rights, Shared Benefits and Pro-Poor Policies*. Retrieved 22 January, 2018, from http://www .fao.org/3/a-x6104e.pdfFAO.

FAO (Food and Agriculture Organization). 2003. *Working with Local Institutions to Support Sustainable Livelihoods*. Retrieved 13 February, 2022, from https://www.fao .org/3/y5083e/y5083e.pdf.

FAO (Food and Agriculture Organization). 2007. "Livestock's Long Shadow: Environmental Issues and Options." Retrieved 28 August, 2020, from http://www.fao .org/3/a-a0701e.pdf.

FAO (Food and Agriculture Organization). 2017. *Zero-Grazing of Improved Cattle Breeds Using Drought-Tolerant Fodder in Uganda*. Retrieved 6 January, 2021, from http:// www.fao.org/3/CA2565EN/ca2565en.pdf.

Fazal, Imran. 2017. "UP, MP May Buy Maha's Instant Beef-Testing Kits." *DNA India*. Retrieved 9 April, 2020, from https://www.dnaindia.com/mumbai/ report-up-mp-may-buy-maha-s-instant-beef-testing-kits-2531209.

Fiems, Leo O. 2012. "Double Muscling in Cattle: Genes, Husbandry, Carcasses and Meat." *Animals* 2: 472–506. doi:10.3390/ani2030472.

First Post. 2017. "To Teach Muslims 'Save the Cow' Message, RSS to Organise Iftar with Only Cow Milk Products." Retrieved 28 May, 2017, from http://www.first post.com/india/to-teach-muslims-save-the-cow-message-rss-to-organise-iftar-with -only-cow-milk-products-3462918.html.

First Post. 2020. "Kerala Elephant Death: Police Make First Arrest; No Evidence Locals 'Fed' Pachyderm Pineapple Stuffed with Firecrackers, Claim Officials." Retrieved 8 February, 2021, from https://www.firstpost.com/india/kerala-elephant-death-police -make-first-arrest-no-evidence-locals-fed-pachyderm-pineapple-stuffed-with-fire crackers-claim-officials-8451501.html.

Fischer, W. J., Schilter, B., Tritscher, A. M., and Stadler, R. H. 2011. "Contaminants of Milk and Dairy Products: Contamination Resulting from Farm and Dairy Practices." In *Encyclopedia of Dairy Sciences*, Second Edition, ed. John W. Fuquay, 887–897 [e-book]. Academic Press.

Flower, F. C., and Weary, D. M. 2001. "Effects of Early Separation on the Dairy Cow and Calf: Separation at 1 Day and 2 Weeks After Birth." *Applied Animal Behaviour Science* 70: 275–284.

Forchtner, Bernhard. 2019. "Climate Change and the Far Right." *Wiley Interdisciplinary Reviews-Climate Change* 10 (5): 1–11.

Forchtner, Bernhard (ed.). 2020. *The Far Right and the Environment: Politics, Discourse and Communication*. Abingdon, UK; New York, NY: Routledge.

Francione, Gary. 2010. "Animal Welfare and the Moral Status of Nonhuman Animals." *Law, Culture and the Humanities* 6 (1): 24–36.

Franklin Vets. 2017. *Theileria*. Retrieved 16 November, 2019, from https://franklinvets .co.nz/dairy/disease-management/theleiria/.

Freeman, Andrea. 2017. "Milk, a Symbol of Neo-Nazi Hate." *The Conversation*. 31 August. Retrieved 7 December, 2017, from https://theconversation.com/ milk-a-symbol-of-neo-nazi-hate-83292.

Freitag, Sandria B. 1989. *Collective Action and Community: Public Arenas and the Emergence of Communalism in North India*. Berkeley, CA: University of California Press.

FSSAI (Food Safety and Standards Authority of India). 2011. *Food Safety and Standards (Licensing and Registration of Food Businesses), Regulations 2011*. Part IV, Section A. Ministry of Health and Family Welfare, Government of India. Retrieved

16 April, 2020, from https://fssai.gov.in/upload/uploadfiles/files/Licensing_Regula
tions.pdf.

Gaard, Greta. 2013. "Toward a Feminist Postcolonial Milk Studies" *American Quarterly*
65 (3): 595–618.

Galgut, Elisa. 2019. "A Critique of the Cultural Defense of Animal Cruelty." *Journal of
Animal Ethics* 9 (2): 184–198.

Gambert, Iselin, and Linne, Tobias. 2018. "From Rice Eaters to Soy Boys: Race, Gender, and Tropes of 'Plant food Masculinity.'" *Animal Studies Journal* 7 (2): 131–182.

Gandhi, Ajay. 2011. "'Informal Moral Economies' and Urban Governance in India."
In *Urban Informalities*, ed. Colin McFarlane and Michael Waibel. Farnham, UK;
Burlington, VT: Ashgate.

Gandhi, M. K. n.d. "Cow slaughter and Cow-protection" Centre for Study of Society
and Secularism. Retrieved 12 February, 2022, from https://www.mkgandhi.org/g
_communal/chap14.htm.

Gandhi, M. K. 1917. Speech on Cow Protection (delivered in Bettiah), 9 October. Retrieved 5 July, 2022, from https://www.sabhlokcity.com/2022/03/gandhi-on-voluntary
-cow-protection-he-disliked-coercion-or-laws/.

Gandhi, M. K. 1920. Speech at Bettiah Goshala, 8 December. *Mahadevbhaini Diary*,
Vol. V. Ahmedabad: Navajivan Publishing House.

Gandhi, M. K. 1927. "Conditions of Cow Protection." *Young India*, 31 March 1927. Retrieved from internet archives of *Young India*, 5 July, 2022, from https://archive.org/
stream/HindSwaraj.yi.10973.33464/yi.10973.33464_djvu.txt.

Gandhi, M. K. 2017 [1920]. "Gandhiji on Cow Protection – Various Articles." Extracted
from *Navajivan*, 8 August 1920. Retrieved 5 July, 2022, from https://shrishri71.word
press.com/.

Gandhi, M. K. 2018. *An Autobiography or the Story of My Experiments with Truth*. New
Haven, CT: Yale University Press.

Gandhi, Maneka. 1999. "Factory Farming and the Meat Industry in India." In *The Meat
Business: Devouring a Hungry Planet*, ed. Geoff Tansy and Joyce D'Silva, 92–102.
London: Earthscan Publications Ltd.

Gandhi, M. Sanjay. 2017. The Many Faces of Cruelty. *Mathrubhumi*. Retrieved 22
July, 2021, from https://english.mathrubhumi.com/news/columns/faunaforum/
the-many-faces-of-cruelty-maneka-gandhi-1.1661360.

Ganguli, Kisari Mohan (trans.). 1896. *The Mahabharata of Krishna-Dwaipayana Vyasa*.
http://www.sacred-texts.com/hin/maha/index.htm.

George, S. 1985. "Operation Flood and Rural India: Vested and Divested interests" *Economic and Political Weekly* 20 (49): 2163–2170.

Ghassem-Fachandi, Parvis. 2009. "The Hyberbolic Vegetarian: Notes on a Fragile Subject in Gujarat." In *Being There: The Fieldwork Encounter and the Making of Truth,*,
ed. John Borneman and Abdellah Hammoudi, 77–112. Berkeley, CA: University of
California Press.

Ghassem-Fachandi, Parvis. 2012. *Pogrom in Gujarat: Hindu Nationalism and Anti-
Muslim Violence in India*. Princeton, NJ: Princeton University Press.

Ghosal, A. K. 1959. "Sarvodaya Gandhian Philosophy and Way of Life." *The Indian Journal of Political Science* 20 (1): 23–30.

Ghosh, Sahana. 2019. "Chor, Police and Cattle: The Political Economies of Bovine Value in the India–Bangladesh Borderlands." *South Asia: Journal of South Asian Studies* 42 (6): 1108–1124.

Gillespie, Kathryn. 2014. "Sexualized violence and the gendered commodification of the animal body in Pacific Northwest US dairy production." *Gender, Place and Culture: A Journal of Feminist Geography* 21 (10): 1321–1337.

Gillespie, Kathryn. 2018. *The Cow with Ear Tag #1389*. Chicago: University of Chicago Press.

Gillespie, Kathryn 2019a. "The Loneliness and Madness of Witnessing: Reflections from a Vegan Feminist Killjoy." In *Animaladies*, ed. L. Gruen and F. Probyn-Rapsey, 77–88. New York: Bloomsbury.

Gillespie, Kathryn. 2019b. "For a Politicized Multispecies Ethnography: Reflections on a Feminist Geographic Pedagogical Experiment." *Politics and Animals* 5: 1–16.

Gillespie, Kathryn. 2021. "The Afterlives of the Lively Commodity: Life-Worlds, Death-Worlds, Rotting-Worlds." *Environment and Planning A: Economy and Space* 53 (2): 280–295. doi: 10.1177/0308518X20944417.

Gillespie, Kathryn. 2021. "An Unthinkable Politics for Multispecies Flourishing within and beyond Colonial-Capitalist Ruins." *Annals of the Association of American Geographers*. doi: https://doi.org/10.1080/24694452.2021.1956297.

Gillespie, K., & Narayanan, Y. (2020). "Animal Nationalisms: Multispecies Cultural Politics, Race, and the (Un)making of the Settler Nation-State." *Journal of Intercultural Studies* 41 (1): 1–7.

Giraud, Eva Haifa. 2019. *What Comes after Entanglement? Activism, Anthropocentrism, and an Ethics of Exclusion*. Durham, NC: Duke University Press.

Giraud, Eva, Haifa. 2021. *Veganism: Politics, Practice, and Theory*. London: Bloomsbury.

Goa Government. 2016. Kamdhenu Scheme (Sudharit). Retrieved 17 July, 2019, from https://www.goa.gov.in/wp-content/uploads/2016/12/1.-KAMDHENU-SCHEME-SUDHARIT-2016-17.Form_.pdf.

Godden, S. (2008). "Colostrum Management for Dairy Calves." *Veterinary Clinics of North America: Food Animal Practice* 24 (1): 19–39.

Goodrick-Clarke, Nicholas. 1998. *Hitler's Priestess: Savitri Devi, the Hindu–Aryan Myth, and Neo-Nazism*. New York: New York University Press.

Gordon, I. (2004). *Reproductive Technologies in Farm Animals*. Oxford: CABI Publishing.

Gould, William. 2004. *Hindu Nationalism and the Language of Politics in Late Colonial India*. Cambridge: Cambridge University Press.

Govindrajan, Radhika. 2018. *Animal Intimacies: Interspecies Relatedness in India's Central Himalayas*. Chicago: University of Chicago Press.

Grillo, Robert. 2016. *Farm to Fable: The Fictions of our Animal-Consuming Culture*. Danvers, MA: Vegan Publishers.

Gruen, Lori (ed.). 2014. *The Ethics of Captivity*. New York: Oxford University Press.

Gruen, Lori, and Probyn-Rapsey, Fiona. 2019. "Distillations." In *Animaladies*, edited by Lori Gruen and Fiona Probyn -Rapsey, 1–10. New York: Bloomsbury.

Guha-Khasnobis, B., Kanbur, R., and Ostrom, E. 2006. "Beyond Formality and Informality." In *Linking the Formal and Informal Economy: Concepts and Policies*, ed. Basudeb Guha-Khasnobis, Ravi Kanbur and Elinor Ostrom, 1–21. Oxford: Oxford University Press.

Gujarat Animal Preservation (Amendment) Act. 2017.https://lpd.gujarat.gov.in/assets/downloads/acts_12042017.pdf.

Gupta, Charu. 2001. "The Icon of Mother in Late Colonial North India: 'Bharat Mata,' 'Matri Bhasha' and 'Gau Mata.'" *Economic and Political Weekly* 36 (45): 4291–4299.

Gupta, D. 2000. *Interrogating Caste: Understanding Hierarchy and Difference in Indian Society*. New Delhi: Penguin Books India.

Gupta, J., Gupta, I. D., and Chaudhari, M. V. 2014. "Dairy Animals." In *Encyclopedia of Agriculture and Food Systems*, Vol. 2, ed. N. K. Van Alfen, 419–434. London: Academic Press.

Hale, Charles R., (ed.). 2008. *Engaging Contradictions: Theory, Politics, and Methods of Activist Scholarship*. Berkley, CA: UCLA Press.

Hall, Stephen J. G. 2002. "Cattle Behaviour." In *Ethology of Domestic Animals: An Introductory Text*, ed. Per Jensen, 131–143. Wallingford, UK: CABI (Centre for Agriculture and Bioscience International);

Hamilton, Lindsay, and Taylor, Nik. 2017. *Ethnography after Humanism: Power, Politics and Method in Multi-Species Research*. London: Palgrave Macmillan.

Hansen, T. B. 1994. "Controlled Emancipation: Women and Hindu Nationalism." *The European Journal of Development Research* 6 (2): 82–94.

Hennelly, William. 2015. "100,000-Cow-Power Dairy Farm in China to Feed Russian Market." Retrieved 12 February, 2022, from https://www.farmlandgrab.org/post/view/25115-100-000-cow-power-dairy-farm-in-china-to-feed-russian-market.

Haraway, Donna. 2008. *When Species Meet*. Minneapolis: University of Minnesota Press.

Haraway, Donna. 2016. *Staying with the Trouble: Making Kin in the Chthulucene*. Durham, NC and London: Duke University Press.

Hardy, K. C. 2019. "Provincialising the Cow: Buffalo–Human Relationships" *South Asia: Journal of South Asian Studies* 42 (6): 1156–1172. doi: 10.1080/00856401.2019.1680484.

Harvard School of Public Health. 2019. "Calcium: What's Best for Your Bones and Health?" *The Nutrition Source*. Retrieved 18 September, 2020, from https://www.hsph.harvard.edu/nutritionsource/what-should-you-eat/calcium-and-milk/calcium-full-story/#calcium-from-milk

Hartigan, J. (2017). *Care of the Species: Races of Corn and the Science of Plant Biodiversity*. Minneapolis: University of Minnesota Press.

Hasler, J. F., McCauley, A. D., Schermerhorn, E. C., and Foote, R. H. 1983. "Superovulatory Responses of Holstein Cows." *Theriogenology* 19 (1): 83–99.

Hawley, J. S. 1983. *Krishna: The Butter Thief*. Princeton, NJ: Princeton University Press.

Hegde, Narayan G. 2014. Forage Resource Development in India. *Indian Journal of Animal Sciences* 84 (7): 715–722.

Hendry, W. F. 1994. "Treatment for Loss of Ejaculation after Para-Aortic Lymphadenectomy." In *Germ Cell Tumours III: Proceedings of the Third Germ Cell Tumour Conference*, ed. W. G. Jones, P. Harnden, I. Appleyard, 353–358. Held in Leeds, UK, on 8–10 September 1993. Oxford: Pergamon.

Herring, A. D. 2014. "Beef Cattle." In *Encyclopedia of Agriculture and Food* Systems, Vol. 2, ed. N. K. Van Alfen, 1–20. London: Academic Press.

Hindu Janajagruti Samiti. 2014. "Heinous Act of Cow Slaughtering." Retrieved 10 February, 2019, from https://www.hindujagruti.org/hindu-issues/cow-slaughter/heinous-act-of-cow-slaughtering.

Hindustan Times. 2016. "Holy or Not: Decade of Loving Deserted Cows," 27 June. Retrieved 4 June, 2018, from https://www.hindustantimes.com/delhi-news/holy-or-not-decade-of-loving-deserted-cows/story-ywRwaSZa1rV6xWImBy9KZM.html.

Hindustan Times. 2017. "Muslim Man Donates Land for Construction of 'Gaushala' in Uttar Pradesh," 3 May. Retrieved 4 June, 2018, from https://www.hindustantimes.com/india-news/muslim-man-donates-land-for-construction-of-gaushala-in-uttar-pradesh/story-ShgNDClfhTEYfGWZcuhQOL.html.

Hobson, Kersty. 2007. "Political Animals? On Animals as Subjects in an Enlarged Political Geography." *Political Geography* 26: 250–267.

Holston, J., and Caldeira, T. 2008. "Urban Peripheries and the Invention of Citizenship." *Harvard Design Magazine* 28: 19–23.

Hörnqvist, Magnus, and Flyghed, Janne. 2012. "Exclusion or Culture? The Rise and the Ambiguity of the Radicalization Debate." *Critical Studies on Terrorism* 5 (3): 319–334.

Hristov, A. N., Oh, J., Lee, C., Meinen, R., Montes, F., Ott, T., Firkins, J., Rotz, A., Dell, C., Adesogan, A., Yang, W., Tricarico, J., Kebread, E., Waghorn, G., Dijkstra, J., and Oosting, S. 2013. "Mitigation of Greenhouse Gas Emissions in Livestock Production: A Review of Technical Options for Non-CO_2 Emissions." Food and Agriculture Organization. Retrieved 2 August, 2016, from http://www.fao.org/3/a-i3288e.pdf.

Hudson, S. J., and Mullord, M. M. 1977. "Investigations of Maternal Bonding in Dairy Cattle." *Applied Animal Behaviour Science* 3: 271–276.

Humane Society International. 2014. "Supreme Court of India Intervenes to Save Thousands of Animals from Nepal's Brutal Gadhimai Festival Sacrifice," 20 October. Retrieved 8 February, 2020, from https://www.hsi.org/news-media/india-supreme-court-gadhimai-ruling-102014/.

Human Rights Watch. 2017. "India: 'Cow Protection' Spurs Vigilante Violence," 27 April. Retrieved 8 February, 2022, from https://www.hrw.org/news/2017/04/27/india-cow-protection-spurs-vigilante-violence.

Human Rights Watch. 2019a. *Violent Cow Protection in India: Vigilante Groups Attack Minorities.* Retrieved 7 August, 2019, from https://www.hrw.org/sites/default/files/report_pdf/india0219_web3.pdf.

Human Rights Watch. 2019b. "India: Citizenship Bill Discriminates Against Muslims," 11 December. Retrieved 7 February, 2022, from https://www.hrw.org/news/2019/12/11/india-citizenship-bill-discriminates-against-muslims.

Hurd, M., and Werther, S. 2013. "Nature, the Volk and the Heimat." *Baltic Worlds* 6 (2): 13–19.

Hurn, Samantha. 2017. "Animals as Producers, Consumers and Consumed: The Complexities of Trans-Species Sustenance in a Multi-Faith Community." *Ethnos: Journal of Anthropology* 82 (2): 213–231.

Iliah, K. 2004. *Buffalo Nationalism: A Critique of Spiritual Fascism.* New Delhi: Sage.

IMARC. 2019. "Indian Animal Feed Market: Industry Trends, Share, Size, Growth, Opportunity and Forecast 2020–2025." Retrieved 25 January, 2020, from https://www.imarcgroup.com/indian-animal-feed-market.

Independent. 2019. "Inside India's Plastic Cows: How Sacred Animals Are Left to Line Their Stomachs with Polythene," 24 February. Retrieved 16 May, 2019, from https://www.independent.co.uk/news/world/asia/india-delhi-plastic-cows-shelters-bjp-modi-gaushala-a8794756.html.

India Times. 2015. "RSS Says Killing or Smuggling a Cow Equivalent to Rape of a Hindu Girl." Retrieved 8 February, 2022, from https://www.indiatimes.com/news/india/rss-says-killing-or-smuggling-a-cow-=-raping-a-hindu-girl-234350.html.

India Times. 2017. "1,500 kg Super Buffalo Yuvraj Is Worth Rs 9.25 Crore and He Makes Rs 50 Lakh a Year Selling Semen!" Retrieved 22 July, 2019, from https://www.indiatimes.com/news/india/1-500-kg-super-buffalo-yuvraj-is-worth-rs-9-25-crore-and-he-makes-rs-50-lakh-a-year-selling-semen-272372.html.

India Today. 2016a. "Muslim Couple Beaten Up in Madhya Pradesh Over Beef Rumours," 15 January. Retrieved 14 November, 2019, from https://www.indiatoday.in/india/madhya-pradesh/story/muslim-couple-beaten-up-in-madhya-pradesh-over-beef-rumours-303965-2016-01-15.

India Today. 2016b. "Beef Market in Rampur, UP Exposed." YouTube. Retrieved 11 January, 2018, from https://www.youtube.com/watch?v=Idv8vbMqgzw.

India Today 2017. "Haryana: 25 Cows Die at Government-Run Shelter Due to Improper Facilities, Lack of Food," 7 July. Retrieved 29 August, 2020, from https://www.indiatoday.in/india/story/haryana-25-cows-die-at-government-run-shelter-1023044-2017-07-07.

India Today. 2019. "Cattle Smuggling: BSF Recovers Cows Tied with IEDs in West Bengal Rivers," 25 July. Retrieved 14 November, 2019, from https://www.indiatoday.in/india/story/cattle-smuggling-bsf-recovers-cows-tied-with-ieds-in-west-bengal-rivers-1573641-2019-07-25.

Indian National Congress. 2010. "Constitution & Rules of the Indian National Congress." Retrieved 12 February, 2022, from https://cdn.inc.in/constitutions/inc_constitution_files/000/000/001/original/Congress-Constitution.pdf?1505640610.

Jadhav, Rajendra. 2018. "India's Milk Powder Exports to Surge on Subsidies, Dampen Global Prices." *Reuters.* Retrieved 15 January, from https://www.reuters.com/article/us-india-milk-exports-exclusive/exclusive-indias-milk-powder-exports-to-surge-on-subsidies-dampen-global-prices-idUSKBN1KH0GQ.

Jaffrelot, C. 2015a. "The Modi-centric BJP 2014 Election Campaign: New Techniques and Old Tactics." *Contemporary South Asia* 23 (2): 151–166.

Jaffrelot, C. 2015b. "What 'Gujarat Model'?—Growth Without Development—and with Socio-Political Polarisation." *South Asia: Journal of South Asian Studies* 38 (4): 820–838.

Jagga, R. (2014). "Over 1.5 Lakh Litre Extra Milk Consumed on Mahashivratri." *The Indian Express*. Retrieved 31 August, 2020, from https://indianexpress.com/article/cities/ludhiana/over-1-5-lakh-litre-extra-milk-consumed-on-mahashivratri/.

Jain, Pankaj. 2014. "Bovine Dharma: Nonhuman Animals and the Swadhyaya Parivar." In *Asian Perspectives on Animal Ethics: Rethinking the Nonhuman*, ed. N. Dalal and C. Taylor, 169–178. New York: Taylor and Francis.

Jal, M. 2015. "Rethinking Secularism in India in the Age of Triumphant Fascism." *Critique* 43 (3–4): 521–549.

Jasanoff, Sheila. 2004. "Ordering Knowledge, Ordering Society." In *States of Knowledge: The Co-Production of Science and Social Order*, ed. Shiela Jasanoff, 1–12. London: Routledge

Jasper, J., and Weary, D. M. 2002. "Effects of Ad Libitum Milk Intake on Dairy Calves." *Journal of Dairy Science* 85: 3054–3058.

Jaton, C. A., Koeck, M., Sargolzaei, F., Malchiodi, C. A., Price, F. S., and Schenkel, F. M. 2016. "Genetic analysis of superovulatory response of Holstein cows in Canada." *Journal of Dairy Science* 99 (5): 3612–3623.

Jauregui, Beatrice. 2016. "Provisional Agency in India: Jugaad and the Legitimisation of Corruption." *American Ethnologist* 41 (1): 76–91.

Jewitt, S. (2011). "Geographies of Shit: Spatial and Temporal Variations in Attitudes Towards Human Waste." *Progress in Human Geography* 35 (5): 608–626.

Jha, D. N. 2002. *The Myth of the Holy Cow*. London: Verso.

Jianqin, S., Leiming, X., Lu, X., Yelland, G. W., Ni, J., and Clarke, A. J. 2016. "Effects of Milk Containing Only A2 Beta Casein Versus Milk Containing Both A1 and A2 Beta Casein Proteins on Gastrointestinal Physiology, Symptoms of Discomfort, and Cognitive Behavior of People with Self-reported Intolerance to Traditional Cows' Milk." *Nutrition Journal* 15 (35): 1–16.

Jitendra, Rajat Ghai. 2016. "Cattle Economy: How Cow Became the Mother of Demigods," 20 July. *Down to Earth*. Retrieved 8 January, 2019, from https://www.downtoearth.org.in/coverage/agriculture/cattle-economy-54972.

Jitendra, Ishan Kukreti. 2017. "Meat Matters." *Down to Earth*. Retrieved 26 January, 2021, from https://www.downtoearth.org.in/coverage/agriculture/meat-matters-57633.

Jodhka, Surinder S. 2014. *Caste in Contemporary India*. London: Taylor and Francis.

Johnsen, J. F., de Passille, A. M., Mejdell, C. M., Bøe, K. E., Grøndahl, A. M., Beaver, A., Rushen, J., and Weary, D. M. (2015). "The Effect of Nursing on the Cow–Calf Bond." *Applied Animal Behaviour Science* 163: 50–57.

jones, pattrice. 2007. *Aftershock: Confronting Trauma in a Violent World: A Guide for Activists and Their Allies*. New York: Lantern Books.

Joseph, Anna. 2016. "Going Dutch: A Model for Reconciling Animal Slaughter Reform with the Religious Freedom Restoration Act." *Journal of Animal Ethics* 6 (2): 135–152.

Joshipura, Poorva. 2015. "India's High Beef Exports Are Linked to Its Milk Consumption." *Huffington Post*, 5 July. Retrieved 18 August, 2019, from https://www.huffpost .com/archive/in/entry/holy-cow-milk-consumption_b_8087156.

Kabeer, Naila, Narain, Nivedita, Arora, Varnica, and Lal, Vinitika. 2019. "Group Rights and Gender Justice: Exploring Tensions Within an Indigenous Community in India." Retrieved 27 January, 2021, from http://eprints.lse.ac.uk/101873/.

Kapoor, Mugdha. 2015. "'Beef Festivals' to Fight Against #BeefBan. How's That for a Protest?" *India Times*. Retrieved 8 February, 2022, from https://www.indiatimes .com/news/india/beef-festivals-to-fight-against-beefban-hows-that-for-a-protest-231355.html.

Karpagavinayagam, M. 2004. *Jaigopal Garodia Foundations v. T. R. Srinivasan. Criminal Law Journal*, 2420 (April 1). Retrieved 12 July, 2022, from https://indiankanoon.org/ doc/805722/?type=print.

Kasturirangan, Rajesh, Srinivasan, Krithika, and Rao, Smitha. 2014. "Dark and Dairy: The Sorry Tale of the Milch Animals." *The Hindu*, 8 November. Retrieved 8 December, 2015, from http://www.thehindu.com/opinion/open-page/the-sorry-tale-of-the -milch-animals/article6578663.ece.

Kaur, Ravinder. 2016. "The Innovative Indian: Common Man and the Politics of Jugaad Culture." *Contemporary South Asia* 24 (3): 313–327.

Kennedy, U., Sharma, A., and Phillips, C. 2018. "The Sheltering of Unwanted Cattle, Experiences in India and Implications for Cattle Industries Elsewhere." *Animals: An Open Access Journal from MDPI* 8 (5): 64.

Kesavan, Mukul. 2015. "Ghoulish Game—The Morality of Protecting the Indian Cow." *Telegraph India*, 12 October. Retrieved 10 February, from https://www.telegraph india.com/opinion/ghoulish-game/cid/1436205.

Khan, M. A., Bach, A., Weary, D. M., von Keyserlingk, M. A. G. 2016. "Invited Review: Transitioning from Milk to Solid Feed in Dairy Heifers." *Journal of Dairy Science* 99 (2): 885–902. doi: 10.3168/jds.2015-9975.

Kikon, Dolly. 2015. "Fermenting Modernity: Putting Akhuni on the Nation's Table in India." *South Asia: Journal of South Asian Studies* 38 (2): 320–335.

Kikon, Dolly. 2020. "The Politics of Dog Meat Ban in Nagaland." *Frontline*. Retrieved 13 January, 2021, from https://frontline.thehindu.com/the-nation/the-politics-of -dog-meat-ban-in-nagaland/article32082833.ece.

Kim, Clare Jean. 2015. *Dangerous Crossings: Race, Species, and Nature in a Multicultural Age*. Cambridge: Cambridge University Press.

King, Anna, S. 2012. "Krishna's Cows: ISKON's Animal Theology and Practice." *Journal of Animal Ethics* 2 (2):179–204.

King, Barbara J. 2018. "Emotion." In *Critical Terms for Animal Studies*, ed. Lori Gruen, 125–140. Chicago: University of Chicago Press.

Kipling, John Lockwood. 1904. *Beast & Man in India*. New Delhi: Inter-India Publications.

Kirksey, E. S., and Helmreich, S. 2010. "The Emergence of Multispecies Ethnography." *Cultural Anthropology* 25 (4): 545–576.

Köhler-Rollefson, Ilse. 2018. "Purdah, Purse and Patriarchy: The Position of Women in the Raika Shepherd Community in Rajasthan (India)." *Journal of Arid Environments* 149: 30–39.

Kornfield, Jack. 2020. "Harmlessness" (trans. Thomas Byrom from the *Dhammapada*). Retrieved 2 April, 2020, from https://jackkornfield.com/harmlessness/.

Korom, Frank J. 2000. "Holy Cow! The Apotheosis of Zebu, or Why the Cow Is Sacred in Hinduism." *Asian Folklore Studies* 59 (2): 181–203.

Knaus, W. 2009. "Dairy Cows Trapped Between Performance Demands and Adaptability." *Journal of the Science of Food and Agriculture* 89: 1107–1114.

Krishnan, Anantha P. 2007. "The Calves of Simhachalam." *ISKCON News*. Retrieved 15 December, 2014, from http://iskconnews.org/the-calves-of-simhachalam/.

Krishna, Nanditha. 2010. *Sacred Animals of India*. New Delhi: Penguin Books Ltd.

Kudaisya, Medha. 2008. "'A Mighty Adventure': Institutionalising the Idea of Planning in Post-colonial India, 1947–60." *Modern Asian Studies* 43 (4): 939–978.

Kudva, Neema. 2009. "The Everyday and the Episodic: The Spatial and Political Impacts of Urban Informality." *Environment and Planning A* 41: 1614–1628.

Kumar, Anshuman. 2019. "Tensions Among Farmers in Uttar Pradesh on the Rise as Stray Cows Run Amok." *The Economic Times*, 2 January. Retrieved 16 August, 2022, from https://economictimes.indiatimes.com/news/politics-and-nation/tensions-among-farmers-in-uttar-pradesh-on-the-rise-as-stray-cows-run-amok/articleshow/67343354.cms?from=mdr.

Kumar, A., Shinoj, P., and Jee, S. 2013. "Do Dairy Co-operatives Enhance Milk Production, Productivity and Quality? Evidence from the Indo-Gangetic Plain of India." *Indian Journal of Agricultural Economics* 68 (3): 457–468.

Kumar, Arun. 2016. "Estimation of the Size of the Black Economy in India, 1996–2012." *Economic and Political Weekly* 48: 36–42.

Kumari, S., Hiloidhari, M., Kumari, N., Naik, N. S., and Dahiya, P. R. 2018. "Climate Change Impact of Livestock CH4 Emission in India: Global Temperature Change Potential (GTP) and Surface Temperature Response." *Ecotoxicology and Environmental Safety* 147: 516–522.

Kurien, Verghese. 2005. *I Too Had a Dream*. New Delhi: Lotus Collection, Roli Books.

Kymlicka, W., and Donaldson, S. 2014. "Animal Rights, Multiculturalism, and the Left." *Journal of Social Philosophy* 45 (1): 116–135.

Lal, Deepak. 2005. *The Hindu equilibrium: India c. 1500 B.C.–2000 A.D.* Oxford: Oxford University Press.

Lammoglia, M. A., Garcez, N., Cabrera, A., López, R. D., Rentería, D., del Carmen, I., and Rojas-Ronquillo, R. 2016. "Behavior Affected by Routine Oxytocin Injection in Crossbred Cows in the Tropics." *Revista Brasileira de Zootecnia* 45 (8), 478–482.

Landes, Maurice, Melton, Alex, and Edwards, Seanicaa. 2016. *From Where the Buffalo Roam: India's Beef Exports*. USDA Economic Research Service. Retrieved 16 June, 2020, from https://www.ers.usda.gov/webdocs/outlooks/37672/59707_ldpm-264-01.pdf?v=4082.5.

Larson, G. J. 1995. *India's Agony Over Religion*. Albany: State University of New York Press.

Lewis, D. 2016. "New Way to Wean Calves Leaves Them Happier and Healthier," *The Smithsonian*, 25 January. Retrieved from https://www.smithsonianmag.com/ smart-news/new-way-wean-calves-leaves-them-happier-healthier-180957919/ #R3KKijx6jegSCRjP.99.

Lockwood, Matthew. 2018. "Right-Wing Populism and the Climate Change Agenda: Exploring the Linkages." *Environmental Politics* 27 (4): 712–732.

Lodrick, Deryck, O. 1981. *Sacred cows, sacred places: origins and survival of animal homes in India*. Berkeley: University of California Press.

Lorimer, Jamie, and Driessen, Clemens. 2016. "From 'Nazi Cows' to Cosmopolitan 'Ecological Engineers': Specifying Rewilding Through a History of Heck Cattle." *Annals of the American Association of Geographers* 106 (3): 631–652.

Ludwig, D. S., and Willett, W.C. 2013. "Three Daily Servings of Reduced-Fat Milk: An Evidence-Based Recommendation?" *Journal of the American Medical Association of Pediatrics* 167 (9): 788–789.

Maan Mandir Gaushala. n.d. *Maan Mandir Gaushala*. Retrieved 6 October, 2017, from http://maanmandir.org/gaushala/.

Maharashtra Animal Preservation Act, 1976. Amended March 2015. http://bwcindia .org/Web/Info&Action/Legislation/MaharashtraAnimalPreservationAct1976(Am endedMarch2015).pdf

Maharashtra Animal Preservation (Amendment) Act, 1995. Maharashtra Act No. V of 2015. http://www.bwcindia.org/Web/Info&Action/Legislation/Maharashtra%20 Animal%20Preservation%20Act%201976%20(amended%20March%202015).pdf.

Makhijani, H. J. 1956. *Gaushalas and Pinjrapoles in India*. New Delhi: Central Council of Gosamvardhana.

Malhotra, Pratishtha. 2016. "Rajinikanth Fans, Can We Stop Wasting Milk Please?" *The Quint*, 26 July. Retrieved 13 February, 2019, from https://www.thequint.com/ entertainment/why-we-should-do-away-with-the-practice-of-immersing-rajini kanths-cut-out-in-milk-every-year.

Mandhani, Apoorva. (2017). "Sikkim State Assembly Passes Bill Prohibiting Cow Slaughter." LiveLaw, 30 August. Retrieved October 6, 2018, from https://livelaw.in/ sikkim-state-assembly-passes-bill-prohibiting-cow-slaughter/.

March of Dimes. (2021). Maternal Death and Pregnancy-Related Death. *March of Dimes*. Retrieved 20 August, 2021, from https://www.marchofdimes.org/complica tions/pregnancy-related-death-maternal-death-and-maternal-mortality.aspx.

Maroney, Heather Jon. 1985. "Embracing Motherhood: New Feminist Theory." *Canadian Journal of Political and Social Theory* 11 (1–2): 40–64.

Mazumdar, Sucheta. 1995. "Women on the March: Right-wing Mobilization in Contemporary India." *Feminist Review* 49: 1–28.

McKenzie, Linda. 2018. "Comparing Cows to Mothers and Children Does Not Work as a Justification for Exploiting Them for 'Ahimsa Milk': Part 8 of a Response to Sivarama Swami." *Vox Vegan*, 15 February. Retrieved 28 February, 2018, from https://

voxvegan.com/2018/02/15/comparing-cows-to-mothers-and-children-does-not
-work-as-a-justification-for-exploiting-them-for-ahimsa-milk-part-8-in-a-response
-to-sivarama-swami/.

Meat and Livestock Australia. 2017. "Market Supplier Snapshot Beef: India." Retrieved 14 November, 2019, from https://www.mla.com.au/globalassets/mla
-corporate/prices--markets/documents/os-markets/red-meat-market-snapshots/
mla-ms_india_-snapshot-2017_r2.pdf.

Meat and Livestock Australia. 2018. "Market Snapshot—Beef—North America (US,
Canada, Mexico)" Retrieved 12 February, 2022, from https://www.mla.com.au/glo
balassets/mla-corporate/prices--markets/documents/os-markets/red-meat-market
-snapshots/2018-mla-ms_north-america_beef.pdf.

Meat and Livestock Australia. 2020. "Global Snapshot: Beef." Retrieved 30 July, 2022,
from https://www.mla.com.au/globalassets/mla-corporate/prices--markets/documents/
os-markets/red-meat-market-snapshots/2020/global-beef-snapshot-jan2020.pdf.

Meat and Livestock Australia. 2021. "Global Snapshot: Beef." Retrieved 11 February,
2022, from https://www.mla.com.au/globalassets/mla-corporate/prices--markets/
documents/os-markets/red-meat-market-snapshots/2021/global-beef-industry-and
-trade-report.pdf.

Mendieta, E. 2011. "Interspecies Cosmopolitanism: Towards a Discourse Ethics
Grounding of Animal Rights." *Logos* 10 .http://www.logosjournal.com/interspecies
-cosmopolitanism.php.

Merriott, Dominic. 2016. "Factors Associated with the Farmer Suicide Crisis in India."
Journal of Epidemiology and Global Health 6 (4): 217–227.

Miele, Mara. 2016. "Killing Animals for Food: How Science, Religion and Technologies Affect the Public Debate About Religious Slaughter." *Food Ethics* 1: 47–60.

Ministry of Food Processing Industries. 2013. "Operational Guidelines for the Scheme
for Setting Up/Modernization of Abattoirs." Government of India. Retrieved 29
January, 2020, from https://mofpi.nic.in/sites/default/files/Revised_12PLan_Aba
ttoir_Guidelines_251113.pdf_o.pdf.

Mishra, Ritesh. 2017. "200 cows die of starvation at a shelter run by BJP Leader in Chhattisgarh." *The Hindustan Times,* 18 August. Retrieved 16 August, 2022, from https://
www.hindustantimes.com/india-news/200-cows-die-of-starvation-at-a-shelter-run-
by-bjp-leader-in-chhattisgarh/story-C1fxj4Pj4DgOcGAtmbBdTN.html.

Mirza, Shireen. 2019. "Cow Politics: Spatial Shifts in the Location of Slaughterhouses
in Mumbai City." *South Asia: Journal of South Asian Studies* 42 (5): 861–879.

Modi, Narendra. 2012. "Janmashtami—the Protector of Cows, Lord Krishna's Birthday." *Narendra Modi's Blog,* 10 August. Retrieved 10 August, 2018, from https://
timesofindia.indiatimes.com/blogs/narendra-modis-blog/janmashtami-the
-protector-of-cows-lord-krishna-s-birthday/.

Mohan, C. Madan. 1989. *Dairy Management in India: A Study in Andhra Pradesh.* Delhi:
Mittal Publications.

Mohan, Dinesh. 2002. "Traffic Safety and Health in Indian Cities." *Journal of Transport
& Infrastructure* 9 (1): 79–92.

Monbiot, George. 2018. "The Best Way to Save the Planet? Drop Meat and Dairy." *The Guardian*, 8 June. Retrieved 13 January, 2021, from https://www.theguardian. com/commentisfree/2018/jun/08/save-planet-meat-dairy-livestock-food-free-range -steak.

Morell, Virginia. 2014. *Animal Wise: The Thoughts and Emotions of our Fellow Creatures.* Collingwood, Melbourne: Black Inc.

Moritz, M. (2008). "A Critical Examination of Honour Cultures and Herding Societies in Africa." *African Studies Review* 51 (2): 99–117.

Morrison, Kathleen D. 2014. "Conceiving Ecology and Stopping the Clock: Narratives of Balance, Loss, and Degradation." In *Shifting Ground: People, Animals, and Mobility in India's Environmental History*, ed. Mahesh Rangarajan and K. Sivaramakrishnan, 39–64. New Delhi: Oxford University Press.

Mosse, D. 2018. "Caste and development: Contemporary perspectives on a structure of discrimination and advantage." *World Development* 110: 422–436.

Mosse, D. 2020. "The Modernity of Caste and the Market Economy." *Modern Asian Studies* 54 (4): 1225–1271.

mowson, lynn. 2019. Making and Unmaking Mammalian Bodies. In *Animaladies*, ed. L. Gruen and F. Probyn-Rapsey, 25–46. New York: Bloomsbury.

Nair, Smita. 2016. "Over 1,900 People Line Up to Become 'Eyes' for Maharashtra's Animal Husbandry Dept to Monitor Beef Ban." *The Indian Express*. Retrieved 8 February, 2019, from https://indianexpress.com/article/india/india-news-india/ over-1900-people-line-up-to-become-eyes-for-maharashtras-animal-husbandry -dept-to-monitor-beef-ban-2939458/.

Naqvi, H., Singh, R., Kumar, S. R., and Pai, S. 2013. "In Lawless Uttar Pradesh It's Rule of the Gun." *Hindustan Times*, 25 December. Retrieved 4 January, 2021, from https://www.hindustantimes.com/india/in-lawless-uttar-pradesh-it-s-rule-of-the -gun/story-WKpeNkUjsBqRUKHLQB05KI.html.

Narain, Sunita. 2019. "India's Cow Crisis Part 3: Brutal to Kill India's Ancient Uber Economy." *Down to Earth*. Retrieved 3 April, 2020, from https://www.down toearth.org.in/news/agriculture/india-s-cow-crisis-part-3-brutal-to-kill-india-s -ancient-uber-economy-62752?utm_source=Mailer&utm_medium=Email&utm _campaign=Down%20To%20Earth-2760.

Narayanan, Yamini. 2015a. *Religion, Heritage and the Sustainable City: Hinduism and Ur-banisation in Jaipur.* Oxford: Routledge.

Narayanan, Yamini. 2015b "Sperm to Slaughter: The Shocking Abuse of Bulls in Dairy Farming." *Huffington Post*. Retrieved 14 February, 2018, from https://www.huffpost .com/archive/in/entry/sperm-to-slaughter-the-sh_b_7516454/amp.

Narayanan, Yamini. 2017. "Street dogs at the intersection of colonialism and informal-ity: 'subaltern animism' as a posthuman critique of Indian cities." *Environment and Planning D: Society and Space* 35 (3): 475–494.

Narayanan, Yamini. 2018a. "Cow Protection' as 'Casteised Speciesism': Sacralisation, Commercialisation and Politicisation." *South Asia: Journal of South Asian Studies* 41 (2): 331–351.

Narayanan, Yamini. 2018b. "Animal Ethics and Hinduism's Milking, Mothering Legends: Analysing Krishna the Butter Thief and the Ocean of Milk." *Sophia: International Journal of Philosophy and Traditions* 57 (1):133–149.

Narayanan, Yamini. 2019a. "'Cow is a Mother, Mothers Can Do Anything for Their Children!' Gaushalas as Landscapes of Anthropatriarchy and Hindu Patriarchy." *Hypatia: A Journal of Feminist Philosophy* 34 (2): 195–221.

Narayanan, Yamini. 2019b. "*Jugaad* and informality as drivers of India's cow slaughter economy." *Environment and Planning A* 51 (7): 1516–1535.

Narayanan, Yamini. 2021a. "Animating Caste: Visceral Geographies of Pigs, Caste and Violent Nationalisms in Chennai City." *Urban Geography*. doi: 10.1080/02723638.2021.1890954.

Narayanan, Yamini. 2021b. "'A pilgrimage of camels': Dairy capitalism, nomadic pastoralism, and subnational Hindutva statism in Rajasthan." *Environment and Planning E*. doi: 10.1177/25148486211062005.

Narayanan, Yamini. (forthcoming). "An Ecofeminist Politics of Chicken Ovulation: A Socio-Capitalist Model of Ability as Farmed Animal Impairment." *Hypatia: A Journal of Feminist Philosophy*.

National Commission for Backward Classes. 2015. *Central List of OBCs*. Retrieved 8 July, 2022, from http://www.ncbc.nic.in/user_panel/GazetteResolution.aspx?Value =mPICjsLiaLv31HvqDjLo2b6bRBzpX69AoP2QYNS1c%2bG5fYPaeM7PeVCET3 GMjhgG.

Natrajan, B. 2021. "Racialization and Ethnicization: Hindutva Hegemony and Caste." *Ethnic and Racial Studies* 45 (2): 298-318. doi: 10.1080/01419870.2021.1951318.

Nauriya, A. 2015. "M K Gandhi and the Founders of the African National Congress," *Mainstream* 53 (41). Retrieved 4 July, 2022, from http://www.mainstreamweekly.net/ article5982.html.

NDDB (National Dairy Development Board). n.d., a. *National Dairy Plan*. Retrieved 28 January, 2022, from https://www.nddb.coop/ndpi/about/brief.

NDDB (National Dairy Development Board). n.d., b. *Milk Production by States*. Retrieved 14 November, 2019, from https://www.nddb.coop/information/stats/ milkprodstate.

NDDB (National Dairy Development Board). (2017). "Facts at a glance: Summary of Operation Flood Achievements." Retrieved 22 December, 2019, from https://www .nddb.coop/about/genesis/significant/facts.

NDDB. (National Dairy Development Board). 2020a. *NDDB Annual Report 2019–20*. Retrieved 7 February, 2020, from https://www.nddb.coop/sites/default/files/pdfs/ NDDB_Annual_Report_2019_20_Eng.pdf.

NDDB. (National Dairy Development Board). 2020b. *Implementation Completion and Results Report (Document of the World Bank)*. Retrieved 5 July, from https://www .nddb.coop/sites/default/files/pdfs/ndpi/NDPI_World_Bank_Evaluation_Report _(ICRR).pdf.

NDTV. (2016). "'Minimal': That's How Minister Describes Beating of Women Over Beef Rumours," 28 July. Retrieved 7 July, 2022, from https://www.ndtv.com/

india-news/minimal-thats-how-minister-describes-beating-of-women-over-beef
-rumours-1437406.

NDTV. 2018a, "Under Modi Government, VIP Hate Speech Skyrockets—by 500%,"
19 April. Retrieved 21 December, 2019, from https://www.ndtv.com/india-news/
under-narendra-modi-government-vip-hate-speech-skyrockets-by-500-1838925.

NDTV. 2018b. "In New Hate Speech, BJP Lawmaker Says 'Hindustan is for Hindus,'"
2 January. Retrieved 21 December, 2019, from https://www.ndtv.com/india-news/
in-new-hate-speech-bjp-lawmaker-vikram-saini-says-hindustan-is-for-hindus
-1794689.

NDTV. 2018c. "'Smuggle, Slaughter Cows, You'll Be Killed,' Warns Rajasthan BJP
Lawmaker," 25 December. Retrieved 21 December, 2019, from https://www.ndtv
.com/india-news/smuggle-slaughter-cows-youll-be-killed-warns-rajasthan-bjp
-lawmakergyan-dev-ahuja-1791811.

Newar, Sanjay. 2016. *A Hindu's Fight for Mother Cow*. Retrieved 3 January, 2020, from
http://agniveer.com/books/a-hindus-fight-for-mother-cow/.

News18. 2017. "Forensic Test Reveals Lynch Victim Was Carrying Beef: Police." Retrieved 22 January, 2019, from https://www.news18.com/news/india/forensic-test
-reveals-lynch-victim-was-carrying-beef-police-1455783.html.

News18. 2018. "'God Punished You for Eating Beef': Ugly Responses to Kerala Floods
Prove Bigotry is Alive and Kicking." Retrieved 2 August, 2021, from https://www
.news18.com/news/buzz/god-punished-you-for-eating-beef-responses-to-kerala
-floods-prove-how-bigotry-is-alive-and-kicking-in-india-1849169.html.

Newby, N. C., Tucker, C. B., Pearl, D. L., LeBlanc, S. J., Leslie, K. E., von Key-
serlingk, M. A. G., and Duffield, T. F. 2014, "An Investigation of the Effects of
Ketoprofen Following Rumen Fistulation Surgery in Lactating Dairy Cows." *The
Canadian Veterinary Journal* 55 (5): 442–448.

New South Wales Government (Department of Primary Industries). 2015. "Cancer Eye
in Cattle." Retrieved 13 February, from https://www.dpi.nsw.gov.au/__data/assets/
pdf_file/0009/584226/cancer-eye-in-cattle.pdf.

NFSU (National Forensic Sciences University). 2019. "Vision & Mission." Retrieved
14≈February, 2020, from https://www.nfsu.ac.in/vision-&-mission.

NMVG (Namo Mission Vande Gaumathram). n.d. "Namo Mission Vande Gaumathram." Retrieved 9 February, 2022, from https://namomissionvandegaumatharam
.com/.

Nibert, D., A. (2013). *Animal Domestication & Human Violence: Domestication, Capitalism
and Global Conflict*. New York: Columbia University Press.

Nisar, Naqshab. 2020. "Forced to Drink Urine: 65-yr-old Dalit Thrashed for Complaining Against 'Influential Man' in UP," 13 October. Retrieved 7 February, 2022, from
https://www.ibtimes.co.in/forced-drink-urine-65-yr-old-dalit-thrashed-complain
ing-against-influential-man-829249.

Nissen, A., Andersen, P. H., Bendixen, E., Ingvartsen, K. L., and Røntved, C. M. 2017.
"Colostrum and Milk Protein Rankings and Ratios of Importance to Neonatal Calf
Health Using a Proteomics Approach." *Journal of Dairy Science* 100 (4): 2711–2728.

Nussbaum, Martha. 1995. "Objectification." *Philosophy and Public Affairs* 24 (2): 249–91.

O'Dea, L., and Woodle, D. E. 1972. India's Approach to Cattle Development: Heifer Project as Catalyst in India's White Revolution. *Iowa State University Veterinarian* 34 (2): 102–106.

Oltenacu, P. A., and Broom, D. M. (2010). "The Impact of Genetic Selection for Increased Milk Yield on the Welfare of Dairy Cows. *Animal Welfare* 19 (1): 39–49.

OneIndia. 2017. "Pigs to Flaunt Sacred Thread to Mark Protest Against Brahminism, BJP in Tamil Nadu." Retrieved 27 August, 2020, from https://www.oneindia.com/india/pigs-flaunt-sacred-thread-mark-protest-against-brahminism-b-2504733.html.

Pachirat, T. 2012. *Every Twelve Seconds: Industrialized Slaughter and the Politics of Sight.* New Haven, CT: Yale University Press.

Padalino, B., Aubé, L., Fatnassi, M., Monaco, D., Khorchani, T., Hammadi, M., and Lacalandra, G., M. 2014. "Could Dromedary Camels Develop Stereotypy? The First Description of Stereotypical Behaviour in Housed Male Dromedary Camels and How It Is Affected by Different Management Systems." *Plos One* 9 (2): 1–7.

Patel, A., and Dutta, S. (2014). India's First Ministry for Cows. Retrieved 31 July, 2016, from http://blogs.wsj.com/indiarealtime/2014/01/14/indias-first-ministry-for-cows/.

Patel, Deven M. 2008 "Kāmadhenu." In *Encyclopedia of Hinduism*, ed. Denise Cush, Catherine Robinson and Michael York. London: Routledge.

Pati, Amulya. 2015. "Jajpur NH Roads, A Safe Corridor for Cattle Smuggling." *The New Indian Express*, 28 March. Retrieved 5 August, 2016, from http://www.newindianexpress.com/states/odisha/Jajpur-NH-Roads-A-Safe-Corridor-for-Cattle-Smuggling/2015/03/28/article2734651.ece.

Pati, Ipsita. 2017. "NRI, Friend Claim They Were Targeted by 'Cattle Smugglers' in Gurgaon." *The New Indian Express*, 28 March, modified 26 September. Retrieved 12 February, 2021, from https://www.hindustantimes.com/gurgaon/nri-friend-claim-they-were-targeted-by-cattle-smugglers-in-gurgaon/story-TCeJuZBzzJVnuaIygoeNnK.html.

Patnaik, Prabhat. 1993. "Fascism of our times." *Social Scientist* 21 (3/4): 69–77.

Patra, A. K. 2016. "Recent Advances in Measurement and Dietary Mitigation of Enteric Methane Emissions in Ruminants." *Frontiers in Veterinary Science* 3, Article 39.

People's Union for Democratic Rights. 2003. "Dalit Lynching at Dulina: Cow-Protection, Caste and Communalism." Retrieved 8 February, 2020, from https://pudr.org/sites/default/files/2019-02/jhajhar_dalit_lynching.pdf.

Perry, Guillermo E., Maloney, William F., Omar Arias, S., Fajnzylber, Pablo, Mason, Andrew D., and Saavedra-Chanduvi, Jaime. 2007. *Informality: Exit and Exclusion.* Washington, D.C.: World Bank Publications.

Phillips, Clive. 2002. *Cattle Behaviour and Welfare.* 2nd Ed. Blackwell Science. Oxford.

Phillips, Clive J.C. (2010) *Principles of Cattle Production*, 2nd Edition. Wallingford, UK: CABI.

Physicians Committee for Responsible Medicine. 2022. *Calcium and Strong Bones.* Retrieved 16 August, 2022, from https://www.pcrm.org/good-nutrition/nutrition-information/health-concerns-about-dairy/calcium-and-strong-bones.

Pick, Anat. 2018. "Vulnerability." In *Critical Terms for Animal Studies*, ed. Lori Gruen, 410–423. Chicago: University of Chicago Press.

Pintchman, T. (2001). "The Goddess as Fount of the Universe: Shared Visions and Negotiated Allegiances in Puranic Accounts of Cosmogenesis." In *Seeking Mahadevi: Constructing the Identities of the Hindu Great Goddess*, ed. T. Pintchman, 77–92. New York: State University of New York Press.

Poonia, Amrita, Payasi, Abhilash, and Kumar, Dharmendra. 2014. "Management Issues and Prospects of Dairy Industry in Varanasi District of Uttar Pradesh, India." *Asian Journal of Dairy and Food Research* 161–62.

Potter, Will. 2009. "The Green Scare." Vermont Law Review 33 (4): 672–673.

Potter, Will. 2011. *Green Is the New Red: An Insider's Account of a Social Movement Under Siege*. San Francisco, CA: City Lights Books.

Prabhu, Maya. 2016. "India's Dalit Cattle Skinners Share Stories of Abuse." Aljazeera, 25 August. Retrieved 8 February, from https://www.aljazeera.com/features/2016/8/25/indias-dalit-cattle-skinners-share-stories-of-abuse.

Pradhan, Bibhudutta, and Chaudhary, Archana. 2021. "Covid May Have Claimed as Many as 5 Million Lives in India." *Bloomberg*, 21 July. Retrieved 10 August, 2021, from https://www.bloomberg.com/news/features/2021-07-21/covid-19-may-have-claimed-as-many-as-5-million-lives-in-india.

Probyn-Rapsey, Fiona. 2013. "Stunning Australia." *Humanimalia: A Journal of Human/Animal Interface Studies* 4 (2): 84–100.

Probyn-Rapsey, Fiona. 2018. "Anthropocentrism." In *Critical Terms for Animal Studies*, ed. Lori Gruen, 47–63. Chicago: University of Chicago Press.

Pullakhandam, R., Palika, R., Rao, S. V., Polasa, K., and Boindala, S. 2014. "Effect of Oxytocin Injection to Milching Buffalo on its Content and Stability in Milk." *Indian Journal of Medical Research* 39 (6): 933–939.

Punjabi, Meeta. n.d. "India: Increasing Demand Challenges the Dairy Sector." Food and Agriculture Organization. Retrieved 12 February, 2022, from https://www.fao.org/3/i0588e/i0588e05.htm.

Rao, Anupama. 2009. *The Caste Question: Dalits and the Politics of Modern India*. Berkeley, CA: University of California Press.

Rashtriya Kamadhenu Aayog. 2021. "RKA Syllabus." Retrieved 7 January, 2022, from https://www.scribd.com/document/489869645/RKA-syllabus#from_embed.

Reese, Jacy. 2020. "Institutional Change and the Limitations of Consumer Activism." *Palgrave Communications* 6 (26): 1-8.

Reuters. 2018. "India Bans Imports of Hormone Oxytocin to Halt Misuse in Livestock Industry," 27 June. Retrieved 16 August, 2022, from https://in.reuters.com/article/india-oxytocin-ban/india-bans-imports-of-hormone-oxytocin-to-halt-misuse-in-livestock-industry-idINKCN1HD14J.

Ribas, Vanessa. 2015. *On the Line: Slaughterhouse Lives and the Making of the New South*. Berkeley, CA: University of California Press.

Rosales, Jon. 2008. "Economic Growth, Climate Change, Biodiversity Loss: Distributive Justice for the Global North and South." *Conservation Biology* 22 (6): 1409–1417.

Rouge, M., and Bowen, R. 2002. *Semen Collection.* Retrieved 15 November, 2019, from http://www.vivo.colostate.edu/hbooks/pathphys/reprod/semeneval/collection.html.

Roy, Ananya. 2011. "Slumdog Cities: Rethinking Subaltern Urbanism." *International Journal of Urban and Regional Research* 35 (2): 223–238.

RSPCA (Royal Society for the Prevention of Cruelty to Animals). 2022. "What Are the Animal Welfare Issues with Sow Stalls and Farrowing Crates?" Retrieved 14 February, 2022, from https://kb.rspca.org.au/knowledge-base/what-are-the-animal-welfare-issues-with-sow-stalls-and-farrowing-crates/.

Sabrang India. 2016. "If the Cow is Your Mother, You Bury Her: Gujarat Dalits Cry Liberation." Retrieved 21 January, 2019, from https://sabrangindia.in/interview/if-cow-your-mother-you-bury-her-gujarat-dalits-cry-liberation.

SAG (Sabarmati Ashram Gaushala). 2013. *Annual Report 2012–13: Sabarmati Ashram Gaushala Bidaj.* Bidaj Farm, Kheda, Gujarat: Sabarmati Ashram Gaushala.

Samanta, Samiparna. 2006. "Calcutta Slaughterhouse: Colonial and Post-Colonial Experiences." *Economic and Political Weekly* 41 (20): 1999–2007.

Sandhu, Kamaljit Kaur. 2016. "Hung from the Neck and Dropped Across the Fence: Viral Video Shows Cruel Side of Cattle Smuggling in Bangladesh." *India Today,* 26 September. Retrieved 20 January, 2021, from https://www.indiatoday.in/india/story/viral-video-cattle-smuggling-bangladesh-343203-2016-09-26.

Santos, Jose Eduardo P. 2011. "Nutritional Management of Lactating Dairy Cows." In *Dairy Production Medicine,* ed. Carlos Risco and Pedro Mendelez, 33–72 [e-book]. John Wiley and Sons, https://doi.org/10.1002/9780470960554.ch5.

Sastri, D. B., and Ramaswami, K. S. 1945. "The Religion and Romance of Cow-Worship in India." *Kalyana Kalpataru* 11 (1): 67.

Savarkar, V. D. 1969 [1923] *Hindutva—Who is a Hindu?* 5th Ed. Bombay: Veer Savarkar Prakashan. https://archive.org/details/hindutva-vinayak-damodar-savarkar-pdf/page/n1/mode/2up/search/first+discernible+source.

Scholten, Bruce A. 2010. *India's White Revolution: Operation Flood, Food Aid and Development.* New York: Tauris Academic Studies.

Scroll. 2016. "'Your Mother, You Take Care of it': Meet the Dalits Behind Gujarat's Stirring Cow Carcass Protests." *Scroll.* Retrieved 21 January, 2019, from https://scroll.in/article/812329/your-mother-you-take-care-of-it-meet-the-dalits-behind-gujarats-stirring-cow-carcass-protests.

Sebastian, Manu. 2017. "Rule Banning Cattle Sale for Slaughter Contradicts the Act Permitting Slaughter of Animals for Food." *Outlook India.* Retrieved 9 October, 2020, from https://www.outlookindia.com/website/story/why-prevention-of-cruelty-to-animals-regulation-of-livestock-markets-rules-2017-/299119.

Sen, Amartya. 1990. "More Than 100 Million Women Are Missing." *New York Review of Books* 20: 61–66.

Sethi, Aarti. 2019. "Mahadev's Gift: Men, Bullocks and the Community of Cultivation in Central India." *South Asia: Journal of South Asian Studies* 42 (6): 1173–1191.

Shah, Ghanshyam, Mander, Harsh, Thorat, Sukhadeo, Deshpande, Satish, and Baviskar, Amita. 2006. *Untouchability in Rural India.* 1st Ed. Sage.

Shapiro, Ken. 2010. "Big Numbers." Message posted to the Animals and Society Institute website (ASI Diary, 25 January). Retrieved 5 July, 2022, from http://www.allcreatures.org/articles/ar-finitude.html.

Sharma, Nidhi. 2018. "Government Dilutes Rules on Cattle Sale in Animal Market." *Economic Times*. Retrieved 9 October, 2020, from https://economictimes.indiatimes.com/news/politics-and-nation/government-dilutes-rules-on-cattle-sale-in-animal-market/articleshow/63690408.cms.

Sharpes, Donald K. 2006. *Sacred Bull, Holy Cow: A Cultural Study of Civilization's Most Important Animal*. New York: Peter Lang.

Shepon, Alon, Eshel, Gidon, Noor, Elad, and Milo, Ron. 2018. "The Opportunity Cost of Animal Based Diets Exceeds All Food Losses." *Proceedings of the National Academy of Sciences* 115 (15) 3804–3809. https://www.pnas.org/content/115/15/3804.

Shinde, R. 2016. "The Most Powerful Weapon of the Gujarat Dalit Revolt." *Huffington Post*, 29 July. Retrieved 7 February, 2022, from https://www.huffpost.com/archive/in/entry/the-most-powerful-weapon-of-the-gujarat-dalit-revolt_a_214 41261.

Shiva, Vandana. 1991. *The Violence of the Green Revolution: Third World Agriculture, Ecology, and Politics*. London: Zed Books.

Shiva, Vandana. 1993. *Monocultures of the Mind: Perspectives on Biodiversity and Biotechnology*. London: Zed Books.

Shiva, Vandana. 1999. "Penalizing the Poor: GATT, WTO and the Developing World." In *The Meat Business: Devouring a Hungry Planet*, ed. Geoff Tansy and Joyce D'Silva, 198–213. London: Earthscan Publications Ltd.

Shiva, Vandana. 2016. *Stolen Harvest: The Hijacking of the Global Food Supply*. Lexington: University Press of Kentucky.

Shiva, Vandana. 2019. "Fake Food, Fake Meat: Big Food's Desperate Attempt to Further the Industrialisation of Food." *Independent Science News*. Retrieved 19 December, 2020, from https://www.independentsciencenews.org/health/fake-food-fake-meat-big-foods-desperate-attempt-to-further-industrialisation-food/.

Shukin, Nicole. 2009. *Animal Capital: Rendering Life in Biopolitcal Times*. Minneapolis: University of Minnesota Press.

Siegel, Benjamin. 2016. "'Self-Help which Ennobles a Nation': Development, Citizenship, and the Obligations of Eating in India's Austerity Years." *Modern Asian Studies* 50 (3):975–1018.

Siegel, Benjamin Robert. 2018. *Hungry Nation: Food, Famine, and the Making of Modern India*. Cambridge: Cambridge University Press.

Sikandar, Zainab. 2020. "Elephant or Cow, Hindutva Doesn't Give Two Hoots About Animal Welfare. Deaths Are Political." *The Print*. Retrieved 22 July, 2021, from https://theprint.in/opinion/elephant-cow-hindutva-give-two-hoots-about-animal-welfare-deaths-political/437520/.

Silbergeld, Ellen K. 2016. *Chickenizing Farms and Food: How Industrial Meat Production Endangers Workers, Animals, and Consumers*. [e-book] Baltimore, MD: Johns Hopkins University Press.

Simoons, Frederick J. 1974. "The Purificatory Role of the Five Products of the Cow in Hinduism." *Ecology of Food and Nutrition* 3 (1): 21.

Singh, Akhilesh. 2014. "Funds from Cow Slaughter Racket Being Pumped into Terror: Maneka Gandhi." *Struggle for Hindu Existence*. Retrieved 22 July, 2021, from https://hinduexistence.org/2014/09/16/illegal-cow-slaughter-rackets-enhance-islamic-terrorism-hindu-muslims-both-are-guilty/.

Singh, Hira. 2008. "The Real World of Caste in India." *Journal of Peasant Studies* 35 (1): 119–132.

Singh, M., Lathwal, S. S., Kotresh Prasad, C., Dey, D., Gupta, A., Saini, M., Lathwal, I., Sharma, B., Kumar, M., and Sharma, V. 2021. "Availability of Feed Sources and Nutritional Status of Hariana Cattle in Different Seasons in the Breeding Tract." *Biological Rhythm Research* 52 (6): 862-868.

Singh Rawat, Virendra. 2019. "UP Tops Up Rs 600 Crore Cow Protection Budget with Special Corpus." *Business Standard*, 29 May. Retrieved 20 June, 2021, from https://www.business-standard.com/article/current-affairs/up-tops-up-rs-600-crore-cow-protection-budget-with-special-corpus-119052900825_1.html.

Sirohi, Smita, and Michaelowa, Axel. 2007. "Sufferer and Cause: Indian Livestock and Climate Change." *Climatic Change* 85 (3): 285–298.

Sirohi, Smita, Michaelowa, Axel, and Sirohi, S. K. 2007. "Mitigation Options for Enteric Methane Emissions from Dairy Animals: An Evaluation for Potential CDM Projects in India." *Mitigation and Adaption Strategies for Global Change* 12: 259–274.

Slater, Joanna, and Masih, Niha. 2020. "As the World Looks for Coronavirus Scapegoats, Muslims Are Blamed in India." *Washington Post*, 22 April. Retrieved 15 January, 2021, from https://www.washingtonpost.com/world/asia_pacific/as-world-looks-for-coronavirus-scapegoats-india-pins-blame-on-muslims/2020/04/22/3cb43430-7f3f-11ea-84c2-0792d8591911_story.html.

Smith-Howard, Kendra. 2017. *Pure and Modern Milk*. New York: Oxford University Press.

Snow, David, Tan, Anna, and Owens, Peter. 2013. "Social Movements, Framing Processes, and Cultural Revitalization and Fabrication." *Mobilization: An International Quarterly* 18 (3): 225–242.

Spataro, Armando. 2008. "Why Do People Become Terrorists? A Prosecutor's Experiences." *Journal of International Criminal Justice* 6: 507–524.

Springmann, Marco, Wiebe, Keith, Mason-D'Croz, Daniel, Sulser, Timothy B., Rayner, Mike, and Scarborough, Peter. 2018. "Health and Nutritional Aspects of Sustainable Diet Strategies and Their Association with Environmental Impacts: A Global Modelling Analysis with Country-Level Detail." *Lancet Planetary Health* 2: e451–61.

Srila Krsnadasa Kaviraja Gosvami (trans. Advaita Dasa). 2000. Sri Govinda Lilamrta. Vrindavan: Rashbihari Lal & Sons.

Srinivasan, Krithika. 2015. "The Human Rights Imagination and Nonhuman Life in the Age of Developmentality." *Journal of the National Human Rights Commission* 14: 289–309.

Srinivasan, Krithika. 2016. "Towards a Political Animal Geography?" *Political Geography* 50: 76–78.

Srinivasulu, K. 2002. "Caste, Class and Social Articulation in Andhra Pradesh: Mapping Differential Regional Trajectories." Retrieved 13 February, 2021, from https://cdn.odi.org/media/documents/2692.pdf.

Srivastava, M. C. P. (1979). *Mother Goddess in Indian Art, Archaeology and Literature.* Delhi: Agam Kala Prakashan.

Staples, James 2017. "Beef and Beyond: Exploring the Meat Consumption Practices of Christians in India." *Ethnos: Journal of Anthropology* 82 (2): 232–251.

Statista. 2022. "Number of Milk Cows Worldwide in 2021, by Country." Retrieved 7 February, 2022, from https://www.statista.com/statistics/869885/global-number-milk-cows-by-country/.

Stevenson, Peter. 1999. "Trade Rules, Animal Welfare and the European Union." In *The Meat Business: Devouring a Hungry Planet*, ed. Geoff Tansy and Joyce D'Silva, 187–197. London: Earthscan Publications Ltd.

Stockler, R. (2015). "Heifer Development: From Weaning to Calving." In *Bovine Reproduction*, ed. R. M. Hopper, 272–275. Oxford: Wiley Blackwell.

Striffler, Steve. 2005. *Chicken: The Dangerous Transformation of America's Favorite Food.* New Haven, CT: Yale University Press.

Struggle for Hindu Existence. 2016. "Five Muslims Held for Slaughtering Cows in Maharashtra," 29 August. Retrieved 16 August, 2022, from https://hinduexistence.org/2016/08/29/five-muslims-held-for-slaughtering-cows-in-maharashtra/save-cow-save-nation-2/.

Subramaniam, Mangala. 2014. "Resisting Gendered Religious Nationalism: The Case of Religious-Based Violence in Gujarat, India." *Gendered Perspectives on Conflict and Violence* 18B: 73–98. https://doi.org/10.1108/S1529-21262014000018B007.

Sur, Malini. 2020. "Time at its Margins: Cattle Smuggling Across the India-Bangladesh Border." *Cultural Anthropology* 534 (4): 546–574.

Swami Vijñanananda. 2010 [1922]. *The S'rimad Devî Bhâgawatam*, Book VII, Chapter XXVII, 686. Kindle Edition.

Tanyas, Bahar. 2016. "Experiences of Otherness and Practices of Othering: Young Turkish Migrants in the UK." *Young* 24 (2):157–173.

TATA. (2017). "Tata Ace HT." Retrieved 6 January, 2018, from http://ace.tatamotors.com/tata-trucks/tata-ace-ht/specifications/tata-ace-ht-specifications.aspx.

Taylor, Bron. 2010. *Dark Green Religion.* Berkeley, CA: University of California Press.

Taylor, Sunaura. 2017. *Beasts of Burden: Animal and Disability Liberation.* New York: The New Press.

Tayob, Shaheed. 2019. "Disgust as Embodied Critique: Being Middle Class and Muslim in Mumbai." *South Asia: Journal of South Asian Studies* 42 (6):1192–1209.

Thapar, Romila. 1996. "The Theory of Aryan Race and India: History and Politics." *Social Scientist* 24 (1–3): 3–29.

Thesaurus. 2022. Milk (tap/exploit). Retrieved 8 July 2022 from: https://www.thesaurus.com/browse/milk.

The Andhra Pradesh Prohibition of Cow Slaughter and Animal Preservation Act, 1977. http://tgahd.nic.in/awelfare/4.Animal%20Welfare%20Acts.pdf (p.21–22).

The Asian Age. 2017. "RSS Plans 'Cow Milk Only' Iftar." Retrieved 8 April, 2019, from https://www.asianage.com/india/all-india/230517/rss-plans-cow-milk-only-iftar .html.

The Bombay Animal Preservation Act, 1954. (Applies to Gujarat) http://www.bareact slive.com/Guj/guj012.htm.

The Chhattisgarh Agricultural Cattle Preservation Act, 2004. http://www.lawsofindia. org/statelaw/2874/TheChhattisgarhAgriculturalCattlePreservationAct2004.htm.

The Dairy Site. 2007. *Blackleg in Cattle*. Retrieved 16 November, 2019, from http://www .thedairysite.com/articles/843/blackleg-in-cattle/.

The Economic Times. 2015. "Gujarat Forensic Sciences University: Creating an Army of Indian Forensic Students." Retrieved 22 January, 2019, from https://economictimes .indiatimes.com/industry/services/education/gujarat-forensic-sciences-university -creating-an-army-of-indian-forensic-students/articleshow/46486887.cms.

The Express Tribune. 2016. "Leonardo DiCaprio Joins Hands with Hindu National- ist Group to Ban Beef." Retrieved 28 October, 2019, from https://tribune.com.pk/ story/1130516/leonardo-dicaprio-joins-hands-hindu-nationalist-group-ban-beef/.

The Hans India. 2015. "South India's Biggest Goshala at Shamshabad." Retrieved 15 May, 2019, from https://www.thehansindia.com/posts/index/Hyderabad/2015-01-18/ South-Indias-biggest-goshala-at-Shamshabad/126532.

The Hans India. 2019. "Animal Welfare Board to File Contempt of Court Plea." Re- trieved 21 January, 2020, from https://www.thehansindia.com/telangana/animal -welfare-board-to-file-contempt-of-court-plea-554409?fromNewsdog=1&utm _source=NewsDog&utm_medium=referral.

The Hindu. 2010. "ISKCON's Largest 'Goshala' Coming Up." Retrieved 16 May, 2019, from https://www.thehindu.com/news/national/andhra-pradesh/ISKCONs-largest -Goshala-coming-up/article15906492.ece.

The Hindu. 2013. "77 heads of cattle seized near Chennai." Retrieved 9 October, 2018, from https://www.thehindu.com/news/national/tamil-nadu/77-heads-of-cattle -seized-near-chennai/article4866685.ece.

The Hindu. 2017. "Make Cow a National Animal: Justice Sharma." Retrieved 3 Septem- ber, 2019, from https://www.thehindu.com/todays-paper/tp-national/make-cow-a -national-animal-justice-sharma/article18685210.ece.

The Hindu. 2019a. "Rajasthan High Court Quashes Cattle Smuggling Case Against Pehlu Khan, His Two Sons and Driver," 30 October. Retrieved 7 February, 2022, from https://www.thehindu.com/news/national/rajasthan-hc-quashes-cattle-smug gling-case-against-pehlu-khan-his-two-sons-and-driver/article29832749.ece.

The Hindu. 2019b. "Cow Is the Only Animal That Exhales Oxygen, Says Uttarakhand CM." Retrieved 2 October, 2019, from https://www.thehindu.com/news/national/ other-states/cow-only-animal-that-exhales-oxygen-says-uttarakhand-cm/article 28718605.ece?homepage=true&fbclid=IwARomP8NJ31YIZ5XdkQGP1Zb6OVcIE XWZRloeNyr4326miP9ZZskA_atXv9E.

The Hindu. 2019c. "More Than 70,000 Cows Died in a Gaushala During BJP Rule." Retrieved 8 February, 2022, from https://www.thehindu.com/news/national/other -states/more-than-70000-cows-died-in-a-gaushala-during-bjp-rule/article26072773 .ece.

The Indian Express. 2015. "Osmania 'Beef Festival' Row: Police Raid Hostels, Detain 30 Students, BJP MLA Raja Singh." Retrieved 4 September, 2019, from https:// indianexpress.com/article/india/india-news-india/beef-festival-row-bjp-mla -arrested-8-organisers-detained/.

The Indian Express. 2017a. "Muslim Man in Ahmedabad to Sit on Fast to Spread Message of Cow Protection." Retrieved 4 June, 2018, from http://indianexpress.com/ article/india/muslim-man-in-ahmedabad-to-sit-on-fast-to-spread-message-of-cow -protection-4744673/.

The Indian Express. 2017b. "New Animal Market Rules Ban Sale of Cattle for Slaughter." Retrieved 6 November, 2017, from http://indianexpress.com/article/india/ cow-slaughter-ban-new-animal-market-rules-ban-sale-of-cattle-beef-ban-4675382/.

The Indian Express. 2018. "Seeking to Curb Illegal Slaughter of Cows, Central Committee to Visit Bengal." Retrieved 14 February, 2020, from https://indianexpress.com/ article/cities/kolkata/seeking-to-curb-illegal-slaughter-of-cows-central-committee -to-visit-bengal-5307267/.

The Karnataka Prevention of Cow Slaughter and Cattle Preservation Act, 1964. http:// www.lawsofindia.org/statelaw/2358/TheKarnatakaPreventionofCowSlaughterand CattlePreservationAct1964.html.

The Madhya Pradesh Agricultural Cattle Preservation Act, 1959. http://www.bareact slive.com/mp/mp044.htm.

The New Indian Express. 2013. "100 Cows Starve to Death at Simhachalam Temple," 15 May. Retrieved 26 December, 2015, from http://www.newindianexpress.com/states/ andhra_pradesh/100-cows-starve-to-death-at-Simhachalam-Temple/2013/05/15/ar ticle1590412.ece.

The New Indian Express. 2018. "Rajasthan: Cow Smugglers Open Fire at Police, Policeman Injured," 4 June. Retrieved 6 December, 2019, from https://www.newindianex press.com/nation/2018/jun/04/rajasthan-cow-smugglers-open-fire-at-police-police man-injured-1823553.html?fbclid=IwARoDWs16EMUOQOPaToxlhOTHqsD2lSF hgQG8-HSY8fzES4xKW_gslVJsSxo.

The New Indian Express. 2020. "Kerala-Grown 'Superfood' Jackfruit Goes Global as a Meat Substitute," 18 May. Retrieved 13 January, 2021, from https://www.newindian express.com/world/2020/may/18/kerala-grown-superfood-jackfruit-goes-global-as -a-meat-substitute-2144909.html.

The News Minute. 2017. "Meat is Dear to Kerala, State Tops in Cattle Slaughter," 19 April. Retrieved 14 November, 2019, from https://www.thenewsminute.com/article/ meat-dear-kerala-state-tops-cattle-slaughter-60581.

The Times of India. 2010. "Dead Calf Used to Milk Cows in Surat." Retrieved 14 November, 2019, from https://timesofindia.indiatimes.com/city/surat/Dead-calf-used -to-milk-cows-in-Surat/articleshow/6290067.cms.

The Times of India. 2013. "Traffickers Use Chili Paste to Torture Animals Taken to Slaughterhouses." Retrieved 12 November, 2018, from https://timesofindia.india times.com/city/chennai/Traffickers-use-chilli-paste-to-torture-animals-taken-to -slaughterhouses/articleshow/24788706.cms.

The Times of India. 2015a. "Dalit Woman Stripped, Forced to Consume Urine in MP," 2 September. Retrieved 7 February, 2022, from https://m.timesofindia.com/videos/ news/Dalit-woman-stripped-forced-to-consume-urine-in-MP/videoshow/48776050 .cms?mobile=no.

The Times of India. 2015b. "Government to Set Up Labs at Ports to Check Illegal Cow Meat Export," 7 October. Retrieved 5 January, 2018, from https://timesofindia.india times.com/india/Government-to-set-up-labs-at-ports-to-check-illegal-cow-meat -export/articleshow/49245226.cms.

The Times of India. 2015c. "Aligarh's Largest Gaushala Survives on Hindu, Muslim Largesse." Retrieved 4 June, 2018, from https://timesofindia.indiatimes.com/ city/agra/Aligarhs-largest-gaushala-survives-on-Hindu-Muslim-largesse/article show/49705256.cms.

The Times of India. 2016a. "Cry for Holy Cows Fails to Draw Funds for Gaushalas." Retrieved 28 May, 2017, from http://timesofindia.indiatimes.com/india/Cry-for-holy -cows-fails-to-draw-funds-for-gaushalas/articleshow/52921244.cms.

The Times of India. 2016b. "Administration Stops Cruel Cow-Pig Fight to Mark Govardhan Puja Celebrations." Retrieved 14 February, 2022, from https://timesofindia .indiatimes.com/city/bareilly/admin-stops-cruel-cow-pig-fight-to-mark-govardhan -puja-celebrations/articleshow/55165592.cms.

The Times of India. 2018a. "Oxytocin Ban to Come into Effect from July 1," 27 June. Retrieved 7 September, 2020, from http://timesofindia.indiatimes.com/articleshow/64769427 .cms?utm_source=contentofinterest&utm_medium=text&utm_campaign=cppst.

The Times of India. 2018b. "Oxytocin Ban Put on Hold till September." Retrieved 25 December, 2019, from https://timesofindia.indiatimes.com/india/oxytocin-ban-put -on-hold-till-september/articleshow/64830926.cms.

The Times of India. 2018c. "Himachal Govt Wants Cow to Be Made 'Mother of Nation.'" Retrieved 7 December, 2019, from https://timesofindia.indiatimes.com/ city/shimla/himachal-govt-wants-cow-to-be-made-mother-of-nation/article show/67084492.cms?fbclid=IwAR2fD7Na2G4HwTdrnnzrhrhDd-q8Zpki5xY -oTza565iq2xhjh-eoA2-Xas.

The Times of India. 2020. "MP Sets Up Country's First 'Cow Cabinet.'" Retrieved 14 February, 2022, from https://timesofindia.indiatimes.com/india/mp-sets-up-coun trys-first-cow-cabinet/articleshow/79293785.cms.

The Tribune. 2016a. "Money from Cow Smuggling Being Used in Terrorism: Police," 29 August. Retrieved 27 July, 2021, from https://www.tribuneindia.com/news/archive/ features/money-from-cow-smuggling-being-used-in-terrorism-police-287198.

The Tribune. 2016b. "8,122 Cows Died Since Jan at Hingonia Gaushala: Rajasthan Govt," 6 August. Retrieved 8 February, 2022, from https://www.tribuneindia.com/news/archive/ nation/8-122-cows-died-since-jan-at-hingonia-gaushala-rajasthan-govt-276859.

The Vegan Society. 2020. "The Vegan Society." Retrieved 13 January, 2021, from https:// www.vegansociety.com/go-vegan/definition-veganism.

The Wire. 2020. "On First Day of Nationwide Lockdown, Adityanath Attends Ram Navami Event in Ayodhya." Retrieved 15 January, 2021, from https://thewire.in/politics/ coronavirus-yogi-adityanath-lockdown-ram-navami-ayodhya.

The Wire. 2021. "In Syllabus for National Exam on Cows, Rastriya Kamdhenu Aayog Unleashes Half-Truths." Retrieved 7 January, 2021, from https://thewire.in/ government/cows-rastriya-kamdhenu-aayog-exam-gau-seva.

Tittensor, David. 2016. "Doing Political Ethnography in a Difficult Climate: A Turkish Case Study." *Ethnography* 17 (2): 213–228.

Tiwari, R., M. Sharma, C., and B. Singh, P. 2007. "Buffalo Calf Health Care in Commercial Dairy Farms: A Field Study in Uttar Pradesh (India)." *Livestock Research for Rural Development* 19 (3): 1–8.

Tomlinson, H. 2016. "Woman and Cousin, 14, 'Gang-Raped for Eating Beef.'" *The Times*, 13 September. Retrieved 28 July, 2021, from https://www.thetimes.co.uk/ article/woman-and-cousin-14-gang-raped-for-eating-beef-pwrz3w87h.

Torres, B. 2007. *Making a Killing: The Political Economy of Animal Rights.* Oakland, CA: AK Press.

Townend, Christine. 2017. *A Life for Animals.* Sydney: Sydney University Press.

Trubshaw, Bob. 1995. "The Metaphors and Rituals of Place and Time—An Introduction to Liminality." Retrieved 4 January, from http://www.indigogroup.co.uk/foamycu stard/fc009.htm.

Truschke, Audrey. 2018. "Anti-Semitism of Hindu Nationalists made me a target of their attacks," *India Abroad*, 5 November. Retrieved from https://www.india abroad.com/opinion/anti-semitism-of-hindu-nationalists-made-me-a-target-of/ article_2c6b47be-e15a-11e8-b1f2-4b62626ebf78.html.

Turner, Emily. 2019. "Poverty Among Workers in the Cashew Industry." Retrieved 21 March, 2020, from https://borgenproject.org/poverty-among-workers -in-the-cashew-industry/.

Twine, Richard. 2010. "Intersectional Disgust? Animals and (Eco)Feminism." *Feminism and Psychology* 20 (3):397–406.

Twine, Richard. 2014. "Vegan Killjoys at the Table—Contesting Happiness and Negotiating Relationships with Food Practices." *Societies* 4: 623–639.

UN in India, n.d. "Scheduled Castes and Scheduled Tribes." Retrieved 21 July, 2022, from: https://in.one.un.org/task-teams/scheduled-castes-and-scheduled-tribes/.

United Nations. n.d. *Universal Declaration of Human Rights.* Retrieved 12 July, 2021, from https://www.un.org/en/about-us/universal-declaration-of-human-rights.

United Nations. 2020. *The State of Food Security and Nutrition in the World 2020.* Retrieved 25 January, 2021, from https://sustainabledevelopment.un.org/index.php?pa ge=view&type=20000&nr=6909&menu=2993.

USDA (United States Department of Agriculture) Foreign Agricultural Service. n.d., a. Custom Query: "Animal numbers, cattle, total slaughter". Retrieved 12 February, 2022, from https://apps.fas.usda.gov/psdonline/app/index.html#/app/advQuery.

USDA (United States Department of Agriculture) Foreign Agricultural Service. n.d., b. Custom Query: "Animal numbers, cattle beginning stock". Retrieved 28 January, 2022, from https://apps.fas.usda.gov/psdonline/app/index.html#/app/advQuery.

USDA (United States Department of Agriculture) Foreign Agricultural Service. (n.d., c). Custom Query: "Dairy milk fluid, production". Retrieved 28 January, 2022, from https://apps.fas.usda.gov/psdonline/app/index.html#/app/advQuery.

USDA (United States Department of Agriculture) Foreign Agricultural Services. 2017. "India, Livestock and Products Annual." Retrieved 20 January, 2020, from https://apps.fas.usda.gov/newgainapi/api/report/downloadreportbyfilename?filename=Livestock%20and%20Products%20Annual_New%20Delhi_India_9-1-2017.pdf.

USDA (United States Department of Agriculture) Economic Research Service. 2017. "India remains the world's largest dairy producer," [press release]. Retrieved 21 January, 2018, from https://www.ers.usda.gov/data-products/chart-gallery/gallery/chart-detail/?chartId=82987.

USDA (United States Department of Agriculture) Foreign Agricultural Services. 2020. "EU-28: Livestock and Products Annual." https://apps.fas.usda.gov/newgainapi/api/Report/DownloadReportByFileName?fileName=Livestock%20and%20Products%20Annual_The%20Hague_European%20Union_09-09-2020.

Valent, P. 2002. Diagnosis and Treatment of Helper Stresses, Traumas, and Illnesses. In *Treating Compassion Fatigue*, ed. C. R. Figley, 1–17. New York: Taylor and Francis.

Valiani, A. A. (2010). Physical Training, Ethical Discipline, and Creative Violence: Zones of Self-Mastery in the Hindu Nationalist Movement. *Cultural Anthropology* 25 (1): 73–99.

Varadarajan, Siddharth. 2015. "The Pink Revolution is Marching On." *The Wire.* Retrieved 8 February, 2022, from https://thewire.in/communalism/the-pink-revolution-is-marching-on.

van der Veer, Peter. 1999. "Hindus: A Superior Race." *Nations and Nationalism* 5 (3): 421.

Verma, Kanika, and Singh, Angad Punia. 2021. "Catalysing India's Bovine Population Through Technology Intervention." *Invest India.* Retrieved 13 February, 2022, from https://www.investindia.gov.in/team-india-blogs/catalysing-indias-bovine-population-through-technology-intervention.

Victor, Reginald, and Bhatt, Kinnari. 2017. "Misconception, Misinformation, Misdirection and Misplaced Aggression—A Case Study of a Murdered Macqueen's Bustard." *International Journal of Environmental Studies* 74 (2): 183–191.

Vij, S. (2016). "New symbol of Hindutva project: Is Gau Raksha the new Ram Mandir?" *Hindustan Times.* Retrieved 21 September, 2016, from http://www.hindustantimes.com/india-news/the-new-symbol-of-hindutva-project-is-gau-raksha-the-new-ram-mandir/story-fPqg5TL2XBE16PooS4kZeM.html.

Voiceless. 2019. "The Co-Founder of the Animal Defenders Office on Australia's Impending Ag-Gag Laws," 29 July. Retrieved 21 December, 2019, from https://www.voiceless.org.au/content/co-founder-animal-defenders-office-australias-impending-ag-gag-laws.

VSPCA (Visakha Society for the Protection and Care of Animals). 2013. "Simhachalam Calves: 2013 Update—12 Months of Liberation for Thousands of Male Calves." Retrieved 13 February, 2015, fromhttps://vspca.org/portfolio/simhachalam-calves/.

Wadiwel, Dinesh. 2018. "Chicken Harvesting Machine: Animal Labor, Resistance, and the Time of Production." *The South Atlantic Quarterly* 117 (3): 527–549.

Wadiwel, D. Joseph. (forthcoming). *Animals and Capital*. Edinburgh: University of Edinburgh Press.

Waikato Times. 2022. "Genetics firm plans to breed non-gassy cows,"4 April. Accessed 1 August, 2022, from https://www.pressreader.com/new-zealand/waikato-times/20220404/281857237055839.

Walby, Sylvia. 1986. *Patriarchy at Work*. Minneapolis: University of Minnesota Press.

Wasley, Andrew, Cook, Christopher D., and Jones, Natalie. 2018. "Two Amputations a Week: The Cost of Working in a US Meat Plant." *The Guardian*, 5 July. Retrieved 2 August, 2020, from https://www.theguardian.com/environment/2018/jul/05/amputations-serious-injuries-us-meat-industry-plant.

Watkins, Stuart. 2018. "The Economic Consequences of Veganism." *Money Week*. Retrieved 13 January, 2021, from https://moneyweek.com/499842/the-economic-consequences-of-veganism.

Webster J. 1993. *Understanding the Dairy Cow*, 2nd Ed. Oxford: Blackwell.

Weis, Lael K. 2017. "Constitutional Directive Principles." *Oxford Journal of Legal Studies* 37 (4): 916–945.

Weis, Tony. 2013. *The Ecological Hoofprint: The Global Burden of Industrial Livestock*. London: Zed Books.

Whittier, W. D., Currin, N. M., Currin, J. F., and Hall, J. B. 2009. "Calving Emergencies in Beef Cattle: Identification and Prevention." Retrieved 13 February from https://vtechworks.lib.vt.edu/bitstream/handle/10919/50696/400-018.pdf?sequence=1&isAllowed=y.

Wicks, Deidre. 2018. "Demystifying Dairy." *Animal Studies Journal* 7 (2):45–75.

Wiley, Andrea S. 2014. *Cultures of Milk: The Biology and Meaning of Dairy Products in the United States and India*. Cambridge, MA: Harvard University Press.

Williams, George M. 2003, *Handbook of Hindu Mythology*. Santa Barbara, CA: ABC-Clio.

Williams, R. E. 1997. *The Political Economy of the Common Market in Milk and Dairy Products in the European Union*. FAO Economic and Social Development Paper 142. Rome: FAO Economic and Social Department.

Wilson, H. H. (ed. and trans.). 1840. *The Vishnu Purana: A System of Hindu Mythology and Tradition*. London: John Murray.

Wood, Ernest, and Subrahmanyam, S. V. (eds and trans.). 1911. *The Garuda Purana*, Chapter 5. Allahabad: Sudhindra Natha Vasu.

World Bank. 2012. "Project Signing: Government of India and World Bank Sign US$ 352 Million Agreement for National Dairy Support Project," 13 April. [press release] Retrieved 12 December, 2020, fromhttps://www.worldbank.org/en/news/

press-release/2012/04/13/project-signing-government-of-india-and-world-bank-sign
-us-352-million-agreement-for-national-dairy-support-project.

World Watch Monitor. 2015. "Indian Beef Ban Hits 'Untouchable' Dalits Hardest." 3 March. Retrieved 8 February, 2020, from https://www.worldwatchmonitor
.org/2015/03/indian-beef-ban-hits-untouchable-dalits-hardest/.

Wrenn, C. Lee, and Johnson, R. 2013. "A Critique of Single-Issue Campaigning and the Importance of Comprehensive Abolitionist Vegan Advocacy." *Food, Culture and Society* 16 (4): 651–668.

Yamin, A. E. 2016. *Power, Suffering, and the Struggle for Dignity: Human Rights Frameworks for Health and Why They Matter.* Philadelphia, PA: University of Pennsylvania Press.

Yarris, Kimberley. 2017. "A2 Milk Facts." Retrieved 13 February, 2019, from https://cdrf
.org/a2-milk-facts/.

Yengde, S. 2022. "Global Castes." *Ethnic and Racial Studies* 45 (2): 340–360. doi: 10.1080/01419870.2021.1924394.Yiftachel, Oren. 2012. "Critical Theory and 'Gray Space': Mobilization of the Colonized." In *Cities for People, Not for Profit: Critical Urban Theory and The Right to the City*, ed. N. Brenner, P. Marcuse and M. Mayer, 150–170. Oxford and New York: Routledge.

Yousefi, Anahita, Bellantonio, Marissa, and Hurowitz, Glenn. 2018. "The Avoidable Crisis." Retrieved 13 January, 2021, from https://www.fern.org/fileadmin/uploads/ fern/Documents/TheAvoidableCrisisPDF.pdf.

YouTube. 2016. "The Barbaric Transports of Cattle in Kerala (India)." Retrieved 27 November, 2019, from https://www.youtube.com/watch?v=IRpOMUAuQc4.

YouTube. 2017. "Periyarites Arrested While on Their Way to a Janeu Ceremony for Pigs." Retrieved 30 October, 2020, from https://www.youtube.com/watch? v=rfyFW5phlpQ.

Yusuf, Hakeem O. 2013. "Harvest of Violence: The Neglect of Basic Rights and the Boko Haram Insurgency in Nigeria." *Critical Studies on Terrorism* 6 (3): 371–391.

Yuval-Davis, Nira. 1993. "Gender and Nation." *Ethnic and Racial Studies* 16 (4): 621–632.

INDEX

ALSO PUBLISHED IN THE SOUTH ASIA IN MOTION SERIES

The Vulgarity of Caste: Dalits, Sexuality, and Humanity in Modern India
Shailaja Paik (2022)

Delhi Reborn: Partition and Nation Building in India's Capital
Rotem Geva (2022)

The Right to Be Counted: The Urban Poor and the Politics of Resettlement in Delhi
Sanjeev Routray (2022)

*Protestant Textuality and the Tamil Modern: Political Oratory
and the Social Imaginary in South Asia*
Bernard Bate, Edited by E. Annamalai, Francis Cody, Malarvizhi Jayanth,
and Constantine V. Nakassis (2021)

Special Treatment: Student Doctors at the All India Institute of Medical Sciences
Anna Ruddock (2021)

From Raj to Republic: Sovereignty, Violence, and Democracy in India
Sunil Purushotham (2021)

The Greater India Experiment: Hindutva Becoming and the Northeast Arkotong
Longkumer (2020)

Nobody's People: Hierarchy as Hope in a Society of Thieves
Anastasia Piliavsky (2020)

*Brand New Nation: Capitalist Dreams and Nationalist
Designs in Twenty-First-Century India*
Ravinder Kaur (2020)

Partisan Aesthetics: Modern Art and India's Long Decolonization
Sanjukta Sunderason (2020)

For a complete listing of titles in this series, visit the
Stanford University Press website, www.sup.org.

CPSIA information can be obtained
at www.ICGtesting.com
Printed in the USA
JSHW042351141222
34936JS00002B/2